D1733455

The Destruction of Pakistan's Democracy

The Destruction of Pakistan's Democracy

Allen McGrath

Karachi
Oxford University Press
Oxford New York Delhi
1996

Oxford University Press, Walton Street, Oxford OX2 6DP

Oxford New York
Athens Auckland Bangkok Bombay
Calcutta Cape Town Dar es Salaam Delhi
Florence Hong Kong Istanbul Karachi
Kuala Lumpur Madras Madrid Melbourne
Mexico City Nairobi Paris Singapore
Taipei Tokyo Toronto

and associated companies in

Berlin Ibadan

Oxford is a trade mark of Oxford University Press

ISBN 0 19 577583 X

Printed in Pakistan at
Mas Printers, Karachi.
Published by
Oxford University Press
5-Bangalore Town, Sharae Faisal
P.O. Box 13033, Karachi-75350, Pakistan.

To Anita

CONTENTS

INTRODUCTION

On 28 October 1954, Pakistan's Governor-General Ghulam Mohammad ordered the police to bar the members of the Constituent Assembly from entering their meeting hall in Karachi. The sole item on the agenda of their aborted meeting was a formal vote on the published draft of Pakistan's new constitution, which had been approved at the Assembly's previous session. Dissolution of the Assembly was legitimized in the following year by Chief Justice Mohammad Munir and the majority of his colleagues of the Federal Court. Thus ended the nation's existence under the dominion constitution which had served as the basis for governing since independence. Under that constitution, Pakistan had ruled itself as a flawed but functioning parliamentary democracy. After Ghulam Mohammad and Munir ended the existence of the first Constitutional Assembly, a weakened form of parliamentary government was restructured from the ruins of the first Constituent Assembly and stumbled on until it was terminated by Ayub Khan's *coup* in 1958. Ayub's rise ushered in the long rule of the military interrupted by periodic efforts to restart democratic government.

In the years prior to the dissolution of the Constituent Assembly, considerable efforts were made to draft a democratic constitution for Pakistan. During that time Pakistanis had not yet taken on the burden of guilt for a democracy that had 'failed', in both their opinion and the estimation of the world. It was also a time when the holding of Islamic beliefs did not automatically brand one as anti-democratic. Rather, the Islamic factions, in this nation founded as the homeland of India's Muslims, showed their willingness to accommodate themselves to parliamentary democracy under a Western constitution.

In Pakistan of the mid-1950s, the dominion-model constitution was subject to what was perhaps the most extensive analysis of any time. It was an analysis utilizing history rather than law and took place in arguments in open court and in the written opinions of those courts rather than in learned journals or academic seminars. This analysis was not possible in England itself where, because of the convention followed by the courts in refraining from passing on the validity of parliamentary legislation, there exists no opportunity to judicially explore issues dealing with the apportionment of powers within the state.

The importance of the clash between the politicians and the Governor-General, which ended in the aborting of the nation's new constitution, was emphasized by a respected American observer. 'Once the first constitution is destroyed, it is doubtful that any succeeding one, no matter how successfully drafted, will ever be truly accepted. A tradition which makes it possible for new leaders to replace old documents with others which appear preferable to them, not only denies constitutionalism but makes reference to it little more than a sham.'[1] The extent to which the events of Pakistan's early years makes that prediction relevant is still being worked out in the nation's politics.

Syed Razi Wasti of Government College, Lahore, and Ijaz Husain Batalvi, senior advocate of the Lahore Bar, who has himself participated in many history-making events in Pakistan, were most generous in their assistance in carrying out this study. Professor Wasti, when he was Quaid-i-Azam Professor at Columbia University, encouraged me to undertake an exploration of this subject, has read my drafts, and has furnished valuable suggestions and information. Mr Batalvi was an invaluable source of information. During much of the period dealt with here, he was a barrister in the London chambers of Mr Pritt, the London barrister who championed the cause of the Pakistan Constituent Assembly after its dissolution. Mr Batalvi and Professor Wasti gave unstintingly of their time and efforts during my stays in Pakistan, and afforded personal introductions and guidance in dealing with the courts and with intellectual and political leaders conversant with the events and issues of Pakistan's early history. I owe a particular debt to Ainsley Embree, now retired director of the Southern Asian Institute at Columbia University, who has, over the course of years, read early drafts of this study, and whose wide knowledge of matters concerning the subcontinent was a most valuable guide.

One of the problems facing an investigator of political events in Pakistan is the absence of personal documentation by participants, even by people who were involved in some of the most important events of the day. This problem was partially addressed here by the opportunity to interview participants, among whom were: Mumtaz Daultana, former Premier of West Punjab; Amjad Ali, Ambassador to Washington and Finance Minister in the second Bogra Cabinet, historian Karl J. Newman, Cologne University, who advised on the drafting of the 1954 constitution; and Altaf Gauhar, former editor of *Dawn* and present editor of *The Muslim*. As a member of the Pakistan Civil Service he was one of the officers in charge at the 1953 East Bengal elections. The co-operation of these participants offered insights from different viewpoints.

The exception to the usual lack of personal reminiscence was the writings of Mohammad Munir, Chief Justice of the Federal (later Supreme) Court, who left several autobiographical writings. It was, therefore, particularly valuable to have had the opportunity to balance his versions of events by discussing the dissolution of the Constituent Assembly with A. R. Cornelius, S. S. Pirzada, Nasim Hassan Shah, L. A. Nizami, and Anwarul Huq. Justice Cornelius, later Chief Justice, served as an Associate Justice on Munir's court, and was the lone dissenter to the court finding in favour of the Governor-General's right to dissolve the Assembly. Mr Pirzada, later Attorney-General and Ambassador, and a well known historian, served before Munir's court as an advocate on behalf of the Constituent Assembly, while Mr Shah, later Chief Justice of the Supreme Court, was an advocate for the Governor-General in the same court battle which determined the fate of parliamentary government in Pakistan. Mr Nizami, as a clerk of the Federal Court, was able to observe that fight from within the court's organization, and former Chief Justice Anwarul Huq knew Munir as a fellow judge and was familiar with his service in the judiciary. These men were most generous with their time, and my interviews of them enabled the construction of what I hope is a balance to the versions of events left by Chief Justice Munir in his writings.

Others who afforded access to valuable information include Moinuddin Siddiqi, librarian of the National Assembly Library, Islamabad. Mr Siddiqi has an impressive dedication to the preservation of the records of Pakistan's early history, and afforded access to constitutional materials otherwise unavailable, including the published copy of the 1954 constitution. In 1991, Professor D. A. Low, of the University of Cambridge, in a short conversation successfully ended what had been my failed search for the personal papers of Sir Ivor Jennings. Jennings, perhaps the most influential British constitutional scholar of his day, was instrumental in shaping the future of Pakistan, not only by advising on the drafting of its constitution, as he had also done in Ceylon and other ex-colonial nations, but by constructing constitutional ideas which were used to legitimize autocracy in Pakistan. To my knowledge, Jenning's unpublished papers at the Commonwealth Institute, London, have not previously been used in an historical study. They provide a unique opportunity to observe the ideas of a scholar-turned-advocate as those ideas progressed from their conception to their embodiment in the court decisions which changed a nation's direction.

CHAPTER 1

PAKISTAN 1947

Although at the time of its birth Pakistan had the fifth largest population in the world and was the world's largest Muslim state, it was an eleventh-hour creation. Only seventeen years before the actual independence of Pakistan had the idea emerged of a separate grouping of provinces encompassing the north-west section of British India with a predominantly Muslim population. In 1930, Mohammad Iqbal, poet and philosopher, first suggested the idea, and only in 1934, thirteen years before independence, was the name 'Pakistan' coined by a group of Muslim students at Cambridge. Pakistan was won by Mohammad Ali Jinnah's skilled negotiations with the British and the Congress Party, but even this victory was certain only in July of 1947, two months before independence, when the British Parliament voted to create two new dominions on the Indian subcontinent. Even then, there were many in India and in Britain who believed (or hoped) that the separation would not be permanent but that Pakistan, unable to stand alone, would be forced to reunite with India.

Addressing the first session of the Constituent Assembly, Jinnah told the members, '...not only we ourselves are wondering, but, I think, the whole world is wondering at this unprecedented cyclonic revolution which has brought about a plan of creating and establishing two independent sovereign dominions in this subcontinent. As it is, it has been unprecedented; there is no parallel in the history of the world.'[1] With the arrival of independence, Jinnah himself appeared to be in a state of shock. Negotiating over the years to achieve Pakistan, when it was achieved he realized that he had never expected to reach that goal in his lifetime and was vague as to what Pakistan would mean in operation. Once he had won his Pakistan it was for those who came after him to make use of it and set new goals.[2] He had envisioned a less abrupt parting of the ways, even harbouring the hope that Pakistan's Constituent Assembly would hold its first meeting in Delhi at the same time that India's Constituent Assembly held its first meeting. He abandoned that hope only when Nehru and Patel adamantly refused to consider the idea despite Mountbatten's backing of Jinnah's proposal.[3] Certainly, he did not have in mind the deep and hostile cleavage which in a short time developed between India and Pakistan. So far was this from Jinnah's mind that on the eve of partition he expressed his intention to return to his home in Bombay after he retired as Pakistan's Governor-General.[4] Jinnah was more rooted in Bombay than anywhere in Pakistan, having built his house there 'brick by brick', as he termed it, and it was Bombay that served as the base of his political life and where he established his law practice.

Pakistan has been called a 'unique addition to modern political thought,'[5] but it was also unprecedented in other ways. The United States of America and Ireland preceded Pakistan and India in gaining independence from the British Empire. Pakistan, however, was not the creation of a new nation out of a wilderness, as were the Thirteen Colonies of North America, nor was it a country with its own territorial and historical definition, as were Ireland and India. Other modern nations, such as Israel and communist Russia, were based on ideology, as was Pakistan, but they had the physical reality of national territory. In contrast, there was no pre-existing territory in which the Pakistan idea of a Muslim homeland had ever existed. Nor were there counterparts of the Wailing Wall or the Kremlin to serve as symbols supporting a Pakistani nationalism. The great monuments of the Muslim Mughal Empire, the Taj Mahal and Fatehpur Sikri among them, as well as the capital of Delhi, were on the Indian side of the partition border. There were no past deeds performed on or for the soil of Pakistan which could inspire the population of the new nation. What was to become West Pakistan had existed in the past only as an undifferentiated part of larger areas such as the Mughal and Afghan empires and British India. It was known to history as the territory crossed by successive armies of invaders on their way to do battle for Delhi and domination of the Ganges plain.

Although poor commercially and industrially, Pakistan enjoyed the advantage of being a developed society based culturally on Islam, which afforded it not only cohesiveness but a tradition of law. Its political, bureaucratic, and religious leaders were accepted by the people, and at independence there existed among the political elite a tradition of democratic government. This tradition, originating from the British, resulted in the development of a structure of parliamentary government with which many of Pakistan's leaders had gained familiarity. Also, the new nation possessed an army trained by the British in their tradition of non-interference by the military in civil affairs.

There did exist questions concerning Pakistan's viability as a state. Shortly after independence, a Pakistani newspaper described the country as having been created by the 'stroke of a pen' and doubted that it could ever be more than 'a geographic entity.'[6] Some British and Indians had not believed that Jinnah would accept such a truncated version of his original demand for Pakistan, which had included an undivided Bengal and Punjab. It was indeed a strange configuration of territories. The east wing of the country, East Bengal, separated from West Pakistan by over 800 miles of Indian territory, had been a marginal acquisition of the Mughal Empire and it was included in Pakistan only because it had a majority Muslim population. When the poet and philosopher Mohammad Iqbal first introduced the idea of a separate territory for Muslims, he had in mind the Muslim areas in north-west India and did not include Bengal. Even the wording of the Lahore Declaration of 1940, which first pronounced the political aim of the Muslim League for a separate nation, did not include the Muslims of Bengal, perhaps because of the distance from the north-west territories and East Bengal's cultural and economic integration with the rest of Bengal. Muslim leaders in Bengal, such as Hussain Shaheed Suhrawardy and A. K. Fazlul Huq, argued before partition for an undivided independent Bengal which would be part of neither India nor Pakistan. They did not prevail, and the Muslim population in eastern Bengal was partitioned from the Hindu section in the western portion of the province. The Hindu west contained Calcutta, the economic and political heart of Bengal. The differences between the two wings of Pakistan were many. East Bengal, an agricultural area considered by the British as being little better than a rural slum, was one-sixth the size of West Pakistan but contained a greater population. West Pakistan was largely arid land with an average annual rainfall of less than twenty inches, its western and northern parts mountainous. In contrast,

East Bengal was situated in one of the largest deltas in the world, watered by over one hundred inches of annual rainfall. Bengal's main physical problem was flooding. West Pakistan's challenge was combating semi-arid conditions by means of irrigation and the drilling of wells.

Their geographic separation on the subcontinent was accompanied by a different world outlook between the two wings, West Pakistan being concerned with affairs in the Middle East, while the eastern wing looked to South East Asia. Even in religion there were differences. An American scholar wrote in the 1950s that West Pakistan, tracing its faith to Arabia and Persian antecedents, tended to look patronizingly on East Pakistan as opportunistic Muslims embracing Islam in preference to outcast status in the Hindu structure. He added, 'In West Pakistan, relationships with Hindus fall in the category of foreign relations; in East Pakistan, with a significant Hindu minority, they are a domestic concern. West Pakistan feels more cleavage from India. The East Pakistanis are still drawn towards West Bengal and regard Calcutta as their metropolis.'[7]

On the positive side for the East Bengal Muslims, many of the local Hindu landlords fled to India at the time of partition. Nearly seventy-five per cent of the land, including most of the largest *zamindari* holdings, belonged to Hindus prior to partition, and the departure of a substantial number of these Hindus allowed for the break-up and distribution of large tracts of land. Land reform legislation was in fact passed by the East Bengal Assembly after independence. As a result, many of East Bengal's farmers held transfer rights to their lands. This fact was reflected in the flexible political power structure of East Bengal, and by example presented a potential threat to the large landlords of West Pakistan who dominated the political structures of Punjab and Sindh and fought any and all attempts at land reform. These landlords were the descendants of the traditional rulers and landowners who had been left in place by the British after the Mutiny. In contrast to East Bengal, West Pakistan was a politically closed society in which very little change was taking place among the economic and social classes.

The Bengalis were long known as the most political people in British India, their politics and parliamentary experience more mature and complex than found in any other province. It was they who gave initial leadership to the Indian national movement, who later embraced violence as a political tool, and it was in undivided Bengal that leftist movements had their greatest following. After independence, the East Bengali farmer took an active interest in politics. Although the East Bengali was poorer than his West Pakistan counterpart, literacy was higher in East Bengal (thirty per cent versus twenty per cent) and East Bengal enjoyed the advantage of a single language, thus facilitating communication on political issues. The East Bengal provincial government when compared to government in West Punjab has been described as being 'more egalitarian in demeanour, more democratic in outlook, more informal, closer to the people in mood and attitude, less haughty...more tolerant of diversity of religious belief and more cosmopolitan in their cultural outlook.'[8] The Bengalis were at a disadvantage, however, because the central government was located in Karachi in West Pakistan, where the distant political voice of East Bengal was weak and Bengalis were under-represented in the bureaucracy of the nation. Furthermore, they had been considered by the British a 'non-martial' people, and as a result Bengalis were little represented in the armed forces. In the minds of some Bengalis, little had changed in their colonial status except the substitution of Karachi for London as the imperial capital and Punjabis for Englishmen as the colonial masters. These new masters masked their own uneasiness in the face of the greater political sophistication of the Bengalis by assuming a pose of racial and cultural superiority. Not surprisingly, many East Bengalis became discontent in this difficult political union with their co-religionists on the other side of the subcontinent.

While East Bengal had one ethnic group speaking one language, West Pakistan was a conglomerate of ethnic and tribal groups each speaking a separate language, many giving their allegiance exclusively to their local leaders and living by their own traditions and customs. West Pakistan was comprised of the western section of pre-partition Punjab, as well as Sindh, which had been separated from Bombay in 1931 and made into a separate province, and the North-West Frontier Province. In addition, there were areas outside of the provinces: Balochistan, geographically the largest political unit in West Pakistan; several units (Kalat, Lasbela, Makran, and Kharan) which comprised the Balochistan States Union; the North-West Frontier States (Amb, Chitral, Swat, and Dir); the Federal Capital area of Karachi; the Frontier tribal areas; and the princely states of Bahawalpur and Khairpur. At the time of independence, Balochistan was ruled by four leaders, each with his own group and territory. These leaders did not agree to rule by Pakistan until 1955, and then, very reluctantly in the face of employment of force by the central government.

The degree of diversity in West Pakistan can be appreciated by observing the differences which existed even within an individual province. Punjab, the most prosperous province, rich in agriculture and known for its industrious population, is an example. The division among the three major groups in the province, the Rajputs, Jats, and Arains, was more significant to many Punjabis than were provincial differences with a Pukhtoon or Sindhi. This diversity was one reason why the Punjab, despite its prominence and strengths in other aspects, particularly its leadership in the bureaucracy and military, did not play as active or unified a role in Pakistan's political scene as might have been expected in the years immediately after independence. Its delegation in the Constituent Assembly lacked unity. Until after Liaquat Ali Khan's death in 1951, however, East Bengal did not take advantage of this weakness and seize the initiative in the Assembly.

The North-West Frontier Province and Balochistan were tribal territories. The British had valued them for their ability to defend the north-west border of British India in return for tribute and the right to be left to their own tribal rule. Within sparsely populated Balochistan the Baloch made up less than fifty per cent of the population, the remaining being Punjabi and Pukhtoon immigrants and more than a score of major and minor tribes and clans. Pukhtoons were the majority in the North-West Frontier, although there, too, an array of tribes existed. In Sindh, the division within the population was made up not so much by ethnic and linguistic groups as by the sharp social distinction between a small elite of landowners and the majority of cultivators who existed almost on the level of chattel. So durable were local factors in what later became West Pakistan that, after completing their conquest of the region, the British found it convenient to avoid any attempt to institute substantial changes of government, opting rather to rule in a significant degree by implementing local customs and utilizing local institutions and structures. As a result, domination by the large landlords continued during British rule.

Britain's administration of the north-west region of the subcontinent had been different from that in the other parts of

India. The rule which Britain established in Bengal beginning in the late eighteenth century was implemented by regulations which thereafter grew in scope and which were extended to other parts of India. The Governor-General ruled in conjunction with a council. In contrast, the north-west corner of the subcontinent, the part which was to become West Pakistan in 1947, was not conquered until later. After the final defeat of the Sikhs in the mid-nineteenth century, a form of government was installed in the Punjab different from that in Bengal. Government in the Punjab was to be by individuals rather than by regulations. It was here that the romantic picture grew of government by individual Englishmen, ruling from the saddle, breaking camp to move from village to village, administering justice in the open fields, man to man, with little as a guide except what the Briton considered his innate sense of fairness and his supposed knowledge of 'his' natives. What need or room for written laws, politicians and assemblies, or haggling lawyers? This tradition was part of the background of such British-trained men as Ghulam Mohammad, Ayub Khan, Iskander Mirza, Chaudhri Mohammad Ali, and Mohammad Munir, who were to play important roles in Pakistan in the years after independence. They were all from the Punjab, and all were former members of the civil, military, and judicial bureaucracies which administered the machinery of government under the British. To them, the efficiency of what the British liked to refer to as the 'steel frame' of autocratic administration would be crucial to the success of any government in independent Pakistan. They had little tolerance for parliamentary democracy or for the interference in the affairs of state by religious factions.

These men differed from Jinnah and the Muslim League leaders, who also formed their political thinking through their experiences under British rule but who were the inheritors of the British constitutional building done prior to independence. Principally because of their experiences in British India, there was no dissent among the top leaders of the Muslim League that Pakistan would have a parliamentary form of government, with a Prime Minister choosing his colleagues in a Cabinet system with joint responsibility. As in many emerging nations, the leaders who led the independence movement were members of a westernized class of professionals and intellectuals identified with parliamentary government. They were persons, like Jinnah, not concerned with religious matters. They were 'Islamic' in that they identified themselves as members of the faith, were willing at times to express themselves by referring to religion in dealing with social and political issues, but were reluctant to introduce Islamic ideology into politics. The leaders of the Muslim League supporting Jinnah were often western-educated, some at English universities or the Inns of Court. Of the original membership of Pakistan's Constituent Assembly, over seventy per cent were lawyers or large landowners. Many were of considerable wealth which enabled them to enjoy the luxuries of European life. They had one goal which might resemble a social policy: as with people anywhere who enjoy economic advantage, they were interested in preserving the *status quo* in order to maintain their economic and social privileges. Because it is the better part of political wisdom not to proclaim such policy publicly, there is little in the Assembly's records dealing with social and economic issues. The task of drafting a new constitution fell to the politicians of the Muslim League, backed by the large landowners. In their backgrounds, the leadership of the League might be compared to the gentlemen of seventeenth and eighteenth century England who laid the foundations of the English constitution. Nor were they very different in mind-set from the American Founding Fathers, landowners, lawyers, merchants, and slave-owners who met in Philadelphia in 1789 to draft a constitution. The men who ruled Pakistan were much like those in other nations before them who had drafted constitutions with the primary purpose of confirming their own privileges, ensuring the success of this effort by crafting a constitution to act as a social contract which the people would willingly learn to live by.

Unlike the Hindus, for many Muslims the opportunities made available during British rule for participation in government had been refused out of fear, suspicion, or pride. Many religious leaders felt they must remain uncontaminated by western ideas for fear that the religious way of life of the people would be subverted, and some refused to support Jinnah's movement for Pakistan because the idea of a nation-state was a western concept. They believed that the Islamic community was universal and should not be broken up by national borders. The goal of these leaders was not a nation-state such as Pakistan but a world-wide Islamic brotherhood. Instead of seeking an independent state, Muslims should put their efforts into converting the subcontinent to Islam and thus turn it into a Muslim homeland, *Dar-ul-Islam*. Shortly before partition, however, the co-operation of the religious leaders was sought by Jinnah and the Muslim League with some degree of success and their help was invaluable in motivating the masses behind the cause for Pakistan.

After independence, some of these religious leaders wished to continue exerting political influence to ensure that Islamic principles would be incorporated into the structure of the new state. They spoke in terms of an Islamic state, but what was meant by such a state was often difficult to understand in modern political terms. While the only true Islamic state recognized in classical Islamic political theory would be one which was identical with the entire community of believing Muslims,[9] no such state had existed in modern times. Even the symbol of Muslim spiritual if not political universality had disappeared with the fall of the Khalifah, the Sultan of Turkey. In the absence of a true Islamic nation, the *ulema* in the past had learned to compromise and live under various forms of government. None of these governments, however, had laid claim to being an Islamic state, while Pakistan had come into existence with the sole justification, in the eyes of some, that it was to be such a state. But even those making such a claim were not necessarily in conflict with their more secular oriented westernized brethren in the Muslim League who advocated a democratic constitution, because under classical Islamic political theory, there did not exist specific Islamic attributes necessary for a government to be acceptable. What was required was that a government be a support for the Islamic way of life. Those advocating a modern western constitution in Pakistan were able to avoid conflict with this goal of classical Islamic theory.

Few of the religious leaders had knowledge of the workings of modern politics. One exception was Maulana Abul Ala Maududi, founder of the Jamaat-e-Islami. Although most of his ideas were similar to those of the religious leaders, he was not one of them. He was a publicist and political activist who advocated an Islamic state. It was his party which furnished the political leadership in the confrontation over constitutional matters between the Islamic religionists and the modernist factions led by Jinnah and the Muslim League. Maududi entered the post-independence period not willing to compromise with nationalism. He considered Jinnah and the other leaders of the Muslim League to be ignorant of Islam and therefore its enemy. He called them 'spineless imitators of the West'.[10] To Maududi, secularism was indistinguishable from atheism, and prior to partition he had declared that democracy was an evil.[11] He would not be satisfied if the new state merely incorporated Islamic ideology, but would find Pakistan acceptable only if it were a truly Islamic state. That meant that where the Koran or *Shariat* had spoken on the law, that must be the law of the land. Only where they were silent could a secular legislature pass laws. In addition, to be Islamic a state must be administered only by those who had become learned in Islam through years of study. Maududi expressed doubt that the people of Pakistan were capable of bringing a true Islamic state into existence at the time of independence. He saw an Islamic state as a goal which could only be brought about gradually. But Maududi warned that the fact that the task would take time was not to be used by Pakistan's leaders as an excuse for a secular constitution. Although he shared with them many basic ideas on the relationship of the state and religion, he criticized the traditional religious leaders for being out of date and reactionary.

By his own design, Maududi's following was small, a select group of some education, and after independence the Jamaat-e-Islami was not able to win more than an insignificant number of seats in any provincial election. Maududi was not a popular orator but more a thinker and pamphleteer and never presented political competition to Jinnah or Liaquat. He was, however, the most articulate spokesman for those demanding an Islamic state, and as such he had broad influence, particularly among students. His Jamaat-e-Islami also appealed to the lower-level bureaucrats who had some western education but had not gone on to the university and did not have the social or economic standing of many of the Muslim League leaders.

The political interplay of the conflicting positions of the two westernized groups, the League leaders and the bureaucrats, and in turn their confrontation with the beliefs of those who wished to see an Islamic state, provided the background to Pakistan's attempt to conduct its political life and to produce a new constitution after independence. Any differences which existed among the Islamic factions were, however, to prove less significant than the differences between the democratic-oriented Muslim League leaders and the autocratic leaders of the bureaucracy. During the early years after independence, the bureaucrats and Muslim League politicians worked together in the operation of government but were to show their fundamental differences when the bureaucracy emerged in 1953 under the leadership of Ghulam Mohammad and established supremacy over the parliamentary forces.

The day before independence, Lord Louis Mountbatten, the last Viceroy of British India, addressed the people of the new dominion of Pakistan. 'Tomorrow two new sovereign states will take their place in the Commonwealth:..fully independent States ...not immature governments or weak, but fit to carry their great share of responsibility for peace and prosperity of the world.'[12] Mountbatten's accolade might have been intended more as a tribute paid by a Briton to British rule in India than it was to the Indians and Pakistanis themselves. The British were leaving behind a system of government of which they were proud. They considered it unique, and some Englishmen even claimed that only they could make it work. The British had, unwittingly, unwillingly, or by design, throughout their rule exported the foundation of their form of government to the Indian subcontinent. The results of this constitutional experimentation in British India dominated Pakistan's early political life.

During the years immediately following independence, Pakistan was influenced by events dating back to the beginning of the transfer of the English form of government to the Indian subcontinent.[13] In the early nineteenth century, Lord Macaulay sensed that the British domain in India constituted what he called 'a state which resembles no other in history and which forms by itself a separate class of political philosophy.'[14] He envisioned this state as being in his time 'covered in thick darkness', and he saw the task as 'to engraft on despotism those blessings which are the natural fruits of liberty'. He acknowledged that Britain could not hold India forever and warned that 'it behooves us to be cautious, even to the verge of timidity.' But if properly instructed, Indians in the future, the very distant future, might demand European institutions of government. Macaulay told Parliament, in words which Mountbatten might have read as a schoolboy, 'Whether such a day will ever come I know not. But never will I attempt to avert or to retard it. Whenever it comes it will be the proudest day in English history.'

Macaulay spoke at a time when the transfer of English institutions of government to India had been under way for almost two centuries.

The transfer had begun on a small scale and for practical reasons. The gentlemen of the East India Company who sailed to the East under Elizabeth's charter, unlike the Mughals, did not come to India to rule but to trade. Nevertheless, a process of governance was necessary to regulate the behaviour of the Company's members who lived at the trading houses from which they conducted their business affairs in India. The governing of the members of the commercial houses, 'factories' as they were then called, was carried out by a president and a council, a form of government which the Company expanded and utilized in some of the territories which it obtained by conquest and treaty. Over time, the ruling power of the East India Company, extending by the early nineteenth century over vast areas of the Indian subcontinent, was truncated by successive legislation of the British Parliament, which assumed for itself the right to supervise the affairs of India.[15] In 1858, following what is known in the West as the Indian Mutiny, the remaining governing powers of the East India Company, which had been exercised in the name of the Crown, were reclaimed by the Crown. By this transfer, the Crown also succeeded to the rights which had been exercised by the original Indian rulers and which had been assumed by the East India Company through conquest or other means of acquisition. In addition, the King of England enjoyed in India all the rights he was entitled to exercise in Great Britain. All of his rights he now delegated to Parliament to be exercised in India by the Governor-General, who was responsible to the Secretary of State. Insofar as Parliament legislated for India, Crown rights were replaced by statute. As theoretical and remote from Pakistan's history as these constitutional concepts might seem, they were to play a decisive role in the nation's politics.

The trauma experienced by the British as a result of the Indian Mutiny led to a change of policy. They would henceforth rule without attempting to change India. But if India was not to be moulded into the designs of the British, some means would nevertheless have to be utilized to prevent the British rulers from again facing the tragedy of another Mutiny, which they considered had been caused in part by their ignorance of how their Indian subjects were reacting to the government imposed on them. To this end Parliament passed the Indian Council Act of 1861, an 'ear to the ground' as it were. The Council Act made the first attempt to introduce an element of Indian opinion into the

Council of the Governor-General. But the opinion was that of Indians appointed by the Governor-General and who could not question, much less discuss, executive business. The Governor-General's Council resembled more the *darbar* of an Indian prince than a form of representative government.

The idea of representative government for India was repudiated by the British even as successive Acts expanded Indian membership in the legislative councils, both provincial and at the centre.[16] Secretary of State for India Lord Morley (1906-10) was co-sponsor of the report which led to the passage of the Council Act of 1909, providing for the first time direct election of non-official members of the Governor-General's Council. Even he was obliged to repudiate publicly the notion that his legislation was moving India towards parliamentary government, a goal which a former Secretary of State had called 'one of the wildest imaginations that ever entered the minds of men.'[17] Britain seemed to lose its way on the path to fashion a government for Macaulay's 'state which resembles no other in history.' One British scholar writing of the early years of this century raised the question: 'For more than twenty years, the Congress [Party] had steadily pinned its faith to a course of constitutional development which was as steadily repudiated by the British Government. And, since no alternative method of advance was proposed, the growth of some distrust in the sincerity of British intentions was only to be expected. Was the real reason for Britain's refusal to give Indians the kind of self-government they desired that she did not want them to govern themselves at all?'[18]

But the talk of political theory was for naught with the arrival of 1914, when British destiny in India became enmeshed in the affairs of war. As was to happen again three decades later, in the First World War the British needed the help of India. To ensure Indian co-operation, the Secretary of State proclaimed that the goal of Britain was the gradual development of self-governing institutions in India. The words used in this announcement were significant. There was the usual warning that nothing ought to be done in haste, but it was proclaimed that India was to have a 'gradual development of self-governing institutions with a view to the progressive realization of responsible government'. Responsible government had a recognized meaning. It meant that India was to have, at a time yet to be determined, a government responsible to the elected representatives of the people. It seemed that a fundamental change was about to come about. Indians hoped that they would soon have a new constitution, one based on the precept Gladstone had urged as Britain's approach to Ireland: 'It is liberty alone which fits men for liberty'.

The Government of India Act of 1919 was intended as a step in the direction of self-government.[19] The existing Central Legislative Council, consisting of 'official members', appointed by the Governor-General, and elected members, was enlarged and a new legislature was created, a bicameral mini-parliament with an elected-majority lower house. The franchise was extended to one-tenth of the adult male population, a number which still encompassed a large illiterate group. The central legislature, however, continued to be restricted in its functions and the government at the centre remained under the control of the Governor-General who was responsible only to the Secretary of State in London. The important changes occurred in the provinces, where the sizes of the Governors' provincial councils were increased and their legislative functions broadened. In addition, certain departments along with their revenues were transferred to the control of the provincial assemblies. Included were the departments dealing with agriculture, public works, local self-government, and education. The 1919 Act was significant because those departments were made responsible to their legislatures. This 'dyarchy' was the first creation of partial responsible government in British India. Nevertheless, the more important departments in each province were retained under the control of the Governor, who also had the right to implement his budget if rejected by the council. In addition, all legislation required his assent.[20]

Any hopes raised by the Government of India Act of 1919 were soon dashed. The Act had been born of British weakness, not conviction. While the war had changed much in Britain, at the top much remained the same. In the fifteen-minister Conservative Cabinet assembled by Bonar Law in October of 1922 were a Duke and six Lords, including Secretary of State for India Lord Peel. The government lapsed back into its old way of thinking about India, but it was too late for any government, regardless of how conservative, to publicly repudiate the goal of self-government. Instead, stress was now placed on the 'gradual' aspect of the constitutional development that Britain had promised as a reward for India's war effort. In 1924, Lord Balfour told his fellow members in the House of Lords that it was absurd to suggest that Indians were in any way inferior. India, he reminded his fellow Lords, had produced some of the world's great religions and was a civilization 'compared with which ours is contemptible in point of date'. But he warned, '...we are different,' and cautioned, 'Free institutions on the British model or on the Dominion model are among the most difficult institutions in the world to manage properly. Free government is very difficult government. The easy government is the government of an absolute autocracy.'[21] Balfour feared that self-government in India would degenerate into autocracy.

When, in 1928, Motilal Nehru chaired a Congress Party committee which drafted the Nehru Report containing constitutional proposals for a self-governing India to take its place among the dominions, the British refused to consider the idea. As a consequence, the opportunity was lost for Indians and Britons to work together in drafting a constitution, and when independence did arrive nineteen years later in 1947, India and Pakistan inherited constitutions which were wholly drafted by the British Parliament with the assent of the Congress and the Muslim League leaders but with very little input by them. It was, however, not only the British who were backing away from Indian self-government. On the Indian side, in the 1930s, leadership was shifting away from the Indian Liberals, a group which included Jinnah, who favoured dominion status. It was now the Congress Party under Mahatma Gandhi and Motilal Nehru's son Jawaharlal who were destined to lead the subcontinent to independence. For them, it was not the words spoken in Parliament but the rifle shots in Jallianwala Bagh which expressed British intentions. These men rejected dominion status and demanded not simply a form of self-government but independence.

Meanwhile, the shadow-play of constitutional reform continued. Because the Government of India Act of 1919 fell short of the increasing demands of the Indian Congress Party, in 1929 the Viceroy, Lord Irwin, was faced with the necessity of breaking through what he termed 'the webs of mistrust that have lately clogged the relations between India and Great Britain'. He announced that dominion status for India was the natural implication of the constitutional reforms which had taken place to that date. Irwin's declaration was followed in the next year by the Simon Report. The report was issued by a commission of Parliament consisting of two Peers and four commoners under the chairmanship of Sir John Simon who visited India over a two year period. Their fact-finding tours met with widespread demonstrations of disapproval because the very existence of such a commission, on which there were no Indians, seemed to many a clear message that Parliament was unwilling to allow Indians to participate in the actual making of their own constitution.

After holding hearings boycotted by the leaders of the Congress Party and Muslim League, the Simon Commission came forth with what has been praised as 'another work of first-rate value to the library of British political science'.[22] The Commission's report was more in the nature of a civics lecture which had become standard fare when Englishmen spoke to Indians on the subject of government, a lecture by now tiresome and irrelevant. The Simon Report repeated the old refrain that the parliamentary institutions which worked so well in Britain carried no guarantee of suitability in India. It supported this assertion by the admonition that Britain's institutions had developed because of conditions 'hardly found outside the English speaking world'. The smallness of Great Britain had fostered a cohesiveness among the electorate. The report continued, 'It seems to us most unlikely that if Britain had been the size of India, if communal and religious divisions so largely governed its policies, and if minorities had had as little confidence in the rule of others as they have in India, popular government in Britain would have taken this form.'[23] The Simon Commission made no recommendation for dominion status, although Lord Irwin continued to maintain that the government's policy remained unchanged.

Before the report of the Simon Commission could have any effect it was mooted by a change of administration in London which affected Britain's Indian policy. Talks followed in three London Round Table Conferences, beginning in 1930. During the conferences, Prime Minister Ramsey MacDonald added momentum to what appeared at the time as a move towards autonomy for India by declaring acceptance of the principle that the central executive in India was to be subjected to the will of the legislature. This principle was made contingent, however, on the coming into existence of an all-India legislature. It was this latter provision in the declaration that frustrated full responsible central government on the Indian subcontinent prior to independence in 1947, because any all-India legislature would have to also include the Indian Princes, 'despotic puppets who had inherited thrones held by the grace of the British crown'.[24] The Princes ruled their various feifdoms which the British kept separate from the rest of British India. Because these Princes were understandably reluctant to surrender their ruling prerogatives to a parliamentary government of all-India, progress toward constitutional change or dominion status was thwarted at the centre of Indian government. As a result, central executive power remained at independence essentially the same as it had been since 1858.

After the London Round Table negotiations were concluded in 1934, the Constitutional Committee created by Parliament considered the requests of the Indian delegation for constituent powers. Constituent power was understood to mean the power to create a constitution or change an existing constitution in whole or in part, and was considered to be synonymous with sovereignty. The granting of constituent powers to the federal legislature of India would have transferred sovereignty over India from Parliament to the federal legislature. The request was refused, and the federal legislature remained subject to Parliament. Changes in the constitution could be made only by the British Parliament under the 1919 Act, and Parliament kept that exclusive right under the next reform measure, the Government of India Act of 1935.

The Act of 1935, which became the basic constitutional document for the new nations of India and Pakistan when they came into existence in 1947, was the last constitution of British India.[25] It reflected the slow evolution of representative government dating back to the aftermath of the Indian Mutiny, and was essentially the next step forward based on the constitutional experiences gained under the Government of India Act of 1919 and the introduction of modified responsible government to the provinces. One purpose of the 1935 Act was to extend a form of responsible government to the centre. Eight years of hearings, conferences, and analyses, culminating in fifty-six days of debate in Parliament, went into the make-up of the 1935 Act, the longest legislation ever passed by Parliament and the most detailed constitution ever written. It went into effect in 1937, but because of the intervention of World War II, the Act had only a brief life prior to independence. Its significance, however, was long-lived. In 1947, it served as the constitutional vehicle for the transfer of sovereignty from the British Parliament to the Constituent Assemblies of the Dominions of India and Pakistan. It also served after independence as the constitution of India for three years. In Pakistan it remained the constitution until 1956, and thereafter large parts of it were borrowed for subsequent constitutions.[26]

As with the preceding Government of India Acts, the most important results of the Act of 1935 took place in the provinces. The respective and concurrent powers of the federal and provincial legislatures were specified in three legislative lists which set out federal, provincial, and joint powers. The provincial governments were similar in structure to that of the federal government, each Governor having power within his province akin to those exercised by the Governor-General on the federal level. It was provided that responsible government would come into existence on both the federal and provincial levels, and the Act attained a degree of success in the provinces, where the elected Indian members of the provincial legislature were conscientious and productive. The Act enlarged the partial responsible government in the provinces to full responsible government, subject to the continuation of emergency powers to enable the British to reassert control if the constitutional experiment were to get out of hand and endanger imperial hegemony. This devolution of greater political power to the provinces had the effect of frustrating the Congress Party leaders in their attempt to exercise influence at the centre and thus forward their move for independence on a national scale. Limitation of power at the centre was, however, at the time not unwelcome to Jinnah because of the difficulties he perceived in protecting the rights of the Muslim minority in any central legislature of a united India.

The changes provided for in the 1935 Act for the federal level were, as with Ramsey MacDonald's 1930 proposal, held hostage by the Princes. Because changes at the centre were premised on the assent of one-half of the rulers of the Princely states to their absorption into the federation created by the Act, and since this required assent was never obtained, the Act affected changes only at the provincial level. Consequently, between 1937, when the Act went into effect, and the outbreak of World War II in 1939, when India came under the rule of the emergency powers of the Governor-General, the federal level continued to operate under the Government of India Act of 1919. Since that Act had provided for only a rudimentary form of federal parliamentary government, the new dominions of India and Pakistan came into existence with little legislative experience at the centre and immediately after the period of the Governor-General's wielding of autocratic emergency powers during war time. When independence came, Jinnah was to be faced with the task of reversing the growth toward provincial separatism and autonomy which had been aided by the constitutional changes brought about by the successive constitutional legislation enacted by Parliament prior to independence.

Chapter 2

JINNAH AND THE MAKING OF A DOMINION

One historian writing of the period of transfer of power from Britain to the dominions of India and Pakistan complained that 'dominion status and the Governor-General's question took up far more time and energy than their real importance warranted.'[1] This conclusion may be true of India, which shed its dominion status and became a republic in 1951, but it is not true for Pakistan, which continued as a dominion and where dominion status and the powers of the Governor-General were used to justify significant constitutional changes eight years after independence.

Although by 1947 dominion status had long been an important element in the history of the nationalist movement on the subcontinent, it was a concept which had a different meaning for different people at different times. After the First World War, the goal of Congress leaders had been that India be admitted as a dominion on the same terms as the existing dominions of the Commonwealth. In 1916, the Muslim League and the Congress Party had joined together to demand in the Lucknow Pact that India be granted dominion status, and this demand was repeated twelve years later in the Nehru Report. By 1929, however, Gandhi and Jawaharlal Nehru had repudiated dominion status as a nationalist goal, demanding instead complete independence for India. At the time, Jinnah wrote to Prime Minister Ramsey MacDonald informing him about this growing nationalist agitation against dominion status. Jinnah warned that 'there was a section in India that was already declared in favour of complete independence, and I may tell you without exaggeration that the movement for independence is gaining ground, as it is supported by the Indian National Congress.' To avoid the consequences, Jinnah urged that the government of Great

Britain immediately state that it was 'unequivocally pledged to the policy of granting to India full responsible government with dominion status.'[2]

Two years after Jinnah's letter to MacDonald, Britain acknowledged the changes which had taken place in the Commonwealth by convention, and embodied those changes in statutory form. The Statute of Westminster of 1931 codified the relationships developed by convention among the Commonwealth members.[3] It did not attempt a definition of a dominion but instead identified the dominions by naming them and enumerating certain general characteristics which they shared.[4] No inference was made that the enumerated characteristics were either all inclusive, exclusive, or permanent. For the purposes of the statute the characteristics were: common allegiance to the Crown, autonomy (undefined), and free association within the Commonwealth.[5] Not stated but implied was that while Commonwealth membership was a free association, it was an association overshadowed by a member's allegiance to the Crown, and the phrase dominion status carried with it a constitutional link with Great Britain and the other dominions. In fact, the dominions were still not in a completely free association with Great Britain, which retained restrictions over some types of constitutional changes. This evolution towards fuller nationhood for the dominions was not paralleled in British India, which had been represented at the conferences which led to the Statute of Westminster but was not included in the statute itself. Instead, Parliament later passed the Government of India Act of 1935 which continued imperial control over India.

The Statute of Westminster offered the potential for further changes in dominion status and the relationships of the dominions with Great Britain. Such changes came about most rapidly in Ireland. When the Anglo-Irish Treaty of 1921 brought to a close Ireland's rebellion against Britain, it was clearly understood by the British and Irish negotiators of the treaty that dominion status, provided for in the treaty, meant that Ireland would remain within the Empire and would retain its allegiance to the Crown.[6] Many Irish considered the acceptance of dominion status a renunciation of the independence for which they had fought during two years of rebellion. So powerful were the symbols of domination attached to dominion status that the Irish nation broke into civil war over the signing of the Treaty of 1921 and what the Irish considered continued subjugation to the British Crown. The Statute of Westminster came ten years after the Anglo-Irish Treaty. The Commonwealth was now statutorily acknowledged a free association of nations and the dominions were allowed to take actions which would change their relationships to the United Kingdom.[7] Such changes in relationship followed in Ireland after Eamon De Valera became President in 1933. De Valera had been a member of the anti-treaty forces in the civil war, and when he came to power he took the opportunity during the period from 1934 to 1937 to undo the provisions of the Treaty of 1921. By 1947, when Pakistan and India gained their independence, Ireland no longer owed allegiance to the Crown, its people were no longer British subjects, and in 1932 the office of its Governor-General had been made 'ludicrous and empty, though not accorded the dignity of being extinguished.'[8] (The Governor-General was replaced by an elected President in 1937.) So antagonistic were relations that Britain and Ireland engaged in a five-year trade war, and Ireland adopted a constitution 'which might have been written for some island in the middle of the Atlantic hundreds of miles from Great Britain (of whose very name it contained no mention).'[9] Yet Ireland remained a Commonwealth member, 'acknowledging in a whisper the Crown as the symbol of its free association'.[10]

In the opinion of some Muslim leaders, dominion status as it had developed would create problems for the Muslim League if India remained united and Muslims were left as a minority unprotected from the Hindus. In a memorandum written in 1939, the noted jurist Zafrulla Khan discussed what he understood was meant by dominion status.[11] He understood it to mean 'that the Indian Central Legislature would cease to be a subordinate legislature and would become a sovereign legislature...'. It also meant that the Governor-General and the provincial governors would, in Zafrulla's words, become 'picturesque symbols to be brought into use mainly on ceremonial occasions'. For Muslims there was much to fear from such a change because 'it is inherent in a Dominion constitution of the Status *(sic)* of Westminster type that the Dominion Legislature is at liberty to convert a Dominion constitution into a republic or a dictatorship or any other type of sovereign government that appeals to it.' As to any constitutional protections for the Muslim minority, Zafrulla warned that 'however complete and elaborate may be the scheme of safeguards which may be embodied in the constitution, there would be nothing to prevent the Sovereign Dominion Legislature to repeal it or amend it out of all recognition...'.

It was agreed by some constitutional experts that by the end of the Second World War dominion status had little to do with the actual type of government under which a Commonwealth member ruled itself.[12] Such a conclusion did not, however, help to define what a dominion was or dispel the widely-held impression that dominion status implied outside domination. Those theoreticians who dealt with the question asserted that dominions were 'virtually autonomous States'.[13] All dominions were included in the Statute of Westminster, and each had a constitution which provided for allegiance to the British Crown. The concept of *virtually* autonomous States was, however, troublesome. To some, Commonwealth membership gave meaning to dominion status. Viceroy Lord Wavell referred to India joining the Commonwealth 'rather than becoming independent'.[14]

Edward McWhinney, one of the academic experts relied on by the British and Indians at the time of independence, later observed that little certainty existed as to the full implication of Commonwealth membership. 'It is characteristic of the rather amorphous definitions in British constitutional law that there was never any exact statement of the boundaries of membership of that British Commonwealth that had grown out of, though not displaced, the old British Empire.'[15]

When Mountbatten arrived in India to replace Wavell in March 1947, he faced escalating communal violence and lack of agreement on a government which could take over upon the withdrawal of the British. The apparent disintegration led him to the conclusion that unless power was transferred quickly there might not be existing authorities, at least in some parts of the subcontinent, to whom authority could be transferred. With his failure to achieve agreement at the Simla Conference in May, Mountbatten concluded that he must begin to move towards the transfer of power immediately. The problem was, as he presented it, 'If we waited until a constitutional set-up for all India was agreed, we should have to wait a long time particularly if partition were decided on. Whereas if we handed over power before the

Constituent Assemblies had finished their work we should leave the country without a Constitution.'[16]

Mountbatten proposed his answer in one of his first staff meetings after arriving in India. If a decision could be reached quickly it might be possible to establish 'some form' of dominion status in India which could be run experimentally until June of 1948, the then scheduled date for British withdrawal.[17] In this way power could be transferred to Indian hands while the British would still be present to offer whatever assistance the new leaders might need.[18] Mountbatten did not spell out the details of what he meant by dominion status, but he knew that the Government of India Act could be amended, and by excising those provisions which maintained British control the Act could be made similar to the basic constitutional structures of the senior dominions. The Governor-General would become the head of the state, limited to his capacity to advise.[19] While the changes would involve a minimum of alteration to the Government of India Act, the problem remained with the use of the term 'dominion status'. As Mountbatten told his staff, the words 'had an unfortunate association in the eyes of Indians and were almost universally misunderstood. Some other formula, some new words must therefore be found.'[20]

Not everyone on the British side was happy with the idea of India and Pakistan as Commonwealth members. An undercurrent of opposition developed at Whitehall among some senior civil servants who were involved with the affairs of the subcontinent.[21] They acknowledged the role the subcontinent would play in Commonwealth defence, considering its location between Europe and Australia. There was also the benefit to British prestige if it could be made to appear that Britain was not being repudiated by its former colonial subjects. At the same time, they argued that the racial, spiritual, and sentimental values which bound together the existing members of the Commonwealth would be absent in the case of India and Pakistan. Further, Britain might be putting herself in a position of owing obligations to Commonwealth members who might not reciprocate. Since the relationship might only be one of appearance, it was argued by some at Whitehall that it would be better to define Britain's relationship with India and Pakistan by treaties rather than through Commonwealth membership. There was fear that the new dominions might turn out like Ireland, whose membership in the Commonwealth provided little advantage and much difficulty to Britain, especially in defence matters. While some thought that India presented an even greater potential problem than Ireland because it was much larger, and that the presence of India and Pakistan in the 'Anglo-Saxon club' would weaken the Commonwealth, these objections were held by only a minority of British leaders. For the majority of British leaders, retaining India and Pakistan in the Commonwealth was a major goal.

There were favorable responses in India to Mountbatten's dominion proposal and the prospect of remaining within the Commonwealth. Representatives of the Scheduled Castes, the Princes, and the Muslim League gave their approval. One attraction of dominion status was that it would come with a constitution, the main features of which had been developed and proven successful in the senior dominions. Mountbatten counselled that acceptance of a dominion constitution would avoid the delays in creating a new constitution after independence. Both India and Pakistan expected that they would draft new constitutions, but until that was accomplished they would, as dominions, have serviceable constitutions under which they could operate. They would be relieved of the immediate pressure to expend energy in constitution-making, energy which might more profitably be directed towards the many problems which the new nations would face. This was an argument which appealed to Jinnah, who was concerned in the months prior to partition about what expert assistance he could obtain to draft a constitution after independence. He sought advice from the Viceroy's staff, and although names like Ivor Jennings and William Radcliffe were suggested, the staff advised that assistance might not be available.[21A]

During their six meetings in the third week of April, Jinnah informed Mountbatten of his willingness to allow Pakistan to become a member of the Commonwealth. Mountbatten's response was not what was expected. As Mountbatten later told his staff, 'All these applicants think they are doing Great Britain a favour by staying in.'[22] Unless the Congress leaders indicated their willingness to join, Mountbatten had serious reservations about offering Commonwealth membership to Pakistan. He curtly informed Jinnah that he 'could not recommend to His Majesty's Government that they should take on such a severe liability as the moth-eaten Pakistan was bound to be.'[23]

Unlike Jinnah, the Congress leaders held back at first. On 22 April, Mountbatten met with Congress leader V. K. Krishna Menon in a long and friendly session over a cup of tea. Mountbatten urged that India come into the Commonwealth in case Jinnah be successful in gaining support among the senior dominions for Pakistan's membership.[24] With only Pakistan in, there would be a disadvantage to India if India remained out, lacking as it would technical and military support and international contacts. Menon told Mountbatten that while Nehru might understand the importance of Commonwealth membership, Congress had burned its bridges in the matter of its future relations with Britain. In January of 1947 the Constituent Assembly of undivided India had capped Congress' long campaign for independence by declaring India to be an independent republic. The new nation was locked into the position of leaving the Empire, and there was a danger that any appearance of backing away from that goal might appear to the left wing of the Congress Party as selling out to the British, an impression which could create opposition to the leadership of Nehru and Patel.[25] Nehru expressed the same concerns in a meeting with Mountbatten on May 10.[26]

The strength of political reluctance on the part of the soon to be independent components of British India to be associated with the dominion concept or with Commonwealth membership can be gauged by Burma's opting for independence with no reference to dominion status and no association with the Commonwealth. As it was reported to the British Cabinet, the Burmese leader Aung San was in favour of accepting Mountbatten's offer of dominion status but opposition at home was too great and 'public opinion would split his party and drive the left wing into the hands of the Communists'.[27]

It was, however, now time for the Congress leaders to re-examine their opposition to dominion status and Commonwealth membership. Mountbatten offered the prospect of speeding British withdrawal, thus allowing Congress rank and file politicians to assume power. He also skillfully engendered fear in the minds of the Congress leaders that Pakistan might be given Commonwealth membership, and if India were not a member it would face a militarily superior Pakistan enjoying access to Britain's military expertise. Mountbatten went so far as to hint that Britain was considering a naval base at Karachi, a threat which achieved its intended effect of frightening the Indian leaders. Another advantage of moving events along at a speedier pace was mentioned by V. P. Menon, constitutional advisor to the Viceroy, who wrote to Sardar Patel that Mountbatten had 'stressed that we should not now delay the question of partition, which was in the best interest of India because he was sure that the truncated Pakistan, if conceded now, was bound to come back later...On the other hand, if there was delay, the uncertainty might lead to renewed agitation on the part of Jinnah and consequent deterioration in the political atmosphere. I agree with [Mountbatten's] observations because our slogan should now be "divide in order to unite".'[28]

After conferences with Mountbatten, Nehru and Patel reached the conclusion that, if dominion status could be given a more palatable name, it would be desirable, at least until a new constitution could be agreed on, which they thought unlikely for some considerable time. But as Attlee warned, secrecy was required to avoid the danger if it be known that 'Congress leaders had privately encouraged this idea'.[29] On 15 May, Mountbatten also had a discussion with Liaquat in which he covered the details of his dominion proposal, and found Liaquat 'surprisingly receptive to the idea'.[30] Mountbatten was quite enthusiastic in his expression of satisfaction, calling what had happened a 'completely changed situation which seemed improbable if not impossible'. He saw it as 'the greatest opportunity ever offered to the Empire and we must not let administrative or other difficulties stand in the way'.[31]

The difficulty which everyone envisioned concerning the use of the term 'dominion status' actually turned out to be less of a problem than was thought. Both India and Pakistan eventually came into existence as dominions in August of 1947 without further extended discussion of the question of what they were to be called. Nehru successfully disposed of the issue by rationalizing that although '...over the last many years, there had been a tremendous sentiment in India in favour of complete independence,' and that while the word dominion was 'likely to irritate because of past associations,' he was now satisfied that 'in theory it could be shown that dominion status was equivalent to complete independence.'[32] Cambridge-educated Nehru had learned the English key to constitutional success, namely, to make a principle of government workable, ratchet up the principle's level of vagueness to a height sufficient to overcome the barrier faced.

On their part, the British busied themselves in draining the concept of Commonwealth membership of most of its past meaning. In the beginning of May, Prime Minister Attlee was made aware that Mountbatten required a loose concept of the Commonwealth, one which would enable him 'to bring in new members without losing the old.'[33] The solution would be a political not a legal one, and Attlee urged that the issue be kept free of the government's lawyers.[34] One month later, he informed the Cabinet that 'it was necessary to find a formula which would allow the greatest number of independent units to adhere to the Commonwealth without excessive uniformity in their internal constitutions or in their relationships with Great Britain, the Commonwealth or one another'. He suggested the name of the new Commonwealth might be 'the Associated States of the Commonwealth'. His Cabinet gave its general approval to the name 'Commonwealth of British Associated Nations'.[35]

Congress leaders were willing to accept the allegiance to the Crown provided the words 'Emperor of India' were no longer part of the King's title.[36] Even the concept of allegiance was undergoing rapid transformation in the last months. It was becoming what the Attorney-General in London suggested as 'some sort of allegiance to the Crown as head of the Commonwealth.'[37] No longer was it to be allegiance to a King who was the monarch of each of the individual nations of the Commonwealth. Instead, he was to be acknowledged by each Commonwealth member as the King of the entire Commonwealth, and what attributes he was to possess were to be left vague. Mountbatten went a step further, proposing that the Crown be eliminated altogether from the Commonwealth and that a President be nominated by the King and elected by the members to head the Commonwealth. He favoured 'some loose form of association within the British Commonwealth' with perhaps 'a form of common citizenship'.[38]

Two weeks before the transfer of power, B. N. Rau, the constitutional adviser looked to by the parties for developing a theoretical foundation for the new order, summarized some of the attributes which distinguished the new dominions of Pakistan and India from the senior dominions. According to a memorandum issued by Rau, because of the allegiance owed by each of the existing dominions to the Crown, none of them enjoyed the right to unilaterally leave the Commonwealth. He quoted one text-writer as setting out the prevailing position of the Commonwealth. 'The Dominions were created as organized Governments under the British Crown, and there is no provision in the constitutions which contemplates that they have the right to eliminate the Crown, or sever their connections with it.'[39] Citations to the Canadian and Australian constitutions and the Anglo-Irish Treaty of 1921 were given to confirm this opinion. The memorandum noted, however, the different conditions under which India and Pakistan were coming into existence: the terms of the Indian Independence Act, which was then being drafted, would not contain the restrictive language of the Statute of Westminster, but instead established 'independent' dominions free to change the Independence Act itself without any reference to Parliament. It was considered significant that the status of the senior dominions developed through convention while India and Pakistan were dominions which would be created by statute. Therefore, any conventions defining the senior dominions were not applicable to India and Pakistan if inconsistent with the terms of the Independence Act. In Rau's words, 'the terms of the Indian Independence Act are wider than those of the Statute of Westminster. In the first place, there is no restrictive preamble to the Act; secondly, section 6(2) of the Act expressly permits repeal of the Act itself...by dominion legislation; finally the name of the Act is significant.'

The name of the Indian Independence Act was also important to Winston Churchill who, like other Conservative Party members, was forced by political reality to accept the passage of the Act but was not reconciled to the idea of India's complete freedom from Britain. As the Act worked its way to final passage in Parliament, Churchill wrote to Attlee, 'The Indian Independence Bill should be called the "Indian Dominions Bills"' because, he maintained, 'Dominion status is not the same as independence although it may be freely used to establish independence. It is not true that a community is independent when its Ministers have in fact taken the Oath of Allegiance to the King.'[40] Attlee disagreed, replying that the Dominion Prime Minister would '...bear allegiance to the King who is the King of all the Dominions.' Attlee saw this as emphasizing 'the complete freedom of every member of the

Commonwealth from control by any other member. I think this is a most valuable counter to the demand for independence outside the Commonwealth as it shows that this demand can be satisfied within it. This is, in fact, the meaning of Dominion Status.'[41]

Mountbatten also had no difficulty with the concept of Indian freedom. In an early broadcast to the people of the subcontinent, he said, 'I should like to make it quite clear that under the terms of the Statute of Westminster, any dominion being independent and voluntarily in full partnership with the other free and independent Dominions, can on its own initiative secede from the Commonwealth at any time it choses.'[42] To Mountbatten the new dominions were not to be 'virtually' autonomous states restricted within the Commonwealth by traditional concepts of allegiance to the British Crown, but were to be independent nations. This became the position adopted by the Cabinet, and the change helped convince Nehru of the acceptability of Dominion Status. Jinnah, however, changed his mind, disappointed that India and not Pakistan alone was to be admitted into the Commonwealth. On this point, Mountbatten ignored Jinnah, who eventually agreed to join India as a Commonwealth member.[43]

Jinnah was also made privy to the thinking of the British on the role of the Governor-General. In June of 1947, Lord Ismay noted from New Delhi the persistence of a good deal of misunderstanding in the country about the meaning of Dominion Status and the powers thereunder of the Governor-General.[44] Because of this misunderstanding, Mountbatten sent Jinnah a memorandum entitled 'Dominion Office Note On Dominion's Governor-General.'[45] This memorandum set out the nature of the office as defined by the Imperial Conference of 1926. A dominion's Governor-General was 'the representative of the Crown, holding in all essential respects the same position in relation to the administration of public affairs in the Dominion as is held by His Majesty the King in Great Britain, and not the representative or agent of His Majesty's Government in the United Kingdom or any Department of that Government.' The memorandum went on to give instruction on a question which was later to be troublesome in Pakistani politics: how the scope and nature of the Governor-General's office in a particular dominion could be determined. The answer given in the memorandum was that there were two sources which were to be consulted. One was the Letter of

Instruction issued by the Crown to the Governor-General, and the other was the terms of the dominion's constitution referring to the Governor-General of that dominion. Because British leaders did not wish to give offence to the aspirations for independence of the Pakistanis and Indians, Letters of Instruction were abolished for these new dominions in the drafting of the Indian Independence Act. This meant that the role to be played by the Governor-General was therefore solely defined by the terms of the Indian and Pakistani dominion constitutions.[46]

Copies of official correspondence with which Mountbatten furnished Jinnah made it clear that by Commonwealth practice all actions of a dominion Governor-General were to be taken on the advice of his ministers.[47] In this regard, a dominion Governor-General had discretionary powers only in the most exceptional situations, his refusal of a dissolution of the legislature being the only one mentioned, and in that situation 'the exercise of discretion must depend upon his finding Ministers who accept responsibility for his actions.' Mountbatten also furnished Jinnah with correspondence from his aide, Lord Ismay, which contained amplification on the role of a Governor-General. 'Under the British constitution which is much in vogue in India at the present time, the King reigns but does not govern. He has, however, an unlimited right to receive information and to give advice which ministers may take or reject on their responsibility.' Like the King, a Governor-General was limited to the tendering of advice.[48] But the concept did not please Jinnah, who wanted expanded powers for the Governor-General of Pakistan, powers which the British were reluctant to include in the Indian Independence Act because they feared Jinnah was seeking dictatorial powers for himself.[49]

The Indian Independence Act was completed by Parliament's draftsmen in London in July 1947.[50] It amended the Government of India Act of 1935, exorcising it of its provisions providing for imperial control, and made the 1935 Act the basic constitutional document of the dominions of India and Pakistan. The federated form of government of British India was continued in both dominions, with functions, duties, and rights enumerated for both the federal and provincial levels. The day before Parliament was to cast its final vote on the Independence Act, Mountbatten arranged conferences at the Viceroy's Palace, inviting Nehru and Patel in one group and Jinnah and Liaquat Ali Khan in another group.

Both groups considered the terms of the Independence Act in separate rooms for a period of an hour and a half.[51] The Chief Justice of the Indian Supreme Court was available to answer any questions concerning the legislation that Parliament was to consider the next day. There were no questions or objections by either group to the terms of the Independence Act.[52]

On 15 August 1947, Pakistan, like India, came into existence specifically identified as an independent dominion with a constitution created by Parliament and modelled on the Westminster form of parliamentary cabinet government. The constitution Pakistan received at independence was similar in structure to the dominion constitutions which had been in operation for many years in the senior dominions of Canada, Australia, New Zealand, and South Africa. Under Pakistan's dominion constitution, the sovereignty previously exercised by Parliament was to be exercised by a newly-created Constituent Assembly of Pakistan.[53] This Assembly was made up of the representatives elected in 1946 to the Constituent Assembly of undivided India from the areas which after independence constituted Pakistan.[54]

The Congress Party had never varied from its position that the legislature of an independent undivided India would be a sovereign body, sovereignty being understood to mean the right to unilaterally amend any constitution which might be in or come into existence at independence. Jinnah and the Muslim League had not disagreed with the theory of legislative sovereignty, but if they were to agree to a united India they demanded safeguards for the Muslim minority within any such legislature. This would have meant a limitation on the constituent powers of the legislature to change the constitution. But after rejection of the Cabinet Mission Plan, there was no further consideration during the negotiations between the British and the Indians of transferring anything less than full sovereignty to the federal level of any new nation that would emerge. The question was whether constituent powers would be transferred to one constituent assembly for an undivided India or would be transferred to separate constituent assemblies if the subcontinent was partitioned. When the sovereign powers exercised by the British Parliament over the subcontinent were transferred to two constituent assemblies, one for the new India and one for Pakistan, limitations of sovereignty were no longer needed because the Muslims would be the majority in their own assembly.

The functions of the federal legislature[55] of British India in enacting ordinary legislation were now to be carried out respectively by the newly-created Constituent Assemblies of India and Pakistan. Separate from that function, those Assemblies also had constituent powers with the initial responsibility in each of the two dominions of drafting any new constitutions. Each Assembly was vested with the power to make any changes it wished to the Government of India Act of 1935 and the Indian Independence Act. Unlike the senior dominions, the independent dominions of India and Pakistan, possessing full constituent powers, were free to make any constitutional changes they wished without obtaining approval of the British Parliament.

The leaders of Pakistan had before them the task of putting their new dominion constitution into operation. Pakistanis had not been called to the barricades to protest British rule. Their principal opponent had been the Hindu majority of the subcontinent, and their reason for insisting that British India be partitioned was not motivated primarily by oppression experienced at the hands of the British, but by fear of future religious suppression by the Hindus. Any thinking as to how this Muslim sanctuary would be governed if it were won was put off by Jinnah and the Muslim League until the time independence was achieved. Jawaharlal Nehru served as the theorist for India's secular state, but Pakistan had no counterpart. The leaders of Pakistan's independence movement had a general idea that the new state would be a democracy of the Western type, but it is uncertain whether their allegiance to parliamentary democracy was based on conviction or convenience.

There was little or no discussion by Pakistan's leaders after independence concerning alternatives to the British system of government. Neither vocal opponents nor enthusiastic supporters existed, but Pakistan had to put a national government in operation in very short order. Not only was parliamentary government familiar, it was already in operation in the provinces. Further, most of the leaders of the Muslim League had been educated in the British tradition, and parliamentary government was the government they knew best. A significant number had legal training and had worked within the system under the British. For them, constitutional government was a familiar package of courts, provincial assemblies, ministerial cabinets, police, and education. These were institutions created by the British and left in place when they departed. The British had finished their role in the subcontinent. It remained for the Pakistanis to take up the task of either discarding the governmental institutions of their colonial past and replacing them with indigenous ones, or of adjusting the inherited institutions to the needs of the new nation.

While he lived, Jinnah was the government of Pakistan. Nothing was done without his concurrence, expressed or implied, and very often with his active participation. It is uncertain how many of those around him knew but never spoke of what the X-rays revealed: the condition of Jinnah's lungs was such that his life-span after independence could only be measured in months. Pakistan seemed to be at a political standstill awaiting direction from its leader. The religious factions raised no demands, east and west wings did not voice their differences, and nothing was done about the new constitution. From the beginning, the people of Pakistan had relied on Jinnah's guidance, and no one could think of Pakistan without him. He had brought into existence a new nation and now his people looked to him to tell them what they should do with the fruits of his victory.

During his long political career Jinnah had built a reputation as an astute constitutional thinker, and it was constitutionalism which characterized his actions in the political arena and in his fight for Pakistan.[56] But in August 1946, Jinnah had made a sharp departure from his past. Stymied in his negotiations for Pakistan, he obtained from the Muslim League a resolution calling for Direct Action. After the vote he told the League members: 'What we have done today is the most historic act in our history. Never have we in the whole history of the League done anything except by constitutional methods and by constitutionalism. But now we are obliged and forced into the position. This day we will bid good-bye to constitutional methods...Today we have also forged a pistol and are in a position to use it.'[57] This was 'Jinnah's Rubicon on the road to Pakistan.'[58] The carnage of the Calcutta Killings followed his call. Direct Action convinced the British that the subcontinent could not be kept united without a bloody civil war. Pakistan was conceded. Having won his valuable prize by actions outside the constitution, would Jinnah be willing to abide by limitations contained in the dominion government which he acquired from the hands of the British?

While as a politician and negotiator for Pakistan's independence, Jinnah operated within the constitution developed in British India, there are reasons to doubt how well he understood that constitution, or, if he did understand it, whether he intended to implement that constitution when it came into existence in its amended form as Pakistan's dominion constitution. In July 1947, while engaged in negotiations for dominion status, Jinnah jotted a note to himself: 'Danger of Parliamentary form of government. (1) It has worked satisfactorily so far in England and nowhere else. (2) Presidential form of government more suited to Pakistan.'[59] In a speech given in Balochistan after independence, he spoke as if presidential rule would be more beneficial for parts of Pakistan than was a legislative form of government.[60] In another speech to officers at Quetta Staff College, Jinnah advocated they study the Government of India Act, which he informed them showed that the executive authority flows from the Governor-General.[61] No recognition was given by Jinnah to the idea that in exercising his powers the Governor-General was to act only on the advice of his ministers.

The first major constitutional act of the new nation of Pakistan was the appointment of a Governor-General. Jinnah's appointment of himself to the office was to have an impact on Pakistan's political development. In the other dominions the Governor-General was by convention expected to be an elder statesman, retired military person, or a member of the aristocracy, and not an active politician. He was appointed by the British Crown on the advice of the dominion ministry, was responsible to that ministry, and was removable by the Crown on the advice of that ministry. It was assumed by many, especially among the British, that Mountbatten would become the Governor-General of both India and Pakistan after independence. Mountbatten coveted the joint office, both as a feather in his cap, showing approval of his work in bringing independence to the subcontinent, and because of what was probably a genuine feeling of respect and affection on his part for the people of undivided India. If there was any barrier to Mountbatten's goal, it was thought by some that it would most likely come from the Indian side of the partition line. The Congress Party, not the Muslim League, had been the leading force opposing

British power, and many of its members had been imprisoned in British jails during the independence struggle. In contrast, few Muslim League leaders had. Nehru, Patel, Gandhi, and many other Congress leaders served lengthy periods of imprisonment after sentencing by British courts. Jinnah and Liaquat Ali Khan, like most Muslim League leaders, never served a day in a British jail for opposing British rule. In fact, as independence and partition approached, the Muslim leaders were none too anxious to see a hasty departure of the British. They were ill-prepared to set up and operate a government for the new state of Pakistan, and it was generally thought that, while some leaders of the Indian Dominion might oppose the appointment of a British Governor-General, Pakistan would see the benefit of a joint Governor-General for both dominions. Much property of the British government which Pakistan was to receive was in Indian territory, and Pakistan might benefit from having a joint Governor-General who would be available to arbitrate any disputes which might arise between the new dominions concerning the division of assets.

While there was no opposition voiced regarding the prospect of a Britisher serving as Pakistan's first Governor-General, Muslim League leaders early raised objections to a joint Governor-General, be he Mountbatten or anyone else. Prior to independence, the office of Liaquat Ali Khan, who was at the time Finance Minister in the interim government of undivided India, issued a memorandum dealing with the office of Governor-General, stating that it was 'inappropriate and opposite to the constitutional practice of the British Commonwealth' to have a single Governor-General for two dominions. 'The Crown is the only connecting link between the Dominions. The appointment of one Governor-General for two Dominions would mean a link between them at the Governor-General's level and not at the Crown level.' The memorandum went on to state that the only reason for one Governor-General would be because the affairs of India and Pakistan were mixed at the present time, but that the requirement of having only one Governor-General 'can be met without doing violence to constitutional practice by the appointment of a Supreme Authority for the interim period when the division of the administration is taking place. He will be His Majesty's Representative for the exercise of the function of the Crown in its relations with the two Dominions (and also the Indian States).

His main function will be to effect the complete transfer of power in a smooth and speedy manner to the two Dominions and to supervise the division of the Civil and Military administrations between the two Dominions.' The Supreme Authority 'would in effect act as arbitrator between the two governments whether he is formally asked to fulfil such a role or not. On the other hand, a common Constitutional Governor-General who is confronted with conflicting advice from the two Dominion Governments will find himself in a difficult and awkward position...Since the Supreme Authority would be appointed with a specific function for a limited period, the disappearance of the appointment would in no way upset or alter the constitutional position of the two Dominion Governments. This would make for a continuity of relationship between the two Dominions and His Majesty's Government.'[62]

While Mountbatten grew to respect Jinnah because he was the one Indian leader he was not able to influence, no personal relationship was established between them. Mountbatten described their first meeting to his staff by calling Jinnah 'a psychopathic case,' and adding that until he met Jinnah 'he had not thought it possible that a man with such complete lack of responsibility could hold the power which he did.'[63] It is difficult to believe that such an attitude, even if not expressed to Jinnah, did not affect the relationship of the two men, but Jinnah took no public notice of it. But among the other leaders of Pakistan, there was widespread dislike and distrust of Mountbatten which made it impossible for them to consider him a neutral statesman. Some were mindful of his close relationship with Nehru, a relationship which had led Mountbatten to disclose the so-called 'Dicky Bird' plan, dealing with the implementation of independence, to Nehru unilaterally in March 1947 and to make changes in that plan when Nehru objected.[64] One Pakistani has commented that accepting Mountbatten as Governor-General 'would have amounted to handing over the position of the Head of the new-born state to a nominee of the Hindu Congress.'[65] So strong and enduring was this feeling that, a decade after independence, the government refused to allow Mountbatten to visit Pakistan.[66]

Some people in Pakistan were also disturbed by Mountbatten's acceleration of the date for British departure. They believed that this was done to weaken Pakistan at its inception, and thus make it possible for India to force reunity. Partition was a thorn in the side of the British. The unity of India, to the extent it existed prior to independence, was of British making and a matter of great pride. Undivided India, their magnificent imperial trophy, was besmirched by the creation of Pakistan, and the division of India was never emotionally accepted by many British leaders, Mountbatten among them. He shared the view of Indian politicians that the aberration called Pakistan would not survive separation from the rest of India. Mountbatten remained of the mind that reunity could be accomplished after the excitement of independence and partition had died down and 'reality' settled in.

Another fear of Mountbatten as Governor-General was the political threat presented by his internationally acclaimed 'charm'.[67] Pakistan was yet without a real identity as a nation aside from its base in Islam, and the most important parts of Pakistan, in Punjab and Bengal, had been precisely those parts of undivided India which had experienced the strongest provincial political development. These were political territories which had joined the Pakistan movement late. Jinnah could not be sure of his political power in those provinces, particularly if he were pitted against Mountbatten's political ability when turned on local politicians, some of whom were lukewarm at best on the need for Pakistan. By grassroots politicking, Mountbatten and the Congress Party might be able to bring Pakistan back into the Indian fold. This was not an unrealistic fear. The Governor-General, although he was a constitutional head of state, was temporarily vested by the Independence Act with extraordinary powers for the first seven months of Independence.

It was a surprise when Jinnah announced that he would be the first Governor-General of Pakistan. He issued no statement giving the reasons why he chose to disregard Commonwealth convention and select himself, certainly no figurehead removed from politics. Churchill appears to have been the only prominent British leader not dismayed by Jinnah's action.[68] The other British leaders, both in India and at home, were angered and disappointed. They considered Jinnah's action one of pure vanity.[69] In later years, Mountbatten related a meeting in which he pointed out to Jinnah that under the dominion constitution of Pakistan, real power would be in the hands of the Prime Minister, to which Jinnah reportedly replied, 'In Pakistan, I will be the Governor-General, and the Prime Minister will do what I tell him.' Mountbatten was convinced that Jinnah, whom he referred to as the 'dying Muslim leader,' was incapable of resisting 'the pomp, the gaudy ceremonials of the top office of the state for which he had worked so hard'.[70]

Jinnah, however, had more than his own personal satisfaction to consider. He was faced with the burden of showing the nation's citizens and the world that Pakistan was really a nation. The fact that after independence three of Pakistan's four provincial governors were British, as were the heads of the army, navy, and air force, did not make this easy. Pakistan was a dominion in the Commonwealth headed by an English King. It had a national assembly which had been split off from the all-India Constituent Assembly elected before independence to serve as the legislature for undivided India, and if a British Governor-General was to head both India and Pakistan the appearance could be created that nothing substantial had been changed by independence and partition.[71] But if not Mountbatten, why not a Pakistani leader who might play the role of a politically neutral Governor-General, as in the other dominions? Most probably it was because the people needed a symbol of their identity, and Jinnah was the symbol of Pakistan. Before independence, the Governor-General symbolized the state and state power. It was the office known to the people. British India had had a Governor-General but no Prime Minister.

Regardless of the reasons for the rejection of Mountbatten and the idea of a joint Governor-Generalship, Jinnah's assumption of the office constituted a departure from dominion practice that the Governor-General should be non-political.[72] Pakistan had in Jinnah not only an active politician as its Governor-General, but its most powerful and influential politician. His very existence in the office of Governor-General would have in itself changed the non-political nature of the office, but beyond that Jinnah also challenged the office's constitutional basis. He insisted that his authority as Governor-General flowed not from the Crown but from the people, whose mandate he claimed he held as a result of the Muslim League's victory in the last election before partition. He dismissed as legal fiction the idea that he held office at His Majesty's pleasure,[73] and consistent with that view he refused to take the oath as Governor-General in the form then in use in the Commonwealth: 'to bear true faith and allegiance to his Majesty'. Instead, his oath was to bear 'true allegiance to the constitution and be faithful to his Majesty'. Further, as Governor-General Jinnah refused to assent in the name of the English sovereign to the ordinary legislation which required the Governor-General's assent under the constitution.[74]

Citing the people's mandate might have made a valid constitutional argument for a Prime Minister but not for a Governor-General. Despite the democratic appearance of Jinnah's views, a Governor-General was an unelected official and for that reason was excluded by convention from any share in political power. It was because he was unaccountable to the people that he was limited to the offering of advice to his ministers, advice which they were free to accept or reject. Jinnah was claiming an expanded political role based on an alleged mandate from the people who never had, nor under the constitution would have, an opportunity to vote on who would occupy the office of Governor-General. The fact that there was little doubt that the people would have voted their Jinnah to any office he wished was beside the point. Jinnah bestowed on the Governor-Generalship expanded unconstitutional political powers which could be and later were used by a successor Governor-General, Ghulam Mohammad, for his own unconstitutional purposes.

Jinnah addressed the problem of building a government at the centre by assuming an active role within the government. His orders were unquestioned. He, not Prime Minister Liaquat Ali Khan, appointed the Cabinet. In the United Kingdom and the other dominions the Cabinet is the Prime Minister's Cabinet and appointees are nominated by him. The Cabinet he chose for Liaquat was a strong one.[75] It included I. I. Chundrigar, formerly a prominent lawyer who later appeared for the Constituent Assembly in the litigation concerning its dissolution, and who then went on to become Prime Minister; Ghulam Mohammad, later to become Governor-General, as finance minister; Sardar Abdur Rab Nishtar, leader from the North-West Frontier Province, who today is buried with Jinnah at the latter's memorial tomb in Karachi; and Bengali leader Fazlur Rahman, who was later to be a leader in the opposition against Ghulam Mohammad when the latter became Governor-General. These men assumed their Cabinet responsibilities at the time of independence. Zafrulla Khan, who enjoyed an outstanding reputation for his judicial service in British India, joined shortly thereafter. The Cabinet represented a geographic diversity and a broad array of talent. The everyday operation of the government was in the hands of the Pakistan Civil Service, which maintained close ties with Prime Minister Liaquat, who supplied its members with as much support as limited resources would allow.

Jinnah undertook the constitutionally unusual move of serving both as Governor-General and as a Cabinet member. He kept the newly-created ministries of Evacuation and Refuge Rehabilitation and that of State and Frontier Regions under his direct control by accepting the portfolios for these Cabinet offices. The latter ministry gave him administrative control of Balochistan. He not only accepted an appointment from the Constituent Assembly as adviser for the writing of a new constitution, but, unique among Commonwealth Governors-General, he served in the dual capacity of Governor-General and President of the Legislature. Jinnah also appointed Sir Archibald Rowland as his financial adviser, Firoz Khan Noon as his special envoy to the Middle East, and Zafrulla Khan to the United Nations to argue the case of the Palestinian Arabs. He appointed a personal representative in Kabul, a post which was later converted to an ambassadorship. His Kabul agent represented to the Afghan government that Jinnah was the only person in Pakistan's government 'who could get things done', making it only a matter of formality to go through any other channel.[76] Jinnah took public positions on controversial political issues such as the separation of Karachi from Sindh. His advice supporting the separation, although quite unpopular, was decisive, and his intervention in the disturbances in East Bengal, urging the Bengalis to accept Urdu as the sole national language, was essential to restoring peace there. Pakistan had a political Governor-General who controlled the Executive, the Cabinet, and the Assembly. Although Jinnah was not the Governor-General envisioned in the dominion constitution, he did not indicate to the nation that he was to be considered unique. Nor did he justify his actions as Governor-General on the ground that he believed the times were exceptional and that in the future the nation should look to the constitution and its conventions when choosing a Governor-General and defining the scope of that office.

Jinnah lived only a short time after independence, and his ebbing energy was so consumed by the political task of state-building that he was unable to accomplish anything toward the drafting of a new constitution. It was his belief that the drafting of a new constitution would require experts from the United Kingdom. He estimated drafting would be 'a stupendous task' taking eighteen months to two years after independence.[77] His references to such a constitution were often in democratic terms. On 9 June 1947, Jinnah told his fellow members of the Muslim League: 'I do not know what the ultimate shape of the Constitution is going to be, but I am sure it will be a democratic type, embodying the essential principles of Islam.' He added, '...democracy is in our blood. It is in our marrow. Only centuries of adverse circumstances have made the circulation of that blood cold...Islam and its ideals have taught us democracy...It has taught equality of man, justice and fair play to everybody.'[78] Apparently, Jinnah saw no inconsistency or conflict in having a democracy based on the principles of Islam, and in fact he later stated that no laws would be passed in Pakistan which would be contrary to the Koran or *Shariat*.[79] He did not, however, give any idea whether the principles of Islam would be incorporated into the constitution itself, and if so what principles, or whether Islam was to be an ideal outside of the constitution acting as an ethical and philosophical basis for that constitution.

Jinnah often referred to the Muslim nature of the state. At Aligarh, three years before independence, he told an audience, 'Throughout the ages, Hindus had remained Hindus and Muslims had remained Muslims and they had not merged their estates—that was the basis for Pakistan.'[80] When he addressed a crowd in East Bengal, urging the necessity of Urdu as the single national language, he rested his plea not on his listeners' loyalty as Pakistanis, but as Muslims. In Peshawar, in April 1948, he reminded his listeners that their government was no longer under foreign rule, 'but it was now a Muslim government and Muslim rule that holds the reigns of this great independent sovereign state of Pakistan.'[81] What did Jinnah mean by Muslim rule? Would he accept a constitution which provided for a government by and for Muslims? What was to be the place and role of any non-Muslims under such Muslim rule? Eighteen per cent of East Bengal was Hindu after partition, and they held twenty-five per cent of that province's seats in the Constituent Assembly.

Before independence, Jinnah had not ventured beyond stating that the minorities would be protected in Pakistan, and would participate in the government. But in his best-known public address on minorities, on 11 August 1947, he appeared before the inaugural meeting of the Constituent Assembly of Pakistan. In a talk which was for the most part extemporaneous and disorganized, Jinnah told the members '...you will find that in the course of time, Hindus will cease to be Hindus and Muslims will cease to be Muslims, not in the religious sense, because that is the personal faith of each individual, but in the political sense as citizens of the state.'[82] Here was the man who had just won the creation of Pakistan on his theory of Two Nations, and some thought he was now denying the validity of that theory. It was as if his mind had drifted back to his younger years and to the ideas he held when he stood forth as a champion of United India. Others understood his speech as a definite statement of intent that Pakistan would be a secular state.[83] In contrast, Jinnah's American biographer asked, 'What was he talking about? Had he simply forgotten where he was? Had the cyclone of events so disoriented him that he was arguing the opposition's brief?'[84] To a biographer who knew Jinnah personally, his 11 August speech was '...an inheritance from the Prophet (PBUH), who had said thirteen centuries before, "all men are equal in the eyes of God...today I trample under my feet all distinctions of caste, colour and nationality."'[85] Jinnah's speech to the Assembly was his sole public statement on minorities after independence.

At the independence ceremonies, four days after Jinnah's Assembly speech, the flag of Pakistan was officially flown for the first time. That flag, the flag of the Muslim League, was three-quarters green, the colour representing the Muslims of Pakistan; the remaining one-quarter was white, representing the non-Muslim population.[86] Liaquat, with Jinnah in attendance, addressed the crowd. '...[T]he State of Pakistan will be a state where there will be no special privileges, no special rights for any one particular community or individual. It will be a State where every citizen will have equal privileges and they will share equally all obligations that come to a citizen of Pakistan.'[87] If the crowd came away from the independence speeches with the idea that Pakistan was a state whose citizens would not be divided politically by religious identification, experience was to prove otherwise. From the beginning of the work on the new constitution, Islam won for itself special privileges, and the non-Muslim population in Pakistan was segregated in electoral groupings which diminished their political power.

Jinnah's statement to the Assembly must be understood in the time-frame in which it was made. While there had been serious communal rioting prior to his speech on 11 August 1948, particularly in the Punjab, Jinnah was speaking to the Constituent Assembly before the carnage of partition occurred. The Radcliffe Boundary Award was not made known until 15 August, four days after Jinnah's speech. It was only then that the territorial identification of Pakistan and India was made public. Muslims began their flight to Pakistan from India, and Hindus and Sikhs began vacating Pakistan territory. The bloodbath accompanying partition was the event which defined the completeness of the separation of India and Pakistan. With it Indian and British thoughts about the 'temporary' nature of the separation lost reality. The picture of the suffering accompanying the act of partition became a scar on the minds of both Pakistanis and Indians, and further increased the separate identity of Muslims and Hindus. The impact was even more serious in Pakistan than in India, since the number of refugees crowding into West Pakistan, in proportion to the area and the number of inhabitants, was much greater than the inflow received in larger India. Because the tragedy of human suffering brought by partition affected Jinnah greatly, when he formed the new government he took the ministry in charge of refugee relief directly under his control.

For the first five months of independence, Jinnah feared that India might succeed in destroying Pakistan.[88] India was withholding some of Pakistan's badly-needed share of the government and military assets left behind by the British, and Nehru's use of the military to assert India's claim to Kashmir was an ominous sign. The conflict over Kashmir added to communal hatred. So did India's ultimatum delivered to the Muslim state of Hyderabad. That ultimatum gave Hyderabad one year to join the Indian Union, with the implication that force would be used if it did not acquiesce. The government of Hyderabad was sympathetic to Pakistan, furnishing desperately-needed finances after independence. It was a state the size of England, and if India was willing to use force to conquer this major Muslim principality, as it had militarily occupied Kashmir, what was to prevent India from using its large army to wipe away what Indian leaders considered the greatest disfigurement on the face of the Indian motherland: Pakistan itself? Fear and suspicion flared further when, on 31 January 1948, the bullet fired by a Hindu fanatic ended the life of 'Muslim-lover' Mahatma Gandhi. The only major public voice for communal understanding in India was silenced. There was little opportunity, even if he desired it, for Jinnah to speak again of unity and reconciliation between Muslim and Hindu, as he had on that one occasion before the Constituent Assembly. In the months that remained to him after independence, Hindus and Muslims were driven further apart. In January of 1948, Jinnah was exhorting an audience to 'sacrifice and die in order to make Pakistan [a] truly great Islamic State.'[89] His audience on that occasion was not a group of *ulema,* but the members of the Sindh Bar Association.

Under the Government of India Act of 1935, politics had been played out on the provincial level. It was at that level, rather than the national, that experience had been accumulated by the majority of leaders who would now govern, and it was on local interests that a politician was able to build his political base, not from participating in government activity on the national level. Despite his enormous prestige, Jinnah was an outsider to local politics.[90] He had been born in Karachi but based his political career in Bombay. Liaquat Ali Khan, his closest political associate, was a refugee to Pakistan from India.

It was in the provinces that Jinnah faced his first political problems. One week after Pakistan came into existence, Jinnah dismissed the ministry of Khan Sahib in the North-West Frontier Province. Because the Muslim League in that province had been in such a state of disorganization prior to the elections of 1946, the Indian Congress Party had been able to form a government with Khan Sahib as Chief Minister. The ministry, although made up of Muslims, had opposed the creation of Pakistan, and when the province voted to join Pakistan, it was anticipated that the Khan Sahib ministry would resign and a new election be held. But maintaining the Congress Ministry in the NWFP had become a test for the National Congress leaders and their ability to make the British bend to their wishes.[91] As a result, the Congress ministry did not resign despite its growing unpopularity, and understandably the existence of such a ministry in a province of Pakistan was anathema to the leaders of Pakistan. Jinnah may have thought that he had obtained a commitment from Mountbatten that prior to independence Khan Sahib's ministry would be dismissed. This commitment was, however, countermanded by the Secretary of

State in London, who gave the reasoning that the dismissal of a ministry which enjoyed a majority in the legislature, as did the Khan Sahib ministry, would be unconstitutional.[92] The problem was left to Jinnah when he became Governor-General at independence. He immediately instructed Governor George Cunningham of the North-West Frontier Province to dismiss Khan Sahib.[93] A Muslim League ministry was thereupon formed which, however, was not able to gain a legislative majority for months and which consolidated its power by arresting 250 of the opposition.[94]

Jinnah purported to act pursuant to Section 51(5) of the Government of India Act, which gave him control over the provincial Governor.[95] Section 51(5) had not been so employed during British rule. Rather, when the British had felt it necessary to assert their control from the centre and a Governor-General wished to remove a provincial ministry, he did so through the exercise of Section 93 of the Government of India Act. The British, believing that this instrument of colonial control would not be necessary after independence, deleted Section 93 from the 1935 Act when they left the subcontinent.[96] Thereafter, what remained was the power of a provincial Governor, based on convention, to dismiss a ministry on the grounds that the ministry had lost the confidence of the provincial legislature, and then only if he could replace the ministry with one which could obtain such confidence.[97] For his part, the Governor-General's involvement in provincial affairs was limited to his right to give instructions to a provincial Governor. For example, the Governor-General could give instructions to a Governor if the latter was not properly carrying out his duties.

The instruction power granted in Section 51(5) of the Government of India Act did not enlarge the powers of the Governor-General in provincial affairs. It made the Governor the agent of the Governor-General but did not increase the power of either the Governor as agent or the powers of his principal, the Governor-General. In the absence of Section 93, Jinnah lacked the power, even with the advice of his ministers, to remove the Khan Sahib ministry so long as Khan Sahib enjoyed the confidence of the provincial legislature. That ministry, however, having opposed the creation of Pakistan and having lost on the issue when the people of the province voted for Pakistan, arguably was in the position of any parliamentary government which had lost an election, making the opposition entitled to take office. The Governor-General could then have utilized the powers vested in him by Section 51(5) to instruct the Governor to bring about a change of administration. The Muslim League was the opposition which had won at the polls.

Several months after removing the Khan Sahib Ministry, Jinnah again acted under Section 51(5) to dismiss M. A. Khuhro from the post of Chief Minister of Sindh. In doing so, Jinnah pushed the bounds of the constitutional limits of the Governor-General even further than he had in the NWFP. On 28 April 1948, Jinnah had Governor Hussain Hidayatullah of Sindh issue a proclamation stating that, on instructions from the Governor-General, he was dismissing Khuhro as provincial Chief Minister. The grounds given were: 'a *prima facie* case has been made out against him for charges of maladministration, gross misconduct and corruption in the discharge of his duties and responsibilities.'[98] Khuhro's government had come into conflict with the central government at the beginning of 1948 when the central government, in order to make Karachi Pakistan's capital, withdrew the city from Sindh and reconstituted it as a federal territory. The Sindh legislature and the Khuhro ministry vehemently fought this move. Despite this opposition, Jinnah supported the establishment of Karachi as the capital of the central government. Khuhro had also clashed with Governor Hidayatullah, who enjoyed the support of Jinnah, when the Governor shuffled portfolios in Khuhro's Cabinet. This action on the part of Hidayatullah exceeded the intrusion of other provincial Governors into the working of the cabinet system.

The new ministries, both to replace Khan Sahib in the North-West Frontier Province and Khuhro in Sindh, proved unsuccessful because they lacked the support of the local Muslim League. After Jinnah's death, Liaquat negotiated with Khuhro and in return for Khuhro's political support the charges against him were dropped. Khuhro soon thereafter returned to power. Khan Sahib's successor managed to maintain his position in the North-West Frontier Province longer, but only by employing political tactics which earned him a questionable reputation.

The most important involvement of Jinnah in provincial government affairs occurred in West Punjab. The Governor of that province, Sir Francis Mudie, was one of the British officials

Jinnah had requested to stay on after independence as a provincial Governor; Sir George Cunningham in the North-West Frontier Province and Sir Frederick Bourne in East Bengal were the others. Each had had an eminent career as a governor in British India. Prior to independence, the Muslim League in undivided Punjab was weak, and when the party scored a victory in the Punjab elections of 1946 it was unable to form the necessary coalition, forcing the central government to retain the emergency rule it had imposed during the war. After independence, the ministry of the Nawab of Mamdot came to power. Mamdot was the President of the provincial Muslim League and leader of its parliamentary party. Mian Mumtaz Daultana, a young politician who was to play an important role in Punjab affairs over the next few years, was his financial minister. A rich landlord, well-read in western literature and political affairs and respected for his intellectual powers, he also gained a reputation for shrewdness and aggressiveness. Mamdot was of a different cut. He had long enjoyed the confidence of Jinnah because of his work for the Muslim League in the movement for Pakistan. But Mamdot had the reputation of not being energetic and of not being a good administrator.

What makes West Punjab politics of unusual interest is not only the fact that the province was Pakistan's most prosperous, but also because Governor Mudie became deeply involved in the politics of the province and has left a good account of that involvement.[99] His communications with Jinnah and Liaquat give us a picture of the workings of provincial politics we do not have for other provinces. 'I have now definitely come to the conclusion that the West Punjab administration can only go from bad to worse if Mamdot remains as Premier,' Mudie wrote to Jinnah on 13 February 1948.[100] Mamdot, according to Mudie, showed 'absolutely no sign of understanding what the premiership of a province implies'. Mudie later added, 'I know that Mamdot has a reputation for honesty. He is a wealthy man and doubtless mere financial considerations do not, in normal circumstances, tempt him. But even if he is personally honest, he encourages dishonesty in the administration and is...not mentally honest. He is prepared at any time to sacrifice the administration to the retention of power and patronage. A very great deal of the corruption and maladministration in West Punjab is directly or indirectly due to him.'[101]

Jinnah was by now a very sick man. Burdened with the cares of the new national government, he would not lightly have stepped into the midst of a party battle in the Punjab. But what he heard from Mudie presented a situation of crisis proportions. 'I see the administration deteriorating every day and I, like everyone else, trace that deterioration to Mamdot,' wrote Mudie.[102] The principal complaint was Mamdot's dealings with the abandoned property of the Hindus and Sikhs who had fled to India at partition. In his letters to Jinnah, Mudie accused Mamdot of using the disposal of that property as political patronage. Mudie stated that he had not investigated these charges himself, but was relying on 'talks which I have had with a great many people, both official and non-official, some of them personal friends of Mamdot'.[103] Jinnah could not ignore these warnings from Mudie. Not only was the Punjab West Pakistan's most important province, but it was because the refugee question was so important that Jinnah had taken the portfolio of refugee affairs himself.

Jinnah summoned Mamdot, Daultana, and the two other members of the Punjab Cabinet to Karachi for meetings in April and May 1948, ostensibly to deal with the refugee question but also to mediate what appeared to some to be growing political tension which had developed between Mamdot and Daultana. The meetings were spirited ones.[104] Despite his long association with Mamdot and the work Mamdot had done in the Pakistan movement, Jinnah was concerned about Mamdot's ability to handle the refugee problem. He thought it better served if the matter were placed in the hands of Daultana, a more efficient administrator. Jinnah suggested to the group that all the ministers resign and that Daultana then be appointed as provincial Premier in Mamdot's place. Daultana indicated reluctance to follow Jinnah's suggestion until an affirmative vote had been obtained from the Punjab Parliamentary Party of the Muslim League.[105] This may have been a proper constitutional point but it annoyed Jinnah. It also developed that Mamdot was reluctant to resign, and Daultana considered that, although Mamdot was not doing a good job on the refugee question, he had known Mamdot for a long time and did not wish to oppose him further.[106] The feudal bonds of the Punjab landowner were stronger than allegiance to the new ruler in Karachi.

The meeting adjourned with the understanding that both ministers would submit their resignations, but Mamdot continued to delay. Both Mamdot and Daultana had reason to believe that Mamdot's resignation would present Mudie with a great deal of political leverage within the province. This would be resented by the Muslim League's other leaders and the rank and file. Not only would it impinge on the exercise of power by local leaders and shift power to the centre through the Governor, but Mudie, being British, was not popular in Punjab political circles. Although Daultana may have been reluctant to oppose Mamdot, a fellow landowner, his reluctance may also have been based on the fact that the nature of the refugee problem made it a no-win situation, not one on which an ambitious politician would want to stake his future career. This was the first challenge by provincial politicians to the central administration after independence, and the affair left Mamdot and Daultana in a state of apprehension, having gone against the wishes of Jinnah. Daultana was careful not to appear publicly to oppose Jinnah, and wrote a contrite letter to Mudie confessing, 'foolishly I went on pressing what I considered to be a minor point when I ought to have yielded my judgment to his...'[107]

There were strong uncomplimentary remarks in the Press about the competence and honesty of the Mamdot ministry, but there were also objections to what was perceived as interference in provincial government by the centre. The Urdu-language *Nawa-i-Waqt* criticized Jinnah, asserting that he was against the choosing of officials by elections and was backing a particular provincial ministry. The readers were reminded of Jinnah's use of the centre's powers against the provincial governments of the North-West Frontier Province and Sindh.[108] The *Civil and Military Gazette* reported that Jinnah had become displeased with the situation because he had been asked by the Punjab parties to the controversy to advise them and then found that they were unwilling to follow his lead. Therefore, according to the paper, 'he now would wash his hands of the entire affair.'[109] On 18 May Jinnah wrote to Mudie: 'I do not wish to intervene...and therefore no reply is to be sent on my behalf to anyone by you. You will adhere to your position as a constitutional Governor, as I explained to you in Karachi.'[110] Mudie thereupon returned the letters of resignation to the ministers and reported to Jinnah that he had 'told them that you had done your best to help them, but must now disassociate yourself from their difficulties which they have to solve themselves...'[111]

Jinnah was attempting to beat a good retreat, one forced on him by the political opposition he encountered from Mamdot enjoying the backing of the Punjab Muslim League. This is how Mudie saw the situation, and how the outcome was announced in the Lahore Press. 'Mamdot to continue as Premier...with the powerful backing of the Press and popular sentiment and the simultaneous "strategic retreat" by the Centre...'[112] Daultana introduced a resolution in the Punjab Assembly that the differences between Mamdot and himself once again be brought to Jinnah to exercise his personal influence and the powers which Daultana alleged Jinnah possessed under the constitution to settle the issue, representing that the parties would be guided by his decision. The resolution was defeated in the assembly by the Mamdot forces.[113] Local political strength, which had been an obstacle to Jinnah's Pakistan Movement, continued to plague him in the Mudie-Mamdot controversy and stood in his way in shepherding power from the provinces to the centre. Although the central government's attempt to influence Punjab politics had been blocked, nevertheless, Mudie was to resume his campaign against Mamdot after Jinnah's death.

CHAPTER 3

PAKISTAN UNDER LIAQUAT

Liaquat's continuation as Prime Minister after Jinnah's death shifted attention to that office and away from the office of Governor-General.[1] He is perceived as favouring an operating cabinet form of government, with the Governor-General as the symbol of authority while the real power would reside with the Prime Minister, as in the other members of the Commonwealth.[2] To this end, he chose as Governor-General Khwaja Nazimuddin, who was willing to act on the advice of the Prime Minister in carrying out the duties assigned to the Governor-General under the constitution. Nazimuddin was, however, like Jinnah before him, an active politician, and his appointment was, therefore, at variance with dominion constitutional practice of a non-political Governor-General. Liaquat also obtained the appointment of Chaudhry Khaliquzzaman as Muslim League President. Khaliquzzaman, not a strong leader and without popular backing, was beholden to Liaquat and his loyalty was assured. Since the Muslim League dominated the Constituent Assembly, Liaquat's control of the League gave him control of that body. Holding the office of Prime Minister, and being the dominant force in the Constituent Assembly and the Muslim League, made Liaquat virtual ruler of Pakistan on the national, although not on the provincial level.[3]

During the movement for independence, Jinnah had succeeded in attracting and retaining a broad spectrum of the Muslim population by avoiding social and economic issues. The cause of 'Islam in danger', and the various arguments supporting the need for Pakistan, told little of how the new government would be set up and operated or how the economy would be structured. By avoiding specifics, Jinnah's Muslim League was able to appeal to landowners, businessmen, lawyers, socialists, intellectuals, and the middle class. By his recourse to religion, the cause of Pakistan had mobilized the orthodox religionists and the lower classes. Each League member was free to create his own image of what Pakistan would be. But the advantage that Jinnah's tactics served in a national movement was a disadvantage when the League faced the question of operating a national state. Pakistan came into existence lacking any social or economic policy which League members could agree to implement.

If there was one point of agreement among the landowners and well-to-do lawyers who made up the League's leadership, it was the fear of communism or other agencies of radical social and economic change. Jinnah made public statements deploring the poverty of his people, and there exists no reason to question the sincerity of those declarations. He was nevertheless not able to take steps to address the problem of poverty by instituting economic programmes. It was the large landowners who occupied the political stage through their domination of the Muslim League. So entrenched and powerful were these landlords in West Pakistan that when millions of Muslims poured into the country after partition, attempts to resettle them on the land vacated by the Hindus and Sikhs who had fled to India was opposed. Lip service was paid to land reform by the Muslim League in West Pakistan, but so long as the large landowners dominated the League and the provincial assemblies there was very little chance of reform being implemented. It is indicative of the difference in East Bengal that its provincial assembly instituted land reform in 1950. Nevertheless, like its counterpart in West Pakistan, the East Bengal Muslim League had limited interest in social or economic change. The League also lacked grassroots support and organization, especially among the lower middle class and small farmers who were becoming politically active in East Bengal. The League's leaders failed to appreciate the growing strength of the demand for greater autonomy in East Bengal, or the strength of the complaints of the Bengali people regarding the economic discrimination they claimed was being practised against them by the West Pakistan-dominated central bureaucracy.

At independence, no Muslim opposition party of any consequence existed. Differences which did exist among the Muslim politicians were at first contained within the League itself, and Muslim opposition emerged only when weaknesses began to appear within the League.[4] Partition had done damage to the framework of the League because much of its strength had been in areas which remained within India after partition, and immigration had created organizational and political problems. Because the Pakistan Muslim League was without an effective national working committee and developed no social or economic programmes, its base of support narrowed to the landowners and more prosperous businessmen and lawyers. But despite its weaknesses, the League dominated the Constituent Assembly and was the sole instrument through which political power could be exercised in that body.

Nearly every member of the Constituent Assembly belonged to one of two parties, the Muslim League or the Congress Party.[5] The latter was made up of the Hindu minority which had been stranded in East Bengal by partition. Distrust of this Hindu minority was strong. Their patriotism was suspect because of their original opposition to the creation of Pakistan, opposition to the defence budget in the Constituent Assembly, continued family and economic ties with India, and the defection to India of a number of prominent Hindu members of the Pakistan government, including a Cabinet Minister. The Pakistan Congress Party was able to offer no strong opposition in the Constituent Assembly, but was reduced to fighting for the protection of its minority interests. Effective parliamentary opposition requires a party capable of assuming the responsibilities of government upon defeat of its rivals. The Congress Party in Pakistan was incapable of playing such a role.

In addition to control of the legislature through the leadership of the Muslim League, Liaquat enjoyed popular support. Like Jinnah, he was identified with no particular province. While not possessing the charismatic personality of Jinnah, Liaquat was an accomplished public orator, able effectively to communicate to large public audiences, and was a skilful parliamentarian. He also enjoyed excellent relationships with the Pakistan Civil Service, and its members looked to him to protect their interests on the political scene.[6] The civil service was under the direction of Secretary-General Chaudhri Mohamad Ali, an effective administrator who is credited with putting the machinery of Pakistan's government in operation after independence. Liaquat relied on the civil service for everyday government at the centre and in the provinces.

The quality of the first Cabinet membership was high, but because its members had been chosen by Jinnah, Liaquat did not exert as much cabinet control as he would have done if its members had been beholden to him for their appointments. A major division existed within the Cabinet reflecting the separation of the country into West Pakistan and East Bengal. Leadership was divided between Ghulam Mohammad, Finance Minister, and Fazlur Rahman, Minister of Commerce. The former was the leader of the West Pakistan forces in the central government, and the latter represented the political strength of East Bengal. Many important issues were decided in meetings between these two men, and their negotiated settlements were presented to the Cabinet where they would often be approved as a matter of form. Rivalry between Ghulam Mohammad and Fazlur Rahman came to the fore in 1949 over the devaluation of Pakistan's currency. Ghulam Mohammad was the loser in the contest, and he, the future Governor-General of Pakistan, experienced a major political defeat in the Cabinet at the hands of the leader of the East Bengal faction. Ghulam Mohammad was a bureaucrat with a low opinion of the parliamentary form of government, and this defeat did not make such government any more attractive to him. These two men were to tangle several years later when Ghulam Mohammad, as Governor-General, and Fazlur Rahman, as leader of the East Bengal members in the Constituent Assembly, clashed in the conflict over the Assembly's attempts to limit the powers of the office of Governor-General.

Liaquat continued Jinnah's policy of attempting to increase the power of the centre at the expense of provincial government. In the provinces, however, Liaquat did not enjoy the same strength as he did on the national level. Some in the local political leadership considered him a refugee and therefore an outsider. His administration was hampered by the fact that he and the Muslim League lacked social and economic policies which might have helped him to build a political base in dealing with local leaders.[7] Liaquat concentrated on asserting control over the Muslim League regimes in the provinces and preparing for provincial elections. Having made Nazimuddin, a Bengali, the Governor-General, Liaquat believed that he could count on the support of the East Bengal Muslim League which controlled the provincial Assembly. But to rely exclusively on East Bengal would have made the centre a captive of that province. Liaquat had also weakened his support in East Bengal when he instructed Nazimuddin to appoint Nurul

Amin to fill the office of provincial Chief Minister, the office Nazimuddin was vacating. This was done without consulting other leaders of the East Bengal Muslim League, and because it left a number of the leaders dissatisfied, the League was weakened in the province.

To provide an alternative leg of political support, Liaquat turned to increasing the influence of the national administration on the political scene in West Punjab. But there Liaquat was faced with the problem of Mamdot and his conflicts with Daultana which had confronted Jinnah. After Jinnah had washed his hands of the matter, the Mamdot ministry continued to enjoy the support of the Muslim League-controlled provincial Assembly. But there was also the Governor of West Punjab to contend with. Governor Mudie's disapproval of Mamdot remained strong, and Jinnah's admonition to rein in his activities had brought about only a temporary abatement of his efforts against Mamdot.

Jinnah's death, four months after his political retreat from the Punjab controversy, gave Mudie the opportunity to resume his campaign openly against Mamdot by taking up his cause with the new Governor-General. Nazimuddin, however, reminded Mudie that it would be improper for the central government to interfere in a matter where the provincial ministry possessed the confidence of the provincial legislature. Writing to Mudie, he said: 'We must recognize that Mamdot has got the support of a very large majority of the Muslim League Assemblymen and it does not pay to have a ministry without support in the Province. This experiment has been tried in Sindh and I am afraid it is not working successfully. Things are bad in the Punjab, but if you force a ministry which has no public support, then that ministry has to resort to nepotism and favouritism in order to win support, and administration thereby suffers. From the reports that I have been receiving about the Sindh Ministry, it appears that interference with administration has increased and is creating a very bad effect on the officials. I would, therefore, advise you very strongly to see that Mamdot is not jockeyed out of office.'[8]

Mudie had had a continuing correspondence with Liaquat during the time he had also been dealing with Jinnah on the affairs of the Mamdot ministry, and as early as February 1948 Mudie had informed Liaquat, as he was simultaneously informing Jinnah, of the dangers of Mamdot. He alleged what he claimed was a 'double-cross' by Mamdot in the matter of the refugees and their resettlement in West Punjab, and advocated that the matter could only be handled by the central government.[9] To do this he suggested the use of Section 104 of the Government of India Act, which allowed the centre to legislate for a province in an emergency. Mudie's rationale for such a move was based on the fact that the refugee problem was not one which was foreseen at the time of partition, and therefore would require some extraordinary government action, particularly in light of the unwillingness of the Punjab and Sindhi landowners to meet the situation by allowing land to be made available to the refugees.

Mudie's advocacy went beyond the particular refugee emergency and attacked the constitutional principal of provincial autonomy. He advocated the rescinding of the changes which had been introduced by the British in the Government of India Act of 1935, granting almost complete provincial autonomy in certain areas of government. He urged that the government be conducted as in the earlier days of British rule, when the central government was empowered to issue instructions on practically any matter it desired. He asserted, without elaborating on his sources, that there 'is a certain feeling that there should be a return to previous practice,' but warned, 'There are strong forces of provincialism that would oppose this...' Mudie made it clear to Liaquat, as he had also asserted to Jinnah, that it was impossible to work with Mamdot, and that Daultana was the only minister functioning efficiently in dealing with the refugee problem. He added that there was fear that Daultana would resign from the Punjab Cabinet and was reluctant to take over leadership. Mudie warned that 'anything might happen,' but assured Liaquat that there was one person Liaquat could depend on in the Punjab. 'I am your man,' Mudie wrote. Mudie had lost the first round against Mamdot when Jinnah refused to take action against the West Punjab ministry, but after Jinnah's death he was determined to win the second round.

In July 1948, Liaquat introduced a bill, which was enacted into law by the Constituent Assembly, giving the central government broad emergency powers to take over the functions of a province. This measure, known as Section 92A of the Government of India Act as amended, restored to the Governor-General the powers which had been removed from the office when Section 93 of the

Government of India Act was repealed at independence. Section 93 allowed for what came to be known as 'Governor's Raj'. The British had employed it against the 'Quit India' movement during the Second World War when they suppressed the Congress Party ministries in the provinces. Section 92A had the potential of being a means of removing the Mamdot ministry if Mudie could convince the central government to employ it in the Punjab.[10]

With the knowledge that Nazimuddin would be sensitive to the constitutional questions raised by any move against a provincial ministry which had the confidence of the provincial legislature, Mudie approached him with the argument that action taken against the provincial ministry under the new Section 92A was not to be equated with the similar and unpopular Section 93. Mudie was aware that the fact he was British might itself give a poor picture to the central government's action under any emergency provision, but he argued that the central government should therefore make all efforts to emphasize what he saw as differences between Sections 93 and 92A. To Mudie, under Section 93 the central government acted with responsibility only to the British Parliament, in which the people of the province had no representation. Now, Pakistan was independent and a Governor was responsible to the Governor-General, as he was before independence. But Mudie saw the relationship as being closer than the Governor's relationship had been to the imperial Governor-General, who was also the Viceroy. In addition, the Governor-General was now responsible to the Constituent Assembly rather than to Parliament. 'It may not perhaps amount to very much in practice,' Mudie admitted to Nazimuddin, 'but there is a difference in theory, which is important if an attack were to be made on the present administration on constitutional grounds.'

On 10 January 1949 Mudie wrote to Liaquat, 'Mamdot has, to everyone's knowledge, defeated the centre, even the Quaid...and the feeling is growing that the centre is powerless, even where the government is hopelessly corrupt and the administration is paralysed...In the present case, it also affects your personal position. It would be fatal to Pakistan to do nothing.' Mudie requested Liaquat to send him instructions to ask for the resignation of the Mamdot ministry and empowering Mudie to dismiss the ministry if Mamdot did not resign. Mudie was prepared to recommend a successor, this time not Daultana, who Mudie now characterized as 'a person whom everybody distrusts...' Mudie offered the opinion that Daultana's failure to take over Mamdot's premiership at the suggestion of Jinnah raised doubts 'whether he possesses the moral courage necessary for a premier...'[11] Mudie suggested to Liaquat that he be allowed to call Firoz Khan Noon as Premier. Mamdot could now sense that Mudie was gaining ground with the central government and held out an olive branch to him. He offered to let Daultana back into his Cabinet, and to hold general elections. The offer had little attraction for Mudie, who by now was disenchanted with Daultana. As for settling the issue of political control in West Punjab by elections, Mudie considered that any elections held while Mamdot remained in office were bound to be corrupt.

On 24 January 1949, Liaquat travelled from Karachi to Lahore, the West Punjab capital, and in what has been called 'an unkind step', dismissed the Mamdot ministry and suppressed the Punjab legislature under the authority of Section 92A.[12] West Punjab was now to be administered by the central government until a provincial election could be held and a new ministry could be chosen. This did not occur for two years. Mamdot and Daultana were both removed from government, and Mudie seemed the victor. He was, but his victory was to be short-lived. In round three, he was to fall victim to Mamdot's skilful use of local political forces.

The dismissal of the Mamdot ministry took place without incident. The *Civil and Military Gazette* offered some constitutional advice, commenting that while West Punjab had greatly deteriorated politically, the central government had assigned guilt with too broad a brush. According to the *Civil and Military Gazette,* although the people were dissatisfied and welcomed Section 92A government, the move was 'retrogressive and anti-democratic. Section 92A should only be employed when it is possible to follow the move with the installation of an efficient and democratic administration which would come into being as a result of elections based on universal suffrage.'[13]

Since Liaquat's Punjab move was the first use of Section 92A, there remained a question as to what type of local administration should be installed until the 'emergency' had abated. Under the practice of cabinet government, the removal of one government was to be followed by general elections. But this, as is true of many other constitutional precepts, was a convention of parliamentary government inherited from the British and not written into the constitution itself. Liaquat did not as yet feel himself strong enough to put his Section 92A government to the test of an election where he might be checked by the strength Mamdot wielded in the Punjab Muslim League. Apparently, an extended period of emergency rule was contemplated by the central government and by Mudie, because considerable attention was given to the question of the interim government.[14]

Mudie had earlier put forth his ideas on the emergency structure of provincial government which he thought suitable for Pakistan. Rule should come from the centre, but since on a day-to-day basis that would be difficult, the actual administration of the province should be left in the hands of the provincial government. Mudie reminded Liaquat of the disaster which befell George III when he attempted to rule the American colonies from London. Mudie advocated that the Pakistan constitution be amended to include a provision similar to that found in the South African constitution, which allowed the central government to take over the administration of a province for a period of five years. The province would be run during the period by a Governor aided and advised by a small council appointed by the central government, with the right of the council to add members as it saw fit. Mudie saw such a system as 'a halfway house' between Section 92A and autonomy. The council would be a 'buffer' between the administration and the people. In his version of Section 92A government, the Governor would be armed with broad discretionary powers, and his advisers would act as a shadow Cabinet. The system would work much like the Viceroy's Executive Council did in British India just prior to independence. Mudie had served on that council.

Mudie proposed that the advisers not actually participate in the running of the government, which would be run by political ministers formed in a Cabinet. The advisers, however, would be armed with the right to conduct inquiries into various subjects if they had any question about the way the ministers were conducting affairs. 'I believe that way we would maintain control between the administration and public and the League, without lowering still further the standards of administrative efficiency.' At first Mudie thought that the advisers should not be eligible as candidates for cabinet posts after Section 92A was lifted. He later moved away from these ideas and advocated that the advisers be allowed to participate in the running of the ministries in the Section 92A government. He saw that the shortage of qualified government officials would make that necessary, and that allowance would have to be made for the advisers to be eligible for government positions when Section 92A government ended. Mudie reasoned that only the advisers would have knowledge of the issues which the government faced during the period of emergency rule, and their experience would be necessary to furnish continuity.

Mudie felt very strongly that the Governor's position must be strengthened. 'My idea is that he should be definitely made the link between the Governor-General and the provinces.' The Governor-General would have the power to issue instructions to a Governor as to how he was to act in various matters while the emergency government continued in existence. 'This means that the Governor can, if he wants to, hold up orders on certain things until he gets the orders from the Governor-General. This would mean some alteration in the [Government of India Act]. . . . What do you think of the idea?' Mudie asked Liaquat. It is easy to see Mudie's service during British rule coming to the fore. To him good government was government by those who knew how to govern, and that was the civil service, not inexperienced politicians.

The newspaper *Nawa-i-Waqt* pointed out the two-pronged nature of the problem presented, editorializing that the advisers neither represented the public nor would be answerable to it. 'If it must be, then they should not be provincial politicians because that would be foisting a ministry on the people.' On the other hand, if the advisers were government officials, the paper warned, this would present the danger of drawing government officials into politics.[15]

Mudie was soon to have more concerns than the structure of the West Punjab government under an emergency administration. This self-styled 'non-politician' had immersed himself deeply in politics and was soon fighting for his political life. His ousted opponent was on the move. In March, two months after the Section 92A regime had been imposed, Mamdot obtained an appointment to the national Muslim League Working Committee. He was appointed to that post by Chaudhry Khaliquzzaman, the national President of the League.[16] In April, Mamdot and Daultana publicly signalled their willingness to act in concert by agreeing on a compromise candidate to head the Punjab Muslim League.

Further trouble loomed for Mudie when Khaliquzzaman arrived in Lahore for a twelve-day visit. Khaliquzzaman, in addition to being the President of the League, was also the chief organizer of the national League. West Punjab was high on his list of provinces needing re-organization, and Mudie furnished a cause which enabled Khaliquzzaman to rally the League in Punjab. Khaliquzzaman spent much of his time in Lahore influencing the newspapers there in support of the League and against Mudie. His efforts were successful and resulted in the newspapers demanding Mudie's recall.[17] Mudie attempted to persuade Liaquat that Khaliquzzaman was engaged in a conspiracy not against him, Mudie, but against Liaquat, and he intensified his attack on Mamdot. 'If he is not brought to public trial, then the result will be the complete triumph of the forces of corruption.'[18] But Mudie sensed his influence with Liaquat ebbing. To bolster his position, he attempted to wean Liaquat away from the Muslim League, claiming that what was needed in the Punjab was a strong leader, and that Liaquat was that man. It was no benefit to Liaquat, according to Mudie, to depend on the support of the League, which he characterized as doomed to continued weakness because of its lack of policy and its inability to ever be a force on provincial issues because of the conflicts within the organization.[19] Mudie urged Liaquat to take those members of the Punjab Muslim League who were personally loyal to him and make them advisers to the Governor under the plan Mudie had proposed. Liaquat should also choose an associate from the Provincial League and appoint him to the central government, thus providing Liaquat a personal link with the local political scene.

Mudie attempted to defend himself from Khaliquzzaman's newspaper campaign by attacking the principal Lahore newspaper, the *Pakistan Times*. Liaquat had delivered a speech at a reception for the British High Commissioner in Karachi to celebrate the birthday of King George. His speech was complimentary to the monarch, causing the *Pakistan Times* to editorialize that '...by no stretch of the imagination can [Liaquat's] speech be regarded as expressing the feelings and opinions of the majority of the Pakistani people.' The paper accused Liaquat of being either 'palpably hypocritical or having lost contact with the people. The king has been the symbol of our slavery for so long that the only feelings for him entertained by our people are those of hatred and rebelliousness.'[20] Mudie was appalled by what he termed 'this paper's pro-Communist campaign...The question...is how long the paper is to be allowed to carry on this Communist propaganda?'[21] Mudie suggested that the government consider taking action and use the Pakistan Safety Acts to close the newspaper. He reminded Liaquat that another newspaper, the *Civil and Military Gazette*, had recently been shut down for less provocation. Sooner or later something must be done, claimed Mudie, 'unless we are to accept the almost inevitable consequences of this propaganda.'

Mudie's downfall came on 22 June, when Liaquat telegraphed him that after meeting with the Working Committee of the Punjab Muslim League, the advisers' plan was adopted, but, and this was the stinger, its members were to be appointed by the Prime Minister on the recommendation of the provincial Muslim League, not the Governor.[22] The advisers were to act as ministers, but must have the agreement of the Governor for any of their official actions. The Governor was 'not to be a merely constitutional head of the Council of Advisers,' but could call for files. While the governor's powers were enlarged, this was a clear defeat for Mudie because the Muslim League, not he, would control the Council of Advisers. Liaquat explained to Mudie that because of the poor relationship between the provincial League and Mudie, the plan as originally proposed by Mudie could not work. Liaquat stated that he would consult with Mudie before any appointments to the Council were made, but this did not satisfy Mudie, and he resigned on 24 June.

Mudie asked that he be relieved of the governorship prior to 8 September and Liaquat suggested Mudie vacate the office by the end of July. Mudie took a parting shot at his victorious enemy, Mamdot. He utilized the provisions of the Public and Representatives Offices (Disqualification) Act, known as PRODA, the measure recently introduced by the Liaquat administration.[23] It enabled charges to be filed, outside the criminal justice system, against government officials and administrators for such political offences as corruption and maladministration. The charges by Mudie against Mamdot were, however, dismissed the following November. The *Pakistan Times* was both satisfied and dissatisfied with the outcome. It welcomed Mudie's resignation because it 'removed the anomaly of a foreigner occupying the office of a Governor in a sovereign and independent State', but also saw it as the result of a 'selfish political battle'.[24] Mudie had been unable to hold the support of Liaquat because, while Liaquat did not need Mudie, he needed the Muslim League in the Punjab. Liaquat also made his peace with the local Muslim League forces in Sindh and the North-West Frontier Province in order to gain their political allegiance. Khuhro, who controlled the Muslim League in Sindh, was back in power soon after Jinnah's death. In the North-West Frontier Province, the administration which Jinnah had installed after independence to replace the Congress ministry found it necessary to arrest the leaders of the opposition in order to maintain itself in power.

Formation of opposition parties began during Liaquat's term of office, and by the end of 1949 twenty-one political parties had come into existence. They were small and few survived their first few meetings. The loosely-knit membership of these parties often consisted of Muslim League dissenters who found themselves unable to exert power within the League, and there were few policy considerations to bind the members together. As a result, there was much shifting in membership, politicians often returning to the League when their prospects of power within the League improved. Several religious parties also came into existence, their principal objective being the creation of an Islamic state.[25] While they represented substantial and important public sentiment, they had limited membership, and made little political headway. Their leaders were unable to compete with the politicians in winning votes, but instead, they usually adopted the approach of lobbying the politicians rather than taking to open political contests. After independence, religious leaders at first generally supported the Muslim League, with some of them in East Bengal later switching their support to the United Front after its formation. Because there were no national elections, any splinter or religious parties, even if they could have mustered support in the provincial elections, would have been limited to influence on constitution-making and politics outside the Constituent Assembly.

Prior to independence, the East Bengal Muslim League was divided into three major factions: the Dhaka, or Nazimuddin faction; the rural vernacular factions led by Fazlul Huq; and

H. S. Suhrawardy's faction centred in Calcutta.[26] Suhrawardy had little support in the rural areas where local issues predominated, but he did have organizational ability and a hold over the politically more active urban literati, especially the student organizations. Fazlul Huq's faction was organizationally weak but enjoyed a broad base of mass support because of its populist positions on the rural issues of landlordism and agrarian debt. His faction was also more reflective of the views of the religious fundamentalists than was Suhrawardy. Nazimuddin's faction was traditional and conservative. It represented the interests of the Muslim landlords in East Bengal and, unlike Suhrawardy's and Fazlul Huq's factions, shared common interest with the political elite in West Pakistan. These men were alternately allies and enemies at various times in the complex political world of Bengal politics during British rule. Each was to play an important role in Pakistan's politics after independence, but it was Suhrawardy who had the greatest influence on the course of national political life.

Suhrawardy, described by Firoz Khan Noon as a 'colourful personality, full of brilliance and charm and also repellent habits,'[27] was perhaps the most dynamic Muslim leader aside from Jinnah. He had served as the Chief Minister of Bengal, forming the only truly Muslim provincial administration prior to independence. His victory in the 1946 election, which led to his formation of the Bengal ministry, was important to Jinnah's campaign for Pakistan because of the poorer showing of the Muslim League in the other Muslim majority provinces. Suhrawardy, as Chief Minister of Bengal during the Calcutta Killings of 1946 which followed Jinnah's call for Direct Action, was blamed by many Hindus for that tragedy. However, when communal trouble again erupted, Suhrawardy took up residence with Gandhi in the Calcutta slums and worked to keep the peace between Muslims and Hindus.[28] Their efforts were credited by many as one of the principal reasons which saved Bengal from the partition slaughter which occurred in the Punjab. As independence approached, Suhrawardy mounted a campaign for an undivided independent Bengal. His efforts were defeated, and after partition he lost out to Nazimuddin, who had the support of Jinnah and Liaquat, in the contest for the chief ministership of the newly-formed East Bengal.

By the time independence arrived, Jinnah had so effectively united the Muslim politicians of Bengal behind him that his support in provincial elections had become a powerful factor. Suhrawardy was the last Bengal Chief Minister under the British, having ousted Nazimuddin in whose Cabinet he served. Suhrawardy had a large following in Calcutta, but Jinnah found Nazimuddin an easier person to deal with; also, his political base was in Dhaka, after independence the capital of the eastern wing of Pakistan. In contrast, Suhrawardy's Calcutta constituency became a part of India.

Suhrawardy waited until March of 1949 to emigrate from India and establish permanent residence in Pakistan. He had won a seat in the Constituent Assembly formed prior to independence for undivided India, but he was deprived of the seat in 1948 when the Pakistan Constituent Assembly adopted a rule limiting its membership to permanent residents of Pakistan. Upon his move to Pakistan from India a year later, Suhrawardy was therefore without a seat in the Assembly and had no chance of obtaining one unless national elections were held.[29] His advocacy of a united Bengal and his delay in moving to Pakistan were held against him and he remained outside the Muslim League.

At first Suhrawardy confined his political activities to West Pakistan rather than his native East Bengal, where, however, his influence grew, and in time he was able to capture the leadership of local forces. He was the first leader with a broad political reputation to go into opposition, attacking the Liaquat administration for suppression, 'vituperative politics', and being an army-backed regime.[30] He also attacked the Pakistan Safety Acts, and criticized the government's policies for the resettlement of the partition refugees. His activities earned him the support of dissatisfied members of the Muslim League in urban areas, particularly in Lahore and Karachi, and he attempted to broaden his political base by his advocacy of participation for non-Muslims in government.

In May 1949, the Muslim League leadership was shocked by its unexpected defeat by an independent candidate in the by-election at Tangail in the East Bengal district of Mymensingh. This defeat exposed Muslim League weakness and encouraged the formation of the East Pakistan Awami League, led by Fazlul Huq and Maulana Abdul Hamid Khan Bhashani. The Liaquat government reacted by setting aside the results of the Mymensingh by-election. When Suhrawardy entered the battle as counsel for the challengers to the government's action, the government responded by imposing a 'gag order' on him under authority of the Pakistan Safety Acts.[31] As an attorney, he was allowed to enter East Bengal to appear in court, but he was forbidden to make political speeches and was required to leave East Bengal as soon as his court appearance was completed. The *Morning News* in Dhaka editorialized: 'To high-handedly curtail [Suhrawardy's] right to say what he wants to say is to put the country dramatically on the high road that leads straight to one-party authoritarian rule.'[32]

Liaquat seemed not to understand or was unwilling to admit that parliamentary government required the existence of viable opposition.[33] Pakistan, to Liaquat, depended on the existence of a strong Muslim League and the exclusion of other parties from government power. His idea of the League's role in Pakistan is exemplified by his definition of the office he occupied. '...I have always considered myself as the Prime Minister of the League. I never regarded myself as the Prime Minister chosen by the Members of the Constituent Assembly.'[34] In 1950, Liaquat became the League's President, departing from the policy of keeping League and government office-holding separate. This move weakened the League by reducing it to a handmaiden of the government. The Chief Ministers of the provinces were encouraged by Liaquat's move to assume the leadership of the provincial branches of the League.

Liaquat's approach to party politics was direct and forceful. Those who would form other parties were traitors, liars, and hypocrites. Words like 'dogs of India' were part of his vocabulary when discussing opposition. He equated opposition to the Muslim League with opposition to Pakistan itself, and made it clear publicly that he would not tolerate the existence of an opposition party as long as he lived. When the East Bengal members in the Constituent Assembly planned a protest day in opposition to Liaquat's proposals for a new constitution, he declared that the government 'shall not tolerate these activities any longer and shall put an end to them in the interest of the existence and stability of Pakistan.'[35] On one occasion his voice reached an emotional pitch while addressing a crowd and declaring that Pakistan was 'the child of the Muslim League'. Those who joined 'mushroom organizations' were 'enemies of Pakistan who aim to destroy the unity of the people'. It was important, according to Liaquat, in the 'interest of true democracy' to have one strong, unified party, and that party must be the Muslim League, 'the mother of Pakistan'. He believed that only 'the real mother could have affection for its offspring'. Opposition parties were foster mothers or stepmothers and 'could never have affection for the child'. He looked to a single party, which he controlled, as the means of continuing his power. If the aborting of parliamentary government was the price, so be it. Liaquat justified his position by picturing Pakistan surrounded by enemies, making parliamentary government a luxury which the new nation could perhaps ill-afford. His desire to consolidate power at the centre through the instrument of the Muslim League made him willing to delay the writing of a new constitution.

The dominion constitution was sufficient for the purpose of carrying out the government affairs of Pakistan, but Jinnah had accepted this constitution only as an expedient means to facilitate transfer of power from the departing British. Constitution-making presents an opportunity for the people of a nation to define themselves. It was now time for the Constituent Assembly to come to an agreement on the terms of a new compact, one which reflected their own thinking rather than only ideas inherited from their colonial past. They were clearly not against retaining some of those ideas, but Pakistanis had to reach agreement on issues which were theirs alone.[36] The two most important issues were religion and the apportionment of legislative representation between the east and west wings.

Religion was the first to surface publicly. In January 1948, Maulana Maududi gave the first of two lectures to the students of the Law College in Lahore. He challenged the students with the assertion: 'Notwithstanding certain similarities of situation the case of Pakistan is not, however, the same as other Muslim countries. This is so, because it has been achieved exclusively with the object of becoming the homeland of Islam.'[37] If a secular constitution and the British civil and criminal codes were to be used instead of the *Shariat* then, Maududi argued, there was no reason to bring into existence a separate Muslim homeland. He sought the support of the law students in moving the Constituent Assembly to declare officially that sovereignty in Pakistan resided in Allah, that the state was no more than His agent, that the *Shariat* be declared the basic law of the land, and that any law then in existence which was in conflict with it be repealed and any such conflicting law which might be passed in the future be declared void.

In his lectures Maududi did show a willingness to co-operate with secular authority and he acknowledged that the sovereignty of God could be delegated. He did not, however, specify how that delegation could take place, but he was willing to see power transferred to the Constituent Assembly by means of a general election. Some matters in the *Shariat* he viewed as not unalterable and immutable and could be dealt with by legislation because Islamic law was responsive to changes in a Muslim society. But change was always to be subject to the guidance of those who were learned in Islamic law. Whether Maududi was now willing to tolerate some form of a democratic constitution was not clear, but he did appear to be moving away from his pre-partition stance that democracy was an evil. Despite what might be interpreted as a more co-operative attitude towards the civil authority, when Maududi publicly declared that he did not consider the conflict with India over Kashmir a jihad, the Liaquat administration arrested him and other leaders of the Jamaat-e-Islami in October 1948. Maududi remained in custody for the remainder of 1948 and most of 1949.[38]

Within the ranks of those Constituent Assembly members who accepted some or all of the ideas propounded by Maududi, there was nothing approaching a consensus. It was all well and good to pronounce allegiance to general principles, but the members of the Assembly had the practical task of translating those principles into words that would make up the nation's constitution. What in the Koran and *Shariat* would assist them in determining the form of government for their modern state? Was there to be no alternative to entering the community of nations with a criminal code mandating that hands must be severed for theft, or having a commercial code which forbade inclusion of interest payments for money involved in a business transaction? Some members would argue that Islamic law was a living law which must be re-interpreted to meet the changes of each new age. Granting that, who was to determine those changes? Could the drafters of the new constitution accommodate those religious leaders who insisted that, since the law of the land was to be religious in nature, the interpretation of the law must be left to religious leaders who had devoted their lives to attaining experience in the knowledge of those laws? According to some religious leaders, interpretation as to what was right or wrong under Islamic law could not be determined by a secular legislature or courts left behind by the British.

While these issues troubled some members of the Assembly, to other Pakistanis the issue was simple. Islam was the reason that Pakistan had been created and the force of religion had been important in winning partition. It was now time to pay the debt owed to Islam. In February of 1949, the Jamaat-e-Islami held a session in Dhaka, attended by 10,000 persons, and passed a resolution demanding the early establishment of an Islamic state based on the Koran. India had already produced a draft of its new constitution and Pakistan faced the challenge in the international community to do the same. It was clear to Liaquat that action on the constitution could no longer be delayed. He announced that the constitution would not be neutral on the religious issues but would create a 'truly Islamic society'.[39] In March 1949, his administration came forward with the Objectives Resolution.

The Objectives Resolution was an enactment which retained importance in Pakistan's constitutional life long after the Constituent Assembly itself was dissolved. It was a short resolution.

> Whereas sovereignty over the entire universe belongs to God Almighty alone, and the authority which He has delegated to the State of Pakistan through its people for being exercised within the limits prescribed by Him is a sacred trust;
>
> This Constituent Assembly representing the people of Pakistan resolves to frame a constitution for the sovereign independent State of Pakistan;
>
> Wherein the State shall exercise its powers and authority through its chosen representatives of the people;
>
> Wherein the principles of democracy, freedom, equality, tolerance and social justice as enunciated by Islam shall be fully observed;
>
> Wherein the Muslims shall be enabled to order their lives in the individual and collective spheres in accord with the teaching and requirements of Islam as set out in the Holy Quran and the Sunnah;
>
> Wherein adequate provision shall be made for the minorities freely to profess and practise their religions and develop their cultures;
>
> Whereby the territories now included in or in accession with Pakistan and such other territories as may hereafter be included in or accede to Pakistan shall form a Federation wherein the units will be autonomous with such boundaries and limitations on their powers and authority as may be perceived;
>
> Wherein shall be guaranteed fundamental rights including equality of state, of opportunity and before law, social, economic and political justice, and freedom of thought, expression, belief, faith, worship and association, subject to law and public morality;

> Wherein adequate provision shall be made to safeguard the legitimate interests of minorities and backward and depressed classes.
>
> Wherein the independence of the judiciary shall be fully secured...[40]

Dawn announced the Objectives Resolution with the headline 'Sovereignty Over The Entire Universe Belongs To God Almighty Alone.'[41] In the Constituent Assembly, Mian Iftikharuddin commented on the headline. 'I see a section of the Press gave it as if they had scored a journalistic scoop by reporting that the authority is derived from the Higher Power. Sir, the authority, whether we say it or not, is derived from that Power. It does not lie in our power to change the law of nature or nature's God. In saying that we have not done anything very extraordinary.'[42] The significance given to sovereignty was, nevertheless, well-placed by *Dawn* in its headline. Sovereignty thereafter remained a problem in the constitutional affairs of Pakistan.[43]

The range of debate on the Objectives Resolution in the Constituent Assembly demonstrated the lack of consensus among the members. For some, such as Ishtiaq Husain Qureshi and Zafrulla Khan, who wished the constitution to be modern and democratic, the stress on Islam was only the acknowledgment of the need to keep religion involved in politics as an ethical foundation. The Objectives Resolution to such men was a statement of morality, not a concrete prescription for the operation of government. For the *ulema*, however, when the Objectives Resolution recited that sovereignty was in God, they understood that in a very concrete sense. It meant not only the acceptance of God into the political structure, but the acceptance of His law as the law of the land. That law was found in the *Shariat*. To most of them, the acceptance of the sovereignty of God meant that the *Shariat* was superior to the constitution itself. The interpretation of the *Shariat* by the *ulema*, not the interpretation of a secular constitution by a secular court, would be the final determination of what was the law of the land. To some *ulema* the Objectives Resolution meant the end of Jinnah's concept of a modern national state.[44]

The Constituent Assembly's debates did not resolve the conceptual differences. The wording of the Objectives Resolution was limited to general terminology in an attempt to accommodate everyone. No mention was made of the *Shariat*, and God's sovereignty was to be delegated to 'the State of Pakistan through its people' resulting in a 'sovereign, independent state of Pakistan'. That state would exercise its powers and authority 'through the chosen representatives of the people'. The Resolution might be read that sovereignty was nicely spread around to please both the modernists and the religious groups: God has sovereignty, the people have sovereignty, and the state has sovereignty. But the Objectives Resolution actually had a specific meaning in regard to sovereignty, a meaning not realized by many at the time. It established that sovereignty did not in any sense belong to the people. The people acted only as a conduit of authority between God and the state, and were limited to choosing representatives who would exercise the 'powers and authority' of the state. These powers and authority were delegated by God and could be exercised by the state only 'within the limits prescribed by Him'.

Democracy was also given a meaning in the Objectives Resolution. It was to be democracy 'as enunciated by Islam'. In attempting to explain Islamic democracy, Liaquat defined it not by stating what it was but what it was not. Islamic democracy was not democracy as understood in either the West or the Soviet Union.[45] Qureshi described it by reciting some of its general attributes. Its 'meaning is richer and is fuller than the principles enunciated in the United Nation's Charter on fundamental rights.'[46] Zafrulla Khan was satisfied because democracy to him was a government which provided for the exercise of authority through the people's representatives, and the Objectives Resolution had met that requirement.[47] That was not what Islamic democracy, as called for in the Objectives Resolution, meant to the *ulema*. One of the religious spokesmen for that group made it quite clear in the Assembly debates: '...[I]t will be limited democracy. The people will have some power, but will not have all the power...Certain things have to be resolved by God and are in His own personal sphere...The principles of Islam and the laws of Islam as laid down in the Koran are binding on the State. The people or the State cannot change these principles or these laws...It might be called by the name "theo-democracy", that is democracy limited by the word of God, but as the word "theo" is not in vogue, so we call it by the name "Islamic democracy."'[49]

While the Objectives Resolution was written in Islamic terms and therefore was acceptable to the religious groups, it did not mention the *Shariat* or attempt to define what Liaquat meant by a 'truly Islamic society', and to that extent did not offend those who wanted a modern constitution. But neither did it resolve the question of what constituted an Islamic state, or to what extent the government should absorb the concepts of Islam.[49] Nevertheless, this first attempt at constitution drafting proved to be the most enduring, and its lack of specifics and its generalities might have been the reason for its longevity. While later constitutional documents came and went, the Objectives Resolution was always there in later years to serve for some as a constitutional *Grundnorm*.[50]

One group particularly displeased with the Objectives Resolution was the Hindus of East Bengal. They were not satisfied with a constitution which merely protected them, but argued that without specific statements within the Objectives Resolution guaranteeing their right of free participation at all levels of the government, including the highest policy-making positions, they would be second-class citizens. They maintained that politics should be separated from religion, and charged that the objectives stated in the resolution would result in a theocratic state in which the growth of dictatorship would be fostered. To them, if sovereignty was in God, as the Objectives Resolution stated, then it followed that sovereignty was not in the people, and the proposed constitution was therefore not democratic. But attempts by the Hindus to amend the resolution were defeated and the Objectives Resolution received almost unanimous Muslim approval.

After adopting the Objectives Resolution, the Assembly promptly appointed a committee, named the Basic Principles Committee, consisting of twenty-five members (one-third of the Constituent Assembly's membership) under the chairmanship of Maulvi Tamizuddin Khan, the President of the Assembly. The committee was to draft a constitution based on the principles agreed upon in the Objectives Resolution. It was divided into sub-committees dealing with such items as federal and provincial relationships, legislative representation, and the judiciary. To these a board of Islamic teachings was added. It was agreed at the start that Pakistan would have a parliamentary government with a bicameral legislature based on a federal structure.[51]

The Basic Principles Committee itself held very few meetings during the twenty months its sub-committees were in existence, and little is known of the nature of the work of the sub-committees themselves. All proceedings were classified as confidential, and although occasional statements were issued, they were brief in nature. Even before the new year of 1950 had begun, impatience with the progress on the constitution began to surface. Liaquat, in no hurry to implement a new constitution and hold a national election, explained the delay to the public by characterizing the task faced by the drafters as one involving 'an unprecedented reconstruction in the realm of political thought and practice'.[52] *Dawn*, being a strong supporter of the Liaquat administration, was not about to criticize him openly on the issue of the constitution. It reminded the government, however, that what seemed like a lack of progress had created considerable public anxiety. *Dawn* suggested, perhaps as a trial balloon for the government, that the next stage of constitution-making need not produce a draft of great specificity, but could give the broad outlines of the structure of the government and the general principles of Islam which were to be a part of the constitution.[53]

Just such an approach was followed by the Liaquat administration. In September 1950, Liaquat submitted to the Constituent Assembly a constitutional draft with the appropriate title, 'Interim Report'.[54] This report was basically the Government of India Act with some of the amendments to that Act made by the Indian Independence Act, and with the Objectives Resolution as a preamble. The report recommended the federation form of government as set out in the Government of India Act, and treated the provinces theoretically as equals for the purposes of representation. It provided for a head of state with extensive emergency powers, including the power to suspend the constitution in whole or in part, and the head of state was to have control of provincial ministries including the right of dismissal. The report also tracked the Government of India Act by providing lists enumerating the respective powers and functions of the provincial and federal levels of government. The proposals of the Interim Report seemed to some to be so similar to the provisions of the pre-independence Government of India Act as to cause one member of the Assembly to comment, 'So far as this Constitution is concerned, if Mr Churchill had been the Leader of this House (which God forbid) he would have drawn up such a constitution.'[55]

Because the Sub-committee on Representation had not completed its report, the Interim Report was vague when it attempted to apportion representation between the east and west wings of the country. It stated only that there would be two legislative houses, a House of the People, elected by direct vote of the people, and a House of Units, elected by the provincial legislatures. The provinces of East Bengal, West Punjab, North-West Frontier, and Sindh were to be equally represented in the House of Units, and Balochistan was also given the status of a province. But the actual number of delegates in each delegation was not fixed, nor was it made clear that the seats in the lower house would be allocated in direct proportion to the population, although that was generally assumed. With East Bengal's majority in the lower house matched by West Pakistan's dominance in the upper house there would be parity between the east and west wings. Both houses were to have equal powers, including the powers of financial allocation, budget, motions of confidence, and removal of the head of state. Differences between the houses were to be worked out by joint session, and the ministry was to be collectively responsible to both houses.

If the generalities of the Objectives Resolution had pleased nearly everyone, the Interim Report seemed to please no one. The religious groups were disappointed because little of the Islamic ideals of the Objectives Resolution was implemented in the Interim Report. The Bengalis were the strongest in opposition.[56] They objected to the fact that Urdu was to be kept as the single national language. What most aggravated them, however, was that they were not granted a legislative majority although they constituted the majority of the population of Pakistan. They saw themselves being turned into a minority by the bicameral provision of the Interim Report.[57] West Pakistan would dominate the upper house because it would have five units to East Bengal's one, and since the houses were to have equal say in enacting legislation, the Bengalis feared that West Pakistan's say in the upper house would, if they voted in a bloc, in effect possess veto power over any legislation proposed by the Bengalis. At the same time, they realized that the Interim Report's formula presented the possibility that the smaller provinces of West Pakistan might be courted as allies against the Punjabis.[58]

The Working Committee of the East Bengal Muslim League called for drastic changes in the report because of what it termed the 'widespread feeling among the people'. The *Pakistan Observer* of Dhaka was less restrained in its criticism of what it saw as the harm to East Bengal. It called the report a 'fatal stab' and 'a shameless conspiracy against the province' by the 'power drunk oligarchical ruling clique in Karachi to impose a dictatorship under the camouflage of Islam.' The Interim Report would turn East Bengal into a colony of West Pakistan 'worse than that of Imperial Britain or France'.[59] The *Observer* saw the centralization of government power as an attempt to reduce the province to the status of another Balochistan, and the absorption of additional taxing power by the central government as making the province into another department of government, similar to Karachi. Even the *Morning News* of East Bengal, which usually reflected the government's point of view in its editorials and letters to the editor, expressed strong opposition to the Interim Report.[60]

The Punjabi members of the Constituent Assembly were at first satisfied that they would have a majority in the upper house. But they soon began to doubt their position as they realized that their upper-house majority would be of benefit to them only if all the provinces of West Pakistan voted as a bloc. The Punjabi politicians and bureaucrats could not be confident that they would always be able to win the votes of the Assembly members from Sindh and the North-West Frontier.[61] Other opposition was voiced in West Pakistan. The *Pakistan Times* argued against over-centralization of government, and expressed dislike for the emergency powers, which it complained were to be exercised in 'partially defined and undefined emergencies' and revealed 'a suspicion of democratic methods and procedures'. The head of state, according to the *Times,* would be a 'virtual dictator'. The paper regretted that the Interim Report had 'failed to discard the limitations imposed by the British-made Constitution of 1935'.[62]

So unfavourable was the initial reception given to the Interim Report in East Bengal that it was withdrawn by Liaquat in November 1950.[63] He had not expected such strong opposition. He assured the Bengali leaders in private that it was not his intention to deny them a majority in the Constituent Assembly, an assurance which the Bengalis found satisfactory. At the same time, Liaquat placated the religionists by declaring that the reason for the withdrawal of the Interim Report was to further ascertain the ideas of those who believed that it had departed from the principles accepted in the Objectives Resolution.[64] A committee of Assembly members was appointed to hold public hearings before beginning work on solutions to the objectionable points of the report which had caused its failure. The Assembly optimistically gave the committee two months for its task of gathering suggestions from the public. As events turned out, the committee did not submit its report for two and a half years. In that period it held public hearings and heard a wide variety of opinions.

The Interim Report rallied many in East Bengal to the cause of autonomy for the province. Bhashani raised the plea that East Bengal faced the future as a colony of the alien rulers of West Pakistan. A committee of action was formed in Dhaka, entrusted with drafting a counter-proposal to the Interim Report. The committee proposed that the constitution contain a provision for two autonomous regional governments, one for West Pakistan and another for East Bengal.[65] There would be a single central assembly, which would have its membership based on population and its jurisdiction limited to currency, defence, and foreign affairs. The central government would be further limited by requiring that there be two Foreign Offices and two regional defence forces, each manned by the people of the region. The central government would be entitled to levy taxes only on specifically enumerated items, and items could only be added to the list with the consent of both regions. The committee members toured East Bengal propagandizing their proposal.

To divert public attention from constitution-making, Liaquat's administration attempted to 'Islamize' the government and thus show that steps were being taken to create an Islamic state even before a new constitution was drafted. He also hoped that progress toward an Islamic state would garner support for his attempt to build the strength of the Muslim League. In February 1951, he set up a commission to bring existing laws into conformity with the principles of the Objectives Resolution. In the next month, the Constituent Assembly instructed the federal and provincial governments to take steps to institute Koranic instructions in schools and universities, and passed a resolution establishing the Institute of Islamic Research, the purpose of which was to 'make the Muslim population of the country truly Muslim'.[66]

Liaquat attempted to offset the dominant position of the East Bengalis in the Constituent Assembly by building a political base for the Muslim League in the provinces of West Pakistan. To this end he had asserted control over West Punjab by his Section 92A action against the Mamdot ministry, courted the support of Khuhro in Sindh, accepted the presidency of the Muslim League, thereby enhancing his personal influence over local League affairs in the provinces, and added five seats to the Punjab delegation in the Constituent Assembly. At the same time, he realized that he could not consolidate national support for his administration until a general election was held. With this in mind, Liaquat intended testing League strength in provincial elections before scheduling a general election. From the withdrawal of the Interim Report in November 1950 to his assassination in September 1951, he held further constitution-making in abeyance and gave his attention to provincial politics. Elections were held in 1951 in West Punjab and 1952 in the North-West Frontier Province, both of which were won by the Muslim League.[67]

CHAPTER 4

GHULAM MOHAMMAD ENDS CABINET GOVERNMENT

Liaquat was fatally wounded as he addressed a political rally in Rawalpindi on 16 October 1951. Ghulam Mohammad, who had resigned just four days earlier from his Cabinet post of Finance Minister because of poor health, was convalescing in Rawalpindi. It was rumoured at the time that Liaquat, aware of Ghulam Mohammad's political ambitions, had intended to send him to Washington, DC, as Ambassador and thus remove him from the political scene. Abdur Rab Nishtar was considered by many to be Liaquat's successor, and it was reported that Liaquat had, in fact, considered appointing him Deputy Prime Minister so as to indicate his wish that Nishtar succeed him. Khwaja Nazimuddin, Governor-General since the death of Jinnah three years earlier, became Prime Minister, and a new Governor-General, Ghulam Mohammad, was announced by Queen Elizabeth II on 18 October. Nazimuddin did not seem to be in anyone's mind as Prime Minister. When he became Governor-General he had removed himself from politics, and his mild manner and non-assertive nature made him appear ideally suited for that office, although not for the office of Prime Minister. Ghulam Mohammad becoming Governor-General was also a surprise because of his serious health problems.[1]

It is not clear how the arrangement came about. It has been suggested that Ghulam Mohammad persuaded Nazimuddin to vacate the Governor-Generalship because he, Ghulam Mohammad, realized it was an office which could be made powerful again.[2] One version of events is that Mushtaq Ahmad Gurmani, Cabinet minister for Kashmir who was stationed in Rawalpindi, accompanied the dying Liaquat to the hospital and summoned Ghulam Mohammad to Liaquat's bedside.[3] They notified other members of the government of Liaquat's death, and also notified Governor-General Nazimuddin, who was vacationing in nearby Murree. Nazimuddin joined them in Rawalpindi. There is uncertainty as to how many Cabinet members assembled in Rawalpindi, but it is known that three men, Ghulam Mohammad, Nazimuddin, and Gurmani, emerged as the most important players. Nishtar was excluded from the meetings held behind closed doors. His presence would not have been welcomed by Ghulam Mohammad.[4] Nishtar's strong political base and the fact that he was from the North-West Frontier Province would make him a poor candidate for manipulation by Ghulam Mohammad and the Punjab interests.

An agreement was struck about the composition of the new government. Nazimuddin vacated the position of Governor-General and become Prime Minister, and Ghulam Mohammad became the new Governor-General. The Rawalpindi meeting was significant not only because it resulted in a realignment of offices within the government, but also because of the way in which constitutional convention was disregarded. The nation was presented with a *fait accompli* by cabal. The *Pakistan Times* noted in an editorial on 19 October that the ordinary procedure would have been to consult the Muslim League Parliamentary Party and the Constituent Assembly concerning who the Prime Minister should be. The paper added, however, that '...in view of the emergency, it was perfectly correct to dispense with *formalities* and give the country a new government as early as possible...The new appointments are likely to be accepted by the people with general satisfaction.' (Italics added.)

The observations of the *Pakistan Times* fairly reflected attitudes which underlay the operation of parliamentary government in Pakistan. An 'emergency', the full implications of which remained undefined, was used as justification for disregarding constitutional practices which attached to a dominion constitution, practices which were slighted as mere 'formalities'. No one raised the point that, unless these formalities or constitutional conventions of the dominion constitution were adhered to, that constitution might become a largely meaningless document.

After the assassination of Liaquat in 1951, Pakistan began choosing its leadership on a geographical basis. No longer did the nation have Jinnah or Liaquat, associated with neither the west nor the east wing of the country. Nazimuddin was a Bengali and Ghulam Mohammad a Punjabi. There were striking differences in the backgrounds and personalities of these two men. Nazimuddin, a member of a distinguished family, was gentle, religious, and well-liked. He had accompanied Jinnah to the 1946 Simla conference, and had a long and successful political career in pre-independence Bengal, serving in the legislature and defeating Suhrawardy for the office of Chief Minister at independence. Sir Frederick Bourne, Governor of East Bengal after independence, who had an opportunity to work with Nazimuddin, then Chief Minister of the province, found him to be an experienced politician and a person of admirable qualities. 'I could not ask for a better man to work with.'[5] Chaudhri Mohammad Ali knew Nazimuddin as an able administrator and a 'happy choice' as successor to Jinnah as Governor-General.[6] Chief Justice Munir considered him 'an angel of a man without guile or smile of a politician,' and a leader who 'clearly understood his constitutional position [as Governor-General] and maintained it throughout his term.'[7] In contrast, Karl Newman, who was at the time Head of the Department of Political Science at Dhaka University, and who knew Nazimuddin, considered him '...a man temperamentally incapable of exercising his powers.'[8] His presence on the political scene strengthened the Islamic factions which demanded that Pakistan and its constitution reflect fully the principles of Islam. For this reason, Nazimuddin was not looked upon with favour by the bureaucrats, who while not overtly anti-religious, supported the position that religion and the *ulema* should not interfere with the affairs of state.

The bureaucracy, which in the past had looked to Liaquat to protect their interests, now had a leader in Ghulam Mohammad, a man whose life was a constant struggle to overcome his physical disabilities. Health problems had prevented him from playing an active role in the independence movement, and only recently he had been seriously disabled by a stroke. It is possible that his physical problems contributed to the acceptance of him and Nazimuddin in their respective offices by both the east and west wings of the country. Punjab politicians found Nazimuddin acceptable because he was not looked upon as an aggressive politician or a strong leader, while the Bengalis concluded that Ghulam Mohammad's physical condition would limit him to a figurehead.

Ghulam Mohammad was to prove a surprise to those unaware of his strength and political inclinations. The personal observations of contemporaries who knew him suggest an intelligent and ruthless leader. As early as 1948, an American official in Pakistan reported that Ghulam Mohammad viewed himself as Jinnah's successor, had gained 'unlimited power' within Liaquat's Cabinet, and had acquired many followers.[9] Chaudhri Mohammad Ali found him 'as quick and sharp as a rapier'.[10] Ghulam Mohammad's chief secretary considered him ill-mannered, vulgar, and overbearing,[11] and Karl Newman considered him 'active, ambitious, and somewhat given to intrigue'.[12] Amjad Ali, serving later as Ambassador to the United States, had a chance to observe Ghulam Mohammad when he chose to 'turn on the charm'. In the diplomatic world, men like Averell Harriman and Sir Stafford Cripps were much impressed with him.[13] 'Absolutely fearless' was the term Ayub Khan used to describe him. 'Whatever else he lacked, he certainly did not lack courage.'[14] Mohammad Munir, at that time the Chief Judge of the Punjab High Court, noted that Ghulam Mohammad assumed the office of Governor-General 'a stricken man, but with the mental grooves of a seasoned bureaucrat and the eyes and the nose of a mountain hawk.'[15]

Ghulam Mohammad's career during British rule had been in the Audit Branch of the Indian Civil Service, serving as finance minister of Hyderabad State at the time of independence. Although he took no active part in Pakistan's freedom movement, he had been a confidant of Jinnah on financial matters before independence and had served on several important missions to negotiate terms of partition.[16] He was appointed by Jinnah as the first Finance Minister in Liaquat's cabinet, and held that office until his appointment as Governor-General. No advocate of parliamentary democracy, Ghulam Mohammad preferred the more efficient government he had experienced during the British Raj. To him, politicians, at least Pakistani politicians, were unprincipled and undisciplined, and the ways of party politics alien and distasteful.[17] He was a strong force as Finance Minister in the Liaquat cabinet, exerting substantial influence in most aspects of domestic policy. As a former civil servant, he was intimately acquainted with the workings of the administration. While he had little public exposure, he nevertheless enjoyed a high reputation in government circles for his administrative skills and knowledge of state finance. Like Jinnah before him, Ghulam Mohammad came to the Governor-Generalship physically impaired, but with the prestige, drive, and ability to utilize the office as an instrument of political power.

The appointments of Nazimuddin and Ghulam Mohammad to their respective posts had constitutional implications which seem not to have been considered at the time. When Nazimuddin was appointed Governor-General to succeed Jinnah in 1948, he was serving as Chief Minister of East Bengal and, therefore, an active politician. He, like Jinnah before him, breached the convention that a non-politician be appointed Governor-General, and he was now re-entering politics as Prime Minister of Pakistan after serving as Governor-General. Ghulam Mohammad had participated in politics just prior to the time of his appointment as Governor-General, as a member of the Constituent Assembly and a Cabinet member. In addition, his appointment contravened another convention, namely, that the office of Governor-General was not to be filled by a former civil servant. This was a strong convention in the senior dominions and during the days of British rule in India.[18] If the Governor-General was to be impartial, it was considered advisable that he not be associated with any one particular interest in the government. Ghulam Mohammad had had a long career as a civil servant, and as events were to show, he was to utilize his connection with the bureaucracy to extend his political power.

Within the bureaucracy, Ghulam Mohammad had only one potentially important rival, Chaudhri Mohammad Ali, who was then the Secretary-General of Pakistan and in this capacity in charge of the Pakistan Civil Service. But while Ali was actively engaged in expanding the role of the bureaucracy in the running of the government, he was seen by some as not having personal political ambitions.[19] On the other hand, Ghulam Muhammad was extremely skilful in building a coalition of senior civil servants and military officers, and thus emerged as the leader of the bureaucratic faction. He was ably assisted by Iskander Mirza, who later became the first President of the Islamic Republic of Pakistan. Mirza, the first Indian Army officer to graduate from Sandhurst, had opted for the civil side of government during his years of service in British India. Although he served in the Constituent Assembly, having been elected on the Muslim League ticket, he was, like

Ghulam Mohammad, known for his pronounced dislike of the legislative process and of politicians. He was a strong proponent of what he referred to as 'controlled democracy'.

Mirza was valuable to Ghulam Mohammad as a connection to the army and its Commander-in-Chief, Ayub Khan. Ayub had been appointed Commander-in-Chief of the army in 1950. He professed to play no part on the political scene during the Liaquat and Nazimuddin administrations.[20] Like all senior officers of the time, he had served in the British Indian army, and publicly claimed adherence to the tradition that the military did not participate in politics.[21] Ayub gave the impression that the task of building the army to afford protection against India was one which consumed his energies and attentions, and that political involvement by himself or his officers would divert attention from that goal. He had one difference with most politicians on international affairs. Ayub and his senior officers favoured a military alliance with the United States, while Liaquat and Nazimuddin supported the maintenance of military ties with Great Britain.[22] The army was to have its way, principally because of the worldwide American military build-up during the Korean War. During the same period, the military strength of Great Britain was ebbing.

Four months after taking office as Prime Minister, it was Nazimuddin's misfortune to fall foul of the language issue in East Bengal. He exhibited a high degree of political insensitivity.[23] Nazimuddin was a Bengali. Having served as a pre-independence legislator and Chief Minister of Bengal, and after partition as Chief Minister of East Bengal, he was aware of how explosive the issue of making Urdu the nation's single official language was. He was also aware that Bengal had a reputation for violence. Since its founding, the Muslim League had been strongly oriented toward Urdu, but to most Bengalis, it was the language of the upper classes and of many of the people who had migrated to Bengal from other parts of India during the late nineteenth and early twentieth centuries, when Calcutta was undergoing its industrial expansion. Now most of those people were on the other side of the partition line, and as a result the support for Urdu was weak in East Bengal. Only a small group of educated persons in East Bengal could understand Urdu, and its official use as the national language meant, for example, that to obtain government employment a Bengali was required to learn Urdu in addition to English, the operative language for much of the business conducted by the government. Urdu and Bengali are written in entirely different scripts, and many an ordinary citizen was unable to understand the Urdu inscriptions on the rupees he carried in his pocket, or on the postage stamps he used. Bengali pride in their own language, the vehicle of some of India's greatest modern literature, was offended by the subservience of Bengali to Urdu. To Jinnah, however, as well as the West Pakistani politicians, Bengali was a Hindu language unworthy of official recognition in a Muslim nation. They also feared it because it represented the cultural unity of Bengal. If this unity were to prove stronger than the religious bond which united the east and west wings of Pakistan, there could even arise a revival of the political agitation by such Bengali politicians as Fazlul Huq or Suhrawardy, who had favoured a united Bengal at the time of partition.

Language was an emotional issue which cut across class lines and mobilized a broad base of the population. Language issues had served to separate Muslims and Hindus in pre-independence days. After independence, this issue served to separate, with the same degree of virulence, Bengalis and those from the provinces of West Pakistan. As Chief Minister of East Bengal, Nazimuddin had been able to quell language riots in March 1949 only by calling for assistance from Jinnah. So important was this issue in the affairs of state that Jinnah, in failing health, made the exhausting air journey to East Bengal, his only visit to the province after independence. Jinnah addressed a large public gathering at Dhaka University on 28 March 1948, urging them in English that it was vital that Pakistan have a single national language and that that language must be Urdu.[24] Jinnah's speech quieted the issue for the rest of the time Liaquat was Prime Minister, but the language issue remained potentially explosive.[25]

Upon becoming Prime Minister, Nazimuddin attempted to continue the language policy of Jinnah and Liaquat. When the issue of Bengali again surfaced, he often referred to it as a 'Hindu plot'. Although a Bengali, he shared the apprehensions Jinnah and Liaquat had had about the danger of Bengali contributing to provincial separateness.[26] The issue exploded in January 1952, when Nazimuddin made his first address in East Bengal as Prime Minister. The speech took place at a large open-air gathering in Dhaka. The subject was not the language issue, but the unity of the country. In the course of his speech, Nazimuddin reminded his listeners that Jinnah had spoken to them on the importance of having one language for all of Pakistan. While the language issue was only one among various passages in Nazimuddin's speech and he gave it no emphasis, it proved to be highly inflammatory. Riots erupted in East Bengal, a general strike was called, and students demonstrated. Lives were lost and property damage sustained. The Hindu minority in East Bengal was united as never before with the Muslim majority. So strong was the reaction that the authorities closed the *Pakistan Observer*, which was one of Dhaka's two English language newspapers and which had been in the forefront of the agitation. The provisions of the Code of Criminal Procedure were applied, but the use of repression only intensified hostilities.

Public reaction when several student demonstrators were killed by police forced Nazimuddin to negotiate with the demonstrators. Agreement was reached whereby an official resolution would be introduced in the Muslim League-dominated East Bengal Assembly, recommending Bengali as one of the national languages. The agreement, however, was not implemented, and demonstrations and violence were renewed.[27] Nazimuddin, as well as the Muslim League, were discredited in East Bengal. It was rumoured at the time that some of Ghulam Mohammad's supporters tricked Nazimuddin into making the mistake he did.[28]

At the end of 1951 the *Nawa-i-Waqt,* a newspaper which often represented the political position of the Islamic faction, criticized what it termed the incompetence of the Assembly. The paper demanded to know: 'for how many hours did the Constituent Assembly meet in more than four years of its existence and how long did its sub-committees set to work on the tasks assigned to them? How much of the constitution had been written and was it not a fact that, except for the Objectives Resolution, not a single line had been drafted?'[29] There had, in fact, been some progress in constitution-making, unnoticed but important. Six weeks after Liaquat's assassination, the Franchise Sub-committee of the Basic Principles Committee reached agreement that there should be legislative parity between Pakistan's east and west wings.[30] Nevertheless, the government felt obliged to issue a news item two days later, saying that all of the sub-committees of the Basic Principles Committee would complete their reports by February 1952.[31]

When February came and the reports of the Basic Principles Committee's sub-committees were not forthcoming, as Nazimuddin had promised the public two months earlier, Governor-General Ghulam Mohammad told a public gathering in Lahore that a great deal of the basic work of the constitution had been completed and that there would be no more delay.[32] But the public continued to lack specific information concerning constitutional progress, and Ghulam Mohammad's assurances did not satisfy Maududi, among others. In a well-publicized speech made in Karachi's Arambagh Park on 8 May, Maududi alleged that the Constituent Assembly had not spent a single day on the framing of a new constitution and that it had lost the confidence of the people. He alleged that the rulers were holding on to power by curtailing the civil liberties of the people. A large-scale campaign was launched to force the acceptance of his version of an Islamic constitution. This campaign involved the distribution of posters and pamphlets and the holding of meetings and silent demonstrations.[33]

Little information about the constitution had reached the public since the Basic Principles Committee had appointed the Suggestions Sub-committee in August 1950. The Basic Principles Committee itself held no meetings for almost two years, awaiting the reports of its sub-committees, but the Suggestions Sub-committee was quite active during that period, holding many meetings to consider a broad spectrum of comments from the public on the constitution. Considerable discussion and debate took place between the religious and secular members of the sub-committee, and progress was made in determining the extent of the Islamic nature of the state.

In May of 1952 the Suggestions Sub-committee submitted its report, and in the period May to July of 1952, there was an acceleration in constitution-making, according to government press releases to the public through *Dawn*.[34] The Judicial and Legislative Representation Sub-committees finished their work, and it was estimated that all of the sub-committees would finish their reports by August of 1952, and that the Basic Principles Committee would submit its report to the Constituent Assembly in September or October. The constitution, it was estimated, would be ready by the end of 1953, and elections under the terms of the new constitution could be held at the end of 1954 or early in 1955 at the latest. There was no objection to this schedule, and as events turned out the estimate proved accurate. In August the Franchise and Judiciary Sub-committees submitted their reports, and the Basic Principles Committee was then able to prepare its report. By this time Nazimuddin had gained control of the Committee through the appointment of new members.[35]

In November 1952, three and a half years after the Objectives Resolution had been adopted, Nazimuddin submitted the Basic Principles Committee Report to the Constituent Assembly.[36] On the day before the report was turned over to the Assembly, the campaign of public demonstrations for an Islamic constitution, begun by Maududi in his Arambagh Park speech in May, reached its culmination when thousands of men paraded with banners and placards in front of the Assembly building in Karachi. Tamizuddin Khan, the president of the Assembly, responded by imposing Section 144 of the Rules of Civil Procedure on the city, enabling the police to suppress political demonstrations and speeches. He also gave a warning to the Press not to make public any information they might have about the contents of the report. The Press was quick to object to this censorship and restriction on its freedom.[37]

Nazimuddin's Basic Principles Committee Report of 1952 was important because, after debate and amendment, it became the final draft of the constitution in 1954. It was an elaboration on Liaquat's Interim Report of 1950. The 1952 report provided for a Council of Ministers which would be led by a Chief Minister who was required to have the confidence of the Assembly. There was to be parity in representation between east and west in both houses, and the apportionment of 400 members was evenly divided in the lower house between the east and the west wings. The five-to-one advantage West Pakistan enjoyed over East Bengal in the upper house, by the equal weight of the units given the provinces in the Interim Report, was abolished by making East Bengal's vote in the upper house equal to the combined vote of all of the provinces of West Pakistan, sixty to sixty. There were to be nine units in West Pakistan in the upper house.[38] Further, the most important legislative matters, the budget, money bills, and motions of confidence were to be exclusively vested in the lower house, the upper chamber being restricted to recommendations in such matters. The report also provided for increased voting weight for some of the smaller West Pakistan units. It was in these units that Nazimuddin had the most influence.

These changes in legislative representation reflected Nazimuddin's policy of increasing the power of East Bengal. Nazimuddin as a Bengali worked to ally the smaller provinces of West Pakistan with East Bengal and against Punjab. It was obvious to the Punjabis that not only was Bengal representation increased in the upper house by the report, but also the greater number of units into which West Pakistan was to be divided provided opportunity for East Bengal's politicians to strike voting bargains with non-Punjabi West Pakistanis. Since the east and west wings started evenly matched with votes in both houses, in any issue contested between the wings either side could prevail only if it could win votes from the other's bloc. The Punjabis feared that the Bengalis would have a better chance of capturing anti-Punjabi votes in the West Pakistan bloc than the Punjabis would have in attracting dissident votes in the Bengal bloc.

The Punjab Muslim League, which at first supported the report, withdrew its support.[39] The newspapers split on the issue of parity. *Dawn* and the *Civil and Military Gazette* editorialized in favour of parity, while the *Pakistan Times* and the majority of papers took the opposite position.[40] The non-Muslim League Bengalis outside the Assembly were also dissatisfied because the report did not go far enough. It did not give East Bengal provincial autonomy, nor did it recognize the fact of the Bengali majority in population, and it also failed to give the Bengali language equality with Urdu.

The Basic Principles Committee Report was the constitutional high-water mark for the religious factions, a position they were later to lose as a result of the Ahmadi riots and the discrediting of their cause by the issuance of the Munir Report. The Basic Principles Committee Report required the head of state be a male Muslim, and recommended that the government should be guided by the principles set out in the Objectives Resolution. In addition, there was a directive provision urging the teaching of the Koran, abstention from alcohol consumption, prohibition of gambling and prostitution, greater propagation of Islam among the people, and measures to bring existing law into conformity with the Koran and Sunnah. Elimination of usury was to be brought about as soon as possible, an agency should be formed to oversee the proper organization of mosques, and the government was to be granted injunctive power to prevent any violations of the provisions of the Objectives Resolution.

Among the concessions in the report was a proposal for an *ulema* board to serve as an expert agency to prevent the implementation of any legislation of the Assembly repugnant to the principles of Islam. Objections to any law of the Assembly which was thought to be in conflict with the Koran or Sunnah could be raised in the legislature by any Muslim member, and adjudication of the challenge was not to be by a court of law. Instead, the bill would be sent to the Governor-General, (who was renamed the head of state), with the objection attached. The head of state would then refer the bill to the *ulema* board appointed by him, which was to give him its views within seven days. If the board unanimously found the bill, in whole or in part, to be in conflict with Islamic principles, the bill was to be returned to the legislature. It could then be passed over the board's objection by a majority of the members present and voting, provided that the majority also contained a majority of the Muslim members present and voting.

The terms were generous but the measure appeared to grant the religionists more than it actually did. Not only were money bills not subject to the review of the *ulema* board but, since the board's finding had to be unanimous in order to have any effect, and since the Governor-General on the advice of his ministers appointed the board members, the outcome of any challenge was in reality controllable by the administration. For this reason *Nawa-i-Waqt*, which usually supported the viewpoint of the religious fundamentalists, attacked the proposed *ulema* board as creating 'a group of religious courtiers whose decision will be guided not by the dictates of the Koran or Sunnah but by the whims and political expediencies of the rulers'.[41]

Those who had hoped for a constitution reflecting modern, secular concepts were also strong in their condemnation. The report was called a 'surrender to Mullahism'. It was labelled a 'recognition of priesthood', and seen as creating a 'medieval theocracy in the twentieth century' by attempting to 'take the country back to the dark days of Islam'.[42] *Dawn* was dissatisfied because the courts were excluded from adjudicating issues of the conflict of legislation with Islamic principle. But if the courts were not to have the final say, the paper advocated that it was better to leave the question of conformity with Islamic principles to the good sense of the majority members of the legislature.[43] It pointed out that the Basic Principles Committee Report went beyond the intent of the Objectives Resolution by including Islam in the constitutional framework. The *ulema* board was criticized because it shifted part of the function of legislating from the chosen representatives of the people to those who had no democratic sanction. *Dawn* went further by criticizing the report as creating something repugnant to the spirit of Islam itself, namely, a class of priests who alone would judge what was in accord with the Koran and Sunnah. This, it was claimed, was bound to lead to dispute from those who were not *ulema* but who believed themselves equally well-versed in Islamic law. *Dawn* could not understand why it was assumed that Muslim legislators, elected by Muslim voters, would be ignorant of the requirements of the Koran and the Sunnah. Certainly, it was reasoned, a large legislative body would contain sufficient numbers of persons well-versed in Islamic law. It was suggested that it would be better to have special Assembly seats for the *ulema* so that expert advice on religious matters could be given within the legislature itself. These experts, according to *Dawn's* suggestion, should themselves be chosen by the people.

The *Pakistan Times* added its objection that the members of the *ulema* board would be 'paid agents of the government and board membership would become a political plum with the membership being in a position of gratitude to those who appointed them'. The *Times* stated that the only way of ensuring the true spirit of Islam would be to 'establish a fully democratic state and leave it to the good sense of the representatives of the people to establish a society which conforms to Islamic ideals.'[44] The religious factions generally did not join in the debate. Many fundamentalists were of two minds. They had gained many of their objectives in the draft of the constitution, and while some believed there was no benefit in adding fat to the political fire, others had strong objections to the political process to which religious questions would be subject. Their equivocation and their resulting failure to speak out in defence of the report undercut the strength of the support for the constitution.

Despite the fact that they had earlier approved the Basic Principles Report, the Punjab Muslim League members of the

Constituent Assembly came out publicly against it. Punjabi opposition grew across the political spectrum, including some of the religious factions of that province.[45] Strong pressure was exerted at the All-Parties Convention held in Lahore on 28 December, and a vigorous opposition campaign was carried on by such papers as *Nawa-i-Waqt* and the *Pakistan Times.* Daultana and Mamdot were strong leaders in the Punjab who took positions against the report. They advocated that the Prime Minister visit the Punjab to assess first-hand the extent of the opposition.

Nazimuddin withdrew the Basic Principles Report and adjourned the Assembly *sine die* on 21 January 1953. He did not give a reason for his action, and it seems to have been done with little or no discussion with the Assembly members. The withdrawal of the report did not have the approval of the Assembly President Tamizuddin Khan.[46] A fact-finding exchange of Assembly members between east and west was arranged and Nazimuddin and eight members of his Cabinet visited the Punjab. A delegation of Punjab Muslim League members were to go to East Bengal to attempt to negotiate a solution to the disagreements on the constitution, but before anything could materialize the attention of the nation was captured by the Ahmadi disturbances. These disturbances and the subsequent dismissal of Nazimuddin as Prime Minister resulted in delay to further work on the constitution.

The Ahmadis are a religious sect which denies the basic tenet of Islam: that Mohammad was the last of the prophets. The members believe in the teachings of Mirza Ghulam Ahmad, who claimed himself to be a prophet. Since Ahmad's death in 1908, the sect had grown to an estimated 200,000 members in Pakistan, and had a number of prominent adherents, including Mohammad Zafrulla Khan, who had been appointed by Jinnah as a member of the first Cabinet and who was serving as Pakistan's Foreign Minister. From its inception, the sect had been the object of fierce opposition, but they had enjoyed the protection of the British. After independence, a campaign had been mounted against the Ahmadis, and by the early 1950s opposition had grown to include a significant number of respected *ulema.* The anti-Ahmadi forces enjoyed the backing of Daultana, now Chief Minister of West Punjab. Daultana may have viewed disturbances as a means of discrediting the move of the religious factions for an Islamic state. Disturbances would also create pressure on Nazimuddin's administration.[48]

On 21 January 1953, a delegation of the *ulema* delivered an ultimatum to Prime Minister Nazimuddin, threatening to resort to direct action if the government did not declare the Ahmadis a non-Muslim minority and if Zafrulla Khan and other Ahmadis in government posts were not discharged. The affair was further complicated by the political manoeuvrings of Daultana, who issued a public statement agreeing with the demands of the anti-Ahmadis and claiming that it was the responsibility of the central government to bring about a solution to the problem. The anti-Ahmadi demands enjoyed strong support, but to accede to their demands for discharge of Ahmadis from the government would have ended any hope of maintaining the principle of equality for Pakistan's minorities.

Prime Minister Nazimuddin attempted to deal with the problem by conciliation, and agreed to meet with a delegation of *ulema*. He personally sympathized with the *ulema* on religious grounds, but when they threatened to take direct action he realized that no government could rule if it gave way to such pressure. Therefore, on 7 March he ordered the arrest of the anti-Ahmadi leaders. This decision caused the Punjab, and particularly Lahore, to burst into violence. The military, with the concurrence of the central government, took action and established military rule.[49] Order was restored within a matter of hours, but military rule lasted for two months. City streets were cleaned up and essential goods were available at controlled prices, giving the public a good impression of military efficiency.

Arrests of religious leaders took place throughout West Pakistan. Maududi and other leaders of the Jamaat were arrested on 28 March. Those arrested remained in confinement, and some were not informed of the charges against them for six weeks. The offices of the Jamaat were raided, money confiscated, and two of the society's newspapers were required to post 32,000 rupees as security under the Press Act.[50] Five days after martial rule was established in Lahore, a military board sentenced Maududi to death for his publication of an anti-Ahmadi pamphlet which attempted to put the blame for the riots on the government. Oddly enough, the pamphlet itself was not banned and it sold 57,000 copies. There were public protests against Maududi's sentence, and although he refused to petition for clemency, his sentence was commuted by the military authorities to fourteen years. Most of the religious leaders were released by the end of 1953 but Maududi remained in confinement for two years.

The strongest Muslim League politician in West Pakistan was Daultana. His roles as Chief Minister of the Punjab and head of the Muslim League of that province placed him in a central position. He, along with a majority of Punjab Muslim League leaders and the central bureaucracy, opposed Nazimuddin's Basic Principles Committee Report because of the increased power they feared it gave to the Bengalis in the Constituent Assembly. They could see that the Bengalis were joining forces with the religious factions, and that this combination would be strong enough to push through the Constituent Assembly a constitution which would be unfavourable to West Pakistan and the bureaucracy. Under the cover of the confusion caused by the riots Nazimuddin used Section 92A to move against this opposition, dismissing Daultana as premier of the Punjab and replacing him with Malik Feroz Khan Noon.[51]

Military rule in the Punjab ended in March 1953. On 17 April, in a surprise move, Nazimuddin was dismissed by proclamation of Governor-General Ghulam Mohammad. In the weeks preceding this dismissal, the nation's newspapers contained many accounts of an existing food crisis, and there were editorials and letters to the editors complaining of government inefficiency. But as serious as the situation was, there was no indication of any political difficulty prior to Ghulam Mohammad's actions against Nazimuddin. In fact, only a week before the dismissal, Ghulam Mohammad had defended the policies of the government in a speech given to the Karachi Rotary Club. Ghulam Mohammad's words about Nazimuddin's administration at the time were quite supportive. He warned that people should give up what he termed 'their old habits of irresponsible and disruptive criticism'. With reference to the existing food shortage, Ghulam Mohammad informed his listeners that decisions had been made 'to do, within a short time, all that is possible to get over the temporary difficulties'.[52] Ghulam Mohammad was referring to a policy statement issued by Nazimuddin a few days earlier setting forth measures his government planned to take to deal with the food shortage. *Dawn* had commented editorially on Nazimuddin's plan with approval and enthusiastically praised him.[53]

Ghulam Mohammad appeared to stay out of politics during his two years as Governor-General. His low profile gave an impression to some that he was content playing the symbolic role of the constitutional head of state. His only public involvement seemed to have been in affairs of the army. But this public impression was deceptive. Some officials who worked with Ghulam Mohammad were alarmed that he was a psychotic obsessed with gaining power.[54] He was suspicious of Nazimuddin's close association with his old enemy, the Bengali leader Fazlur Rahman, and feared that Nazimuddin would remove him as Governor-General. By the end of 1952, Ghulam Mohammad's health had deteriorated to such a point that he performed the ceremonial duties of his office with difficulty, and his speech was greatly impaired. Ill as he was physically, he retained a remarkably clear mind, and remained a consummate flatterer. His strength lay in two areas of growing importance, the civil service and the army. He was also establishing contact with Suhrawardy and other members of the Awami opposition in East Bengal.

It does not seem that Nazimuddin foresaw his dismissal. Ghulam Mohammad called a meeting of the Cabinet, and when it was assembled he curtly demanded the resignation of Nazimuddin and the other Cabinet members. Nazimuddin later narrated what had occurred.

> His Excellency the Governor-General suggested to me that I and my colleagues should meet him at his residence. When we met him at his residence at 4:00 p.m., he demanded our resignations. I told the Governor-General that constitutionally and legally he had no right to make such a demand because he was purely a constitutional Governor-General. I also told him that I commanded the confidence of the Legislative Assembly and the country and, therefore, was entitled to remain in office. The fact that only recently the Legislative Assembly passed my budget by an overwhelming majority was a clear proof of the fact that I had the Legislative Assembly and the country behind me. For these reasons I refused to tender my and my colleagues' resignations.[55]

Upon refusing to resign, he was dismissed by Ghulam Mohammad. Nazimuddin termed the action an 'illegal and unconstitutional course...against the basic principles of democracy'.[56] When he returned to the Prime Minister's house after the meeting and attempted to reach Queen Elizabeth in London to advise her to remove Ghulam Mohammad as Governor-General, he found his telephone cut and his house surrounded by a police detachment.[57]

Nazimuddin was aware that he could have called an emergency session of the Constituent Assembly but hesitated because, as he put it, 'The Assembly was threatened with all kinds of military action…and I advised them not to create trouble at the time.'[58] In a radio address to the nation the next day, he counselled the people to be calm. 'I have always asked my countrymen, and even at this juncture, beg of them to be true Muslims and hold fast according to the Koranic injunctions to the covenant of Allah and be not divided.'[59] Nazimuddin stated that it was important that nothing be done that might weaken Pakistan domestically or embarrass it internationally. In part because of the muted reaction to his dismissal, little notice was payed outside Pakistan to the unconstitutionality of Ghulam Muhammad's act.

The Pakistan Times reported widespread political arrests in Punjab,[60] but most politicians chose to remain silent and those who did speak up stated their approval of the Governor-General's action. Suhrawardy approved without reservation. He was happy to see a Muslim League Prime Minister fall from power, especially an old political enemy who had replaced him at independence as the political leader of the Bengalis. Now, he urged Ghulam Mohammad, it was time to take the next step and dissolve the Constituent Assembly, the body which had refused to seat Suhrawardy when he moved from India to Pakistan. Ghulam Mohammad received a large number of letters and telegrams of praise. There were no public demonstrations and *The Pakistan Times* was able to report that the *coup* was a complete success and had been well-received in Washington.[61]

In his proclamation, Ghulam Mohammad gave as his official reasons for Nazimuddin's dismissal the food shortage, the need for more vigorous action on the general economic problems of the country, and the need for law and order. He proclaimed, 'I have been driven to the conclusion that the Cabinet of Khwaja Nazimuddin has proven entirely inadequate to grapple with the difficulties facing the country.'[62] Despite this assertion about general Cabinet incompetence, Ghulam Mohammad re-appointed most of its members after Nazimuddin was dismissed.

Pakistan was suffering a loss of income caused by the fall in commodity prices following the end of the Korean War, and disputes over Punjab agricultural prices led to a man-made grain shortage. But these were not conditions which had suddenly appeared, some economic difficulties having been inherited from the Liaquat administration.[63] Nazimuddin had been weakened by his failure to win the support of the Punjab leaders and people for the constitutional proposals which were pending at that time. At the same time he was weakened in Bengal, even within the ranks of the Muslim League provincial party members, because of his unwillingness to include greater provincial autonomy in his proposed new constitution and his recent support of Urdu. But despite these events Nazimuddin had succeeded in having the Constituent Assembly pass the annual budget after the Ahmadi riots had subsided, thus demonstrating that his administration held the confidence of the Assembly. What better explains Ghulam Mohammad's action was the fact that the new budget proposed by Nazimuddin called for a cut in defence expenditures by one-third.[64] This was an unprecedented move, and was bound to alarm Ayub and the army.

During the two years Ghulam Mohammad had occupied the office of Governor-General, he had seen nothing to change his opinion about politicians or what he considered their unwillingness or incapacity to give the country the leadership he believed it needed. Mohammad Munir, who knew Ghulam Mohammad well, believed that Nazimuddin's dismissal was a calculated act designed 'to feel the pulse of the nation.'[65] The civil service was now gaining in strength and effectiveness, emerging from the complete disorganization in which it existed at partition.[66] This did not mean, however, that the members of the civil service opposed the drafting of a new constitution or believed the politicians should be removed and replaced with civil administrators.[67]

Not a voice was heard in protest to Nazimuddin's dismissal, an event which the American Ambassador described to Washington as 'one of the most popular *coups* in history.'[68] It was, however, a *coup* which was not generally recognized as a *coup* at the time. Ghulam Mohammad was able to strip Nazimuddin of all political support while six of the nine members of Nazimuddin's Cabinet were reappointed by Ghulam Mohammad. The three who were permanently dismissed along with Nazimuddin were the most influential Muslim League members and potentially the most difficult for Ghulam Mohammad to control. They were replaced by three figures with little political strength. Included in the dismissal was Sardar Abdur Rab Nishtar, who was not only a strong West Pakistani leader possessing political influence not under the control of Ghulam Mohammad, but was also a supporter of the religious factions. With the dismissal of Nishtar, the last of Jinnah's Cabinet choices was removed from the administration. Fazlur Rahman, the East Bengali leader and long-time foe of Ghulam Mohammad, was also dismissed. There were now no Bengalis in the Cabinet. Most of the members of the Cabinet accepted Ghulam Mohammad's invitation and remained. As Ayub Khan put it, they did so 'without demur, if without avidity'.[69]

By his dismissal of Nazimuddin and the shuffling of the Cabinet, Ghulam Mohammad was also eliminating the Muslim League as an independent voice in the central government. Although dismissed as Prime Minister, Nazimuddin remained for a while as President of the Muslim League. Leadership of the League left him in a position of power, even though not holding government office. However, when Nazimuddin appointed the Working Committee of the Muslim League (its executive committee), seven of the thirteen nominees refused to serve because Mohammad Ali Bogra, the new Prime Minister appointed by Ghulam Mohammad, was not included as a member.[70] In the Assembly, the Muslim League Parliamentary Party elected the new Prime Minister as its leader shortly after Nazimuddin's dismissal. By repudiating Nazimuddin, the Muslim League surrendered whatever remaining claim it had to leadership on the national level. The dismissal was also an attack on the Constituent Assembly. Ghulam Mohammad was demonstrating that the confidence expressed in Nazimuddin by the Assembly meant nothing. He was now exercising power similar to Jinnah, also a politically active Governor-General who appointed a Prime Minister independent of the Constituent Assembly.[71]

Ghulam Mohammad attempted to deal with the constitutional issues raised by the dismissal by issuing a statement through the Law Minister, A. K. Brohi, criticizing 'undue emphasis on certain conventions as they are known to the British constitutional practice'.[72] Brohi was referring to the modern British and Commonwealth constitutional convention that a Prime Minister who had the confidence of the legislature, as did Nazimuddin, could not be removed by the head of state, whether King or Governor-General, without replacing the dismissed Prime Minister with a person possessing the confidence of the legislature.[73] While this constitutional practice was well-recognized in the Commonwealth, it was a matter of convention rather than a rule of law which could be enforced in a court of law. In conformity with English constitutional practice, the Pakistan constitution made no mention of a Prime Minister, his duties, or his tenure of office.

Brohi's statement denied that those conventions could be read into the Pakistan dominion constitution. He relied on a distinction between constitutional convention and constitutional law, and he cited the fact that the Cabinet and Prime Minister were creatures of convention. Brohi argued that while the conventions which had grown up around government practice in Britain played a serviceable role in the constitutional mechanics of Great Britain, such conventions were not applicable in Pakistan. He maintained that ministers in Pakistan were not the same as ministers of the British Cabinet, who had no statutory recognition, while in contrast Pakistani ministers were specifically provided for in the Government of India Act of 1935 and served at the pleasure of the Governor-General.[74]

Dawn reflected the reaction of the national Muslim League to the dismissal. This paper was caught off-guard, like most of the nation, and limited its first editorial to taking exception to the 'method by which the change has been effected', and repeating parts of the statement Nazimuddin had issued the day after his dismissal concerning his description of and his reaction to the dismissal.[75] Two days after its first editorial, *Dawn* expanded its views. 'The Governor-General's communique explaining his action had force at point, and much that he said in it could not but have met with ready response in the public mind. But the spirit of the Constitution is even more important than its letter, and the use of such powers by the Head of State is not to be lightly regarded if democratic institutions are to be firmly established in Pakistan . . . Nazimuddin's protest has its own validity and both the Muslim League and the Party will have to review the situation in all its far-reaching implications.'[76]

There was a divergence of opinion within the Muslim League concerning Nazimuddin's dismissal, and that divergence was dictated to a large extent by provincial considerations. In contrast to *Dawn's* comment, the Punjab branch of the League reflected in its statement the discontent existing in that province arising from Nazimuddin's dismissal of the Daultana ministry during the

Ahmadi riots. The Punjab Muslim League issued a statement claiming the dismissal 'echoed the will of the rejoicing millions of people; it will go down in history as the most courageous and sublime act ever dictated by a deep sense of patriotism.'[77] The League in East Bengal, however, viewed the dismissal of a Prime Minister from Bengal quite differently. Its President charged that the dismissal was 'against the canons of constitutional propriety. Even if it was conceded that constitutionally the Governor-General was within his rights to dismiss the Cabinet, the manner in which it was done was against the conventions of a democratic state.' He saw the danger to the League itself and pleaded that '...[I]t was the duty of devoted Muslim Leaguers to uphold the cause of the Muslim League and save it from being killed so ruthlessly.'[78]

Strong criticism in East Bengali newspapers concentrated on the dismissal of a Bengali Prime Minister by a Punjabi Governor-General. The *Morning News* of Dhaka showed an understanding of the workings of convention in a parliamentary system of the Westminster model when it expressed the opinion that, although the Governor-General possessed extraordinary powers under the constitution, these powers were subject to conventions and what it termed 'democratic practices', and were powers which were not actually to be used. Although the members of the Cabinet held office 'at the pleasure' of the Governor-General, in any government that considered itself operating as a parliamentary government, this did not vest him with the right to remove a ministry which enjoyed the confidence of the Constituent Assembly.[79]

The views expressed by the *Pakistan Times* are of particular interest because, unlike *Dawn* and the *Morning News*, this West Pakistan newspaper had been a strong critic of Nazimuddin and had advocated his removal. The 21 April headline of the *Pakistan Times* read: 'Decision Hailed...Messages From All Over the Country.' Maintaining its usual anti-Nazimuddin stance, it characterized Ghulam Mohammad's action as 'courageous, wise and statesmanlike.' It regretted that democratic government had not been operating more effectively, for then what it considered a failed administration such as Nazimuddin's would have been removed earlier in the normal course of the operations of the democratic process. The dismissal heralded a new era, according to the *Times*, and Pakistan could now look to powerful friends abroad for help in achieving prosperity and stability. Yet even the editors of the *Times* sensed that all was not right. The dismissal exposed 'the true operation of Pakistan's political system behind the facade of parliamentary forms'. Perceiving an 'undercurrent of disquiet about the constitutional propriety' of the Governor-General's action, the editors seemingly contradicted themselves and termed the dismissal 'undesirable'.[80]

Robert Trumbull of the *New York Times* reported from New Delhi that Nazimuddin's dismissal was viewed as a 'constitutional curiosity that intrigues the entire British Commonwealth'.[81] One might question just how intrigued the other parliamentary democracies actually were. The constitutional issues involved in Nazimuddin's dismissal received little attention in the British Press, which treated the change not as a constitutional crisis, but as an expedient political move. *The Times* of London congratulated Ghulam Mohammad for short-circuiting the 'political intrigues of which public life has recently been far too full'.[82] The *Economist* hailed the 'courageous, timely and dramatic' action of the Governor-General, who had made 'a realistic appraisal of the situation and by acting with at least some semblance of constitutional legality, has prevented a possible *coup d'etat*'.[83] Nazimuddin's dismissal was hardly noticed in Washington, Pakistan itself being at the time of little interest in the American capital.[84]

CHAPTER 5

THE 1954 CONSTITUTION AND THE DISSOLUTION OF THE ASSEMBLY

After the Ahmadi riots ended in March 1953, and the Army had returned to barracks in May, an investigative commission was appointed. It was chaired by Mohammad Munir, at that time Chief Justice of the Punjab High Court, and consisted of one other member of that court, M. R. Kayani. Munir shared many of Ghulam Mohammad's ideas about the superiority of bureaucracy over the legislative process of government. At the conclusion of the investigation, he issued the Munir Report, which supported Ghulam Mohammad and his Punjab bureaucracy by criticizing the way the politicians, such as Daultana and Nazimuddin, had handled the riots. Also, during the hearings held by the commission, Munir pressed the *ulema* and religious political leaders who appeared as witnesses to define a Muslim. The results, published in 1954, stressed the inconsistencies in the answers given, and were used to discredit the usefulness of the Islamic leaders as participants in constitution-making. The conclusion the report was intended to reach was quite clear. If the religious leaders could not agree among themselves on something as basic as who was a Muslim, how reliable could they be in advising as to what Islamic principles should be reflected in the constitution?[1]

The hearings of the Munir commission were symptomatic of a change on the constitutional scene which took place as a result of the Ahmadi riots. The strongest voices in constitutional debate were now those arguing for a secular constitution. The new Prime Minister, Mohammad Ali Bogra, and the new Chief Ministers of Punjab and East Bengal, Noon and Chaudhry Khaliquzzaman, were known to hold ideas opposed by the religious factions, and Brohi, a respected Karachi lawyer, legal scholar, and advocate of a secular constitution, was now Law Minister. Many in the religious communities had had their sensibilities shocked by a 1952 article of Brohi's which appeared in *Dawn* entitled, 'Thoughts on the Future Constitution of Pakistan'.[2] From the beginning of the constitutional debates, Brohi had supported Islam as a means of furnishing a general basis for democratic government, but in his article he denied that Islamic principles could go beyond that. He maintained that it was erroneous to expect the constitution of a nation to improve individuals or society itself.

The reaction to his article had been so strong that Brohi felt obliged to trim his position. He issued a disclaimer asserting that his remarks should be understood as limited to those parts of the constitution 'which dealt with the distribution of sovereign power within the state'.[3] But now reaction to the riots and the dismissal of Nazimuddin checked the political strength of the religious leaders. Nazimuddin had been the most prominent national leader sympathetic to the constitutional aims of the religious community.

Ghulam Mohammad hoped to take advantage of the existing secular mood on constitutional matters. He planned to work within the Assembly and obtain constitutional legislation which would provide a temporary and partial constitution, based primarily on the Basic Principles Committee Report but omitting any reference to the Islamic nature of the state. Like India, Pakistan would be declared a republic. He also wished to see the dissolution of what he considered to be an unrepresentative Constituent Assembly, and to obtain the election of a new assembly, which would not be a sovereign body and over which the Governor-General would exercise a right of veto. The new assembly would, if all went as Ghulam Mohammad planned, pass constitutional legislation amending the Government of India Act to allow for his One Unit Plan uniting the provinces of West Pakistan. To achieve these goals, he needed the support of the Muslim League. While the weakness of the League had been exposed by the dismissal of Nazimuddin, it was still the only significant party in the Constituent Assembly. The party had to be utilized if Ghulam Mohammad wished to work within the parliamentary framework, a necessity for him because there was no other way he could legitimize his rule.

Ghulam Mohammad's proposed interim constitution would have weakened the Bengali-Islamic coalition which was forming in the face of rising Punjabi power. His proposed interim constitution made no concession to demands to include Islamic principles, and by depriving it of its sovereignty would have radically changed the Assembly, which was the only forum of power available to the Bengalis on the national level. By means of his One Unit Plan, Ghulam Mohammad would have further increased Punjabi power at the expense of East Bengal. His justification for an interim constitution was that it would allow the government to make a showing to the public that some progress was being made in drafting a constitution, and allow some further time to work out important problems not yet resolved. It would, however, confirm the Governor-General as the dominant factor on the political scene, and by abolishing the Assembly's sovereignty would have addressed for Ghulam Mohammad his principal problem: he now controlled the Cabinet, but did not control the Constituent Assembly.

East Bengal, with its majority population, naturally caused concern to the politicians and bureaucrats of West Pakistan. But the unity of East Bengal was deceptive. Although the population of East Bengal was larger than that of West Pakistan (fifty-six per cent to forty-four per cent) and the members of the Constituent Assembly had been elected in the 1946 election in proportion to population, East Bengal did not have an Assembly majority. At the time of independence, the East Bengal Assembly had elected a number of non-Bengalis as part of the province's delegation to the Constituent Assembly. What later appeared as perhaps an act of misplaced generosity was, at the time, motivated by a spirit of patriotism and unity. These non-Bengalis had resided in the then Congress dominated North-West Frontier or in one of the Muslim-minority provinces of India in 1946, when the Assembly was elected. Their chances of successfully competing in the 1946 election had been limited by the existing political situation in those areas. Liaquat, I. H. Quraishi, Abdul Qayyum, and Ghulam Mohammad were among the non-Bengalis receiving seats. Iskandar Mirza, although from a Bengal family, had spent little time in his home province and was allied with the Punjabi bureaucrats. He also was given a seat. Suhrawardy praised this gesture made by his fellow Bengalis as matchless generosity and self-sacrifice in the interest of the nation. In his opinion, the actual numbers in the delegation from Bengal was, however, a secondary consideration because Bengalis, with their high political consciousness, tended to influence the deliberations of the Assembly out of proportion to their actual numbers.[4] They also controlled the Muslim League Parliamentary Party and thereby controlled the passage of legislation in the Assembly.[5] Nevertheless, the grant of Bengali seats to non-Bengalis left the Bengal Muslim League a minority in the province's forty-four member delegation to the Constituent Assembly. Aside from the eleven seats which were given to the non-Bengalis, thirteen Assembly seats were held by Bengali Hindus; thus the Bengal Muslims held only twenty seats in the delegation.

Ironically, the division between the Hindus and Bengali Muslims within East Bengal was caused in part by the Muslim League politicians who were in control of the East Bengal Assembly and administration. Hindu and Muslim members from East Bengal were divided by the separate electorates which existed for minorities in East Bengal. This was the same separate electorate system first created under British rule when the Muslim minority in India demanded a means of protection against the Hindu majority. The pre-independence elections of 1946 had been held on the basis of separate electorates, and as a result, when the Pakistan Constituent Assembly came into existence, there were seats separately elected by the minorities. The issue was not of importance in West Pakistan, since the flight of the Hindus and Sikhs at partition left that part of the country with a miniscule minority population. In contrast, the eighteen per cent of the East Bengal population who were Hindus held twenty-five per cent of the Constituent Assembly seats from the province after partition, a significant voting bloc.

The Hindus protested against separate electorates after partition. They were a minority, but unlike the Muslims before independence, they were a minority which wanted the right to full political participation, not protection. The Hindus resented having to vote in a separate category where they voted only for Hindu candidates, with the result that the Hindu voter had no influence on who was elected in the majority Muslim category which would be in control of the government. In contrast, a joint electorate, in which all votes were counted together, would have enhanced the value of the vote cast by a minority voter because any candidate would be running as a general candidate. A member of a minority community would be eligible to be one of the general candidates, and perhaps of even greater importance, the minority-community voter would possess a vote which would be in the interests of a Muslim candidate to attempt to win. The Hindu voter would have an opportunity to participate in the election of an office holder who would be active in running the government, instead of voting only for a candidate who would, in effect, be limited to representing Hindu interests.

The Muslim League in East Bengal felt that it was to its advantage, because of its decreasing strength, to keep the Hindus isolated and prevent them from effectively supporting dissident Muslim factions, such as represented by Suhrawardy and Bhashani. In 1952, the Muslim League pushed a law through the East Bengal Assembly which provided for adult franchise and separate electorates, providing categories for Christians and Buddhists and further dividing the Hindus by setting up two categories, one for Caste and one for Schedule Hindus. Having thus compartmentalized East Bengal, it was important for the Muslim League political leaders from that province to keep West Pakistan compartmentalized by provinces.

The conundrum faced by the Bengali Muslim League leaders was that, while separate electorates rendered the minorities powerless against the Muslim League majority in both the East Bengal and the Constituent Assemblies, it made the Hindus and other much smaller minorities of East Bengal voting blocs available to be wooed by the Punjabis. What East Bengal was able to do by striking an alliance with the smaller provinces of West Pakistan against the Punjab, in the future the Punjabis or a united West Pakistan could do against the Bengalis by making alliances in the Constituent Assembly with minority bloc members from East Bengal. Perhaps realizing this, Suhrawardy was a long-time opponent of separate electorates. If they were abolished he saw no reason why West Pakistan could not be united.[6]

The idea of one electoral unit for West Pakistan did not originate with Ghulam Mohammad's 1953 constitutional proposals. It had been discussed as early as 1948 as a countermeasure to the growth of provincialism. By some it was seen also as a means to greater efficiency in government. The argument was frequently made that the existence of the various provinces was the result of British imperialist rule, which had muted the demands for independence by fragmenting the political base of the nationalists and presenting a facade of local popular government. Now, it was argued, Pakistan could be brought together, separated only by the geographic division between the east and west wings. When One Unit was first proposed after independence, the Muslim League was reluctant to endorse the idea without the consent of the smaller provinces of West Pakistan, and because of the absence of that consent it was not included in the Objectives Resolution. Also, when the Objectives Resolution was proposed in March 1949, West Pakistan did not yet feel the political threat from Bengal. When Liaquat introduced his Interim Report twenty months after the Objectives Resolution, it was too late to propose the unification of West Pakistan. The Bengali members had by then begun to exert their strength in the Constituent Assembly, and any such proposal would have disrupted the unity between east and west wing members which the Muslim League had succeeded in maintaining within its ranks. That unity had enabled the League to pass legislation through the Assembly by first obtaining a consensus in the League's Parliamentary Party, and then moving the proposed legislation through the Assembly usually with little or no floor debate and little discussion.

The Pakistan Times of Lahore supported one unit for West Pakistan, maintaining that it was the only fair way of preventing one province, East Bengal, from dominating the others.[7] In August 1953, the One Unit idea, having been rejected the previous autumn, surfaced again when *Nawa-i-Waqt*, the Urdu voice of the Muslim League, endorsed the idea as a measure of combating what it saw as growing provincialism. The paper asserted that the idea was gaining support. Even in East Bengal, the *Pakistan Observer* expressed willingness that the idea be given a try.[8] This was consistent with the position taken by some Bengalis who believed there was a better chance of East Bengal gaining autonomy in a federation where East Bengal was balanced by a united West Pakistan, thus alleviating Punjabi fears of Bengali domination based on population. The matter of West Pakistan's unity, however, received no serious attention in the Assembly until September 1953, when it was revived in Ghulam Mohammad's proposals for an interim constitution.

Under the One Unit Plan as it re-emerged in 1953, the Punjab, to assuage the fear the smaller provinces harboured of Punjab dominance, would settle for forty per cent of the voting power in the one unit, a share which was less than its entitlement based on population.[9] This, however, still gave potentially greater control to the Punjab than might first appear. Not only would the smaller provinces no longer be able to ally themselves with East Bengal and, in effect, be politically trapped within the one unit, but within that unit the Punjab would have the largest single voice and the possibility for controlling the entire wing by gaining only eleven per cent of additional votes from among the smaller provinces. Also, Punjabis were dispersed in sufficient numbers throughout the other provinces of West Pakistan to give them considerable political power within those provinces. The East Bengal leadership in the Constituent Assembly worked very actively with the Assembly members from North-West Frontier and Sindh to defeat the One Unit Plan.

Nazimuddin's replacement as Prime Minister, Mohammad Ali Bogra, was not chosen by the people nor did he represent any political party, but was the personal choice of the Governor-General. Bogra, like Nazimuddin a member of the Bengali landed gentry, had entered politics in 1937, serving one year in the Bengal legislature. His principal government service had been as a diplomat, most recently as Ambassador to the United States, a post which he filled successfully. What made him attractive to Ghulam Mohammad was that he was a Bengali. His appointment as Prime Minister would continue the fiction that, because the offices of Governor-General and Prime Minister were divided between the two wings of Pakistan, East Bengal enjoyed its share of government power.

Another of Bogra's attractions for the Punjab group of bureaucrats was his lack of an independent constituency. Without such a base, it was thought that he could not be other than a tool of Ghulam Mohammad. The Punjab group also perceived that for their purposes, his personal weaknesses made him a suitable candidate. Munir was of the opinion that Bogra was the 'last man who should have been considered for the position of prime minister'.[10] Ayub Khan saw Bogra as somewhat of a scatterbrain with whom it was often difficult to have an adult conversation, and Amjad Ali, who succeeded Bogra as Ambassador in Washington, considered him 'trivial' and not a very effective person.[11] Others later evaluated him as self-indulgent and lacking the strength of character and sense of purpose that the office of

Prime Minister demanded. He has been called a 'pathologically pro-American' political non-entity whose one strong point was his popularity in Washington.[12] This made him valuable to Ayub and the military in their efforts to obtain foreign aid. He lived in fear of Ghulam Mohammad, at times acting like a child trying to avoid the wrath of a dominating and violent father.[13] The Cabinet which Bogra was supposed to lead was not chosen by him. All but three of its members were inherited from the Nazimuddin Cabinet, the other members were appointed by Ghulam Mohammad and all of the Cabinet was from West Pakistan. Bogra, a Bengali, was isolated in what was supposed to be his Cabinet. Only in the Constituent Assembly did East Bengal retain power.

Now, with the success of his *coup* dismissing Nazimuddin, and with Bogra at the helm of the Assembly, Ghulam Mohammad had reason to believe that the chances of success for his interim constitution in the Assembly were good.[14] But the situation was changing for Bogra. He was soon caught between the power of the Governor-General and that of the Bengali-dominated Constituent Assembly, and without a power base of his own was forced to jump one way or the other. In making his choice, he could not ignore what was occurring in his home province. The year in which he was appointed to replace Nazimuddin, 1953, was a politically turbulent one in East Bengal. Feeding this turbulence was the popular perception that the province was being short-changed economically by the central government in the allocation of resources and thwarted politically by Punjabi control of the central government. Intense political activity resulted in the formation of several new anti-Muslim League political parties in East Bengal.

Initially, the new parties had limited membership and exerted little influence on the political scene, but in the second half of the 1953 they gained greater and broader support.[15] The East Bengal Awami League had been formed by Maulana Bhashani in 1949. Bhashani, former President of the Assam Muslim League, was a religious leader with little formal education, and his following was overwhelmingly peasant. The Awami League dealt with sensitive issues of local concern in East Bengal—the food situation, nationalization of the jute industry, establishing Bengali as one of the national languages, and the holding of a general election based on universal adult suffrage. It also called for the release of 'political prisoners', including students who were being held in detention. A march held in conjunction with the first meeting of the party was lathi-charged and tear-gassed by the police, and nineteen of the party's top leaders, including Bhashani, were arrested.[16]

While the Awami League had by far the highest membership and the best organization of any new political party in East Bengal, it was thought that by itself it was not capable of defeating the entrenched Muslim League in the province's election, scheduled to take place after the elections in West Punjab and North-West Frontier. In 1951, it had joined with Mamdot in the Punjab as part of the All Pakistan Awami League under Suhrawardy's leadership. In spite of Suhrawardy's strongly-held belief in the necessity of making any national party a non-communal one, the new party was limited to Muslims. In the Punjab election, influential figures from the North-West Frontier, West Punjab, and Sindh joined the party, and it was able to capture thirty-two seats in the West Punjab Assembly. The party, however, began to disintegrate in the Punjab shortly thereafter. Probably discouraged with the election results, most of the party's leaders began to return to the Muslim League which they had left earlier because they had been denied a place on the party's election slate. The Awami League next entered the 1952 provincial election in the North-West Frontier, but because it failed to make a good showing Suhrawardy was forced to turn his attention to Bengal.

Most of the new smaller parties in East Bengal had political aims which differed from the Awami League only in emphasis. Soon the idea of a united front of the parties gained widespread popularity, leading to pressure on the Awami League in the form of student demonstrations. This resulted in the parties agreeing on a platform known as the Twenty-One Points. The parties joined under the name of the United Front and prepared for East Bengal's provincial election scheduled for 1954. Despite having managed to win elections in West Punjab and the North-West Frontier Province, the Muslim League was concerned about the East Bengal election which had been postponed several times. But while the Muslim League leaders from East Bengal in the Constituent Assembly were aware that there was discontent in the province, they did not fully appreciate its extent.[17] They did realize that they would weaken their position with the voters of East Bengal if they did not strongly oppose Ghulam Mohammad's interim constitution, which would have increased the power of the Governor-General at a time when that office was occupied by a powerful and aggressive West Pakistani politician. They also had to show some progress in the drafting of a new constitution which would at least provide for majority representation for their province in the Assembly.

When the Assembly reconvened in September 1953, there was no discussion or debate concerning Nazimuddin's dismissal five months earlier.[18] On the surface at least, it was as if the event had not occurred. A Briton, who had served in the Indian Civil Service and stayed on in Pakistan as a businessman and newspaper reporter, found the country enjoying 'outstanding stability' by what he considered Middle East standards. Writing from Karachi shortly after the Assembly convened, he noted, 'There have been no *coups d'etat*...No one has attempted to set himself up as a dictator, and the existing Constitution, though only a patchwork legacy from British India, has been respected. With occasional lapses, the government has allowed freedom of speech and free expression of opinions in the Press. The two makers of Pakistan, Jinnah and Liaquat Ali Khan, were both aristocrats and to some extent autocrats, but they were careful in their scrupulous observance of democratic forms, and even in the early critical days, when the country was struggling to make good against the sea of trouble, did not assume unduly great powers. The qualities of the present Prime Minister [Bogra] are those of a good democrat and no man is less likely to attempt to set up a dictatorial regime. Islam is perhaps the most democratic of all religions, and it follows that the Pakistanis, as Muslim people, are enthusiastic for democracy. In fact, on a wide view, this is the most healthy feature of the Pakistan outlook.'[19]

After attending to budget matters, the Constituent Assembly took up the constitution. Mohammad Ali Bogra warned the members that there had been too much delay in producing a new constitution.[20] His statement was greeted by the members pounding on their desk in agreement, and cheers arose from the crowded visitors' gallery. Progress did follow. The *New York Times* reported, 'Scoring a major success in his sixth month as head of the Muslim state, Mr Mohammad Ali effected unity among provincial heads.' The paper reported the Assembly members as favouring a constitution, republican in form, and predicted that a constitution would be produced containing 'many ideas included in the United States Constitution and some of the more secular aspects of Islamic law.'[21]

Bogra began to shift his political position and, as Ayub Khan observed, was attempting 'to get free of the Governor-General's apron strings'.[22] He now joined his fellow Bengalis in the Assembly by announcing that his administration would go ahead with Ghulam Mohammad's interim constitution but would not agree to the proposal that the Governor-General be given the power to dissolve the Constituent Assembly, asserting that the Assembly was a sovereign body. Starting with little weight himself in the Assembly, Bogra as Prime Minister did provide the Bengali faction with a symbolic leader against the Governor-General. The actual leadership of the Bengali faction, however, remained in the hands of Fazlur Rahman, with the backing of Nazimuddin. This faction was willing to support Bogra as their nominal leader because he was a fresh face on the political scene and did not carry with him the image of inefficiency which Nazimuddin had with some of the public. Bogra later proved effective in winning support in Sindh for the new constitution.[23] The East Bengali members of the Assembly not only formed alliances with the religious community, but also courted the smaller West Pakistan provinces to counter-balance the alliance which was forming between Ghulam Mohammad and Suhrawardy, who shared the common bond of favouring the dissolution of the Assembly.

Bogra faithfully submitted the Governor-General's interim constitutional plan to the Assembly, which overwhelmingly rejected it. On 7 October he re-introduced the Basic Principles Committee Report. With two exceptions, the report remained the same as it had been when withdrawn from Assembly consideration eleven months earlier. The principal exception reflected a compromise on Assembly representation, to which the politicians of the east and west wings had succeeded in reaching agreement.

The compromise was incorporated into the report and popularly known as the Mohammad Ali Formula. It provided that the lower house was to consist of three hundred members elected on the basis of population, and the upper house would consist of fifty members, equally divided among the five units, who would be elected by the legislatures of the units. Revising the proposal made the previous November by Nazimuddin in his Basic Principles Committee Report giving East Bengal equal voting weight in the upper house against all of the West Pakistan provinces, the new formula called for the upper house to consist of five units, each with equal voting weight.[24] East Bengal, as only one of the five units, would have a minority in the upper house, while the reduction of the West Pakistan units from nine, as previously provided for in Nazimuddin's constitutional plan, to five, reduced the vulnerability of the west wing to incursion by the Bengalis. East Bengal continued to have a majority in the lower house based on population.

The election of the President, and some important motions and differences between the houses on legislation, would be submitted to a joint session in which there would be parity between the east and the west. Another important change was a new provision requiring any measure to gain a concurrence of at least thirty per cent of the members of each of the five units making up the upper house. This was designed so that the Bengalis could not carry a proposal by a simple majority.[25]

The Basic Principles Committee Report as amended received the approval of the Cabinet, the provincial Chief Ministers, (including Noon, Chief Minister of Punjab) and the members of the Muslim League Parliamentary Party.[26] The Assembly politicians, including those from the Punjab, were now in agreement on the troublesome issue of legislative appointment.

Bogra urged Assembly members to complete their consideration of the report by the adjournment of the session, which would probably be in November.[27] The members were given two weeks to study the approximately 250 clauses of the report. They were also given printed workbooks, each page of which had at the top a single clause of the report with the remainder of the page blank for their notes.[28] The *New York Times* reported from Karachi: 'The enthusiasm and active interest of the Pakistan legislators in working on the constitution has been interpreted by diplomats here as the most encouraging sign in recent years.'[29] The next day, the paper added that if constitution-making 'seems to be slow it also seems to be going forward on firm ground. The problems are being solved in an atmosphere of patriotic concentration.' This is how it appeared in public. There was, of course, much negotiating and deal-making, endemic to the legislative process, going on behind the scenes.[30]

Opposition to parity had disappeared, but it soon re-emerged in the Punjab and among the parties in East Bengal opposed to the Muslim League. The part of the Mohammad Ali Formula which caused the most comment was the thirty per cent voting provision.[31] This provision, designed to limit Bengali power, proved to be of little solace to the Punjabis because it worked both ways. By exercising their veto power under the thirty per cent provision, the Bengalis could block the industrial and military plans of the Punjabis. Further, this compromise provision in the constitutional draft was cited by both the *Pakistan Times* and the *Pakistan Observer* as being a defective way of legislating and one which would turn the Constituent Assembly into a mere debating society, because any legislation could be defeated by a thirty-one per cent negative vote in any one of the five units of the upper house.[32] The formula was, however, approved by the Assembly. The nation was declared an Islamic Republic, and further concessions were made to the religious groups by providing that a challenge to any law on religious grounds would not be restricted as a right of Assembly members only but could be made by any citizen. This concession was balanced by making the country's highest court rather than the *ulema* board the final arbiter of any such challenge, and it was envisioned that any Islamic changes in the present secular law would be gradual.

In the West, the *New York Times* saw the efforts to exclude anything repugnant to the Koran as 'an obvious and sensible solution,' and editorialized that the Mohammad Ali Formula was not unlike the solution which the United States had adopted in its constitution to address the issue of representation at the federal level.[33] Pakistan earned the praise of the paper as 'one of the world's newest and largest countries...a stable and progressive Muslim nation, a staunch ally of the free West and a bastion of democracy in Asia.'[34] *Dawn* welcomed the Mohammad Ali Formula as both satisfying the spirit of democracy, which was the concern of the Bengalis, and the requirements of federalism. The latter was of interest to the Punjabis, who hoped to use the federal units as their safeguard against a Bengali legislative majority.[35]

On 27 October the Assembly began a paragraph-by-paragraph consideration of the Basic Principles Committee Report and the Mohammad Ali Formula amendment.[36] The sessions continued for fifty-five days and included night sessions, causing the *New York Times* to run a headline reading 'Karachi Sets A Pace In Muslim World'. The *Times* reporter sent the following dispatch from Karachi:

A key to the way the changing Muslim world may go politically in the next few decades is being forged in the Constituent Assembly of Pakistan, largest of the Islamic nations.

In an atmosphere of western Parliamentary procedure at its most decorous several men and two women have been working since October 7th to frame a constitution by June.

They are working on the assignment with a determination that resists fatigue during the long hours of debate on the 350 proposed amendments and the phraseology of 255 clauses in the sixteen-part report. As a clause is adopted—more than 100 have been cleared—the lawmakers seem refreshed.

In the rotunda, foreign envoys take notes of these developments. Observers from many other Muslim countries are attending.

The lawmakers' wives watch proudly from their reserve seats and Pakistan nationals in the press section write almost feverishly to meet the demand of the forty-three vernacular and three English newspapers.

About the only cabinet member absent recently was Prime Minister Mohammad Ali. He has been indisposed for two weeks but is following developments over the radio and by sending frequent word through his aides who visit him at almost any hour.[37]

By 14 November 1953, the Assembly had approved 130 paragraphs of the new constitution. On that day, Brohi moved that further consideration of the report be postponed, stating: 'In these 130 paragraphs all the essential aspects of the constitution have been covered in regard to that part which deals with the Islamic character of the constitution as also the most controversial part, namely, the federal structure. We have also covered the ground with regard to the provincial set-up under our proposed constitution.'[38] Begum Shaista Suhrawardy Ikramullah of East Bengal, H. S. Suhrawardy's cousin and political ally, did not agree. She objected to any further delay. 'Every time we pass one or two clauses we make a lot of fuss about it and say that it is Islamic and then put the whole thing in cold storage.' So strongly did she feel that, although she had been a member of the League for years and acted now with 'a heavy heart', she announced that because of the delay, 'I...register my protest and resign from the Muslim League party today.'[39] Nurul Amin of East Bengal was mindful of the need for prompt action on the constitution but he noted that the Assembly had sat for fifty-five days, some days with more than one session and on many occasions sitting till late hours at night. 'We have already made sufficient progress with regard to the Report. Major hang-ups have been resolved very happily.'[40] As an experienced politician, it was important to Nurul Amin to test the waters back home in East Bengal to see how the voters would accept what the Assembly had done to this date.

An adjournment was agreed on after a drafting committee was appointed. The committee was made up of 'the best brains in Pakistan', and included such prominent politicians as Tamizuddin Khan, Nishtar, Fazlur Rahman, D. N. Dutt, Pirzada, and Brohi.[41] The drafting committee was charged with seeing that during the next two to three months, when the Assembly was in recess, the amended Basic Principles Committee Report would be drafted in the formal language of a constitution and be ready when the Assembly reconvened to consider the remaining clauses of the report. The Assembly seemed confident that the remaining clauses would give little difficulty. There were expressions of satisfaction in the Assembly that the Muslim League's promise of an Islamic state was now fulfilled.[42]

The Constituent Assembly had produced the basis of a constitution which brought that body in direct conflict with the Governor-General at a time when his power was growing. The civil service had gained control of patronage and, unlike many politicians, its members understood day-to-day government. As a result, the bureaucrats had increased their operating power in the central and provincial governments. In contrast, the Muslim League had not expanded its membership or improved its structure, and therefore offered an inadequate base to organize and galvanize the politicians or enable their power to balance the growing strength of the bureaucracy.

With the bureaucracy as his base of power and his successful dismissal of Nazimuddin, Ghulam Mohammad controlled the central executive. But the defeat of his interim constitution, and the progress the Assembly was making in approving the Basic Principles Committee Report and the Mohammad Ali Formula, demonstrated his lack of control over the Assembly. Without that control Ghulam Mohammad could not influence the making of the new constitution and thus avoid losing control to the East Bengal majority. His failure to win a concession uniting West Pakistan pushed him into a political danger zone.

Ghulam Mohammad had been successful in subverting cabinet government when he dismissed Nazimuddin because he was aided by what he argued was the lack of certainty as to the conventions of cabinet government. He justified his move on the grounds that the conventions which defined cabinet government in Great Britain did not apply in Pakistan. Now he faced a different situation in attempting to subvert the Constituent Assembly. It was unequivocally stated in Pakistan's dominion constitution that the Assembly had the right 'in the first instance' to draft a new constitution.[43] If Ghulam Mohammad moved forcibly against the Assembly, as he had against Nazimuddin, he would topple the remaining constitutional structure under which Pakistan had operated since independence.

When the Assembly adjourned in November 1953, the Bengali members returned home to campaign in the provincial elections scheduled for March 1954. Sixteen million persons cast their ballots.[44] The results were shattering to the League, which won only ten seats in the provincial assembly of 239, now controlled by the United Front. The magnitude of the Muslim League's loss was so great that it surprised even the United Front leaders.[45] The United Front's Twenty-One Points, on which the party fought the elections, contained a demand for provincial autonomy on all matters except defence, currency, and foreign affairs. The Constituent Assembly itself was threatened by the elections. The Muslim League members of the Assembly from East Bengal were urged by many of their constituents to resign because, it was argued, as a result of the recent provincial elections they now represented no one. The United Front called for the election of new members of the Constituent Assembly on the basis of direct adult franchise and demanded that no further action be taken on the constitution until new Assembly members were elected.

Political power in East Bengal passed into the hands of Suhrawardy and Huq. Their arrangement for exercising that power was later described by Suhrawardy. 'It was settled with Fazlul Huq that while I would support him for the Chief Ministership of East Bengal, he would support me and follow my guidance in central politics.'[46] Suhrawardy, who had remained in the political wilderness since he was deprived of his Assembly seat in 1948, was the principal spokesman advocating dissolution of the Assembly. To him the Constituent Assembly was not democratic because it was not representative. Earlier, he had urged the Assembly to end its 'miserable undignified existence' by voluntarily amending the Independence Act which, he admitted, could be interpreted as allowing the existence of the Assembly until it had completed the task of drafting a new constitution.[47] Suhrawardy contended that although legally the present Assembly had the right under the existing constitution to write a new constitution, he had the backing of morality. He assured Ghulam Mohammad that the country would overlook any unconstitutional actions if steps were taken to 'exorcise the fascist demon and to establish democratic institutions'. Suhrawardy claimed drastic evils required drastic remedies. He nevertheless attempted to put his suggestions in the best constitutional light by reasoning: '...after all, the dissolution of a legislature before a general election is normal practice and nothing to be afraid of.'[48] Suhrawardy and Ghulam Mohammad were publicly of one mind on the issue of dissolution.

While the East Bengal elections gave rise to the argument that the Assembly had become unrepresentative and should dissolve itself, the first attempt at promulgating a new constitution could only be made by the existing Constituent Assembly unless that body voluntarily surrendered that right.[49] *Dawn* saw the importance of adhering to the dominion constitution. 'If the existing constitution was not followed, any further constitution would be mortgaged to the heritage that the first constitution had been disregarded.'[50] *Dawn* went on to editorialize that changes in the Assembly should be made only by the Assembly itself. Pressure was on the Assembly, if not to make outright concessions to East Bengal in the form of greater autonomy, then at least to complete the constitutional draft and bring into existence a new legislative body by fresh elections.

Bogra responded by opposing any change in the membership of the Constituent Assembly, claiming that the body was a sovereign one created by the Indian Independence Act and was not affected by provincial elections. He took the position that the elections could not be considered a mandate against the present East Bengal membership in the Constituent Assembly because the United Front had not made the dissolution of the Assembly a part of its election platform.[51] The Awami League had in fact refrained from making the Constituent Assembly's dissolution part of its election platform, knowing that such dissolution would create delay in finalizing the constitution. Not that the Awami League was being solicitous of the constitution, but to appear to advocate delay would have cost them support among the religious factions in Bengal who favoured the passage of the constitution because of the religious concessions that it contained. Bogra also argued that proposals to dissolve the Constituent Assembly were not practical, pointing out that the Assembly had completed three-quarters of the work involved in drafting the new constitution.[52]

After a four month recess, the Assembly reconvened on 14 March 1954. It first devoted itself to financial matters, and returned to its constitution-making on 5 April. On 7 May, Bogra moved that Bengali be used along with Urdu as the national language, and that other languages be considered in the future when appropriate. English was to be continued in official use. Bogra's motion was passed by the Assembly.[53] After adopting the motion, the Assembly then began a paragraph-by-paragraph consideration of a non-controversial draft of the judicial section of the new constitution and the other remaining clauses of the Basic Principles Committee Report.[54]

While the Assembly was progressing towards the final version of a constitution, in April 1954, the *Pakistan Times* reported that the central government was arresting political opponents in Punjab and Karachi, using the Public Safety Acts in order to strengthen its grip on West Pakistan.[55] Then in May the political scene was upset by an unexpected event in East Bengal. Three months after the East Bengal elections, the United Front's power was undermined by alleged remarks of Fazlul Huq, the United Front Chief Minister of East Bengal. In a speech to an audience in Calcutta, Huq was reported to have stated that he would seek to join East Bengal with West Bengal with the co-operation of India.[56] Huq denied that he intended his remarks in the way that they were being publicly interpreted, but Bogra labelled him a 'self-confessed traitor'.[57] Using Huq's mis-step and the emergence of serious labour trouble in East Bengal, the central government imposed Section 92A of the Government of India Act and took control of the province. This was a move which aided not only the Muslim League members in the Constituent Assembly, whose party had been so disastrously defeated at the polls, but also Ghulam Mohammad and the central administration, who were challenged by the United Front's advocacy of provincial autonomy and the abolition of the Public Safety Acts.

Fazlul Huq was removed as Chief Minister. The provincial cabinet was dismissed and the East Bengal Assembly was not allowed to meet. (It did not meet again until 22 May 1956). The central government appointed Iskander Mirza as governor. Mirza, as mentioned earlier, although from a Bengali family and having been born in that province, was for most of his political career allied with the Punjab bureaucrats. He was widely known for his espousal of 'controlled democracy', and made it known that he believed parliamentary government had failed in East Bengal and would be restored only when he determined the province was ready. Huq and thirty-two members of the recently-elected East Bengal Assembly were placed under house arrest, the Communist Party banned, and the Air Force was utilized to drop leaflets to the population. Ten thousand troops and a Navy frigate were reportedly sent to East Bengal.[58] Mirza threatened martial law, and warned there were enough troops plus 40,000 police available in East Bengal.[59] Censorship was imposed on the Press, with 319 political arrests being made straight away, and over 1,000 more following before a month had passed.[60] These arrests included members of the provincial assembly. Meanwhile, arrests continued in Karachi, including four journalists, a college lecturer, and a doctor.[61] The detainees were sentenced under the Public Safety Acts to one year imprisonment for 'activities prejudicial to public safety'.[62] Committees were set up in East Bengal to investigate 200,000 workers and to weed out 'communists'.[63] There was no reaction from the public to the central government's takeover in East Bengal. During the summer of 1954, the newspapers were filled not with political news but almost exclusively with accounts of widespread floods and an epidemic in East Bengal. Mirza's expeditious handling of these disasters made him popular, and deflected potential opposition.[64]

The central government threatened Huq with treason prosecution for his Calcutta statement, but took no action upon his assurance that he would retire from politics.[65] The power of the United Front was now suppressed, and the central executive controlled both wings of the country. Firoz Khan Noon had been appointed to replace Daultana as Punjab Governor at the time of the Ahmadi riots. Noon was a strong proponent of uniting West Pakistan in one unit and was considered a supporter of Ghulam Mohammad. The central executive now controlled the provincial governments in Pakistan's two principal provinces, West Punjab and East Bengal, and the ministries of the North-West Frontier Province and the government of Balochistan were under the influence of the central bureaucracy. Only the Chief Minister of Sindh could be looked to by the Muslim League Bengali members of the Assembly for support outside the Assembly.[66] Their Hindu fellow-Bengalis opposed their constitutional efforts because of the Islamic nature of the new constitution. For the present, however, the suppression of the United Front removed the pressure for changes in the Constituent Assembly membership.

In July, at the invitation of the Assembly's constitutional drafting committee, Sir Ivor Jennings arrived in Pakistan on leave from his post as Vice Chancellor of the University of Ceylon. Prior to independence, Jennings had been recommended by Mountbatten's staff to Jinnah, who had expressed a need for a constitutional expert to assist in the drafting of a new constitution for Pakistan. It was not until 1954, however, that his services were utilized.

The election results in East Bengal brought renewed activity on the issue of the unification of West Pakistan.[67] Fazlur Rahman and Nazimuddin continued their political campaign among the smaller provinces of West Pakistan to fight the inclusion of the One Unit Plan in the constitution, offering to surrender a number of Assembly seats to these smaller provinces. But not all Bengalis were opposed to the unification of West Pakistan. Suhrawardy accepted the idea, believing that unification of West Pakistan could aid the claim for greater autonomy for East Bengal.[68] On this issue he differed with the Nazimuddin-led group of Bengalis in the Constituent Assembly who opposed One Unit. The members of the Muslim League Parliamentary Party, meeting on 3 September, rejected the One Unit Plan and decided not to re-open constitutional matters already settled.[69] A sub-committee was appointed to resolve some matters concerning allocation of power between the central and provincial governments, with 10 September 1954 given as the date for the sub-committee to report back, but with the admonition that the report must not disturb the federal structure and must be in accord with the Mohammad Ali Formula.

On 7 September, the Assembly amended and adopted part of a report submitted by the Committee on Fundamental Rights. The

Assembly was now approaching the long-awaited goal of finishing a new constitution. On 15 September, Bogra stood before the Assembly and announced: 'Mr President, I am grateful to God that at long last we have crossed the last hurdle in Pakistan.'[70] But although the Assembly had previously reached an agreement on the relationship between the centre and the units which included the Mohammad Ali Formula, now the Punjabi members, under pressure from Ghulam Mohammad, switched away from their approval of the formula. Firoz Khan Noon, Chief Minister of West Punjab, led the attack, with a proposal which he labelled Zonal Federation.[71] Essentially, his plan gave more autonomy to the provinces than would the Mohammad Ali Formula. Noon's proposal was calculated to defeat the Mohammad Ali Formula by attracting those in East Bengal who were advocating greater autonomy for their province. But the main Bengali support for provincial autonomy was outside the halls of the Assembly, in the ranks of the United Front, and was not capable of bringing about a change of the vote on the Mohammad Ali Formula. Noon's proposal faced the further difficulty that Zonal Federation would have diminished the power of the central government, and it was unlikely that Ghulam Mohammad would have accepted it even if the Punjabi politicians could have gained its passage in the Assembly.

Noon's eleventh-hour delaying tactics were condemned in the Assembly by Nazimuddin, who usually remained on the sidelines during debates. This time, however, he accused Noon of bringing the matter up only because it was quite apparent that the constitution would be agreed on within the week.[72] Nazimuddin raised the question as to why Noon had not brought his plan forward at an earlier date. Noon had served on the Basic Principles Committee for three years, yet, as Nazimuddin pointed out to the Assembly, it was only now that he 'suddenly discovered that the whole of West Pakistan was supposedly unanimous for Zonal Federation, without a single word having passed in any meeting; without a single gentleman saying a word about it'. Even if it were wise at this late date, argued Nazimuddin, to consider Zonal Federation, no one knew what it was and no one could point to any example of it having been put to use. Noon made an argument which excited the usually unexcitable Nazimuddin when he criticized the Assembly for being in too much of a hurry in passing the constitution.[73] To Nazimuddin this was ridiculous. It was precisely the long period of time spent on the constitution which gave the constitution's enemies their greatest argument. The next day's edition of *Dawn* described the debate as a stormy one.

There were rumours that Ghulam Mohammad had requested the assistance of the army in order to close down the Assembly but that Ayub had refused, and there were also rumors that Ghulam Mohammad intended to file PRODA charges against twenty-two Assembly members.[74] In what appeared to be defensive moves in anticipation of Ghulam Mohammad's reaction to the new constitution, the Assembly on 20 September abolished the Public and Representative Offices (Disqualification) Act (PRODA), leaving pending charges under the Act unaffected.[75] Ever since it was passed during Liaquat's ministry, the Act had been a powerful executive weapon.

The Assembly next went on the offensive over the issue raised by Nazimuddin's dismissal the previous year. On 21 September the Constituent Assembly amended the Government of India Act. The amendments precluded the Governor-General from acting except on the advice of his ministers. All ministers were to be members of the Assembly at the time of their selection and continue to hold office only so long as they retained the confidence of the legislature.[76] The Cabinet was declared to be collectively responsible to the Assembly, and would be required to resign if any one of its members lost the confidence of the Assembly. The Assembly stated that their purpose was to give 'legislative sanction to certain accepted principles and conventions connected with the formation and working of government in a parliamentary system of government...'[77]

In effect, the Assembly was codifying conventions of the constitution into statutory form. As statutory law, the former conventions of cabinet government could now be enforced in court by the Assembly against the Governor-General, and the Assembly had thus fashioned a judicial weapon which it did not possess when Ghulam Mohammad replaced Nazimuddin with Mohammad Ali Bogra.[78] These legislative restrictions on the Governor-General put in statutory form provisions which were also in the Basic Principles Committee Report and which would become law when the constitution went into effect. The Assembly was moving in September to protect itself and the new constitution during the interim.[79]

Reaction to the Assembly's curbing of the Governor-General was divided. *Dawn* supported the Assembly's actions and carried the headlines 'Parliament Made Supreme Body.' 'The Constituent Assembly of Pakistan yesterday laid down in clear and unambiguous terms that from that day the supreme authority in the country shall be the Parliament.'[80] *The Pakistan Times* was of the opinion that the Governor-General should be no more than a ceremonial figure, and that the actions of the Assembly had been justified for that reason, but it held to its previously stated position that the Assembly should be dissolved.[81] An article in *Nawa-i-Waqt* called the Assembly's action a 'step from democracy to fascism', and accused its members of wishing to perpetuate their power and create 'Prime Minister dictatorship'.[82] In East Bengal, there was strong opposition expressed to the moves taken by the Muslim League Bengalis in the Assembly against the Governor-General. This was due to the failure of the Assembly to acknowledge the wishes of the people of the east wing to have the representatives in the Assembly changed after the March election.

On 21 September, the Assembly voted its approval of the constitution in the form of the Basic Principles Committee Report as amended.[83] None of the members from the Punjab voted on the constitution. Of the forty votes cast, eleven were Hindu members from East Bengal who voted against the constitution because they considered it Islamic. The vote in favour was twenty-seven.[84] There was much satisfaction and congratulations given to Bogra for his successful moving of the Basic Principles Committee Report to final passage. The Assembly then adjourned until 27 October, concluding what *Dawn* called an 'historic session'.[85]

The approved clauses of the Basic Principles Committee Report were drafted into a formal constitutional document by the drafting committee and on 15 October sent for printing to the Government Printing Office, which published the document under the title *The Draft Constitution of Pakistan, Confidential.*[86] This document was submitted to Jennings who made extensive but minor changes on the draft.[87] The date of 25 December, the anniversary of Jinnah's birthday, had been announced earlier by Bogra as the date the new constitution was to go into effect.[88] After seven years of bargaining and drafting, the Assembly had completed its mission of giving the country a constitution. Two weeks after the Assembly approved the constitution, Chief Justice Munir, addressing the

Lahore Bar Association, spoke of the new constitution in terms which reflected no negative opinion on his part.[89]

The major components of the 1954 Constitution were the Objectives Resolution as a preamble, the Government of India Act of 1935 perpetuated through the Basic Principles Committee Report, the concessions to the Islamic factions, and the Mohammad Ali Formula. It also contained a new section dealing with guaranteed fundamental rights.[90] The document asserted that it was a constitution framed by the Constituent Assembly as representative of the people of 'the sovereign independent State of Pakistan'. The nation was now to be a republic, ultimate sovereignty residing in Allah with 'authority which He has designated to the State of Pakistan through its people for being exercised within the limits prescribed by Him in a sacred trust.'[91] It is useful to note that the same non-committal identification of the location of sovereignty remained as in the Objectives Resolution. What was added was reference to Jinnah, who, it was said in the constitution, had repeatedly 'declared that Pakistan would be a democratic State on Islamic principles of social justice'.[92]

A new bicameral legislature, to be called Parliament, was to replace the Constituent Assembly.[93] But this new body was not to be the sovereign power of the state, as is the British Parliament. The constitution itself, as in the United States, not Parliament, was declared to be the supreme law of Pakistan, and would be 'binding upon all legislatures, courts, authorities, and persons'.[94] No legislature, either national or provincial, was competent to enact any law repugnant to the Koran or Sunnah, except where certain specific financial matters were involved, and any violation could be challenged in the Supreme Court (successor to the Federal Court).[95] The courts were granted the power of judicial review, the power to declare void any legislation which contravened the constitution.[96] The provisions of fundamental rights, guaranteed in the constitution, were broad and comprehensive, and were enforceable against the government by the Supreme Court.[97]

The representational apportionment made by the Mohammad Ali Formula was to include six seats for women,[98] and reserved seats for Hindus and other minorities in East Bengal were continued.[99] Broad emergency powers remained with the government, including the right of the head of state to issue emergency orders. Such orders were subject to the approval of the Parliament, but only after a period of six weeks were the orders required to be submitted to Parliament.[100] The office of Governor-General was replaced with that of President, who was required to be a Muslim and who was given the power to summon and prorogue Parliament and was empowered to dissolve if he found that a ministry could not be formed which had the confidence of that body.[101] Provisions were made for a Prime Minister who was to appoint the other ministers in a Cabinet to be collectively responsible to Parliament and remain in office only so long as they retained the confidence of Parliament.[102] The federal structure of the Government of India Act was maintained, the new constitution containing a schedule defining the powers of the national government, the provincial governments, and those powers which were to be concurrently exercised.[103]

Politically, the most significant aspect of the new constitution was the power of the former Governor-General, now President. As extensive as those powers might read, the President was reduced to 'a mere figurehead'.[104] Except in those limited situations where specifically granted discretionary powers by the constitution, the President, in whom were vested the executive powers of the state, was to act only on the advice of his ministers.[105]

The new constitution, a modern western model, had the concurrence of the Islamic factions. It contained an agreed-on formula for the apportionment of representation between the east and west wings, and provided for extensive guaranteed individual rights which were enforceable by the courts exercising judicial review. It was a document which one western observer characterized at the time as 'not unique or even unusual…not unlike many federal constitutions in the world,' Canada and India being examples.[106] The results were noteworthy in that they demonstrated the ability of the secular and religious political leaders in a Muslim society to reach a compromise on a western-style democratic constitution.[107] The religious leaders were willing to accept the constitution, and in return the secular politicians were willing to see that the constitution reflected a religious orientation, an orientation containing religious preferences within a democratic constitutional framework. The most important concession to the religious groups was a board of review, but the members of the board were to be appointed by the government and any vote had to be unanimous to be effective. Legislation rejected by the board was to be returned to the legislature. It was the legislature which had the final word, and disputes were to be resolved by a secular court.

The religious fundamentalists remained vital to the efforts of the Bengali members of the Assembly to complete the drafting of the new constitution. The majority of the *ulema* and Maududi supported the new constitution, and were careful not to take any action or make statements which might endanger or delay adoption. They wished to preserve the benefits they had obtained in the draft of the constitution, and were concerned as well about the further ascendancy of the secular views held by Ghulam Mohammad and the central bureaucracy. When they did speak out, it was in favour of implementing the constitution drafted by the Assembly. One of the principle *ulema* organizations reported that a resolution declaring 22 October Constitution Day had been passed in seventy-seven mosques in Karachi during Friday prayers.[108] Maududi's Jamaat-e-Islami declared that the new constitution was to a very large extent Islamic in character and urged its adoption.[109]

Opposition to the constitution came from East Bengal and expressed the views of many of those opposed to the Muslim League Bengal bloc in the Assembly. The *Evening Mail* of Dhaka reported growing sentiment for the Governor-General to declare an emergency and dissolve the Assembly.[110] The *Pakistan Observer* claimed that the Assembly had no authorization from the people of Pakistan but was a creature of British law, and should be dissolved.[111] From a sickbed in Switzerland, Suhrawardy again called for dissolution and indicated his non-opposition to any form of unity which the people of West Pakistan might agree on.[112] Rumors circulated in Karachi that the Governor-General was about to dissolve the Assembly.[113] Nevertheless, the Constituent Assembly felt confident. *The Islamic Constitution of the Republic of Pakistan*, the final version of the constitution containing Jennings' revisions, was published by the Government Printing Office[114] and on 23 October *Dawn* reported that the Punjabi members of the Assembly, at a meeting called by Noon, had abandoned the claim for One Unit and Zonal Federation.[115] The Assembly, as one observer noted shortly afterwards, 'had finalized its mission of giving the country a constitution'. There was certainly not total agreement, 'but generally speaking there was satisfaction that at least a constitution had been framed'.[116] Bogra was ready to begin a campaign to sell the new constitution to the people for implementation on 25 December.[117]

With a completed constitution in hand, Bogra, against the advice of some of his ministers, left Pakistan on a diplomatic mission to the United States.[118] He had received an invitation from President Eisenhower two months earlier, but another explanation for leaving at such a crucial time seems to be that he feared a meeting with Ghulam Mohammad, who was absent from Karachi during the time the Assembly had moved against him.[119]

With the Assembly adjourned and Mohammad Ali Bogra out of the country, the field was left open to the Governor-General. Ghulam Mohammad returned to Karachi and calculated what moves he should make, both to maintain the advantage he had gained by dismissing Nazimuddin, and to prevent West Pakistan from becoming politically weakened, in his view, by the new constitution. If he did not take action he would be considered to have acquiesced in the Assembly's newly-passed statutes and the new constitution which defined his role as a figurehead, the role intended by the drafters of the Independence Act of 1947. Mirza took leave from his post as Governor of East Bengal to join him in Karachi.

Ghulam Mohammad's first move was to pardon several influential politicians, enemies of the Bengalis in the Assembly, from actual sentences, and dismiss pending charges of disqualification under PRODA.[120] Included in the group were Khuhro of Sindh and Daultana of West Punjab. Both were members of the Assembly and commanded strong support among the members from their provinces. They could be counted on to fight the new constitution and advocate One Unit. As the *New York Times* reported Ghulam Mohammad's move, 'The effect of the Governor-General's actions was to release into the political arena a group of influential men who may unseat Mr Mohammad Ali and his Administration, unless the Prime Minister can convene a Constituent Assembly within the next few days to test the legality of the Governor-General's ruling. The latest development in the contest is expected to give impetus to opposition plans in Punjab and East Pakistan to delay adoption of the Constitution scheduled to come before the Constituent Assembly in its next scheduled meeting next week.'[121] Outside of the Assembly, Ghulam Mohammad was gathering the components of an opposition bloc which would include Suhrawardy, Huq, the United Front parties, and the tacit approval of the Army.[122] He also intensified pressure on the Punjab members of the Assembly to retract their approval of the new constitution. He was successful despite the fact that his concept of a centralized government ran counter to the wishes of many of the members to retain power in the provinces. It was reported that on 21 October thirty-five Muslim League leaders, including two members of Bogra's Cabinet, met to show their support of Ghulam Mohammad,[123] while in Sindh, the Muslim League leaders expressed their confidence in the Constituent Assembly and requested that it finalize the constitution.[124]

On 22 October, the day declared by the *ulema* as Constitution Day, a resolution was passed at a mass meeting of 30,000 persons in Lahore opposing any attempt to dissolve the Constituent Assembly. The principal speaker at the meeting criticized the call for dissolution. '...[N]ow, after seven years, when constitution-making is in the final stages, certain elements have come out with the mischievous demand to dissolve the Constituent Assembly merely to serve their selfish end. The demand is in fact designed to destroy the Islamic character of the Constitution.'[125] Similar meetings were held in Hyderabad, Larkana, and Quetta. Posters appearing on Karachi walls and in other cities called for early enforcement of the new constitution.

The next day the Punjab Muslim League Parliamentary Party met to consider a last-ditch stand against passage of the constitution in the upcoming Assembly vote, which had been rescheduled for 28 October. Those at the meeting were critical of their representatives in the Assembly, presumably because of the representatives' initial agreement to the Mohammad Ali Formula. There was a sense of defeat among the Punjabis, which limited their actions to the passage of what *Dawn* labeled 'a tame resolution'.[126] The party instructed its Assembly representatives to attempt one more time to obtain passage of a form of Zonal Federation, and if that move failed, the representatives were to report back for further instructions. According to the *Dawn* report, the party unanimously rejected the idea that the Punjab members of the Assembly would resign from the Assembly if they did not get their way. Realizing that they would have to live with the new constitution, the Punjab now favoured an amendment to the constitution which for five years would allow its amendment by a simple majority vote of the Assembly, provided that at least thirty per cent of both West Pakistan and East Pakistan in joint session voted in favour of the amendment.

That evening, Bogra, who had been recalled by Ghulam Mohammad from the United States mission, arrived in Karachi. At the time Ghulam Mohammad's summons arrived, Bogra had made an agreement with the United States for both economic and military aid. The latter was a token and would not go far towards modernizing the Pakistan Army.[127] When it became known in Washington that a political crisis was brewing in Pakistan, the United States announced that it was increasing military aid fourfold, raising the amount to $105,000,000. United States officials expressed the hope that this change would help Bogra, who was viewed by many in the West as 'the United States' favourite Pakistani'.[128]

Bogra returned to Pakistan despite his fear of the Governor-General and his apprehension that he might be arrested.[129] He was accompanied on his return by Ayub, who had been with the Prime Minister in the United States, and Mirza, who had been dispatched to London by Ghulam Mohammad to meet Bogra and escort him home. Ayub and Mirza kept Bogra under surveillance to prevent him from meeting with a delegation from the Assembly. The delegation had travelled to London to inform Bogra that Ghulam Mohammad planned to dissolve the Assembly, and to advise him to contact Queen Elizabeth to have her dismiss the Governor-General.[130]

According to *Dawn*, when Bogra landed at the Karachi Airport he was met by the largest crowd since those which had greeted the popular Liaquat.[131] He was able to announce that he had been successful in obtaining large grants from the United States. He assured the cheering crowds that he was aware of the growing anxiety of the people for a new constitution and that the new constitution would be in effect by 25 December. He also told them that Pakistan would be declared an Islamic republic, a proposition which was not favoured by Ghulam Mohammad. When questioned about newspaper reports citing the existence of a political crisis, Bogra laughed and replied, 'what crisis?' Deny the crisis though he may, Bogra was returning to face a Muslim League whose Parliamentary Party had lost its unity and was now divided by the Punjabi members' stand-off against the majority on the upcoming vote on the new constitution. But Bogra did command the majority in the Assembly, if he had the courage to utilize it. He shrugged off the suggestion that a reshuffle of the Cabinet was in the offing.[132] According to a report by the American news magazine *Time*, Bogra was then separated from his wife and taken to the Governor-General's residence for a meeting which he very much dreaded. When he arrived he was ordered to wait in an ante-room.[132A]

Ayub Khan gave the following account of what happened at the Governor-General's residence.

> The Governor-General was lying in his bedroom upstairs. He had very high blood pressure and an agonizing backache which compelled him to lie flat on hardboard. He was bursting with rage, emitting volleys of abuse, which, luckily, no one understood. Chaudhri Mohammad Ali ventured to say something and received a volley; then Iskander Mirza said something and got another. We were pleading with him to give another chance to Mohammad Ali [Bogra]. His only reply was an angry growl, 'Go, off you go.' He kept on saying 'No, no.' All he wanted was to shoo us off.
>
> We marched out of the bedroom in single file, Iskander Mirza at the head, Chaudhri Mohammad Ali following, and I bringing up the rear. I was about to step out of the room when the nurse attending the Governor-General tugged at my coat. I turned and found myself facing a different man. There he was, the sick old Governor-General who a moment ago was insane with anger, now beaming with delight and bubbling with laughter. I said in my heart, 'You wicked old man!'[133]

General Mohammad Musa, later Commander-in-Chief of the Pakistan Army, attended the meeting and gave the following description of events.

> Ghulam Mohammad's orders were definite and firm. He was not prepared to reason them out or listen to any arguments. He had made up his mind to do away with the Constitution, call in the Army and hand over the Government to Field Marshal (then General) Mohammad Ayub Khan...The atmosphere in the Governor-General's House that evening was tense. In the room adjacent to the Governor-General's Office was sitting the Prime Minister, Mr Mohammad Ali...He was completely shaken, vague, confused and nervous.[134]

According to Musa, Karachi was filled with rumours that evening. Ignoring the existence of the completed draft of the constitution which was to be voted on by the Constituent Assembly within a week and to go into operation on 25 December, the Governor-General asked Ayub Khan to take over the government for the purpose of producing a constitution. When Ghulam Mohammad announced that he had decided to dissolve the Constituent Assembly and turn the government over to the military, Ayub rebuffed him.[135] Those at this meeting did finally agree, however, that the Constituent Assembly would be dissolved, and Ayub declared the Army's support for a united West Pakistan. Ayub would enter a new Cabinet as Defence Minister while remaining as Commander in Chief of the Army. He would thereby show the nation that the Army backed the dissolution and the new government. Mirza was to become Interior Minister, and the politically enfeebled Bogra was to remain as Prime Minister.[136]

The next day Ghulam Mohammad imposed press censorship and issued a proclamation:

> The Governor-General, having considered the political crisis with which the country is faced, has with deep regret come to the conclusion that the constitutional machinery has broken down. He therefore has decided to declare a state of emergency throughout Pakistan. The Constituent Assembly as at present constituted has lost the confidence of the people and can no longer function.
>
> The ultimate authority vests in the people who will decide all issues including constitutional issues through their representatives who are to be elected; fresh elections will be held as early as possible.[137]

Bogra, who a few days earlier had described those who wanted to dissolve the Assembly as fomenting 'open treachery against the country,'[138] followed Ghulam Mohammad with a statement to the public:

> The destiny of the country could no longer be left to the caprices of an Assembly which instead of safeguarding the interests of Pakistan, was becoming increasingly subject to internal strain and bickering. Constitution-making by the present Constituent Assembly has resulted in developments which threatened to imperil our national unity. It has provoked personal, sectional, and provincial rivalries and suspicions.[139]

Bogra appeared later with Ghulam Mohammad at a joint news conference, and nodded assent when asked whether he agreed with the Governor-General's action. When asked why he had agreed to the dissolution of the Constituent Assembly, he replied, 'I did not have a gun to my head.'[140]

On 27 October, Tamizuddin Khan cancelled the next day's meeting of the Assembly, and announced he would challenge the dissolution in court. He cancelled because he had learned 'on very reliable authority' that the government was determined to take steps to prevent the meeting.[141] Earlier that day, the Deputy President of the Assembly and the leader of the Hindu opposition party were refused admission to the Assembly building by the police, who said passes were required. Later, several other members were prevented from entering. A small number of army troops appeared in parts of the city but were not needed to play a direct role in the actual closing of the Assembly. They were there for what Mirza claimed were 'security reasons'.[42]

Ghulam Mohammad's proclamation had not specifically stated that the Assembly was dissolved, but on 28 October he achieved that end by his use of Section 144 of the Code of Criminal Procedure, banning all public meetings for a period of two months.[143] On the same day, a meeting of a new Cabinet, selected by Ghulam Mohammad, was convened at the Governor-General's place, and it was announced that Ghulam Mohammad, not Bogra, would preside at Cabinet meetings.[144] In London, *Round Table,* the influential journal of Commonwealth affairs, later offered its understanding of the events in Karachi. 'What is most encouraging for the future of democracy in the country is that the government has constantly shown high regard and respect for the rule of law.'[145]

CHAPTER 6

GHULAM MOHAMMAD'S PAKISTAN, 1954

Ghulam Mohammad had neutralized the Cabinet and the office of the Prime Minister by dismissing Nazimuddin, thus freeing himself from the restraints of ministerial advice. He had at his disposal the emergency and police powers of the state with little constitutional restraint on how they were to be used. These powers were, however, sufficient to dissuade the politicians from blocking him. Constitutional form was carefully observed when the consent of Prime Minister Bogra was obtained for the dissolution of the Assembly, but this was only a gesture. Not only had consent been obtained under pressure, but Bogra did not have the confidence of the Assembly in giving his consent. Nevertheless, the approval of the Prime Minister to the dissolution enabled Ghulam Mohammad to appear to be acting constitutionally. Bogra's consent also eliminated the possibility of the Assembly requesting the Queen to remove Ghulam Mohammad. Such a request would have had to be forwarded to the Queen by Bogra as Prime Minister.

The ending of parliamentary democracy was a constitutional *coup*. This does not mean that the military was not a factor. Ghulam Mohammad was allied with Ayub in opposition to the new constitution. While he was careful not to make any move which the Army might oppose, Ghulam Mohammad was satisfied with the Army remaining in the background. It was a political game he was playing in October of 1954, and he was setting the rules.

Press censorship was imposed after the Governor-General's emergency proclamation, and the newspapers in Pakistan were unable to report political events, turning instead to economic and international news. The foreign Press found Pakistani politicians reluctant to discuss the action taken against the Assembly.[1] As a result, the only source of information came from the government itself through Mirza and Bogra, who held press conferences with the foreign Press. Mirza acted as the chief spokesman.[2] He led off with a full-scale attack on democracy. According to Mirza, the electorate was bound to act 'foolish', as they had in the East Bengal elections.

This was so because they were 'illiterate' and needed further training in democratic institutions. Until that was accomplished there would be a need for 'controlled democracy'.[3] He charged that democracy had 'run riot during seven years in Pakistan' and claimed that the masses of the country were not really interested in politics and needed to be protected from making political blunders.[4] He also warned the religious parties to stay out of politics, and later threatened to shoot the East Bengal political leader, Bhashani, if he returned to Pakistan from self-imposed exile in England.[5] *The Times* of London reported Mirza as having stated that the people wanted an honest government and they would get it. 'They would also get law and order and prompt justice. There was no point in having the fine British administration with good traditions that Pakistan had inherited unless it was run the British way. A district officer or magistrate must be given the full powers to deal with any situation. Politicians could make policy, but they must not interfere.'[6] He denied that the new regime was military rule. What had occurred was 'purely administrative action'. It was actually democratic, Mirza asserted, because 'ninety-five per cent of the Pakistan people disapproved of what had been going on in the Assembly.' Mirza did not disclose the source of his information on public sentiment.

At his press conference Bogra claimed that a 'deadlock' had existed in the Constituent Assembly which meant that it could 'not function effectively' and for that reason had to be dissolved. He avoided the question put to him as to why a state of emergency was necessary if there existed a difference between political parties and regions on the make-up of the constitution, matters which could have been worked out by ascertaining the will of the majority. He admitted that the situation 'was not a question of law and order' but was a matter of political differences.[7] His rationale for the Governor-General's emergency decree was that it was only temporary. Emergency decrees, he claimed, had been used in the past even for such comparatively minor matters as price controls. 'Pakistan has been having a series of emergencies for years now.'

Bogra admitted, however, that 'a grave question of legality was involved in the Governor-General's decision to suspend representative government in Pakistan.' When reporters pressed him for the source of the Governor-General's powers to proclaim a state of emergency and dissolve the Assembly, Bogra answered: 'This is a constitutional question. It is for you to find out.'[8] Although he was still being reported publicly as claiming that dissolution had been necessary because of the 'bitter and violent conflict between factions and various provinces,' Bogra's comment on the dissolution's legality appeared to some observers to be giving approval to Tamizuddin's public challenge to the dissolution which had been made previously. Asked if he still believed the Constituent Assembly was a sovereign body, Bogra evaded the question, and when asked if the Assembly was dissolved he replied: 'That is one interpretation. I am not a constitutional expert. I do not know.'[9]

In its last edition before censorship was imposed, *Dawn* had discussed the situation, stating that some observers thought it possible 'that a complete deadlock might have followed later this week if the Punjab's and the Frontier's demands for changes in the Constitution were not accepted. It seems to have been felt that rather than prolong the agony, it would be better to cut it short.'[10] The paper would have preferred the Assembly to have completed the constitution, 'good, bad or indifferent', and to have provided an easy means of amendment and means of electing new members of the Assembly, thus curing the 'evils that the abuse of democracy had created'. 'However, some other and more powerful people have devised a different remedy and applied it...Let it not be claimed that it has been constitutional, nor let it be claimed that it has been democratic.' *Dawn* pointed out that Pakistan's independence had been won by legal and constitutional means and was a nation based on law and the constitution. It was therefore of the greatest importance 'that the legality of the action lately taken should be proved beyond doubt and dispute'. If Ghulam Mohammad's action was not legal then the very foundation of the nation was shaken, 'and all other actions that follow from that original action would assume the same character...and the whole future of the country will be built on something dubious in the eyes of the law'.[11] *Dawn* urged that the constitutional question as to whether the Governor-General possessed the right to dissolve the Constituent Assembly needed full discussion and a decision by the nation's highest court. After censorship was lifted, the paper ran a series of articles discussing the legal questions raised by dissolution.[12]

The Pakistan Times had been advocating dissolution even before Ghulam Mohammad made his move against the Assembly. It editorialized that 'few tears would be shed' over the dissolution because the Assembly had become a body 'rocked by petty intrigues' and 'riven by personal rivalries and factional jealousies', and had failed to exert the control which was its duty to exert over the central government.[13] But a week later the paper voiced concern that: 'It seems to be a fact that there is no existing legal provision which allows the Constituent Assembly to be suspended or dissolved by the Governor-General.'[14] Like *Dawn*, its editors urged a full discussion of the issues raised. To *Nawa-i-Waqt*, however, the issue was simple. The Governor-General had performed a 'courageous' and 'patriotic' act.[15] In East Pakistan, newspaper editorials and letters to the editors ran strongly in support of the dissolution.[16]

The Army had increased in strength and was growing in importance behind the political scene. The ever-present opinion that India was a threat to Pakistan's existence, and the Kashmir dispute with India, made it ill-advised for any Pakistan government to deny the Army a sizeable portion of the nation's resources, as Nazimuddin had discovered when he attempted to reduce military appropriations in his budget. Beginning in 1952, the domestic resources were augmented by a significant amount by United States military aid now that Pakistan was well-established as a Cold War ally. This aid came as a result of an alliance with the United States arranged by the Pakistan Army independent of any involvement with, and perhaps against the wishes of, the civil government of Pakistan.[17] In 1953, Ayub Khan paid an informal visit to the United States, which resulted in President Eisenhower's announcement of February 1954 granting further military aid to Pakistan. Three months later, the two countries signed a mutual defence agreement. This build-up, of course, increased the power of the military leadership, as had their role in the suppression of the Ahmadi riots where their efficiency had received public notice.

The military leaders were particularly proud of their accomplishment in winning the friendship of the United States. Ghulam Mohammad could conclude that, so long as he retained the approval of the Army, there was no reason why the nation could not be returned to the traditions of the viceregal rule of the British Raj and the Jinnah administration. By the end of 1953, the American Ambassador was reporting that there were rumours in Karachi of a change of government and a military takeover.[18]

Like all senior Pakistani officers, Commander-in-Chief Mohammad Ayub Khan had served most of his career in the British Indian Army and was not yet willing to violate openly the British military tradition that soldiers should not interfere in politics.[19] However, the base of army strength was in the Punjab, and Ayub could see that base threatened by a developing Bengali-Islamic majority coalition which would probably dominate the national elections to take place under the new constitution. Since assuming command shortly after independence, Ayub had been fully engaged in equipping the Army, a task now close to completion. Consequently, he was free to turn his attention to political affairs, and he was convinced of the necessity to combine the provinces of West Pakistan into a single political unit in order to balance the voting strength of the Bengalis in the Assembly.[20] Ayub, therefore, was willing to show the Army's support of Ghulam Mohammad by agreeing to serve as Defence Minister while remaining Commander-in-Chief. His presence in the cabinet, unlike Mirza's, seems to have been largely for appearances' sake, and he resigned when the new Constituent Assembly came into existence.

Ghulam Mohammad dispatched a delegation to meet with Suhrawardy, who was hospitalized in Switzerland, and Suhrawardy issued a statement expressing the opinion that the Governor-General had the power to dissolve the Assembly and urging the Governor-General to continue using his powers against the Assembly.[21] Suhrawardy was elated, claiming that by dissolving the Constituent Assembly the Governor-General had accepted his contention that the Assembly was an unrepresentative body. But by a 'representative' body for constitution-making, Suhrawardy did not want one responsible to the people but one composed of persons not aspiring 'to being political leaders or being returned in an election by the people'.[22] But even Suhrawardy was troubled by the make-up of the new government, fearing that, with Ayub and Mirza as the strongest members of the new Cabinet, Pakistan was on the threshold of a military dictatorship. Ghulam Mohammad pacified Suhrawardy by offering him the Cabinet portfolio of Law Minister, coupled with the promise that in time he would be made Prime Minister. The bait was too tempting for Suhrawardy. To the astonishment of friends and foes alike he accepted Ghulam Mohammad's offer. Suhrawardy, a self-styled democrat, was incorporated into the new autocratic administration and worked closely with Mirza, who soon replaced the ailing Ghulam Mohammad.[23] Fazlul Huq, who only shortly before had been branded a traitor by the central government and stripped of his provincial office, was also won over to the new regime with the spoils of office, being made Interior Minister. If there might have been opposition from East Bengal to the new regime at the centre, that opposition was now neutralized by the co-opting of the two top Bengali leaders outside the Constituent Assembly.

No public protests were made by the members of the Assembly. Opposition would have required acts of personal courage against an angered Governor-General who controlled the police and enjoyed the backing of the Army. At the critical time after the Assembly's dissolution there was no leader capable of effectively championing the cause of democracy. In part, non-opposition to Ghulam Mohammad was the result of his command of the forces of coercion, but in addition, he also enjoyed the advantage of Jinnah's example. The first and highly-revered Governor-General had ruled autocratically without signalling to his people that his approach was not to be taken as a guide for future constitutional conduct. Ghulam Mohammad's usurpation of power seemed, therefore, less of a violation of the dominion constitution than it really was.

The Governor-General in his dissolution pronouncement had promised elections, and many politicians responded by turning their attention to what had to be done to win at the next polling. (Ghulam Mohammad's promise, a ritualistic part of any *coup*, was never fulfilled.) To many in the general population, the battle between the Constituent Assembly and the Governor-General was as remote as were the grand affairs of state in those not too distant days of the British Raj when government was conducted from New Delhi and Simla. No public protest erupted, no processions or student demonstrations took place, and no further agitation occurred in the mosques.[24] The man in the street seemed unconcerned, perhaps because he had little comprehension of what was going on. Even among the educated members of the public, the significance of the dissolution was not understood. To some it was just an ordinary change of government. Ghulam Mohammad received a hero's welcome when he visited East Bengal in November.[25] The politicians on the committee formed to greet him became so enthusiastic in showing their feelings for their new leader that they nearly came to blows over the question as to which members should have precedence in welcoming him. Even had the promised elections been held, government would exist at the sufferance of an all-powerful Governor-General.

The leaders who might have have wanted to oppose Ghulam Mohammad had little to guide them. Although the British had originated and fostered parliamentary democracy on the subcontinent, they provided little guidance in implementing it in Pakistan after independence. The advice Governor Mudie gave Liaquat reflected the negative view of democracy's prospects on the subcontinent expressed earlier by such British leaders as Morley and Balfour, and in the Simon Report. These men had pronounced that, as admirable as were attempts to transplant parliamentary democracy to the subcontinent, English liberties and forms of government were fragile plants which grew best, and perhaps only, in the security of the English political garden.

Viewing what Ghulam Mohammad had brought about, it was easy for a Pakistani to wonder: Had the British been correct? Looking back to the events of this period, a Pakistani historian echoed the predictions of the British by concluding that western democracy was 'not a dress which can be imported and donned for the occasion'.[26] A British observer who was in Pakistan at the time made a particularly painful comparison: '[T]he chances of British forms of democracy proving transplantable to Pakistani soil were probably, anyhow, from the start, intrinsically poorer as compared to the Indian.'[27] Even if a Pakistani politician were to disagree with those verdicts of failure, there was little precedent available to him as a guide in confronting the problems raised by the Assembly's dissolution. Britain, the sponsor of Pakistan's dominion constitution, had itself in modern times not experienced a political event similar to the dissolution of the Assembly.

Parliamentary democracy, which was the basis of dominion government, was not without its blemishes in the eyes of many newly-independent nations at mid-century. It not only came tainted with the recollection of the colonial past, but was also remembered for the inability of the liberal democracies to deal prior to the Second World War with problems of the Great Depression and the threats of fascism and communism. As a result, there was appeal in the idea of government and economy being controlled by an elite few rather than the many. The 1950s witnessed 'the spectacle of nearly half the world's population professing democracy and struggling to work the novel and difficult system, but at the same time not quite convinced if it would succeed and far from persuaded if it was the best alternative'.[28] It was in such a political climate that Ghulam Mohammad launched his attack on Pakistan's parliamentary democracy. While democracy lacked leadership, the forces opposing did not. Ghulam Mohammad and Mirza were as capable as they were ruthless.

Like many Pakistani bureaucrats, Ghulam Mohammad's career had begun and developed within the 'steel frame' of the autocratic government of British India, and like others he carried over an admiration for the efficiency which had been attained under that system. It was a feature of British rule that, while their Indian government might be autocratic, it brought with it the idea of possible development towards independent parliamentary government at some time in the future. When they departed from the subcontinent in 1947, Pakistan came into existence as an inheritor of a system which the English, over the centuries, had developed both at home and in the Commonwealth. Part of that system was the liberties afforded to the people living under it, liberties which, however, were not unconditionally guaranteed. Citizens of Britain and of Pakistan had no rights against the state. In Britain such rights were only what Parliament said they were, and in Pakistan a citizen's rights were what the successor sovereign to Parliament, the Constituent Assembly, said they were. Even when Parliament or the Assembly established a constitutional right for the citizens of their respective nations, such a right was not guaranteed against action by a future Parliament or Assembly because all future Parliaments, being themselves sovereign, could not be limited by a predecessor.

Despite England's absence of guaranteed human rights, the rights enjoyed by her citizens have been extensive. These rights are found not only in the statutes of Parliament and in the conventions of the constitution, but the courts have also established a wide array of rights: the right against self-incrimination, of peaceful assembly, of fair hearing, of limited freedom of the Press, and against the taking of property without compensation, are examples. A. E. Dicey characterized the role of the judiciary under the English Constitution by claiming: 'A large part, and many would add the best part, of the law of England is judge-made law.'[29] Court-established rights have come into existence over the years not in derogation of or in conflict with parliamentary sovereignty, but by the courts 'interpreting' the meaning of the spirit of the laws of Parliament, that is, by the courts declaring what they believe Parliament would have passed if Parliament had considered the specific right in issue.[30]

Nevertheless, none of these court-established rights are guaranteed because they too can be abolished at any time by Parliament. The idea of rights enforceable against the government, or a Bill of Rights as that found in the American constitution, is as alien to an English lawyer today as it was to Blackstone. This absence of guaranteed fundamental rights has led one English commentator to label his country's constitution 'Gothic'.[31] But the position taken by Sir Ivor Jennings better typified the British attitude, at least the attitude of the English elite to which he belonged. 'In Britain we have no Bill of Rights, we merely have liberty according to law; and we think—truly, I believe—that we do the job better than any country which has a Bill of Rights or a Declaration of the Rights of Man.'[32] Neverthless, regardless of how well or badly that 'job' might be carried out, there is no recourse afforded a citizen when the government goes wrong.

The absence of guaranteed fundamental rights had been raised as an issue by Indian leaders during the independence movement. In 1929, the report of the Nehru Committee stated, 'Our first care should be to have our fundamental rights guaranteed in a manner which would not permit their withdrawal under any circumstances.'[33] This demand was also pressed at the London Round Table Conferences. But the Englishmen against whom the protection would apply were the ones who wrote the final report on the Conferences and they did not share the Indians' distrust of British power. The 1934 report, therefore, denied the necessity or advisability of stating fundamental rights in any constitutional document for India. The report reasoned, 'We are aware that such provisions have been inserted in many constitutions, notably in those of the European States founded after the war. Experience, however, does not show them to be of any practical value. Abstract declarations are useless unless there exist the ways and means to make them effective.'[34]

One effective way to make such rights enforceable against Parliament was by vesting the courts with the power of judicially reviewing parliamentary legislation and declaring such legislation invalid when found to be in violation of a guaranteed right. Because this would mean infringement of Parliament's sovereignty, no such judicial power was considered by the committee. As a result, the Government of India Act of 1935 contained no mention of the rights of an individual except those rights protecting British property rights and the right of the British to pursue professional and other employment in India.[35] Consistent with the absence of constitutional safeguards for fundamental rights in Great Britain itself, no such safeguards came into existence in British India. When independence came, the Indian Independence Act also made no mention of fundamental rights.

To understand the political environment in Pakistan, it is also helpful to recognize some of the instruments of coercion available to the government at the time Ghulam Mohammad seized power. The police powers and criminal justice system which had existed in British India continued in existence after independence. As in Great Britain and the Commonwealth nations, state criminal matters were administered under a penal code. Work on the Indian Penal Code was begun by Lord Macauley when he became Law Member on the Council of India in 1834, and was adopted after a number of revisions in 1862. The Code, in essence, provided for punishment after a trial at which the government proved that the accused had violated the provisions of the Code. But Britain was the conqueror as well as the law-giver in India, and for that reason had need for stronger means of controlling an alien and potentially hostile people who might challenge Britain's right to rule them. To meet this need, preventive detention was instituted, to operate in addition to the Indian Penal Code. In employing preventive detention the government was not limited by the Penal Code's requirement that only persons who had committed acts in violation of the Code could be imprisoned. The government was free to use preventive detention to detain those who might in the future commit an unspecified act which the government considered to be threatening to good order or the security of the state.[36]

The origins of the preventive detention employed by the Pakistan government go back to the Bengal State Prisoners Regulation III of 1818, which later was made applicable to all of British India. A prohibited act under preventive detention need not be a crime, but could include any act which might be considered by the government as prejudicial to public safety or tranquillity. The purpose of Regulation III was to allow the government to detain a suspect when sufficient evidence did not exist to convict him of a crime under the Penal Code, or when public proceedings under the Penal Code might be inconvenient or embarrassing for the government. The Governor-General in Council was the sole judge of the necessity of using these extraordinary powers, which allowed the summary arrest and detention of an individual for an indefinite period of time, and the attachment of his estate, all without giving the accused recourse to being heard in a court of law. The detainee had no right to be informed of the reasons why he was detained, or to be represented by an attorney. A warrant of confinement was sufficient authorization to hold a person, and the courts were excluded from inquiring into the detention upon being shown that detention was within the terms of the Regulation. The only safeguard provided in the Regulation was the requirement that a detainee's case be reviewed by a government official every six months during his imprisonment.[37]

Police powers similar to those allowed under Regulation III were enumerated in the Indian Code of Criminal Procedure and utilized extensively on the local level in British India and later in Pakistan. Unlike Regulation III, which during British rule could be exercised only by the Governor-General in Council, the Code of Criminal Procedure provided for preventive detention exercised by local magistrates.[38] Section 144 of the Code of Criminal Procedure, which was continued in force after independence, was a most effective suppressant of political opposition. This section of the Code allowed a magistrate to prohibit certain acts, such as the making of a speech or the holding of a procession or a public meeting, on the grounds that it might lead to a disturbance of the peace. Magistrates were civil servants under the direction of the provincial government, and a magistrate could easily reach the conclusion during an election campaign that the speech of an opposition leader was more likely to result in a riot than would the speech of a government minister. Section 144 also allowed a magistrate, without proof that a crime had been committed or the public peace violated, to require an arrested person to furnish security for the keeping of the peace and for good behaviour. Upon failure to post the required security, imprisonment for a period of up to one year could be imposed.

The various forms of preventive detention were continued in force after independence by the ministry of Prime Minister Liaquat Ali Khan. Citing the problems of partition and conflict with India over Kashmir, the Liaquat administration introduced, and the Constituent Assembly enacted, Public Safety Acts in 1949 and 1950 similar to the provisions of the Acts in British India modelled on the Bengal Regulation.[39] Under the Government of India Act of 1935, prior to independence, police powers had been vested exclusively in the provincial governments. In 1952, the powers of the federal government were broadened to make police powers a federal affair to be shared with the provinces.[40] At the same time, the Constituent Assembly attempted to mitigate some of the harshness of preventive detention by providing for a number of safeguards.[41] But these safeguards were limited, and none detracted from the fact that the preventive-detention powers enabled long periods of incarceration to be meted out to a person at the discretion of the government. Similar detention acts were promulgated in each of the provinces by the provincial assemblies.[42]

The operation of preventive detention and related police measures became important parts of civil administration in Pakistan during the dominion period. 'In practice there had been quite enough arrests to convince the most sceptical that the power of preventive detention is a reality...[T]he former hirelings of the alien rulers who had sent obstreperous politicians to goal in 1939-46, became loyal and valued servants of the state, fully capable of sending obstreperous politicians to gaol in 1947-56.'[43] What gave these police measures great potency was the fact that they could be used interchangeably, and no citizen was protected by a right against double jeopardy. If the government failed in its attempt to detain a person on the first try because the court freed that person for good reason, the government could simply re-arrest him on any of a number of other security measures. After independence, the citizens of Pakistan were subject to police measures which the British ordinarily did not feel the need to rely on during their rule in peace-time.[44]

Unlike Great Britain, where the judiciary was a source for the development of fundamental rights and a protector of citizens against the arbitrary acts of the government, the courts in Pakistan were restricted by Constituent Assembly legislation limiting the scope of a court's ability to monitor infractions of personal liberty. As an example, the Assembly made the basis of the validity of an arrest and detention under the Public Safety Acts the arresting authority's satisfaction that the person was apt to commit a prohibited act. 'Satisfaction' was considered a state of mind of the arresting authority which the courts were denied the right to question. A court was not to substitute its judgment for that of the arresting officer. While a detainee was given the right to show that his detention had been ordered on grounds other than those stated in the arresting order, for a prisoner lacking access to investigators or other means of gathering information this was a meaningless right. The detention statutes also gave the government ample opportunity to frustrate any attempt by a court to obtain information which would enable it to form a reasonable opinion even as to whether the arrest was made for the reasons covered by the statute. Mohammad Munir, when he was Chief Judge of the Punjab High Court, gave a good picture of preventive detention in operation when he vented his frustration in one of the cases before his court.

> In almost every case of detention under the Public Safety Act, the authority ordering the detention, when questioned by the court about the reason for the detention, mechanically repeats the formula of 'public safety and maintenance of public order', and displays a positive disinclination to the matter being probed further. While such disinclination is understandable where high affairs of state are concerned, I do not see why in ordinary cases, as for instance, where a man is arrested for defying law and order, intending to lead a banned procession, fomenting labour discontent, or communal hatred, or for otherwise endangering the public peace, the authority ordering the arrest should not take the court and the public into confidence by giving a broad hint as to the reasons for the action taken. In such cases the court does not desire to go into details or to ask for disclosure of the material on which the authority ordering the arrest formed his opinion, except to the extent that such information is relevant to the question whether the action taken was bona fide.[45]

Munir's protest had no effect, and preventive detention remained unchanged. A detainee was left without meaningful rights and could look to neither the constitution, the Constituent Assembly, nor the courts for protection against the police powers of the state.[46]

In another area of political control, Pakistan inherited from the British a law which enabled the government to control the Press. In 1931, in the face of growing nationalist activity, the British put into effect the Indian Press (Emergency Powers) Act, which gave the government the right to require a security deposit from any newspaper publisher or any other person who controlled a printing press. It was a prohibited act to publish or distribute unauthorized newspapers or to 'encourage or entice any person to interfere with the administration of law or with the maintenance of law and order'. A violator was subject to the forfeiture of his security deposit without recourse to a judicial hearing, and the offending newspaper could be banned. This measure was continued in Pakistan,[47] and was used in Karachi in 1949 when the Assembly, under Liaquat's leadership, banned foreign newspapers for a period of up to a year and ordered censorship of three local newspapers for a period of up to three months because the papers were indulging in writings which the authorities found prejudicial to the interests and stability of the state.[48] The Press Laws, however, were infrequently utilized by the government, and during the constitutional debates the Press carried a full variety of opinions. Nevertheless, the Press Acts were important when the government wished to take action to suppress opinion, such as after the Assembly's dissolution, and their very existence on the statute books was a deterrent to an editor who wished to take a strong position against the government.

After independence, the Liaquat administration re-instituted a measure which the British had made a part of the Government of India Act at the time of its passage in 1935 and which became important in Pakistan's political affairs. Section 93 empowered the Governor-General of British India to suppress a provincial ministry. Fearing that the power granted by Section 93 would render useless the newly-gained responsible governments under the 1935 Act in the provinces, Indian leaders prior to independence obtained a commitment from the British Indian government that the emergency powers of the section would be employed only in exceptional situations, and that the ordinary functioning of the provincial government would not be interfered with.[49] The British abided by their commitment fairly well until the Second World War brought with it increased nationalist agitation. The use of emergency powers during the war was unpopular, and when the British withdrew from the subcontinent they amended the Government of India Act to remove Section 93. It was, however, re-enacted during the Liaquat administration as Section 92A to the Government of India Act, and became a part of Liaquat's policy of concentrating power at the centre. Liaquat made the first use of this power against the Mamdot ministry in West Punjab.[50] The Constituent Assembly did not resist this lessening of provincial autonomy. Perceived danger from India, the Kashmir dispute, and the problems of the refugees created a crisis mentality that made the strengthening of the central government acceptable.

Emergency powers in the constitution, such as those contained in Section 92A, proved a temptation to solve political problems by autocratic means. Powers were not granted by the legislature to the executive to meet a specific emergency situation, but were, as in British India, a part of the constitution readily available for use by the executive branch when the executive concluded that an emergency existed.[51] It was easy after independence for those who commanded the instruments of police power to perceive an 'emergency' in any political situation they found undesirable, and no politician could help but be influenced by the knowledge that the central government was willing to exercise such powers. Liaquat's exercise of the centre's Section 92A powers to remove Mamdot was a model for centre-province relationships. Consequently the autocratic government of British colonial rule was continued in Pakistan. 'The line of authority still ran from a central government to its local agents. Provincial autonomy never became a reality and recalcitrant local politicians were speedily removed from office.'[52]

Under the parliamentary system, the Constituent Assembly had the responsibility not only to legislate, but to act as a monitor of the actions of the executive branch.[53] But with reference to the executive's use of the police, the Assembly exerted no effective control.[54] Ordinarily, oversight of human rights and control of the executive is addressed by the parliamentary procedure of adjournment motions, whereby private members of the Assembly can address objections to the government bench. However, in the seven-year history of the Constituent Assembly, fifty-six such motions were made but only three or four were discussed. The others were dismissed or withdrawn for various reasons.[55]

On 26 January 1949 Liaquat put in place another instrument of political control when he introduced the Public and Representatives Officers (Disqualification) Act, PRODA, for passage by the Constituent Assembly.[56] This statute had no counterpart in British India. It provided that the Governor-General or a Governor could issue an order charging a minister or deputy minister of the federal or provincial governments, or a member of the Constituent Assembly or a provincial legislature, with misconduct in any matter relating to the accused person's office. Charges could also be filed by any politician or citizen upon the posting of a security of five thousand rupees, the deposit to be forfeited by the person who brought the action if the charges were not substantiated. Misconduct, in the terms of this legislation, included 'bribery, corruption, jobbery, favouritism, nepotism, wilful maladministration, wilful misapplication or diversion of public monies...and any other abuse of official power or position or any abatement thereof...'[57] The maximum penalty was disqualification from public office for a period of ten years. Charges were tried by a tribunal consisting of two or more judges of a High Court, those members to be appointed by the Governor-General or a Governor at his discretion.

PRODA was an expression of lack of confidence in Pakistan's politicians to operate the government honestly and efficiently as the constitution intended. In a democratic government, the failures of government officials are usually addressed by the voters through the election process, and corruption or misdeeds of politicians amounting to crimes are prosecuted under criminal law against politicians as they are against a private citizens. For any cases falling outside of such safeguards, there exists the impeachment process. In place of these normal procedures, PRODA created political crimes, with a new separate body of political procedures which would be subject to the influence of the Governor-General or a Governor by means of exercising his right under the statute to choose the judges who would sit on the tribunal to try the offence.

PRODA became more than a symbol of the government's lack of confidence in the democratic process. It soon became a tool used by the government and politicians in dealing with political enemies. Politicians with five thousand rupees at their disposal for a filing fee could burden an opponent with the necessity of preparing for and defending a PRODA charge, thus diverting the opponent's attention and placing him under a political cloud while the slow process of adjudication of the charges wound on. Before PRODA was abolished by the Constituent Assembly in September 1954, it was widely used, and introduced destabilizing confusion into the legislative process, affording the central government a means of inhibiting opposition on both the federal and provincial levels. For example, during one period all but one minister in the Sindh government were subject to PRODA charges. The statute was also used as a political tactic by members of the Constituent Assembly against each other. The many charges which were filed disrupted the legislative process and contributed to damaging the public image of politicians as compared with the bureaucrats. While cases of wrongdoing and corruption by civil servants were not uncommon, they did not attract the amount of public attention PRODA directed to the activities of politicians.[58]

How the Liaquat administration and the Constituent Assembly viewed the balance between liberty and security was exemplified by the passage of the Rawalpindi Conspiracy Act. This legislation was introduced in the Constituent Assembly by the Liaquat administration in 1950 in response to the discovery of a conspiracy made up of civilians and high-ranking military officers of the Pakistani Army who allegedly had communist connections.[59] The provisions of the Act removed the trial of the conspirators from the ordinary military and civilian courts and subjected them to a special procedure and tribunal. The trial was to be held in secret, without a jury, police statements could be entered in evidence without the requirement that the police officers responsible for the statements be sworn and be available for cross-examination, no records of the proceedings were to be kept, no disclosure to the public of the procedures was to be allowed, no judgement would be published, and there was to be no right of appeal. Mian Iftikharuddin, leader of the opposition Azad Party, argued in the Constituent Assembly that the procedure provided for was one that would be expected at the Reichstag trials conducted by the Nazis.[60]

Pursuant to the Act, a military tribunal was set up before which eleven military officers and four civilians were tried. Some were convicted and sentenced to imprisonment. Little is known of what transpired before the military board. No notes were allowed to could be kept by those who participated, and access to the file of the proceedings remains closed. D.N. Pritt, the English barrister who later appeared in the litigation which followed the dissolution of the Constituent Assembly, was barred from appearing on behalf of the defendants who had retained him in the Rawalpindi case. Without a constitution containing guaranteed fundamental rights, there was nothing to bar the government from exercising such powers against its citizens or political foes.[61]

Despite the existence of the means of repression, Pakistan, until Ghulam Mohammad's act of physically dissolving the Assembly, was not a police state. The Assembly members were unhampered in their law-making activities, the public was free to express itself on political questions, the Army had returned to barracks after the Ahmadi riots, and the Press was free from censorship for nearly all of the period. Yet, the means of oppression available to the central government were of overriding importance. They were not the 'cause' of democracy's termination any more than a gun is the cause of a murder, but they did afford Ghulam Mohammad the sense of confidence that he had at his disposal the means to achieve his goal of destroying the Cabinet and the Assembly.

Pakistan remained a conservative country ruled by a conservative elite. It had not been disturbed by revolution in the change from colonial rule to independence. Continuity of the established social and economic elite of large landowners in West Pakistan was not questioned by the mass of the people. There was little activity at either end of the political spectrum. Communists were active but easily kept in check, and no totalitarian party emerged on the right. The always-perceived threat from India, while it caused the allocation of resources away from civil purposes and to the military, had the benefit of focusing the people on a common effort, which in turn fostered a sense of nationhood which had not been apparent at independence.

As in other democratic societies, everyday government in Pakistan was in the hands of a bureaucracy. Despite its very disadvantageous start after independence, the bureaucrats established what Keith Callard evaluated at the time as 'a workable system of responsible government'. From his on-the-scene experience he reported in 1956, 'That the country has survived is largely due to the worth of the public services. A central government was established and has succeeded in administrating the affairs of a nation of eighty million inhabitants. The armed forces have not meddled in politics but have been ready to support the civil administration when required. Some aspects of bureaucratic control have been arbitrary and irresponsible, but the structure has held together and has made possible the future establishment of a working system of responsible government.'[62] During the same period Leonard Binder's interviews with members of the civil service, most of them Punjabis, led him to conclude that there was little preference among them as to any particular form of government or particular ministry. They were principally concerned with preserving their own rights and the position of their agencies. He found that the involvement of the civil service in government did not go beyond keeping routine functions in operation.[63]

Writing in 1964, Henry Goodnow claimed that, in the two-year period from April 1951 to April 1953, especially in the Punjab, 'the elected representatives had exerted more influence on the conduct of public administration than they did before that time or have since.' The Muslim League had won a clear majority in the 1951 Punjab elections and, as Goodnow concluded, 'Apparently, the civil servants deferred to the duly constituted cabinet.'[64] The fact that Ghulam Mohammad was a bureaucrat gives no idea of how great his following was in the ranks of the bureaucracy, many of whose members may have been as surprised by Ghulam Mohammad's *coup* as were the politicians.

Changes took place in the bureaucracy because of the approach the government took to economic development. Under the dominion constitution, industrial policy and its implementation was assigned to the provincial governments. This arrangement appeared to some bureaucrats in the central government to be inappropriate in the face of Pakistan's need for a national economic plan, and they were successful in winning the Constituent Assembly to their view. Shortly after independence the Assembly began to enact a series of amendments to the constitution, and enacted legislation transferring the responsibility for industrial development to the national government.[65] Many fiscal powers were also moved from the provinces to the centre, while at the same time the taxing powers of the central government were being enlarged. To accommodate these moves, administrative machinery was set up by the central government under the supervision of various advisory and development boards. Although the Prime Minister and industrial leaders served on some of these boards, economic affairs came into the hands of the bureaucracy. The potential powers made available to the bureaucracy are illustrated by the extent of the legislation passed by the Assembly. For example, it provided that no new industrial project employing more than fifty workers could be established without obtaining a licence from the government. The government could attach to the issuance of such licenses a vast number of conditions, including dictating the location of the new industrial project and the type of materials which must be used in any manufacturing. Substantial penalties were prescribed for the infringement of any regulations or conditions of the licence.

Between 1947 and 1951, these economic measures placed significant control of the scarce resources of Pakistan under the bureaucracy. During this time, the political leaders did not concern themselves with the process of economic development, leaving even the formation of policy to the bureaucrats, who in time came to command sources of political patronage not at the disposal of many of the politicians. Ghulam Mohammad, as Finance Minister from 1947 to 1951, was in a central position to dictate economic policy and to establish patron-client relationships between the bureaucracy and the financial and industrial communities. He could thereafter depend upon their support in any conflicts with the politicians.

By default, the bureaucrats became stronger relative to the politicians, who had little contact with what ordinarily would have been their main basis of support, the electorate. On the national level of the Constituent Assembly, that support had not been developed because, in the absence of national elections, there was no need or opportunity for the Assembly members to go to the voters. Such an election would not take place until constitution-making was completed. Nor had the politicians made the Muslim League into a political party with broad-based support. As a result, Ghulam Mohammad took over a government which afforded him access to dictatorial powers at a time when there existed no political party with a leader who could oppose him.

One of the most important differences between Ghulam Mohammad's Pakistan and the nation as it was under Jinnah,

Liaquat, and Nazimuddin was that the Constituent Assembly no longer possessed the sovereign power of the state. The importance of this change, brought about by Munir, can be appreciated when it is remembered that the Civil War of the seventeenth century, so important in the development of the English constitution, was a struggle between Parliament and the Crown over the location of sovereignty within the state.[66] This is an issue of importance in any society but it is particularly important in a newly created nation such as Pakistan of the 1950s. Unless there is agreement as to where secular sovereignty within the state resides, sovereign power, as in Pakistan's experience, becomes a prize to be seized by the strongest. When Munir denied the existence of the Assembly's sovereignty, he destroyed Pakistan's existing constitutional basis. He did further harm when he did not indicate where sovereignty resided. He thereby created a vacuum which was an opportunity for Ghulam Mohammed. The absence of a constitutional foundation is a harm which has lived on in Pakistan since Ghulam Mohammed left office.

CHAPTER 7

A CLASH OF IDEAS

Thus far Ghulam Mohammad had carried out a *coup* which was remarkably successful. Part of this success was due to the fact that what he accomplished was not recognized as a *coup*. Yet he had captured the office of Prime Minister by forcing Nazimuddin out of office, and he had dismissed the Assembly with the public approval of Bogra, his hand-picked successor to Nazimuddin. One man, the Governor-General, now controlled the government. When Tamizuddin Khan announced that he would raise in court the question of the Governor-General's powers, Ghulam Mohammad was faced with the first challenge to his accumulation of power. While the office of Prime Minister had developed by convention, the existence and role of the Constituent Assembly were matters not only of convention but also of specific provisions in the dominion constitution. Ghulam Mohammad's right to rule could be defeated by a court decision interpreting the constitution in favour of the Assembly.[1]

In contrast to the Assembly, which had not established itself in the consciousness of the nation, the courts were not only popular but, in theory at least, independent. When Pakistan came into existence, the judiciary enjoyed a high degree of prestige and popularity with the people. Indianization had occurred early in the judicial branch of the government of British India, and achieved widespread positive results. As early as 1929, one-half of the judges of the Punjab were Indian. By 1932, one-half of the judges of the High Court of the Punjab, including the Chief Justice of that court, and sixty-four per cent of all judges below the High Court, were Indian.[2] As one western scholar observed, by independence the people of the subcontinent had developed 'a passionate love of litigation,' and what he termed an 'affection' for courts.[3] Court decisions were widely distributed, often printed in full in the newspapers, and were read and discussed by the educated sectors of the public. There was a degree of familiarization with the court system which did not exist between the people and the Constituent Assembly. To suppress the courts would have made the *coup* apparent to the public.

The challenge to Ghulam Mohammad came from a man whom he had probably never pictured as a potential antagonist. A quiet, modest political figure, Tamizuddin Khan had filled the office of Assembly President since the death of Jinnah in a way that earned widespread respect. Not a bold man, he nevertheless was willing to start a lonely campaign, with few dependable political allies and relying principally on his own limited financial resources, against a Governor-General who had the coercive forces and financial resources of the state at his disposal. Pakistan has remembered Tamizuddin Khan by naming avenues in some of its major cities in his honour, a tribute noticeably denied to Ghulam Mohammad.

Since no national election would be held until after the new constitution went into effect two months later, members of the Assembly could not take the issue of the dissolution to the electorate. The courts were the only hope. There they could argue that, as a sovereign body, the Assembly could not be dissolved without its consent. If its members could obtain a favourable ruling from the court, their stand would have the backing of law, and they would have ground to stand on in continuing their opposition to the Governor-General. Although the members of the Assembly feared Ghulam Mohammad, they did move against him to protect the Assembly and the new constitution until it went into effect on 25 December. The statutory measures taken by the Assembly to curb the Governor-General on 21 September indicated that they did not think in terms of protecting the Assembly by relying on the right under constitutional convention to go to the Queen. Instead, they made it a requirement by statute that the Governor-General act only on the advice of his ministers, and that those ministers be members of the Assembly and have the Assembly's confidence. What had been convention was now statute, and therefore could be enforced in court.

If the Assembly needed the judiciary, the same was also true of Ghulam Mohammad. When he dismissed Nazimuddin and dissolved the Constituent Assembly he became in fact the supreme ruler of Pakistan, but his dissolution of the Assembly was not sanctioned by the dominion constitution or its conventions, and he had dissolved the only body in the government with the constitutional authority to frame a new constitution. As discussions in the Press showed, the country (and perhaps Ghulam Mohammad himself) were uncertain as to the constitutionality of what had occurred. Neither the Governor-General nor anyone else outside the Assembly was given the power by the terms of the constitution to dissolve the Assembly. Perhaps for that reason the word 'dissolution' had not been used in the Governor-General's proclamation of 24 October.[3A] Tamizuddin Khan pointed out that any new Assembly resulting from the election that Ghulam Mohammad had promised in that proclamation would 'have no legal status if it does not derive its sovereignty from the present Constituent Assembly'.[4] Ghulam Mohammad could not be confident how long the initial support of the Army and the public would last if his assumption of power were to be perceived as lacking the sanction of law. He needed to make a convincing public showing that his right to rule was legitimate under the constitution.

On 8 November 1954, Tamizuddin Khan filed a petition with the Chief Court of Sindh based on a recently-enacted statute had effected a constitutional change by allowing the courts to issue writs restraining illegal actions by the executive.[5] He requested that writs be issued against the Governor-General and the members of the new Cabinet which Ghulam Mohammad had selected and installed after his 24 October proclamation. If granted, the writs would require the Governor-General to cease interfering with the Constituent Assembly and restrain the new ministers from functioning as a cabinet. Tamizuddin Khan's petition claimed that the allegation in the Governor-General's proclamation, namely, that the constitution-making process had broken down, was not true, that the Assembly was in fact a sovereign body, and that there existed no provision in the constitution which would allow a Governor-General to dissolve the Assembly.

The filing of his petition presented dangers for Tamizuddin Khan.[6] He and those supporting the Assembly against Ghulam Mohammad's dissolution were apprehensive that the Governor-General would employ the police to prevent any action being taken in court. Aware of such a danger, S. S. Pirzada, the attorney who drew up Tamizuddin Khan's petition papers, did so at home rather than hold meetings with Tamizuddin Khan in his downtown law office.[7] On the day prior to the court filing, a junior attorney, Moulvi Sahib, took the papers to be filed from Pirzada's home to his own. The next morning, another associate of Pirzada, acting as a decoy, left Pirzada's downtown office for the Registrar's office at the Sindh Chief Court, creating the impression that he was on his way to file court pleadings. At the same time, Moulvi Sahib left his residence through the back door and, disguised as a *burqa*-clad woman, walked some distance until he could hail a bicycle-rickshaw to take him to the court building. Meanwhile, Pirzada's other associate was arrested and detained by the police as he reached the court-house. While this was happening Pirzada reached the court in a borrowed diplomat's car. There he joined Moulvi Sahib who had succeeded in filing the petition papers with the Registrar. They then retired to the court library where they thought they would be safe from the police until the case was called on the court docket.

The Registrar immediately sent the petition to the Chief Justice. When the police found that the arrested attorney did not have the petition and then discovered that the petition had been filed, they attempted to obtain it from the Registrar, who no longer had the document. Recognizing the importance of the petition, Chief Justice Sir George Constantine placed the matter on the court calendar for 2.00 p.m. that day and sent a warning to the Inspector General of Police that any interference with the proceedings would be treated as contempt of court. Before 1.00 p.m. news of the filing had become public, and when the judges assembled for the scheduled hearing the courtroom was crowded. Pirzada appeared at the hearing on behalf of Tamizuddin Khan, and after a two hour argument the matter was set for a full hearing at a future date. The question of the constitutionality of Ghulam Mohammad's dissolution of the Assembly was now before the court and the public.

A political settlement was attempted. Iskander Mirza knew Pirzada personally, having retained him as attorney in another case. According to Pirzada, Mirza, accompanied by Ayub Khan, approached him with the suggestion that Pirzada go to Tamizuddin Khan and propose a compromise which would result in the withdrawal of the court petition. Mirza succeeded in obtaining a meeting with Tamizuddin Khan and a settlement was agreed on.[8] Ghulam Mohammad's dissolution of the Assembly was to be withdrawn and the Assembly would then meet and dissolve itself. A new Cabinet would be formed, one-half of its members to be nominated by the Governor-General and one-half by Tamizuddin Khan. A new Constituent Assembly would be elected and that Assembly would approve the new constitution. When this proposed settlement was communicated to Ghulam Mohammad he rejected it. He was afraid that the members of the Assembly would not live up to the settlement once he had allowed them to reassemble. He was also concerned that if the court was asked to enter an order making the settlement enforceable, such an order might be construed as confirming that the Assembly was a sovereign body. After the settlement attempts failed, offers were made to Tamizuddin Khan to become a minister in the new government but he refused.

Tamizuddin Khan and those Assembly members who supported him wanted D. M. Pritt to represent the Assembly.[9] Since 1910, Pritt, a London barrister, had represented causes against government actions throughout the Empire and the Commonwealth. He was best known most recently for his defence of Jomo Kenyatta in the Kenya Mau Mau conspiracy trial. For fourteen years, he had served as a leftist Labour Party Member of Parliament. He was known in Pakistan because of his previous retention by the defendants in the Rawalpindi Conspiracy Case of 1951, the country's most famous political prosecution to that date. Contact was made with Pritt who was at the time in Singapore. Such was the perceived possibility of police action against the Assembly members or Pritt that Tamizuddin Khan and his small group of supporters feared using the mail or cable, and instead arranged to meet Pritt in Colombo to discuss the case. After that meeting, Pritt entered Pakistan to appear in the Sindh court by the ruse that he was a doctor being summoned to Karachi by a sick patient. He succeeded in entering Pakistan incognito only because the police, anticipating his arrival, mistakenly thought he would be on a plane from London. While they searched the London flights, Pritt arrived undetected on a flight from Colombo. He was careful not to have anyone meet him at the airport and not to telephone Tamizuddin Khan until he arrived at his Karachi hotel.

Meanwhile, the Governor-General made his preparations. He dispatched the government's Law Secretary, Sir Edward Snelson, to Ceylon to confer with Sir Ivor Jennings, who had returned to his post at the University of Ceylon after completing his work on the final draft of Pakistan's constitution prior to the dissolution of the Assembly.[10] Jennings agreed to return to Pakistan as an adviser on litigation and also to help prepare a new constitution for the Governor-General.[11] Having access to public funds, Ghulam Mohammad did not have the same financial problem as Tamizuddin Khan and the Assembly. He was able to offer Jennings a retainer which amounted to over seven times the annual compensation paid to Pakistan's Chief Justice of the Federal Court, and in addition Jennings received a generous living allowance while in Pakistan. The money was well-spent by Ghulam Mohammad, for Jennings proved to be the ideal person to mastermind Ghulam Mohammad's court defence and to justify the Assembly's dissolution.

While Jennings was considered an outstanding constitutional expert of the day, particularly on Commonwealth matters, he was not being retained as a scholar but as an advocate. This meant that he would not be falling back on his vast store of constitutional law and history to reach an objective conclusion on constitutional questions. Instead, he had a client, Ghulam Mohammad, and Jennings was hired to prove that Ghulam Mohammad's dissolution of the Assembly was justified under the dominion constitution and the principles of English and Commonwealth law. The evolution of Jennings' ideas to that end is a fascinating example of the workings of the mind of a very talented scholar and lawyer.

Jennings returned to Pakistan on 26 November and began immediately to develop Ghulam Mohammad's case. The task before him had been discussed several weeks earlier in a *New York Times* dispatch from Karachi.[12] According to that account, 'academics have been searching law books for a source of the Governor-General's powers...In the informal opinion of constitutional lawyers here the authority of the Governor-General is derived from powers latent in the British Crown.' Much of the searching most likely included the works of Jennings, who was the most voluminous author on the subject of cabinet government and Commonwealth constitutions. The reporter pointed out that the constitutional experts had not been able to find any substantiation for their conclusion in any written law, but rather that their conclusion fitted into what one lawyer described to the *Times* as the 'highly involved and complex structure of British law'. The newspaper report made reference to Nazimuddin's dismissal the previous year, when Bogra had been appointed Prime Minister pursuant to authority said to have been derived 'from the Crown', and nobody had then challenged that authority.

It would be necessary for Jennings to construct a theory of the powers vested in the Governor-General by the constitution broad enough to encompass a right to dissolve the Assembly under the circumstances in which Ghulam Mohammad had acted. This theory had to be creditable enough to convince the courts. When the Government of India Act was originally enacted in 1935, it continued the broad powers which the Governor-General had enjoyed under the Government of India Act of 1919 and its predecessors. As representative of the Crown and the chief executive officer of India, he acted on Instruments of Instruction issued by the Crown with the approval of Parliament and was responsible to Parliament through the Secretary of State. He remained the potentate described by Ramsey MacDonald as 'surrounded by pomp and awe; ceremony walks behind and before him and does obeisance to him.'[13]

While responsible government was provided for in the provinces under the Act of 1935, reserve powers were granted to the Governor-General in areas enumerated as his 'special responsibility,' where he acted 'in his discretion' or on 'individual judgment'.[14] These areas included defence, financial matters, protection of minorities, and 'peace and tranquillity,' areas broad enough in scope to enable any Governor-General to temporarily and partially return to absolute rule when he determined it to be necessary. He enjoyed the right to assume control not only over certain areas of legislation, but also over the whole of the legislative process if he deemed, in his discretion, that the provisions of the Act of 1935 were not being properly carried out. Perhaps the greatest check on legislative growth was the Governor-General's right to legislate on his own, upon his certification that such legislation was necessary for the safety or tranquillity or 'to protect the interests' of India. The Governor-General also possessed the power under the Act to prohibit the legislature from considering certain matters, and to suspend the operation of legislative government. In the exercise of these powers, the Governor-General acted on the advice of the Secretary of State in London.

The Governor-General appointed the members to his Council of Ministers who were, in accordance with parliamentary practice, to be members of the Federal Legislature and who enjoyed the confidence of the legislature.[15] Convention required that he act on the advice of his ministers, but since the terms of the Act gave the Governor-General freedom to act without their advice with reference to so many important affairs of government, the scope of his ministers' roles was limited and the prospect for the development of cabinet government was impaired.

When the Government of India Act was amended by the Indian Independence Act of 1947, the powers of the Governor-General were radically changed. He was now to 'represent His Majesty for the purposes of the government' of each of the dominions of Pakistan and India.[16] He remained the titular repository of the executive power of the state, and all executive actions were still to be performed in his name including the appointment of the top government, judicial, and military leaders as well as the provincial governors. But also like the King, all of the Governor-General's powers were subject to convention and were understood to be executed only on the advice of his ministers. He no longer possessed the power to act on his own discretion or individual judgment, and no longer did he exercise 'special responsibilities'. His powers were also changed so that he no longer possessed the right to dissolve the legislature or legislate on his own authority. In addition, he was no longer a part of the central legislature, although the provincial Governors remained a part of their respective legislatures.

In reviewing events, Jennings discarded as a possible defence that part of the Governor-General's proclamation which stated that the Constituent Assembly had lost the confidence of the people. To Jennings, the confidence of the people raised a political question, not a legal one.[17] He also rejected as a defence that part of the proclamation which claimed that the Assembly had broken down. To Jennings such a conclusion, when stated by the Governor-General, was not conclusive. Instead, he initially turned his attention to the seventeenth-century English decision in the *Case of Shipmoney*, which had supported the utilization of power by the Crown similar to the power that the Governor-General had utilized against the Assembly.[18] But he answered his own argument by recalling that the *Shipmoney* holding had been overruled by Parliament after the fall of Charles I, and the rule was established that an emergency sufficient to justify unilateral action by the

Crown or executive was justified only when a court of law took notice of the existence of that emergency.[19]

Having found no legal bases for the Assembly's dissolution, Jennings turned to history in the hope of justification, and there he looked to the Crown prerogative of the English monarchy. The approach he took was itself not unusual. When a case of first impression involving social or political issues, such as *Tamizuddin*, comes before a court, a judge sometimes will search the past for events, deriving principles applicable to the issues under consideration. If the search into history uncovers events which the judge concludes are relevant, he can then claim that he has 'discovered' the law in historical precedent, much as he would discover precedent in a past decision of the courts.

Jennings used a historical approach, but chose to utilize English history and to make no reference to the history of Pakistan just prior to and following independence. Pakistan's history would have presented difficulties for Jennings. In order for the Crown prerogative to have any meaning in *Tamizuddin*, the presence of the Crown in Pakistan would have to have survived the withdrawal of the British. But the events surrounding the transfer of power by the British indicated that it was the intent of the parties involved that Pakistan was to come into existence as an independent dominion. Jinnah had accepted a dominion constitution as an expedient, not because there was any desire to maintain the Crown as part of the Pakistan government. Nor did the people of Pakistan have a nostalgic attachment to the monarchy as did many in the senior dominions, initially populated as they were by settlers from the British Isles. Jinnah might have differed with his Congress counterparts on the timing of the British withdrawal, but he and the Muslim League had a history of opposition to British rule which left little ground supporting the continued existence of the Crown on the subcontinent.

Thus, Jennings avoided Pakistan's history and based his arguments solely on English history and the history of the British in India. He started his historical review with the East India Company rule in India from 1660 to 1772, when the first Regulation Act had been passed under prerogative instruments from the Crown.[20] Although the Company had ceased to be a trading company in 1833, it continued to govern on behalf of the Crown.[21] Jennings gave consideration to the fact that after 1858, when the right to govern India was taken from the Company and reverted to the Crown,[22] India was thereafter ruled by a series of parliamentary Acts of which the Government of India Act of 1935 was the latest.[23] Jennings saw nothing in the 1935 Act affecting the existence of the Crown's prerogative.[24]

When Parliament passed the Indian Independence Act in 1947, Pakistan became a dominion, and would remain so until the option was exercised by Pakistan to abolish dominion status. Until that option was exercised, in Jennings' opinion Pakistan was subject to the same prerogative rights of the Crown as applied in the other dominions. The fact that the Crown's prerogative rights were not specifically preserved in the 1947 Indian Independence Act was not a problem to Jennings, who concluded that such rights could be taken away by Parliament only by specific language.[25] What Jennings referred to as a 'mere omission' he concluded had no effect on prerogative rights. Jennings also concluded that the Indian Independence Act presumed the Crown's prerogative rights by providing that the Governor-General 'shall represent His Majesty for the purpose of the government of Pakistan'.[26]

In a lengthy memorandum, Jennings informed the government that the Government of India Act and the Indian Independence Act did not provide what Jennings termed 'a complete constitutional scheme' because they did not provide an answer for a situation such as the one facing the nation, namely, the failure of the constitutional machinery to function after the Assembly had been dissolved. The Government of India Act did have such a provision when it was originally enacted in 1935, but the right of the Governor-General to exercise power at his discretion, and to step in and operate the constitutional system, had been deleted from the Government of India Act when it was amended at independence. As Jennings pointed out, this constitutional void would not have arisen in Pakistan if it were still a colony, because the omnipotent British Parliament could pass any legislation necessary to address the problem.[27] But since in theory a constitutional vacuum could not exist, Jennings concluded that it was necessary in the Dominion of Pakistan to fall back on the Common Law under which the monarch filled a vacuum by the exercise of his or her prerogative rights through the Governor-General. Based on this reasoning, Jennings concluded that the prerogative had never been abolished, but had remained in abeyance since the eighteenth century, during which time India was ruled by statute.[28]

Even if he were correct on the continued existence of the Crown's prerogative in Pakistan, Jennings knew that prerogative rights could not be exercised in the absence of a legislature, and he was concerned that there was no statute authorizing the calling of a new Constituent Assembly.[29] Jennings found his answer in the reign of William and Mary. With the flight of James II in 1688, there was no longer a monarch and there was also no legitimate Parliament. The Parliament which William and Mary summoned was not summoned by a lawful monarch. Jennings reasoned, 'logically there could be no Parliament because there was no monarch and no monarch because there was no Parliament, but logic must bow to necessity...'[30]

This solution, worked out to resolve the crisis of William and Mary in the seventeenth century, Jennings saw as passing into English Common Law and thence into the Common Law of Pakistan. The prerogative rights of the Crown, therefore, encompassed the power to call a new legislature in Pakistan. 'The problem of Pakistan is simple,' advised Jennings. 'It has a monarch, whose functions have lawfully been delegated to the Governor-General. It is not merely within the power of the Queen to fill the lacuna: it is her duty to do so. However tenuous the relations may be, and however anxious the citizens of Pakistan may be to break the bond, the people of that country are British subjects owing allegiance to the Queen and therefore entitled to peace, order and good government, through the instrumentality of her deputy, the Governor-General.'[31]

So strong did Jennings find this line of reasoning that it carried him to the point of asserting that the Queen had even greater power in independent Pakistan than she had in England, because Pakistan had been conquered territory and therefore the Crown was not faced with the traditional limitations placed on it at home. As satisfactory as Jennings found this theory, he was apprehensive about having to rely on the prerogative of the Crown, knowing that that argument contradicted the belief held by Pakistanis that they had won full independence and that the British were no longer involved in their government.[32]

Jennings concluded that the prerogative rights of the Crown, regardless of what description or scope was attributed to those rights, were to be exercised under the terms of the Indian Independence Act by the Governor-General, and those prerogative rights would enable him to call a new Assembly. But Jennings still had the task of justifying the dissolution of the old Assembly.[33] On this point he could not rely on the events following the flight of James II, because William and Mary bore no responsibility for dissolving the old Parliament. In contrast, Ghulam Mohammad was responsible for the Assembly's dissolution. He was asking Jennings to find a justification to counter Tamizuddin Khan's public charge that it was because there was nothing in the constitution which allowed a Governor-General to dissolve the Assembly that Ghulam Mohammad had not actually stated in his proclamation that the Assembly was dissolved.

Jennings found a way out of this quandary. He believed that the Indian Independence Act gave the Governor-General the right to assent to all legislation of the Constituent Assembly.[34] The Assembly in the past had amended the dominion constitution to provide for additional Assembly seats, and had done so without obtaining the Governor-General's assent to such legislation.[35] As a result, in Jennings' opinion, the Constituent Assembly changed its nature and therefore ceased to exist as a result of its unconstitutional action. 'There is no reason,' Jennings advised Ghulam Mohammad, 'to ask whether the Governor-General's Proclamation of 24 October 1954 dissolved the Constituent Assembly, no such Assembly was in existence.'[36] Jennings did, however, note a weakness in his position. There was no time limit which attached to assent. It could, therefore, be given now for past Acts. Jennings, however, did not dwell further on this point. He was satisfied that the Assembly had changed its composition without assent and therefore did not exist at the time Ghulam dissolved it.

A ruling that the Constituent Assembly did not exist not only would have immediate consequences affecting the operation of the government, it would also involve departure from the convention followed in England and Pakistan by which the courts refrained from passing on the legality of anything done by the sovereign power. In England, Parliament possessed that sovereignty, and in Pakistan it resided in the Constituent Assembly. Jenings' argument would have required a court to hold that the legislation of the Constituent Assembly, creating new seats by amending the Government of India Act, was invalid. No court had exercised such power in Pakistan. A court could give effect to Jennings' argument and exercise the power to invalidate the questioned legislation only if the Constituent Assembly was not a sovereign body.

Jennings' argument would also have expanded the assent powers of the Governor-General in contradiction to existing constitutional convention. In the time of Jinnah, the Constituent Assembly had established the practice that a statute legislating a constitutional enactment, such as the one amending the constitution to add Assembly seats, did not require the assent of the Governor-General. In effect, the disregarding of the existing practice dealing with assent would do away with a convention of the constitution which Pakistan had chosen to establish for itself. While part of Pakistan's constitution was written in the Government of India Act and the Indian Independence Act, like the constitutions of England and the other dominions much of the constitution was developed by practice and was unwritten. Conventions were a part of all of these constitutions, a part without which the constitutions could not operate. Conventions were so integral to the constitutions of the United Kingdom and the nations of the Commonwealth that they have been called 'the motor part of the constitution'.[37] '[N]either statute nor prerogative, that is common law, explains much that is vital in the governing of the Dominions. That governing rests essentially, as in the United Kingdom, on conventions of the constitution...'[38] The office of Prime Minister, the requirement that the monarch and the Governor-General act only on the advice of ministers who have the confidence of Parliament or the Assembly, the existence of the Crown prerogative, and the restraint of the courts in not invalidating parliamentary or Assembly enactments, are but four of the many examples of constitutional conventions. Jennings was to contradict himself in Pakistan. Nineteen years earlier he had written in his *Cabinet Government* that 'conventions were not only followed but they have to be followed.'[39] This was not the advice that he gave to Ghulam Mohammad. Instead, he considered Pakistan's constitutional convention dealing with the Governor-General's assent to legislation but chose to override it with the English constitutional convention of Crown prerogative.

The atmosphere in Karachi was tense when Tamizuddin Khan's case was called before the Sindh Chief Court. It was now two months since the Assembly had been dissolved. Ghulam Mohammad had begun moving immediately after the Assembly's dissolution to obtain support from the provincial Assemblies in West Pakistan for his One Unit Plan. The members of these Assemblies were well aware of how the ministry in East Bengal had been extinguished by the central government only months before. Members who opposed the idea of West Pakistan unity were threatened with arrests, and opposition to the unification plan, which had been strong in the smaller provinces, evaporated. Enough force had been used by Ghulam Mohammad in the preceding year and a half to give him a ruthless public image. In the general population there was fear of him and respect for the forces he commanded.

On the opening day of the hearing of Tamizuddin Khan's petition, the courtroom was filled to capacity. The newspapers reported that many citizens sat on their prayer mats in the open space before the Pantheon-domed Sindh court building. Tamizuddin Khan was represented by D. N. Pritt, S. S. Pirzada and I. I. Chundrigar.[40] Jennings appeared as adviser to the government's counsel. At the opening of the court session, Jennings was questioned by the court concerning the rights of a Governor-General to dissolve a legislature. He responded that since Pakistan was a dominion, the Crown had the right to dissolve the legislature if it decided that the legislature no longer represented the people.[41] Since, however, Jennings considered this a political not a legal argument, he added that even if that power did not exist, the court did not have the power to grant the requested writs because the statute which established the court's jurisdiction to grant such writs had been passed by the Constituent Assembly but had never received the assent of the Governor-General.[42] Such assent, Jennings maintained, was required under the dominion constitution. When Jennings tried to continue, the Assembly's lawyers demanded the right to cross-examine him on what he said. They realized his constitutional theories would have great weight with the court. Rather than being subjected to cross-examination, Jennings refrained from making further statements to the court.[43]

As satisfied as Jennings was with the soundness of his position on assent, he was aware that no Governor-General from Jinnah to Ghulam Mohammad had ever raised the question. Since independence it had been accepted that the Government of India Act required the assent of the Governor-General only for ordinary legislation, not legislation which dealt with changes in or additions to the constitution. This constitutional formality of assent was carefully observed by Jinnah in structuring the government.[44] After independence Jinnah was both President of the Constituent Assembly and Governor-General. Under the constitution the Constituent Assembly had two distinct functions, the ordinary legislative function, previously the concern of the Federal Legislature of undivided India under the Government of India Act, and the function of legislating a new constitution. The Assembly met in separate sessions to carry out these functions.[45] It kept one set of records when it met as the ordinary legislature, and a separate set when it met in its constitution-making capacity to draft a new constitution or to pass interim legislation adding to or amending the existing constitution. Jinnah certified, as President of the Constituent Assembly, all measures passed in the capacity of a constitution-making body, and pursuant to the rules of that body, all such measures became law upon being published in the official gazette.[46] As required by the Government of India Act, Jinnah assented, as Governor-General, to all ordinary legislation.[47]

This practice of assent, established by the Constituent Assembly under Jinnah, had not been placed in question by either of Jinnah's successors in the office of Governor-General. Nazimuddin had been a member of the Constituent Assembly, and the third Governor-General, Ghulam Mohammad, had also served as a member of that body. Each was aware that, according to the Assembly's practice, the assent of the Governor-General was not necessary for constitution-making legislation. For the seven years after independence, each Governor-General, including Ghulam Mohammad, had carried out without demur the provisions of constitutional legislation passed by the Assembly without receiving his formal assent. In addition, the judicial branch of the government had considered the question of assent during those seven years, and on each occasion had concluded that the assent of the Governor-General was required only for ordinary, not constitutional, legislation.[48]

In his *Autobiography*, Pritt gave his reaction to Jennings' position on assent. 'I can understand most vagaries of lawyers and litigants, but I just cannot understand why a government, challenged as to the validity of some important action on its part, which must obviously be determined on its merits sooner or later, should attempt to win the case by a point which leaves the matter undecided on the substance, and thus leaves the whole constitutional position of the country in suspense.'[49] Pritt was referring to Jennings' reliance on one part of Section 6(3) of the Indian Independence Act which provided: 'The Governor-General of each of the new Dominions shall have the full power to assent in His Majesty's name to any law of the Legislature of the Dominion...'[50] The section, if used in the way Jennings advocated it be used, gave rise to the question of the Constituent Assembly's sovereignty. Did the assent provision of Section 6(3) mean that the Assembly could validly legislate the new constitution into existence only with the assent of the Governor-General, and was consequently less than a sovereign body?[51]

In its argument before the Sindh Chief Court, the government attempted to have the court first consider the necessity of assent of the Governor-General to all legislation. This would have enabled the court to dispose of Tamizuddin Khan's petition on the ground that there was no jurisdiction vested in the court to act since the amendment to the constitution granting jurisdiction had not received the Governor-General's assent. Jennings felt that this argument was very strong, and hoped that the court would be persuaded by it, thereby making arguments on the other issues of the case unnecessary.[52] The court denied the government's motion to limit argument to the issue of assent, and thereby forced an argument on the issue Jennings considered 'the great weakness in the case', namely, that there was no provision in the constitution which allowed the Governor-General to dissolve the Assembly.[53] Jennings' report to the government prior to the argument had contained the conclusion, 'The principal difficulty in this case is that there is no clear and definite legal provision under which the Proclamation of 24 *(sic)* October 1954 can be justified.' Jennings was troubled by the fact that the Constituent Assembly would have been dissolved on 25 December 1954 under the provisions of the new constitution. 'The question for the Court was whether the Assembly was to be dissolved by the Governor-General as and when he saw fit, or by the Constituent Assembly when it had completed its job.'[54] The government side was relieved when neither Tamizuddin Khan's lawyers nor the Sindh Chief Court capitalized on what the government considered the main weakness in its case.[55] The government relied on the prerogative of the Crown to vest the Governor-General with the power to dissolve the Assembly.

After oral argument in the Sindh Chief Court, a period of fifteen days elapsed before the issuance of the court's judgment. During this time Mohammad Ali Bogra was in New York. He had kept regular contact with Tamizuddin Khan during the litigation through Dr A. M. Malik, a member of the deposed Cabinet, and it was agreed that, if the ruling was in favour of Tamizuddin Khan, word would be sent by courier from Karachi to New York. Bogra was then to notify the Queen that the Pakistan government requested the removal of the Governor-General. Because of the concern about police interference, two couriers were dispatched to Bogra. They were sent separately as soon as courthouse 'leaks' made it apparent that the court would decide in favour of Tamizuddin Khan. One courier got the word to Bogra just as the judgment was announced in Karachi, but Bogra did not contact the Queen.[56]

The Sindh Chief Court unanimously decided in favour of Tamizuddin Khan. The judges of the court decided that the court did have jurisdiction, and that the actions of the Governor-General in dissolving the Constituent Assembly and appointing a new Cabinet were beyond the powers granted him in the dominion constitution. They restated the proposition that the Constituent Assembly was a sovereign body. In its opinion, which Chief Justice Munir was later to call 'a disappointing document,' the Sindh Court exhibited no difficulty in identifying and disposing of the issues in the case. Justice Bakhsh Memon concluded, 'I am unshaken in my belief that the Governor-General had no power of any kind to dissolve the Constituent Assembly.'[57] He called attention in his extensive opinion to the fact that, 'The language employed by the Proclamation (dissolving the Assembly) is somewhat extra-ordinary...It does not even say in clear and specific terms that the Constituent Assembly is "dissolved". Normally whenever any order is passed, it indicates the provision of law under which the power is exercised...Those responsible for the draft could not think of any provision of law.'[58] To Justice Bakhsh the proposition that dissolution of the Assembly by the Governor-General was not permitted under the Independence Act was 'simple'. In the written judgement of the court, Chief Justice Constantine found that there was no case in the senior dominions where dissolution of the legislature takes place except by expressed provision in the constitution.[59] Constantine continued, 'When we turn to sub-section (3) of Section 6 we find that the Governor-General's full power to assent...is not to be controlled by Her Majesty...The necessity of assent was required in the Government of India Act in respect of the Federal Legislature: no corresponding provision necessitating consent in respect of the Constituent Assembly was inserted in the Independence Act.'[60]

Their colleague, Justice Vellani, observed that specific powers and rights were not assigned the Crown in the Indian Independence Act or the Government of India Act as amended, and for this reason the Crown could not assume any role in Pakistan's affairs. It was clear to Judge Vellani that Parliament had intended that the Crown be excluded from the operation of the Pakistan Government.[61] As to the Governor-General's rights and powers, Vellani concluded: 'His Majesty's own intervention to give validity or force to the measures of the Constituent Assembly was not to be required. It is anomalous to say that the intervention of His Majesty's representative is required.'[62] On the point which so concerned Jennings, the right and power of the Governor-General to dissolve the Constituent Assembly, Vellani held that this power had specifically been taken from him in the Independence Act.[63]

The Sindh Court held that Section 6(3) could not be interpreted to limit the sovereignty of the Constituent Assembly, and therefore, as Chief Justice Constantine so held, Section 6(3) could not be read to require the assent of the Governor-General to validate constitutional legislation passed by the Constituent Assembly. 'The intent [of Section 6(3)] is not to create the necessity of assent where none has been prescribed.'[64] He understood the section to mean that where assent was made necessary, for example, by another section of the constitution or by another statute, Section 6(3) granted the necessary power to the Governor-General to exercise the required assent. Constantine approached the reading of Section 6(3) in the following way: 'The key to the interpretation of the Act is provided by the preamble—the independence of Pakistan. The purpose of Section 6 is to efface the supremacy of the Parliament of the United Kingdom, and to confer power unfettered by any control from the United Kingdom, upon the Legislature of the Dominion...'

The Sindh Chief Court held that the Constituent Assembly's purported dissolution was a nullity in law and both it and the office of its President were still in existence. The court issued a writ of mandamus restraining Ghulam Mohammad from preventing petitioner Tamizuddin Khan from performing the function of his office of President of the Constituent Assembly. The opinion was received favourably in the Press and among the members of the Bar.[65] The support the Governor-General had received when he dissolved the Assembly was eroding three months later because he had failed to make any further mention of elections. The favourable reaction was also based on the esteem in which Tamizuddin Khan was generally held and the respect which the public had for the courts. Nevertheless, no other Assembly members joined in the small group around Tamizuddin Khan, and there was little financial support forthcoming to defray his costs of litigation.[66]

The decision caused Jennings to re-examine his constitutional theories. The testing of those ideas in argument before the Sindh Court, the give and take of argument of counsel, the questioning of the judges, and the well-reasoned opinions of the judges, caused Jennings and the government's team to again consider the principal difficulty in the case, the lack of any clear and definite legal provision under which Ghulam Mohammad's dissolution proclamation could be justified. They reconsidered utilizing the argument that an emergency existed at the time of dissolution and the Governor-General's action, if not justified on the law or terms of the constitution, was justified on the maxim '*salus populi suprema lex*', (the safety of the people is the supreme law). But their further research did not change what Jennings had previously concluded.[67] Seventeenth-century precedent established that emergency powers could be used by the Crown only if the administration of justice had so broken down that the courts were no longer operating. Jennings again faced the limitation established after the *Shipmoney* case, allowing the arbitrary exercise of prerogative rights by the Crown only when war or civil disturbance justified military rule itself. Jennings' litigation report concluded with regard to the research of this issue: 'It was therefore decided that an argument on these lines could not be sustained, and that any attempt to produce so weak an argument would react upon better arguments.'

The government appealed to the Federal Court, Pakistan's highest judicial tribunal. Jennings considered that if the government was to win the case it would have to be the assent argument which would carry the day on appeal. He assured the Governor-General that he saw no weaknesses in this argument if it was considered strictly as a legal question. Nevertheless, Jennings admitted that there had developed what he termed the 'traditional' view of assent. 'For seven years everybody has been talking about the "sovereignty" of the Constituent Assembly...The government and Federal Court have assumed for seven years that assent was not needed.' In over one hundred cases, Acts of the Constituent Assembly had been assumed to be valid. He concluded, 'The fact that the "traditional" interpretation is wrong has therefore to meet a good deal of opposition and argument and has to overcome a good deal of passive resistance. There is a reasonable prospect that the Federal Court will come to the right decision but it would not be surprising if they took the wrong one.' But Jennings admitted ambiguity in the statute to the extent that it was '*possible* to interpret the Indian Independence Act to read that the Governor-General's assent was required only for ordinary legislation and not for legislation dealing with the making or amending of the constitution.'[68]

While Jennings continued his search for a defence, Ghulam Mohammad remained willing to have his dispute with the Assembly decided in the courts, but only so long as the case went his way. If the litigation did not go well in the Federal Court, the government was prepared to ignore the court's decision. In a memo to the Governor-General, Jennings wrote: 'In short there is a six-to-four chance of getting a favourable decision but it would not be very surprising if the decision was against the Government. The possibility has been foreseen and the necessary drafts have been prepared to carry out His Excellency's policy whatever the decision might be. All the documents needed have been drafted and they will be ready for immediate issue once the decision of the Federal Court is known, whether it is for or against the Federation.'[69] Jennings was referring to Emergency Ordinance No. 9 of 1955 which Ghulam Mohammad later issued after he won before the Federal Court. The ordinance allowed him to administer the country on an emergency basis.

When the case reached the Federal Court, the Chief Justice of the court, Mohammad Munir, called a conference of the parties to discuss the possibility of settling the case. He urged the parties to reach a settlement because, he told them, the issues involved were political rather than legal issues, better decided by the people through the political process.[70] Tamizuddin Khan responded to the suggestion of the court by proposing a compromise. The Constituent Assembly would meet, but it would not frame a new constitution provided that the Governor-General would call, within a reasonable and specific time, a new Constituent Assembly based on adult-franchise elections. The existing Constituent Assembly would then dissolve itself. Munir let it be known that he favoured this proposal as a basis for negotiations.[71] The government, however, refused to negotiate, Ghulam Mohammad fearing that if he allowed the Assembly to meet they might not consider themselves bound by any agreement reached with Tamizuddin Khan.[72] This refusal was criticized in the Press, and Munir expressed disapproval of the government, which he saw as obliging the court to decide the case because it had been filed, despite the fact that the issue raised was political rather than legal.[73] Later, during one of the initial court sessions, Munir again expressed his opinion to the counsel for the Assembly. 'This is a political case. You should have brought it to the *marches* (the people), but as you have brought it to us and we are seized with it, we will decide it.'[74]

Pritt did not appear on behalf of Tamizuddin Khan on appeal. Tamizuddin Khan and his supporters in the Assembly did not have sufficient funds to pay him a fee, and the members turned down Pritt's offer to serve *pro bono* for even this would have involved paying Pritt's living expenses. Most of the funding of the litigation was supplied by Tamizuddin Khan personally. He was a man of modest means, now without his income as Assembly President. The litigation was proving a financial burden for him. Two businessmen did provide limited financial help, and Chundrigar and Pirzada contributed their services and paid their own living expenses when the case moved to the Federal Court in Rawalpindi. Money of any significance, however, was not forthcoming from the members of the Assembly, and Tamizuddin Khan did not solicit any from them.[75]

Pritt's departure was a loss for the Assembly's cause. He had the ability to grasp issues rapidly and present them in an energetic way to the court. Coming as he did with an international reputation, not only was he able to ward off any badgering from the court, as one might expect from Munir, but his presence served to attract attention to the Assembly's cause outside of Pakistan. The Assembly's case would now be argued by Chundrigar. He had served as governor of West Punjab at a time when Munir was chief judge of the Punjab High Court and they were on a friendly basis. He was capable but not as effective in arguing to the court as Pritt had been. Pirzada's background in constitutional law would be an asset, but as junior counsel he would not be arguing the case to the court.

The government brought in Sir Edward Diplock, Q. C. (later Lord Diplock) to argue its case. Diplock was of a friendly and outgoing nature in contrast to the taciturn Jennings, and his calm, measured presentation of his argument to the court was in marked contrast to Pritt's style. Jennings was in court each day and drafted the arguments which Diplock as barrister was to argue. It was quite clear from what was said in the government strategy conferences and from casual remarks made outside the courtroom that Diplock did not agree with all of Jennings ideas[76] but these ideas proved to have great weight in court. Nasim Hassan Shah, who later became Chief Justice of the Pakistan Supreme Court, had just returned from earning a doctorate in political science from the Sorbonne and joined the government's team as a junior member. There was little need for him to research the constitution and historical issues raised.[77] Not only had Jennings and Diplock brought from England most of the materials they were to use in argument to the court, but Jennings had written the most widely known work on cabinet government and had written many of the most authoritative constitutional works used in the Commonwealth. Much material which Diplock cited to the court was not available in Pakistan libraries. This was a formidable team Chundrigar and Pirzada faced.

Although the prayers of the *muezzin* sounded outside the Federal Court in Rawalpindi when the full bench convened in April 1955, nothing in the courtroom served as a reminder that this was a land of Islam. Punctured by what Munir terms the 'sonorous sounds of Latin,' the argument of distinguished counsel was a battle Munir claimed to be 'the greatest ever fought in legal history'. Jennings, with a bit more perspective and restraint, described the issues as 'fundamental principles of constitutional law of interest throughout the Commonwealth'.[78] Each day for a fortnight, the courtroom overflowed with spectators, all of whom were aware that the most important case in Pakistan's history was being argued. The audience reflected the anxiety of the nation. Munir later described the scene. 'The whole attention of the country was rivetted on the litigation before the Federal Court which instead of going back to the Koran and Sunnah was going back to England, to the days of Bracton and Lord Mansfield, and was engaged in expounding the traditions of democracy, and the Crown's prerogative in the British Colonies, possessions and dominions.'[79] What was argued before Munir and his colleagues in robes and wigs involved an attempt to define the nature and scope of the Commonwealth in the mid-1950s.

The court heard seven days of argument by counsel. At the conclusion of the final argument, the Justices assembled in conference. Chief Justice Munir planned a press release announcing the decision of the court. He had hoped the decision would be unanimous, but there was one dissenter. Justice A. R. Cornelius arrived at a different conclusion from the one reached by Munir. Cornelius had made a career in the judicial branch of the Indian Civil Service and had served as Law Minister in Liaquat's Cabinet in 1951. He was convinced that Ghulam Mohammad had pressured and influenced the other Justices during the time the case was being argued before the court.[80] Munir inquired: 'Well, Cornelius, have you considered your decision?' Cornelius replied: 'I have tried to persuade myself but have failed to persuade myself to find with the opinion of Your Lordship.'[81]

After the conference Munir wrote the majority opinion of the court to which Cornelius wrote a dissent.[82] Munir, like Jennings, was not able to find in the dominion constitution any empowerment of the Governor-General which allowed his dissolution of the Constituent Assembly. But this he dismissed as a 'lacuna' in the Independence Act. He insisted that to understand the role of Pakistan's Governor-General it was necessary to go 'far back in history and to trace the origin and development of the British Empire itself'. Proceeding to do so, he started with the principle that all acquisition of territory by British subjects, whether by cession, conquest, or settlement, was on behalf of the Crown. At this point the Crown's prerogative was unlimited. Thereafter, the right to legislate for an acquired territory was vested in Parliament by the transfer of that right by the Crown, with the reservation of prerogative rights, however, remaining with the Crown. Exercising this delegated right to legislate, Parliament had provided constitutions for each of the senior dominions. The one exception was Ireland, which framed its own constitution, later approved by the British Parliament. With that exception, the constitutions of all of the senior dominions provided that the Crown's prerogative rights would be exercised in the dominion through the Governor-General, who was appointed by the Crown on the advice of the King's ministers and was responsible to His Majesty's Government.

In 1931, Parliament enacted the Statute of Westminster. The preamble of that statute stated that dominions were 'autonomous communities within the British Empire, equal in status, in no way subordinate one to another in any respect of their domestic or internal affairs, though united by a common allegiance to the Commonwealth of Nations'. The Governor-General remained the representative of the Crown in a dominion but acted on the advice of his dominion ministers.

Meanwhile, India's constitutional development followed its own path. The Government of India Act 1919 had given a measure of responsible government to the provinces which was extended in the Government of India Act of 1935. But the latter Act did not change the control exercised by Parliament over the executive and legislative functions of the Government of India. That control was not removed until 1947, when Parliament enacted the Indian Independence Act. This transfer of the right to legislate from Parliament to the new dominions of India and Pakistan, Munir saw as in no way different from the earlier constitutional developments which had taken place in the senior dominions. Consequently, to him the Independence Act did not affect the Crown's prerogative rights, which were exercised after independence by the Governor-General as the representative of the Queen. According to Munir, the Governor-General, as representative of the Crown, remained a part of the legislature because that was historically his position in the senior dominions, and Pakistan and India, being dominions, were in no different position in this respect.

To Munir, British rule did not entirely leave Pakistan at independence. Remaining behind were the prerogative rights of the English Crown which were to be exercised by the Governor-General. Munir acknowledged that this might appear to most people to contradict independence itself. No so, he argued. The prerogative rights might be British, but the Governor-General was Pakistani and, as was shown in the senior dominions, being a dominion meant that the nation was autonomous. And besides, restrictions on a dominion's independence could always be eliminated by following India's example and voting to cease being a dominion.

According to Munir, the independence Jinnah gained for his country was restricted by the prerogative rights of the English Crown. He adopted the argument made to the court by Diplock that Pakistan did not become independent in 1947. It had attained a status like the senior dominions, 'virtually indistinguishable from independence'.[83] As a dominion, Pakistan possessed the power to become fully independent by the Constituent Assembly voting to end dominion status. Since the Assembly had never so voted, Pakistan's independence, according to Munir's reasoning, was incomplete. Pakistan therefore remained subject to the prerogative rights of the Crown. The leaders who gained independence in Pakistan and India in 1947 could have opted, as did Burma, for complete independence. Instead, they chose to enter what Munir referred to as a 'gentlemen's agreement' and accepted dominion status.[84] 'And if the legal incidence of association with the Commonwealth under a common head hurt their pride or was offensive to their sensibilities, and the Constituent Assembly shared that feeling, it could have done away with all these so-called indices of inferiority within a day...The Constituent Assembly was unwilling to take big decisions, and they can hardly have any grievances if, on the present occasion, the position is restated to them.'[85]

The independent dominion status referred to by Parliament in the Independence Act was intended, thought Munir, to distinguish Pakistan from the senior dominions, which like Pakistan were autonomous in that they had the right to govern themselves, but which were not as independent as Pakistan because of clauses in the Statute of Westminster which rendered them incompetent to change their constitutions by unilateral legislative action. Any changes in the constitutions of the senior dominions could be effective only with the consent of Parliament. Pakistan's independent status did not, however, affect the allegiance which Pakistan, as a dominion in the Commonwealth, owed to the Crown. Citing the seventeenth-century English case, *Postnati*,[86]

Munir saw allegiance arising from the fact that the citizens of all of the dominions were British subjects. This was not only a personal connection between citizen and Crown; it also defined the relationship among the states themselves. To Munir, it was this allegiance which bound the Commonwealth members together. Membership in the Commonwealth could be severed by a dominion but it could not be severed unilaterally. Severance required the consent of the United Kingdom and all of the other dominions in the Commonwealth. The Statute of Westminster had made the Crown the symbol of the free association which existed among the Commonwealth members without changing the Crown as the object of allegiance owed by all the subjects of a dominion. Munir acknowledged, however, that allegiance was not indispensable for Commonwealth membership. This was demonstrated by India maintaining its membership in the Commonwealth after it became a republic.

Jinnah had specifically changed the oath of Pakistan's Governor-General. He and his successors, Nazimuddin and Ghulam Mohammad, recited the oath: 'I do solemnly affirm true faith and allegiance to the Constitution of Pakistan... and I will be faithful to His Majesty...'[87] Munir's reasoning on this wording was that, while allegiance is sworn to the Constitution and not the Crown, '...if allegiance to the Crown is a necessary incident to the Constitution of Pakistan, then allegiance to the Constitution obviously implies allegiance to the Crown. Further, it does not make the slightest difference whether the Queen is described as the Queen of Pakistan or the Head of the Commonwealth of which Pakistan is a member.'[88] Allegiance to the Crown was, according to Munir, intact in Pakistan and so was the exercise of the Crown's prerogative. Munir saw examples of the exercise of this prerogative when the Governor-General appointed, in the name of the Crown, the Commander-in-Chief of the armed forces, the commissions of all military officers, members of the civil service, appointed judges of the Federal and High Courts, and ambassadors, and assented to ordinary legislation. Munir pointed out that even the court writs which were petitioned for by Tamizuddin Khan, if issued, would bear the Royal Coat of Arms.

Munir then turned to the path which had been laid out by Jennings, the necessity of the Governor-General's assent to legislation as justification for Ghulam Mohammed's dissolution of the Assembly. It was on this point that Munir based his decision in the case. He pointed out that it was a body called the Legislature of the Dominion, not the Constituent Assembly, which had been vested by the Indian Independence Act with the entire power to make laws. The legislature of the Dominion did not actually exist, but would be created by the vote of the Constituent Assembly, presumably after the Assembly adopted a new constitution in which the yet-to-be-decided makeup, powers, and duties of the Legislature of the Dominion would be set out. Until this new legislature was voted into existence by the Assembly, the Independence Act provided that all legislation was to be enacted by the Assembly.[89] From this fact Munir reasoned that any right to legislate exercised by the Assembly could only be derived from the right to legislate vested by the Act in the Legislature of the Dominion. The yet-to-be-created Legislature of the Dominion was significant to Munir because, under Section 6(3) of the Independence Act, the Governor-General was given the 'full power to assent to any law of the Legislature of the Dominion'. He concluded that since constitution-making was done by Assembly legislation, it followed that the Governor-General's assent which applied to the Legislature of the Dominion also applied to the Constituent Assembly and, therefore, to all of its legislation, constitutional and otherwise. In Munir's opinion there was no ambiguity in the Independence Act. Its requirement on assent was clear and simple. Although it had not been followed in the past, what he considered to be the only correct reading of Section 6(3) was, he believed, binding on the court.[90]

The conclusion reached by Justice Cornelius in his dissenting opinion was entirely different.[91] To him, it was irrelevant to compare the Assembly with the Legislature of the Dominion because of the fact that the latter did not exist and was not even described in the Independence Act. It was a name only. It would come into being only if the Assembly chose to vote it into existence, a step the Assembly had no duty to take but could instead exercise its constitutional power to create a substitute. In contrast, the Assembly was in existence and had been created in the Independence Act as a sovereign legislature equal to the British Parliament which had given it life.

Cornelius answered Munir's interpretation of Commonwealth history with his own understanding of the meaning of a dominion.

He maintained that the important historical fact was that Pakistan had been created with complete independence, and he pointed to what he believed to be clear differences in the status of the senior dominions and the new dominion of Pakistan. The Statute of Westminster had declared the senior dominions autonomous and equal nations, but Justice Cornelius pointed out that equality existed only among the dominions themselves. When the Commonwealth was referred to as a free association of free people, 'free people' had to be understood in a qualified sense. The dominions enjoyed the advantage of representative government according to the British pattern, but the senior dominions were not equal and free *vis-a-vis* the English Crown. In that relationship their status was one of allegiance. Further, the King was part of the legislature of each of the senior dominions, made so by specific provisions of their constitutions. Their Governors-General, unlike the Governor-General of Pakistan, while obliged to act on the advice of the local ministers, were in addition subject to Crown Instructions. Also of significance was the fact that the senior dominions could not change their constitutions without the approval of the Parliament.

Cornelius stressed that Pakistan was not just a dominion but an independent dominion. As such, the Crown had no presence in Pakistan, played no role in its legislative process, and Pakistan owed no allegiance to the Crown. In the Indian Independence Act, Britain, bowing before the strength of 'Quit India' and acknowledging her own weakness, had left the subcontinent. The Independence Act stated in unequivocal terms that 'His Majesty's Government would have no further responsibility in Pakistan.'[92] A similar statement had never been made by the British concerning the senior dominions. Furthermore, Pakistan professed no allegiance to the Crown, and the Queen was not the Queen of Pakistan as she was for the senior dominions. She was acknowledged in Pakistan only as the Head of the Commonwealth, significant as a symbol. As Cornelius expressed it, 'Her Majesty is indeed a mere symbol, although as Queen of Pakistan a more substantial position might perhaps have been claimed.'[93] The Crown had been removed from Pakistan's national legislature by the Independence Act, and that legislature was not subject to restrictions of Parliament. Also, the fact that at independence Pakistan was not incorporated by reference into the Statute of Westminster and made one of the dominions covered by that statute, demonstrated to Cornelius that Pakistan was intended to be a different kind of dominion.

Cornelius believed that allegiance had a definable meaning. The giving of allegiance made the giver a sworn vassal. He maintained that while this was a medieval concept, it was still apt when applied to royalty, and royalty continued to play a part in the senior dominions. The Statute of Westminster acknowledged the right of the senior dominions to self-government, but it did not affect the allegiance owed the Crown, which remained in the constitutions of those dominions. In contrast, there was no obligation of allegiance expressed in the dominion constitution of Pakistan.

Membership in the Commonwealth itself did not carry with it the concept of allegiance. To Cornelius, the Commonwealth had evolved into a club, and that club tolerated great divergence of status among its members. There were no club rules requiring allegiance to the Crown or any connection with the Crown beyond acknowledging the British Sovereign to be the Head of the Commonwealth. Cornelius supported his picture of the Commonwealth by citing the constitutional history of the Irish Free State, one of the dominions named in the Statute of Westminster. He recalled what the Irish Free State had done since the passage of that statute. It had unilaterally abolished the oath of allegiance to the British Crown (1933), excluded its citizens from the definition of British Subjects (1935), abolished the office of Governor-General (1935), and adopted a form of constitution (1937) which eliminated any reference to the Crown except to grant the Crown the power to act on behalf of the nation, on the Irish government's advice, in external affairs. Despite these actions, it was not considered by the United Kingdom or the other dominions that Ireland had excluded itself from the Commonwealth.

To Cornelius, by 1947 any concept of common allegiance to the Crown had 'become obscured to the vanishing point.'[94] This was certainly true in Pakistan and India, Cornelius reasoned. By granting independence, Parliament was reacting to the subcontinent's insistence to 'quit India', and the temper of the people was shown by the speed with which independent India framed a new constitution making itself a republic. But like Ireland, India accepted the British Sovereign as the Head of the Commonwealth.[95] Cornelius asserted it was general knowledge that the attitude of the people of Pakistan was no different from that of the Indians concerning the connection with the British rulers. This was clearly shown by Jinnah's refusal to accept the existing oath which required the Governor-General to bear 'true faith and allegiance to His Majesty'. It was significant to Cornelius that Pakistan's oath was different from the oath of allegiance which was taken by all of the Governors-General of the senior dominions. Instead, Jinnah and his successor Governors-General took an oath that required he should bear true allegiance to the Constitution and be faithful to His Majesty.

To demonstrate that the Crown was not present in Pakistan's legislative affairs, Cornelius quoted an earlier court decision written by Munir when he was Chief Justice of the Punjab High Court:

> The assent to the bills, however, is still given by the Governor-General to the Governors in the name of His Majesty but that is because the Crown is the symbol of the free association of the members of the British Commonwealth of Nations and not because His Majesty exercises any control over it in the form of revoking the assent or authority of the Governor-General or disallowing the act. The Governor-General is the head of the Government of the Dominion, and is there by reason of the will of the Government and not by the will of the British Government or that of His Majesty, His Majesty in such matters having no will at all.[96]

Cornelius did not agree with Munir that the Governor-General's right to assent to all legislation was so clearly expressed in the Independence Act that it could be read with only the meaning given it by Munir. To do so, one would have to overlook the previous findings of the courts and the practice established when Jinnah was Governor-General and which had been followed by all of his successors, including Ghulam Mohammad, and in all sessions of the Constituent Assembly. Cornelius agreed with the decision of the Sindh Court that the Governor-General's 'power to assent' was the grant of a capacity only and was not accompanied by any right or duty to assent. At best, the wording of the Independence Act dealing with assent was ambiguous, and therefore the practice of not requiring the assent of the Governor-General to constitutional legislation should continue undisturbed. In support of this conclusion, Cornelius quoted a noted American constitutional authority:

> ...Where a particular construction has been generally accepted as correct, and especially when this has occurred contemporaneously with the adoption of the Constitution, and by those who had the opportunity to understand the intention of the instrument, it is not to be denied that a strong presumption exists that the construction rightly interprets the intention.[97]

He then applied this reasoning to the facts before the court.

> ...Here, the greatest organs and agencies of the State have been consciously and unanimously holding a certain belief, and have been acting upon it in numerous respects affecting the most fundamental rights of the entire people... These circumstances should, in my opinion, furnish an argument of almost insuperable character, in favour of upholding what has been the practice hitherto in regard to assent to constitutional laws.[98]

Cornelius would grant Tamizuddin Khan the writs sought even though the legislation authorizing such writs had not been assented to by the Governor-General, because to do otherwise would be an insult to the independence of Pakistan. Cornelius believe that 'the question of assent by the Governor-General was purely a domestic matter for Pakistan to settle for itself; and the three great limbs of the State had settled it, and were content with the settlement for seven years.' Pakistan, Cornelius maintained, was 'an autonomous State, not an academy for the advancement of a particular school of political philosophy. It would be a denial of the autonomy of the State of Pakistan to declare that its opinion in this matter is wrong.'[99]

In March of 1955 the Federal Court handed down its decision.[100] It found in favour of the Governor-General and against Tamizuddin Khan. The order of the Sindh Court, allowing the writs nullifying the Assembly's dissolution, was vacated. No mention was made by the Federal Court of the Governor-General's right to dissolve the Assembly. Instead, Munir avoided the issue by resting the opinion of the court solely on the lack of jurisdiction of the Sindh Court to issue the writ, premising his conclusion on the single point that the statute amending the constitution and creating jurisdiction in the court to issue the writ had not received the assent of the Governor-General. Jennings' idea had carried the day against the reasoning of Cornelius. Munir asserted that assent was 'as necessary to the validity of legislation as the law which requires a document to be under seal or registered. It is a formality which cannot be dispensed with except by proper amendment of the Constitution.'[101] By insisting on this 'formality' Munir threw the nation into chaos. Most of the major legislation in effect in Pakistan became invalid for lack of the now-required assent.

CHAPTER 8

MUNIR AND JUDICIAL POLITICS

Chief Justice Munir played a crucial role in Pakistan's political history, dominating the court which would decide who would exercise the sovereign power of the state, the Constituent Assembly or the Governor-General. Like Ghulam Mohammad, Munir was a Punjabi. Born on 3 May 1895, in Patiala State, which now lies in the Indian Punjab, his grandfather was a Viceroy's Commissioned Officer in a Punjab regiment and his father a graduate of the Lahore Medical School who for part of his medical career served as a government doctor.[1] Munir took an undergraduate degree at a local college before earning an MA in economics and politics from Government College, Lahore, in 1916. After a short period as Professor of Economics in Peshawar and Sialkot Colleges, he earned a law degree from the University Law College, Lahore, and entered practice in Amritsar. He later moved to Lahore, where he practised before the High Court and taught a course in the law of evidence at his alma mater. In 1928 he began the writing of his *Principles and Digest of the Law of Evidence*, a task which was to take him seven years. During that time, Munir also carried on a busy and lucrative law practice. When his work on evidence was published in 1935, it won him recognition at the Bar as a serious legal scholar. That work was to have long life as an authoritative statement of the law of evidence, and its later edition is still available in public library collections of Pakistan law.

Munir made his entry into public life in 1937, at the time of the implementation of the Government of India Act of 1935. In his first government post he was charged with adapting existing law to the new constitution. His movement up the government ladder was rapid. The office of Assistant to the Advocate-General of Punjab was specifically created for him, making him the *ex officio* public prosecutor for the Punjab. In 1940, three years after entering government service, Munir became president of an appellate tribunal created to hear cases arising out of newly-passed income tax legislation. The appointment was controversial because he lacked experience with tax law. When his opponents seemed to be in a position to block his appointment, Munir was able to muster enough political clout to have his appointment approved by the Governor-General. In 1942, he was appointed Judge of the High Court of Punjab, an appointment which was also the subject of controversy. As Munir himself characterized the situation, there were some who thought he had been appointed through the 'backdoor', possibly referring to the strength of his political backing. Munir remained on the bench during the years of Pakistan's movement for independence and, therefore, did not actively participate in nationalist activities. Prior to independence, however, he did give a speech in favour of an independent Pakistan. Having violated the strict rule against a judge participating in political activities, he was reprimanded by the senior judge of his court.

After independence, Munir came in contact with Ghulam Mohammad when, in 1948, he was appointed to serve as chairman of a commission to evaluate the pay-scale of Pakistan's civil servants, while at the same time, he remained Chief Judge of the Punjab High Court. Ghulam Mohammad was Finance Minister in Liaquat's Cabinet, and the appointment of Munir to the commission was within his jurisdiction. Pay for government servants had become a pressing issue for Pakistan because the new nation had inherited a pay-scale with many inequities which had arisen during the time of British rule. Ghulam Mohammad had very definite ideas on the subject. As a strong advocate of free enterprise, he believed it was important that the best talents in Pakistan be attracted to the private sector. In his view a public servant did not need talent or imagination, but honesty and willingness to endure the humdrum existence of a public job. He was quite outspoken on the subject and the ideas he expressed were well-known in government circles.

Chaudhri Mohammad Ali, then Secretary General of Pakistan, held the opposite position on the subject of public pay. He believed that in an undeveloped country it was vital that the government have at its disposal the means to plan economic growth. This required qualified civil servants, and those servants could be attracted to government careers only if the existing pay-scales were revised upward. When Chaudhri Mohammad Ali heard that Munir's commission was going to adopt Ghulam Mohammad's ideas on government pay, he went to Liaquat and requested that the Prime Minister confer with Munir in order to 'put the problem in a balanced perspective'. Liaquat did speak with Munir, but to no avail. When Munir submitted the report of his commission, it reflected Ghulam Mohammad's opinions. The report stated that the committee 'did not think it to be the right policy for a state to offer such salaries to its servants as to attract the best available talent. The correct place for our men of genius is in private enterprise and not in the humdrum career of public service where character and a desire to serve is more essential than outstanding intellect.'[2] Not only did Munir conform to Ghulam Mohammad's position on the subject of pay, but he reported his conversation with the Prime Minister to Ghulam Mohammad, who came to the conclusion that Chaudhri Mohammad Ali had attempted to interfere in financial matters, the area Ghulam Mohammad considered his domain. Ghulam Mohammad felt aggrieved, but he had carried the day. His pay policy was put into effect through the instrument of Munir. It should be added, however, that this policy proved a failure and was reversed shortly thereafter by Cabinet action.

The Ahmadi riots of March 1953 played an important role in Munir's career. Munir, then Chief Judge of the Punjab High Court, was appointed to be the chairman of a two-judge commission to investigate the riots. The commission's findings, referred to previously, were published in what has become known as the Munir Report.[3] In the report, Munir was strongly critical of the political views of the religious factions which had participated in the disturbance, as well as those religious leaders who expressed their political opinions at the commission's hearings. The Munir commission held 117 hearings and compiled 2,600 pages of testimony. The report which was submitted to the government by the commission was a comprehensive summary of the political and constitutional problems associated with the creation of an Islamic state within western concepts of constitutional government. Mainly authored by Munir, and bearing all the characteristics of his clear writing style and intellectual grasp of broad social issues facing Pakistan, the report has been utilized by western scholars as virtually the sole source of facts dealing with the 1953 Punjab religious disturbances and their aftermath.

The Munir Report reflected the attitude of Ghulam Mohammad and Mirza that religious leaders should renounce political activity and that Islam be kept out of government. The report was effective in serving the central bureaucracy to this end. It not only discredited the religious faction in politics by denouncing that faction for the violence which had occurred in the Punjab, but it also contained a condemnation of the competence of the politicians, citing the inability of Daultana's Punjab ministry to react to what the report states could have been controlled as a local police matter. One observer, who was in Pakistan at the time of Munir's later appointment to the Federal Court, commented, '[Munir's] view in the constitutional crisis facing Pakistan as expressed in [the Munir Report] gave little justification for any fear that he will be inclined to view the prerogatives of the Crown narrowly.'[4]

Munir used the report to give a picture of how he viewed proper government conduct. '[This inquiry] has given us an opportunity to ask our officers, on whom lies the burden of administration, to bear this burden in the tradition of the steel frame, when we saw the erect figure of a district officer in the middle of an excited procession, a soft smile on a firm mouth, determination written on his face.' In 1913, Lloyd George had used the term 'steel frame' to describe the Indian Civil Service, than a preponderantly British institution. Munir's use of that term furnished a sharp contrast to the ministerial government in Pakistan which he saw as 'remorselessly haunted by political nightmares'. Munir wondered if law and order could not better be administered by some other form of government, implying that democracy meant 'the subordination of law and order to political ends'.[5] He revealed the importance of his roots as a former British government servant, roots which he shared with Ghulam Mohammad, Mirza, and Chaudhri Mohammad Ali, who controlled the central government after the assassination of Liaquat in 1953. To each of them, it was not democracy but efficiency in government, as they had experienced it under the autocracy of British India, that was the goal of good government. Munir shared their background and ideals. He approved of Ghulam Mohammad's dismissal of Nazimuddin, believing that Nazimuddin's alleged inability to cope with the law and order situation had provided a plausible ground for his removal. Munir never seemed to have been troubled by any constitutional questions raised by Ghulam Mohammad's action. Nor did he address the question of why it was necessary after the riots for the military to be so long and extensively involved in the government functions in the Punjab.

The questions raised by the Ahmadi disturbances soon reappeared before Munir in his judicial capacity. As significant as the Munir Report was, the case of *Umar vs. The Crown* had a longer-lasting and greater impact on the history of Pakistan. The case raised for the first time the question of the limits of the role to be played by the military in the civil affairs of the nation.[7] The imposition of martial law during the Ahmadi riots had resulted in a number of rioters being arrested, tried, and sentenced by Army boards convened for the purpose. An accused rioter by the name of Umar Khan was one of the persons sentenced by an Army board. He appealed his sentence in the Punjab High Court after the Ahmadi disturbances were quelled by the military. There were two questions presented by the case: granting that military action was initially justified by the facts, was military rule necessary for the period it existed, and was it necessary for military tribunals, rather than civil courts, to try civilian offenders such as Umar Khan?

While the demonstrators had been unruly and at times violent, they were not armed for insurrection, and, as the Munir Report had found, the protesters could have been controlled if the government had acted with ordinary police forces. During the disturbances, the civilian government kept functioning and the civil courts were open. Nevertheless, regulations were issued by the military that were applicable to the civilian population, and the military instituted tribunals to try civilians who were in violation of those regulations. The disturbances were put down six hours after martial law was declared.[8] Military rule, however, continued for a period of several months, and the military performed some of the functions of the civilian government, although there was no showing that the civilian government was not capable of handling these functions on its own. During the period of military rule, and while the civilian courts were open to try offences by civilians, Umar Khan, a civilian, was tried and sentenced to death by a military board for conspiracy to manslaughter resulting from a mob action during the riots. The sentence was later commuted to life imprisonment by the military commander.[9]

At the conclusion of military rule, the Constituent Assembly passed indemnity legislation, holding harmless all actions taken by the military during its rule, a common practice in most countries after the use of military rule. What was unusual about this indemnity legislation was that it also continued in force all sentences passed by the military during the emergency. Umar Khan appealed his military sentence to the Punjab High Court, raising the argument that the sentence imposed on a civilian by a military tribunal could not be kept in force beyond the termination of military rule. The conviction and sentence were upheld, the court basing its decision on the ground that the challenged *ex post facto* indemnity law was within the power of the Assembly.

Munir, in his written opinion, acknowledged that military law was not law but rules devised to deal with emergencies, and was justified only on the basis of necessity.[10] He also acknowledged that military tribunals were not courts but boards, having as their sole purpose the assistance they could render to the military commander during a disturbance. He recognized that in the precedents examined from other Anglo-American jurisdictions, no sentence of a military tribunal, such as the sentence received by Umar Khan, could continue in existence after the necessity for the sentence terminated with the end of the emergency which was the justification for military rule.

A point which is unexplained in Munir's High Court decision is its extensive citation of, but unwillingness to follow, the guidelines promulgated by the British during their rule in India to control the functioning of the military.[11] When military assistance was resorted to by the civil government in British India, the military was not allowed to assume civilian functions where such functions, including the courts, could continue to operate under civilian authority. In this respect, the British had continued in India the traditions followed at home. According to regulations, martial law was justified only when it was necessary to assist the civilian authorities. The nature of that assistance was to be measured by the need of the civilian authorities to meet the emergency. The rule was explained by A. V. Dicey and was quoted by the Jamaat-e-Islami in its protest against the way the Pakistan government had utilized military force against a civilian population during the Ahmadi riots.

> Martial law, in the proper sense of that term, in which it means the suspension of ordinary law and the temporary government of a country or part of it by military tribunals, is unknown in the law of England...Soldiers may suppress a riot as they may resist an invasion, they may fight just as they may fight foreign enemies, but they have no right under the law to inflict punishment for riot or rebellion. During the effort to restore peace, rebels may be lawfully killed just as enemies may be lawfully slaughtered in battle, or prisoners may be shot to prevent their escape, but any execution (independently of [law applied to military personnel or occupied territory]) inflicted by a court martial is illegal and technically murder.
>
> ...As necessity creates the rules so it limits its duration; for if the government (government by martial law) is continued after the courts are reinstated, it is a gross usurpation of power. Martial law can never exist where the courts are open and in the perfect unrestrained exercise of their jurisdiction.[12]

In *Umar*, Munir did not pass opinion on the issues of the military exercising civilian functions or the need to set up military tribunals when civilian authorities were operating concurrently and the civil courts were open. By giving no weight to those factors in his decision, he, in effect, judicially accepted for Pakistan a concept of military rule broader than that which the subcontinent had experienced under the British. Munir was not in disagreement with the principle that military rule is not itself based on law but on the absence of law, and that it is an expediency resorted to and justified by necessity.[13] In a society such as Pakistan which governed itself by the rule of law, the absence of law could be justified only by a state of affairs which threatened the maintenance of government by law, and the determination of the existence or non-existence of such a state of affairs is a question of fact within the exclusive province of the courts to determine. Whether such a threat exists, in other words, whether military rule is justified by necessity, is most decisively answered by whether or not the courts are open and operating. If they are, then the civil authority is capable of trying civilians, and the military tribunals are precluded from doing so because it is not necessary that they so function. This test is applied by courts throughout the Anglo-American jurisdiction.[14]

In his decision in *Umar*, Munir avoided the accepted principles of military rule by not addressing the fact that the civil courts were open and capable of trying Umar Khan. Instead, the court upheld Umar Khan's sentence, not by relying on the precedents found in Anglo-American cases dealing with civil disturbances, but instead, by citing cases arising from British suppression of the Irish and African peoples in the nineteenth century.[15] In the cases relied on, the British judiciary had allowed the colonial military authorities powers beyond those they would have been allowed to exercise at home or in other colonies during times of peace. Convictions of civilians by military boards were upheld by the Privy Council in several cases where civilian courts were functioning at the time of the trial and sentencing. Munir relied on cases which have been called 'forgotten episodes' which had 'provided a few fragmented rules'.[16] An American constitutional historian has commented on these cases, calling them 'harsh', and adding, 'the many vigorous protests from eminent legal authorities suggest that such measures are looked upon as usurpations and wholly out of harmony with the genius and spirit of English institutions.'[17]

Munir was utilizing cases which represented Britain the conqueror rather than Britain the law-giver. What resulted was a law of military rule in Pakistan not based on the restrained regulations for the use of the military which the British had found sufficient to control India. Instead, he relied on law which had arisen from the actions of the British authorities taken amidst the bitter armed conflicts with conquered peoples in revolt in Ireland and South Africa, and applied that law to his own countrymen in peacetime.

In *Umar*, Munir established the character of military rule in Pakistan. He did so by avoiding Umar Khan's plea that the civil courts were open and that he should have been tried there. Instead, he concentrated on the legal point of the legislature's right to delegate authority to the military *ex post facto*. Since the issue of the necessity of trial of a civilian by a military board was bypassed, necessity in effect ceased to be a pre-requisite for the use of military rule in Pakistan as it had been in British India. By negative implication, military rule now had the legal sanction of being an optional form of government.[18]

In June 1954, a brief notice appeared in the *Pakistan Times*.[19] It announced that Mohammad Munir, then Chief Judge of the Punjab High Court, had been appointed by Governor-General Ghulam Mohammad to replace the retiring Chief Justice of the

Federal Court, Pakistan's highest court. At the time of his appointment, Munir was probably the most prominent judge in Pakistan, because of both his legal scholarship and his court opinions. He was also well-known for his work on various committees, including the Radcliffe Commission which had determined the boundary line between India and Pakistan at independence, as well as his recent Munir Report.

The appointment had an unusual aspect. It was customary for appointments to the position of Chief Justice of an appellate court to go to the senior Associate Justice then sitting on that court. That procedure was not followed. Munir had on several occasions been offered a seat on the Federal Court as an Associate Justice but he had declined. He had actually sat for one month as an additional or acting judge on the Federal Court in 1952, but requested that he be allowed to go back to the High Court of Punjab. Although the Federal Court was the highest court in the country, it handled comparatively few cases. As Chief Justice of the Punjab High Court, Munir wielded much more judicial power than he would as an Associate Justice on the Federal Court. The Punjab High Court was a busy one and heard some of the country's most important cases. Munir also preferred being Chief Justice of the Punjab Court, which he dominated, to being Associate Justice of the Federal Court. A number of the Associate Justices on the Federal Court had earlier served under Munir as judges on the Punjab High Court and looked to him as their mentor. When the first Chief Justice of the Federal Court retired in June 1954, Munir agreed to accept the Chief Justiceship. He became Chief Justice after the senior Associate Justice of the court, A. S. M. Akram, a Bengali, wrote to the Governor-General agreeing to waive his seniority rights in favour of Munir.[20]

From his written court opinions, the Munir Report, and from his other writings, Munir was known as a person of wide intellect, capable of clear expression of his often strong views. He enjoyed the esteem of his fellow judges but was feared by many of the lawyers who appeared before him in court. Harsh treatment was often meted out to the advocate who displeased Munir by making what might appear to him an irrelevant argument. In contrast, he was jovial in social situations. Like Ghulam Mohammad, Munir was a man who often used rough language in private conversation. While domineering on the bench, he was considerate of his staff and exhibited an ability to change his mind when arguments counter to his own proved attractive to him. Through the strength of his personal character and his judicial ability, Munir was to dominate the Federal Court until his retirement in 1960, writing most of the major opinions of that court. From the day of his appointment, there was never a doubt as to where he thought the political power in Pakistan should reside. He was definitely the Governor-General's man, and his career before appointment to the Federal Court had demonstrated that he believed in strong authority in the central executive.

There are reasons to believe Ghulam Mohammad made it quite clear to Munir just what decision he wished the court to reach in *Tamizuddin*, and that he applied pressure on Munir to obtain the desired result.[21] According to a private secretary of Ghulam Mohammad, while the case was pending before the Federal Court Ghulam Mohammad communicated with Munir by coded written messages on a regular basis.[22] Delivery was allegedly made between the two men by one of Ghulam Mohammad's private secretaries. Ghulam Mohammad also made at least one visit to Munir at his home. He drove to Munir's residence in his official car with flags flying and escort. With *Tamizuddin* pending at the time, this was effective notice to Munir and the political community of the Governor-General's involvement in the issues which were pending before the court.[23] The visit caused comment in the legal community as it was a breach of the carefully-adhered-to rule of separation of the judiciary from contact with the executive or the legislative branches of the government. So strict was this rule of conduct in practice that the first Chief Justice of the Federal Court had declined to associate with Liaquat when he was Prime Minister even on a social basis. In later years, Justice Cornelius was to comment that the Governor-General had been effective in influencing not only Munir but also the other Justices who voted in the *Tamizuddin* majority.[24] It is easy to understand what Munir meant when he said years later that Tamizuddin Khan came to court with a case he could not win.[25]

There was no doubt in the minds of the Assembly's lawyers that in *Tamizuddin* the deck was stacked against them.[26] Four months before he dissolved the Constituent Assembly, Ghulam Mohammad had made Munir Chief Justice of the Federal Court, and it was assumed that Munir approved of Ghulam Mohammad and his policies. Munir also served as Acting Governor-General on one occasion when Ghulam Mohammad was absent from the country. The Chief Justice, however, was only one of six votes on the bench, and his ability to influence the outcome of litigation depended on factors other than his rank and forceful personality. When Munir joined the Federal Court, one of his protégés, Justice Mohammad Sharif, who had served under him on the Punjab High Court, was already a member of the Federal Court. This was a vote the Assembly's litigation team believed Munir could count on, but the court also had two sitting justices to whom the Assembly's lawyers looked to oppose Munir and Sharif and who it was thought would favour the Assembly's position on appeal. One of these justices was Shahabuddin, who not only was as strong-minded as Munir but had already taken a position on the question of the necessity of the Governor-General's assent to constitutional legislation. The Assembly's lawyers remembered that when sitting on a PRODA panel of two judges in 1951, Shahabuddin had ruled that the Governor-General's assent was not necessary for all legislation. Cornelius, the only non-Muslim on the court, was believed to share Shahabuddin's views on the question of assent. The other two members of the court were non-committal on the issues and not personally allied with either the Munir or Shahabuddin groups. Neither of the other two justices was considered to be strong. They were therefore viewed as 'swing-votes' by the Assembly's lawyers.

As the *Tamizuddin* case moved through the Sindh High Court, an unusual change took place in the composition of the Federal Court. Justice Shahabuddin was temporarily assigned by the central government to fill the office of Governor of East Bengal in the absence of the Governor. Such an appointment was unexpected because it was the practice to have the Chief Judge of the High Court of a province fill in for an absent Governor. Ghulam Mohammad replaced Shahabuddin with S. A. Rehman, who had served under Munir on the Punjab High Court and was considered by the Assembly lawyers to be a protégé of Munir's and very much under his influence. The change meant that Munir now commanded three votes including Sharif and Rehman, and Cornelius was isolated. With a three-to-one imbalance, and with Shahabuddin's strength absent, the Assembly lawyers now had to face the prospect that the fifth judge, Justice Akram, might be influenced by the power of the Munir camp, and would probably be less inclined to take a position against Munir now that it meant joining Cornelius who stood alone. The Assembly lawyers believed that Akram had earlier buckled under the Governor-General's pressure to step aside and allow Munir to become Chief Justice although Akram was the senior member of the court at the time. By the Assembly lawyers' tally, they faced the prospect of losing in the Federal Court by a four-to-one margin, a count which turned out to be the eventual outcome of the case.

Munir's behaviour during the oral argument in court was a noticeable feature of the *Tamizuddin* hearings. Nasim Hassan Shah, who observed the court proceedings from the government table, remembers Munir as being 'vitriolic' in response to Chundrigar's arguments on behalf of Tamizuddin Khan.[27] Pirzada, who sat at the Assembly table in court, remembers Munir as being 'less than dignified'.[28] Munir frequently interrupted Diplock during his argument on behalf of the government until Diplock informally mentioned to Munir, when they met out of the courtroom, that he was not accustomed to such treatment when he argued before the Privy Council, and politely indicated that Munir was interfering with the development of his argument. Thereafter, Munir let up on Diplock but not on Chundrigar.[29] His comments and demeanour toward the latter was such that Chundrigar considered resigning from the case.[30] Chundrigar had the ability to make a good argument but, as Munir well knew, was easily disturbed by questions or interruptions from the bench and tended to lose his train of thought. Munir's treatment of Chundrigar was unusual considering the friendly relations between the two men over the years, but it did serve Munir's purpose of demonstrating to the other members of the court how strongly he believed the government's case should prevail.

When, on 21 March 1955, Munir issued the court's decision at the conclusion of the case, it devastated the political structure of Pakistan. It has since been called '...a momentous ruling, one from which Pakistan has never fully recovered.'[31] Because the statute upon which Tamizuddin Khan had brought his case was declared unconstitutional on the ground that it lacked the Governor-General's assent, forty-three other laws, which had been amended or added to the dominion constitution since independence and which also lacked the assent of the Governor-

General, were likewise unconstitutional. As a result, the entire structure of Pakistan's government was affected. For example, the provincial legislatures were all improperly composed and, therefore, most of their legislative enactments were invalid; the provincial governors had issued 143 Acts which had the force of law but were invalid; the establishment of the State Bank of Pakistan, along with its power to regulate currency and exercise exchange control, were invalidated; and all of the many pre-independence laws of British India which had been amended to apply to Pakistan were invalid, as was Section 92A, which had been used to suppress the provincial ministries in West Punjab and East Bengal.[32]

There was no doubt in Munir's mind that his opinion would bring sweeping changes in the existing form of government. But, according to Munir, these changes were caused not by the Governor-General but by the Constitutional Assembly itself. Munir stated: 'If the result is disaster, it will merely be another instance of how thoughtlessly the Constituent Assembly proceeded with its business...[W]e have no option but to pronounce [the legislation upon which the writ was based] to be void and to leave it to the relevant authorities under the Constitution or to the country to set right the position in any way it may be open to them.'[33] After Ghulam Mohammad dissolved the Constituent Assembly he and his new Cabinet were the only 'relevant authorities' of the central government in existence.

Munir did not want to take on the question of the Governor-General's right to dissolve the Assembly; he therefore pursued what appeared the simpler path: he would accept Jennings' argument that the writs undoing the dissolution were invalid because the Sindh Chief Court's jurisdiction to issue such writs was based on a statute which, lacking the assent of the Governor-General, was unconstitutional.[34] But this approach involved a departure from the past practice of the English courts, which for centuries had not assumed the right to invalidate a statute of Parliament, recognizing that Parliament was the sovereign power of the state.[35] The Pakistan courts had followed that practice after independence, when it was generally assumed that Parliament's sovereignty had been transferred to the Constituent Assembly.[36]

Had the Federal Court of Pakistan continued to follow that practice in *Tamizuddin,* there would have been only a single question for it to answer: did the Constituent Assembly, by enacting Section 223A, the statute vesting jurisdiction in the courts to grant the requested writs, intend that such writs be issued under the facts presented to the court by Tamizuddin Khan? If the court interpreted Section 223A to indicate that such had been the Assembly's intent, the court's inquiry would be finished. Convention would obligate the court to allow the writs because, the Assembly being sovereign, any action by it was legal and constitutional.

Munir faced this barrier of precedence by declaring that the Assembly had 'lived in a fool's paradise if it was ever seized with the notion that it was the sovereign body of the State.'[37] With one sentence he swept away the sovereignty of the Assembly, the basis upon which Pakistan's constitutional government had been anchored since independence.[38] He also armed the courts with a powerful political weapon in the form of judicial review.[39] This new judicial power enabled a court to invalidate any law of the legislature when in the opinion of the court the law violated the constitution.[40] The judicial review exercised by Munir was rooted in politics.[41] Seven years after Pakistan's independence, he was following in the footsteps of Chief Justice John Marshall of the United States Supreme Court, who, fourteen years after America's independence, created judicial review.[42] It was a power not mentioned in the United States constitution. Marshall created judicial review by a 'stroke of political genius, salted with lawyerly adroitness.'[43] Like Munir, Marshall had conceived of a nation run by a strong central government with the states in a subordinate role. Also like Munir, he had developed a prejudice against the legislative process. Marshall believed that government should be run by and for the members of his class, the conservative creditor-capitalists who dominated the Federalist Party. Utilizing the power of judicial review, Marshall was able to carry out many of his ideas through his court decisions, broadly interpreting the language of the constitution granting powers to the federal government and limiting the powers reserved to the states. In the three decades after creating the power of judicial review, Marshall utilized it to implant his social and political philosophy in the early history of the United States.[44] A description given of Marshall could very well apply to Munir many years later. '[H]e saw the law as a servant, not as a master of the functions and goals of government and...he used the Court as a means of achieving the goals he was after however he had to bend or twist the law to achieve them. Scorning past legal precedence to fabricate his own, turning tiny technical points into rulings and far-reaching political principles, ...he ran his Court with a realistic gusto as refreshing in retrospect as it would be deemed improper, even indecent, today.'[45]

Munir and Marshall worked amid similar political clashes in their respective new nations. They were both Chief Justices who dominated their courts, both had strong political ties, and both were dealing with constitutional concepts applied in a period when institutions were in transition from colonial status to independent state. Munir was also able to introduce into Pakistan's constitutional and political history his own ideas of government. Like Marshall, he believed in a strong central government run by a strong executive, the civil-military elite which had emerged in West Pakistan.[46] Because he dominated his court, most of the significant decisions of the Pakistan Federal (later Supreme) Court were written by Munir until his retirement as Chief Justice in 1960, and reflected his political philosophy of a strong executive.

Because the opinions of Munir and Cornelius were lengthy, complex, and ranged widely in their discussion of legal and historical precedents, any public discussion of the court's opinions would have to originate in the comments and analysis of members of the legal community with the background to understand the issues.[47] But the issues discussed in the case were beyond the training of most members of the Pakistan Bar at that time.[48] In addition, Pakistan was without a body of legal literature, such as the law reviews and journals which are common in the United States, Great Britain, and the Commonwealth, and Pakistani lawyers and law professors were unaccustomed to writing on legal subjects.[49] Nor were there journals which discussed the theory or history of Pakistan's government. Jennings had brought books and documents from England, and used them to build the historical theories which Munir accepted in his decisions, and most of the materials relied on by Jennings were not available in Pakistan at the time.

The *Tamizuddin* case could have been discussed in letters to the editor, columns, or the special articles which were such a prominent part of Pakistan's journalism and which had been so widely used to discuss constitutional issues during the time the Constituent Assembly had been drafting the new constitution. But the dissolution was followed by a period of censorship, and even for those who understood the opinions and had an opportunity to express their views, there was the threat of contempt of court.[50] During this period, and for a considerable time after, any unfavourable comment about a judicial decision would have subjected the commentator to sanctions by the court for contempt. Munir had been a member of the Punjab High Court prior to independence when that court gained a reputation for using contempt powers freely.[51] There was private discussion of the opinions by some of the judges who were not members of the Federal Court, and some retired judges did let it be known confidentially that they disapproved of the decision.[52] But no judge would deem it proper to make public any comment on a decision issued by a fellow member of the judiciary, particularly when the decision was that of the highest court.

As a result of the legal community's silence, the public remained ignorant of the reasoning used by the courts to support the *Tamizuddin* decision. The Press, lacking a source of information which would have enabled it to understand what the Federal Court decision had done, was not surprisingly superficial in its comments. This was in marked contrast to the knowledgable discussions which had regularly appeared on the editorial pages and in letters to the editor during the time the constitution was being debated and drafted in the Assembly. During the time the court had the case before it, the East Bengal *Pakistan Observer* justified its opposition to the Assembly's case by generalizing that experience was 'a great principle in its own right' and that 'over and above the legal sovereignty of the legislature was the political sovereignty of the people.'[53] *Dawn* stated that it was satisfied that the Federal Court's decision had cleared the air and brought stability. The decision 'ends the state of suspense, silence, doleful prognostications and averts chaos'.[54] The *Pakistan Times* hailed the decision as a 'very healthy' one.[55]

Criticism did arise because of the continued failure of the Governor-General to call elections for a new Constituent Assembly and because of the greater powers he had assumed by executive order.[56] On his part, Ghulam Mohammad interpreted *Tamizuddin* as a green light allowing him to exercise unchecked power. He had already had his staff draft a constitution which provided for a head of state who would be assisted by ministers to be appointed by him. The head of state and his ministers would have broad powers and would not be responsible to the legislature.[57]

A week after the *Tamizuddin* decision, Ghulam Mohammad issued the Emergency Powers Ordinance which Jennings had prepared for him, in which he declared a 'grave' emergency in order to augment the emergency he had declared when he dissolved the Assembly, and which was still in effect.[58] The order granted him power to validate laws which he selected from among those passed by the Assembly but invalidated by the court, omitting the Acts passed in September by the Assembly curtailing his powers. He implemented his One Unit Plan, made provisions for a future constitution, and assumed the right to give the nation an annual budget validated on his signature alone. He also abolished the jurisdiction of the courts to entertain any action against the government arising from his proclamation dissolving the Assembly. All court actions, pending and future, brought in challenge of the dissolution proclamation, were quashed.

Ghulam Mohammad's Emergency Powers Ordinance was issued at a time when no central legislature existed and there was no indication that one would soon be brought into being, when the provincial government of East Bengal was suppressed by the central government, and while he was employing threats against members of the legislatures of West Pakistan to amalgamate the provinces into one unit. It was the exercise of complete authority by the executive. Although at first the Awami League and others had reacted favourably to the dissolution of the Assembly because they anticipated that it would soon be followed by Ghulam Mohammad lifting the ban against the provincial government in East Bengal, Ghulam Mohammad and Mirza disabused them of any hope in that direction.

Dawn expressed approval of the Governor-General's emergency decree with what may have been intended as sarcasm. It praised Ghulam Mohammad's actions, claiming that the One Unit Plan made 'romantic reading because it fulfils the romance of unity where diversity has been the canker in the rose. Like mist before the sunshine, let that diversity now melt, disperse and vanish.'[59] In contrast, while it disapproved of the Assembly as it was constituted, the *Pakistan Times* expressed uneasiness about the obvious violation of fundamental law by the Governor-General, and charged that he had 'virtually assumed the powers of an absolute ruler and the Government over which he presided is responsible to nobody'.[60] The paper interpreted his actions as having brought about a revolution and expressed fear of dictatorship.[61] In East Bengal, the *Pakistan Observer* echoed the *Times* in objecting to the Governor-General's intention to implement a new constitution on his own, and Fazlul Huq claimed that the country would not accept government by ordinance.[62]

The Governor-General's response to such criticism came through another Bengali, Suhrawardy, now Law Minister in the new regime. He threatened that opposition to the Governor-General would lead to revolution, a military-backed dictatorship, or martial law.[63] *Dawn* and the *Pakistan Times* admonished Suhrawardy, claiming such talk would undo what *Dawn* perceived as the good impression created by Pakistan in solving its constitutional problems by the rule of law.[64]

Within a few days of the court delivering its decision in *Tamizuddin*, the government received a surprise. The case of, *Usif Patel v. The Crown* came up on appeal to the Federal Court challenging the validity of Ghulam Mohammad's emergency order.[65] It was the province of Sindh and not the federal government which was the party in the case, and therefore the federal authorities had received no notice of the date when the case would be considered by the court. When the government became aware that the case was to be argued, a brief was prepared containing the arguments Jennings wished to have placed before the Federal Court on such issues as the scope of the Governor-General's emergency powers and Crown prerogative. Jennings was encouraged by the government's success in *Tamizuddin*, and sensing the favour with which the Munir court looked on Ghulam Mohammad, he began to reconsider arguments which he had previously discarded. The brief which he prepared was sent to Diplock, who was at the time in Lahore.[66]

Unfortunately for Jennings, *Usif Patel* came up for argument at the Karachi session of the Federal Court while Diplock was still in Lahore and the brief was on the way to him. The federal government's advocate who appeared on short notice in *Usif Patel* did so without having seen Jennings' brief. Chief Justice Munir rendered the court's decision after argument in *Usif Patel* invalidating Ghulam Mohammad's emergency order and indicating that the government was required to call a new Constituent Assembly.[67] But the decision was only a temporary setback for Ghulam Mohammad. In the same month that *Usif Patel* was decided, *Special Reference No. 1 of 1955* came before the Federal Court.[68] In that case, the government was able to have its full argument heard, and the court proved willing to grant the government everything it requested, undoing whatever inconvenience *Usif Patel* had created for Ghulam Mohammad.

Special Reference No. 1 of 1955, decided after *Tamizuddin*, furnished a further example of how Munir's court could accommodate Ghulam Mohammad in his consolidation of power. *Tamizuddin* had left complete executive and legislative power undisturbed in the hands of the Governor-General. The court, however, had reached this result not by finding that Ghulam Mohammad acted constitutionally. Instead, it had held that the Constituent Assembly acted unconstitutionally in granting jurisdiction to the courts without obtaining the assent of the Governor General for such a constitutional change, and, therefore, was without a remedy for the dissolution. But Ghulam Mohammad needed a ruling that would confirm that his dissolution of the Constituent Assembly was legal and that he could rule in the Assembly's place during the period of the emergency which he had created. With a large part of the country's laws nullified, such havoc wracked the legal system that a judicial determination on the constitutional issue of dissolution left open in *Tamizuddin* was necessary.[69]

Problems remained for Ghulam Mohammad to which Jennings' theories had still not provided an answer. The Government of India Act of 1935 had empowered the Governor-General in British India to dissolve the Federal Legislature, but that power had been removed by the Indian Independence Act.[70] When the Constituent Assembly was created by the provisions of the Independence Act, no mention was made of a right of the Governor-General to dissolve the Assembly. The Assembly, operating on the premise that it was a sovereign body which could be dissolved only by its own action, had passed a rule (Rule 15) providing the requirement of a vote of two-thirds for dissolution.

In *Special Reference No. 1 of 1955* Ghulam Mohammad asked the court for an advisory ruling.[71] The court interpreted the reference as stating three facts which the court assumed to be true: first, the Constituent Assembly had been unable to provide a constitution and instead made itself into a perpetual legislature; second, the Assembly had become totally unrepresentative; and finally, the Assembly had asserted that assent of the Governor-General was not necessary for constitutional legislation. The third asserted fact, the requirement of assent, had been decided in *Tamizuddin*. As to the second fact, the unrepresentative nature of the Assembly, Jennings had earlier concluded that it was a political question and not a proper matter to be ruled on by the court.

The first fact, the assertion that the Assembly had failed to produce a constitution, became the issue in *Special Reference No. 1*. Jennings, the person who had approved the final draft of the constitution, now through Diplock was in effect denying that the document existed. Munir knew that the provisions of the Basic Principles Committee Report had been approved and that all that remained at the time of the Assembly's dissolution was the final vote on the published form of the constitution. He had, prior to the dissolution, addressed the Lahore Bar on the new constitution. Now he was to decide a case based on Ghulam Mohammad's assertion of the fact that the Assembly had been unable to produce a new constitution.

Munir requested that the dissolved Assembly enter opposition to the Governor-General and suggested that they obtain the services of Pritt for this purpose, ordering the government to pay Pritt's fees and expenses. Pritt agreed although he was not convinced that the Assembly would receive a fair hearing. The Assembly litigation team members believed that Munir was determined to hold against the Assembly and that Pritt's presence was being used to give the appearance that the issues were argued fully and fairly. Pirzada and Chundrigar again served with Pritt. They entered opposition to Facts No. 1, 2, and 3, arguing that it was not possible for the court to render sound advice unless it evaluated the truth of the facts asserted by the Governor-General's request. They requested the court to allow them to challenge the truth of facts one and two. Munir denied the request on the grounds that the Federal Court was an appellate court, and fact-finding was not an appropriate function for such a court, stating that he saw 'nothing unusual' in employing the advisory opinion procedure instead of having the matter tried on the facts in a trial court. The result was that in reality only the Governor-General was allowed to present a case. The attorneys for the Assembly were prevented from offering their version of events and were limited to arguing the law using only the Governor-General's facts.

The Assembly's attorneys were aware of the one-sided nature of the advisory proceedings, and when the court refused to allow them to offer evidence to rebut the facts submitted by the Governor-General, they decided to withdraw their client from the case before a decision was reached by the court, in order to protest the unfairness of the proceedings.[72] Their intention, however, became known through the indiscreet statements made by a junior attorney of the Assembly's litigation team. Munir learned of their plans prior to issuing his decision and he attempted to thwart such a move by offering to the Assembly the right to file an affidavit of facts at the end of the hearing. On the record, this would have created the impression that the facts of both sides in the litigation had been considered by the court in reaching its decision. The Assembly's attorneys considered such an eleventh-hour production of evidentiary facts meaningless. Pritt and Pirzada were in favour of standing by their original decision to withdraw their client from the case, but Chundrigar thought such a move would be politically ill-advised. Chundrigar prevailed. An affidavit was filed setting forth the facts in opposition to the petition for an advisory opinion. Munir then decided the case, basing his reasoning in the decision on the Governor-General's facts as if they had been substantiated by evidence. Not surprisingly, the court rendered an opinion giving the Governor-General the advice the Governor-General wanted, based on the facts submitted by him.

What Munir decided in *Special Reference No. 1* can be briefly summarized.[73] He now acknowledged that the complete right and power to frame a new constitution resided solely with the Constituent Assembly, with no time limit set for the completion of this task.[74] Munir acknowledged that the prerogative of dissolution could not be read into the terms of the Independence Act or into the warrant of appointment issued to the Governor-General from the Crown. He reasoned, however, that while the Crown's prerogative powers to frame a constitution for Pakistan were replaced by the statutory terms of the Indian Independence Act, such replacement had to be understood to be operative only so long as the Constituent Assembly carried out this task in an expeditious manner. The words of the Independence Act, specifying that the responsibility for the drafting of a new constitution was vested in the Constituent Assembly 'in the first instance', indicated that an indefinite life for the Assembly was not contemplated.[75] According to Munir, the Crown's prerogative to dissolve the Assembly had been withdrawn by the Independence Act only so long as the Assembly performed its assigned task within a reasonable time. Only if the Independence Act were read to create the Assembly as a perpetual legislature could it be concluded that the British Parliament had intended that the Act was to replace the Crown's prerogative permanently.

Munir held that the British Parliament, when it enacted the Independence Act, 'never imagined that...the Constituent Assembly for Pakistan would beat the world record,' and for seven long years would not be able to introduce a draft constitution for enactment. To support this conclusion he did what he had earlier refused to allow the Assembly's attorneys to do: he introduced facts into the record. He reviewed the time it had taken other nations in the nineteenth and twentieth centuries to produce constitutions. Although known to him to be a fact, Munir disregarded the existence of the new constitution and accepted the Governor-General's claim that the Assembly had not produced a constitution seven years after independence. This justified, in Munir's view, the return of the Crown's prerogative rights to Pakistan. He reasoned: '...if the Assembly was unable or refused to perform the function assigned to it [to produce a constitution 'in the first instance,' IIA §8(1)], and on the contrary assumed the form of a perpetual legislature, the right in that event to dissolve it was not taken away by the Act.'[76] Munir held that the Assembly was rightfully dissolved by the Governor-General exercising those rights as the representative of the Crown.

Munir gave two other grounds which justified the use of the Crown's prerogative by the Governor-General to dissolve the Assembly. He concluded that the Independence Act could not be read to exclude the exercise of the Crown's prerogative if the Governor-General was satisfied that the Assembly had become unrepresentative, a point Jennings had previously concluded was a political question not proper for a court to decide. Finally, Munir adapted a variation of Jennings' idea that the Assembly could be dissolved even in the absence of any authorization for such dissolution because the Assembly did not exist. Munir found that, by illegally claiming from the time of independence that the Governor-General's assent was not necessary for all legislation, the Assembly 'never functioned as it was intended by the Indian

Independence Act to function. As a result, the prerogative to dissolve remained all along with the Governor-General.'[77]

Having established the grounds supporting the Assembly's dissolution, Munir looked to English history to justify the calling of a new Constitutional Assembly by the Governor-General, a subject not mentioned in the Independence Act. 'Before elections were regulated in England by law, the King exercised his prerogative right under common law to convene the Parliament. The number of knights, citizens and burgesses summoned, and the counties, cities and boroughs that were to return them were both determined by the King, and all election disputes were settled by the King-in-Council.'[78] Having thus established this as his starting proposition, Munir then recited details of the use of this prerogative right from the reign of Henry VII. 'I have gone so far back in English history,' wrote Munir in his decision, 'merely to illustrate the simple point that in the absence of a statute the representation of the Realm in Parliament was at the discretion of the King...which gradually developed into rights in Common Law.'[79] In 1947, according to Munir, the Parliament had used this prerogative, which had been surrendered to it by the Crown, to set up the first Constituent Assembly. 'That being the legal position, it follows that Pakistan being a Dominion and the Governor-General here representing the King for the purposes of the Government of the Dominion, he is possessed in this matter of the same powers as in the absence of a statute were or are exercisable by the King.'[80]

The Munir court next reconsidered the power of the Governor-General to rule by ordinance in the absence of a sitting legislature, the right it had struck down in *Usif Patel.* The court now examined the crisis of the nation after *Tamizuddin,* a crisis caused by the invalidation of forty-four constitutional enactments of the Constituent Assembly because they lacked the assent of the Governor-General. The court found that this result justified the use of emergency powers by the Governor-General, provided the Governor-General's powers be exercised only temporarily until a new Constituent Assembly could be convened. The emergency powers Munir referred to were not the emergency powers granted the Governor-General in the constitution, the use of which would have subjected his actions to the approval of the Constituent Assembly, but special and extraordinary powers he created for the present situation.

To support Ghulam Mohammad's use of these non-constitutional emergency powers, Munir found it necessary to move beyond the constitution to what he claimed was the Common Law, to general legal maxims, and to English historical precedent. He relied on Bracton's maxim, 'that which is otherwise not lawful is made lawful by necessity', and the Roman law maxim urged by Jennings, 'the well-being of the people is the supreme law.' What appealed above all to Munir was Cromwell's rationale, 'if nothing should be done but what is according to law, the throat of the nation might be cut while we send for someone to make a law.' Munir supported the maxims by making reference to a number of famous cases in English constitutional history dating back to the *Saltpeter Case* of 1606.[81] None of the cited cases, however, supported his position that the Crown could exercise emergency powers in peacetime or outside of the nation's constitution. Munir found support by following Jennings lead, and maintaining that the reign of William and Mary had been legitimate because of what he termed the Law of Civil Necessity. Relying on the proposition that the Crown, as part of the legislature, retains residual discretionary prerogative powers of acting in place of Parliament when Parliament is not in session because of an emergency,[82] Munir created a legal doctrine not recognized in Anglo-American jurisdictions but which was to have a continued life in Pakistan.[83] In later years, he attempted to distinguish his Law of Civil Necessity from martial law.[84]

It was in *Special Reference No. 1* that Munir made his claim that the court was building a bridge to save the constitution. Pritt, however, had a different interpretation. 'The Government won the point of procedure [in *Tamizuddin*], and had thus taken up the best part of a year not getting a decision on a vital and urgent constitutional matter but in preventing it being decided...We had a very interesting legal struggle [in *Special Reference No. 1*], but in the end the Court did not feel equal to deciding in our favour, and thus telling the government that it had not only acted illegally but had in effect been governing the country for a year or more against the constitution.'[85]

Ghulam Mohammad had seized the power of the state, and because the Constituent Assembly was denied a judicial remedy, the Governor-General's position as the ultimate power of the state was now confirmed. The new Constituent Assembly, which the court required Ghulam Mohammad to call, was not a sovereign body, and the Governor-General now enjoying virtual veto power over all of its legislation. It also followed from the court's decision on sovereignty that the Assembly could be dissolved by the Governor-General for political purposes. Nothing remained but the form; the substance of the government envisioned in the dominion constitution had been brought to an end in *Tamizuddin*.

The Governor-General called a Constituent Assembly made up of members who were to be elected by the provincial assemblies. It was to convene at the hill station of Murree on 7 July 1955 for the purpose of drafting a constitution.[86] Although *Dawn* saw this latest order of the Governor-General as getting the country 'back on the rails',[87] the *Pakistan Times* disagreed. It recognized that the Governor-General now possessed the power to dismiss the Assembly at any time because that power had not been denied him in the *Tamizuddin* case. According to the *Times:* 'A body which is created by an executive edict and lacks the people's mandate which can only be secured through a direct appeal to the entire people, would only serve to provide some sort of democratic facade for a structure with is essentially dictatorial.'[88] Although it had long been in the forefront of critics of the Constituent Assembly, the *Times* pointed out that the members of the new Assembly were elected by provincial legislatures which had been created after the Indian Independence Act. These existing provincial legislatures had no such mandate under the Independence Act, and therefore the new Assembly could not validly carry out the constitution-making tasks now being entrusted to it by the Governor-General. The only road to follow, urged the *Times*, was to reconvene the old Assembly which could reinstate the laws struck down as a result of *Tamizuddin* and which could pass a law calling for the election of members to a new Assembly.[89]

The Governor-General's move was also opposed by Munir's predecessor, Chief Justice Abdul Rashid, who considered the new Assembly unconstitutional because it was not in conformity with the Independence Act. In addition, the former Chief Justice considered the new Assembly legally defective because it was not a Constituent Assembly as understood in a dominion government, and it was only such an Assembly which was empowered by the Indian Independence Act to create a new constitution.[90] Suhrawardy, who had long been an advocate of dissolution, also had doubts about the representation of the new Assembly, recognizing that its make-up was a departure from the constitution.[91] In East Bengal, the *Pakistan Observer* editorialized that a constitutional convention would not be in accord with the Indian Independence Act and the proposed membership was unconstitutional.[92] Articles in the *Observer* agreed with positions taken in the *Pakistan Times* that the new Assembly would labour under the restriction of having to obtain the assent of the Governor-General to any constitution, that the Governor-General was now free from the constitutional restriction of acting only on the advice of his ministers, and that the new Assembly actually had little power and would be illegal.[93]

This Second Constituent Assembly experienced none of the delays which the First Constituent Assembly had encountered in reaching its 1954 draft of the constitution. The substance of the new constitution was agreed on in private meetings held among Ayub, Mirza, Gurmani, Khan Sahib, Suhrawardy, and Chaudhri Mohammad Ali. It was agreed that West Pakistan was to be integrated into One Unit, each wing was to have full regional autonomy, parity was to exist between them at the centre, and election would be by joint electorate.[94] A draft of the proposed constitution was drawn up by Chaudhri Mohammad Ali in the same form and with the same structure as the 1954 draft, which in turn had employed the structure of the Government of India Act of 1935. As with the final 1954 draft, the new draft was submitted to Jennings for his review and approval,[95] and on 15 April Bogra announced that the constitution was ready for submission to the convention.[96]

The 1956 draft appeared to provide for parliamentary government of the Westminster model, but in actuality it gave the President (formerly the Governor-General) many opportunities to exercise unfettered power. In reality, the Constituent Assembly would be allowed a role in law-making only so long as its activities did not displease the President. Under the new constitution the President would possess emergency powers to suppress the central government and Section 92A powers to suppress any of the provincial ministries. He would also control budgetary legislation to be considered by the Assembly, enjoy extended scope of political patronage, have assent over all legislation, which after *Tamizuddin* amounted to a veto power, and possess a right to dissolve the legislature.[97]

Munir's service to the executive did not end with Ghulam Mohammad. After Ghulam Mohammad resigned as Governor-

General and Iskander Mirza became President under the 1956 Constitution,[98] Munir soon established a relationship with the new leader. Meetings of the two men were infrequent but were described by Munir as 'informal and intimate'.

> When I used to be in Karachi either on my way to Europe for vacation or for a Supreme Court Session at Karachi, it was my practice to sign the Visitors' Book at the Government House, and I invariably received an invitation for a meal. Thus my relations with Iskander Mirza became more and more intimate, and whenever I happened to be in Karachi and he went out on hunting excursions, of which he was very fond, I was often asked to join.
>
> And as the present President [Ayub Khan] was then the Commander-in-Chief, was also a close friend of Iskander Mirza and was equally fond of shooting, he was always a member of the shooting party.[99]

Munir was aware of the significance of his relationship with Mirza.

> ...I had been a judge for six years before Independence but in accordance with the traditional requirements which governed the conduct of pre-Independence judges I had never sought or cultivated friendship or familiarity with any member of the executive. We were following the traditions of the British judiciary and strictly adhered to some generally accepted rules of conduct.
>
> In those days a judge was almost a social recluse. He hesitated in joining or going to a club, never sought an elective office, seldom attended a wedding or a private dinner and did not go about speech-making or addressing or participating in seminars, symposiums, debates, inaugurating or attending or presiding over every conceivable function. Cards he never played outside his house...
>
> I was conscious of the fact that being the head of the judiciary, it was not right for me to have such close associations with the head of the executive...'[100]

He offered the following justification.

> When Pakistan came into being, the shortage of manpower was acutely felt, and judges began to be put on different special assignments. Special assignments were entrusted to me, and I accepted them unhesitatingly, because I then felt that we could no longer maintain an attitude of detachment or isolation and whenever and wherever required had to put our shoulders to the wheel. It was this sense of duty that brought me in close contact with Heads of State including General Iskander Mirza.[101]

The relationship of the two men grew, Munir soon serving as an unofficial adviser to Mirza.[102] He fulfilled this function despite the fact that he was then Chief Justice and litigation involving the government was before his court. The relationship paid off for Mirza when he dissolved the Second Constituent Assembly in 1958 and placed the country under martial law. Munir and his court were available to place a judicial stamp of approval on what had taken place. Now, unlike *Tamizuddin* three years before, the power of the executive was so secure that no pretence was needed that the dissolution was constitutional or even based on necessity. In *Dosso v. Federation of Pakistan*, Munir found:

> It sometimes happens, however, that the Constitution and the national legal order under it is disrupted by an abrupt political change not within the contemplation of the Constitution. Any such change is called a revolution, and its legal effect is not only the destruction of the existing Constitution but also the validity of the national legal order...For the purpose of the doctrine here explained, a change is, in law, a revolution if it annuls the Constitution and the annulment is effective...Thus the essential condition to determine whether a Constitution has been annulled is the efficacy of the change...Thus a victorious revolution, or a successful *coup d'etat* is an internationally recognized legal method of changing a Constitution. After a change of the character I have mentioned has taken place, the national legal order must for its validity, depend upon the new law-creating organ. Even Courts lose their existing jurisdiction and can function only to the extent and in the manner determined by the new Constitution.
>
> ...If what I have already stated is correct, then the revolution having been successful, it satisfies the test of efficacy and becomes a basic law-creating factor.[103]

Munir found it acceptable to forget the old constitutional order and accommodate the court to the new regime. The justification for such a shift was successful revolution, which Munir later characterized as 'legalized illegality'.[104] To Munir, any *coup* was a revolution if successful and if, like the British Raj, it legitimized itself by its efficiency. 'This change is a political act beyond the proper scope of judicial opinion, which would be no more than "academic declarations" which could do nothing to change the event but could encourage civil war. Such a result would not only be harmful to the nation but would destroy the jurisdiction of the Courts.'[105] Munir attempted to garner respectability for his legal theory of revolution by claiming it was based on Hans Kelsen's *The Pure Theory of Law*, but Kelsen subsequently took pains to deny that his work could serve as a basis for Munir's theory of revolution, and Kelsen's theory was itself later repudiated by the

Pakistan Supreme Court.[106] Munir's decision in *Dosso* set the constitutional stage for Ayub Khan's 1958 military takeover of the government, which took place one day after the court's decision was announced.

Acceptance of government employment by judges after retirement was a matter of concern in Pakistan because the prospects of such employment could be a serious distraction from the impartial conduct necessary in the judiciary. There was a mandatory retirement age of sixty for judges. Some judges, fearing that their pensions would not be sufficient, looked to the government as a source of income after they reached mandatory retirement age. The adverse effect this could have on judges hearing cases in which the government was a party was a problem serious enough to be addressed in Munir's presence by the chief advocate of the Federal Court at ceremonies honouring Munir on his retirement.[107] These considerations, however, did not deter Munir from accepting a government assignment to Tokyo immediately after his retirement, or from later accepting a cabinet post in the Ayub administration. Munir acknowledged that the acceptance of a cabinet post by a former Chief Justice was 'somewhat odd', but justified his conduct on the grounds that he wished to aid in fostering the development of political parties and because times were 'not normal'.[108]

Munir remained on the bench until 1960. After the dissolution decisions, he was at first satisfied with the political changes his court had sanctioned. By the time of his retirement, however, he had departed from his position that the dissolution opinions were based on the law and English history. Those decisions faced growing unpopularity as lawyers came to understand the significance of the written opinions and the nation found itself increasingly under the hand of autocratic government. Munir began to shift the responsibility for what had happened away from himself. He attempted to exculpate himself in a speech to the Lahore Bar Association on the occasion of his retirement from the bench. At that time, he explained to the lawyers that his decisions were what lawyers call 'result oriented'. The term Munir used was 'pragmatic approach' to constitutional questions. His method, he claimed, was not to look to the law books on important constitutional issues but to look around to discern what reality was and base his conclusions not on what the law was but on what he thought it ought to be or had to be. Applying this approach, Tamizuddin Khan had been unrealistic when he challenged the Governor-General. Munir told his audience:

> The basic point that is not to be overlooked for a moment in [the dissolution] cases was that a forcibly-ejected ministry had come to a court of law for recognition of its right to remain in office and for obtaining from the court process for its restoration, and the [Sindh Chief Court] had issued enforceable writs against a *de facto* government.

Munir asked the lawyers: 'With all your experience and knowledge derived from textbooks and law reports can you recall to your mind anything even reminiscent of any such situation?' Although nowhere in his opinions had Munir expressed concern as to whether the writs could be enforced against the government, he now told the lawyers that had the court allowed the writs to stand, '...I am quite sure that there would have been chaos in the country and a revolution would have been formally enacted, possibly by bloodshed.'[109]

Later in his life he gave details as to what he possibly had in mind when he told the lawyers in Lahore of a revolution which would have been 'formally enacted'. He revealed in his writings that when the dissolution cases were being heard, he was impressed that Ayub Khan had publicly indicated his support for Ghulam Mohammad by accepting the post of Defence Minister. The growing restlessness of the Governor-General's power was also signalled to by Diplock, who in open court stated that military rule was being considered. This announcement came at the same time that Jennings let it be known that the institution of such rule would be justified under the circumstances. Munir attempted to ward off any implication that his judicial opinions had been political subterfuge, and were intellectually dishonest, by pleading for the sympathy of posterity. The mental anguish caused to the judges, he wrote towards the end of his life,

> ...was beyond description...No judiciary elsewhere in the world had to pass through what might be described as judicial torture...[W]ho could say that the coercive power of the State was with the court and not with the Governor-General? At moments like these public law is not found in the books; it lies elsewhere, viz.: in the events which have happened.

Munir reduced the erudite sophistry of his dissolution decisions to naught by his admission that Tamizuddin Khan had lost his case before he even entered the courtroom because 'the Governor-General was in possession of the coercive power of the State...'[110]

Chapter 9

PAKISTAN, THE 'UNDOUBTED FAILURE'

The police who barred the entrances of the Constituent Assembly's meeting place in Karachi prevented the members from casting their votes to formalize the new constitution which they had adopted in their previous meeting. On 28 October 1954, the Assembly, which until then had been an operating political body and had produced a new constitution, became a 'failure'. That is how Ghulam Mohammad branded it and that is how it has been remembered.[1] But it was the success, not the failure, of the Assembly which brought about its demise. It had succeeded in producing a constitution which was democratic and therefore unacceptable to Ghulam Mohammad. The intervention of the coercive power wielded by the Governor-General, not failure within the Assembly or defects in the new constitution, brought about the termination of parliamentary democracy. Because there was no doubt that under the dominion constitution it was the Assembly which had 'in the first instance' the right to produce a new constitution, it was necessary for Ghulam Mohammad to convince the public that the politicians of the Assembly had failed in their task. He accomplished this by Munir's decisions after the Assembly's dissolution. To Ghulam Mohammad and Mohammad Munir, demeaning politicians was an easy game to play. While politicians are essential in any free and democratic society, they are vulnerable. Democracy itself is a messy form of government, made up in large part of talk and clashes among competing interests. The political representatives of these interests are easily demeaned as bickering and self-seeking, many times appearing less stable or attractive to the public than the seemingly efficient bureaucrat or the soldier. Unfortunately, historians and political scientists often lack first-hand experience of working in a political process. From a distance, the day-to-day activities of a politician in a democratic society may appear to consist of little more than meaningless arguments, jockeying for power, and unprincipled compromises.

That is the picture of Pakistan's politicians that exists in the West. Although the reputations of Jinnah and Liaquat have survived untarnished, the images of Pakistan's other politicians of the period have not. Munir was successful in leaving the impression that it was the politicians who were to blame for bringing about the end of democratic government, a charge which effectively directed attention away from Ghulam Mohammad's destructive conduct. For example, the politicians are often derided for the fact that in the eleven-year period between independence and the military takeover by Ayub in 1958, there were seven different ministries, an indication of political instability. What is often forgotten, however, is that for over half that period, the six years between independence and Ghulam Mohammad's dismissal of Nazimuddin's Cabinet, there were only two Prime Ministers, Liaquat and Nazimuddin, and that the change of administration which did occur was caused not by political instability but by Liaquat's death. The politicians entered their period of irresponsibility *after* Ghulam Mohammad dissolved the first Constituent Assembly and Munir stripped it of its sovereignty. As a body which thereafter had little real responsibility, its members often acted irresponsibly. This does not imply that prior to the dissolution Pakistan's politicians were above approach. There undoubtedly was ample corruption and Chicago-style rigged elections. But Pakistan's versions of these political flaws were not so flagrant as to set the nation apart from other democratic societies during their formative periods.[2]

In fact, it is difficult to find another group of politicians who have been confronted with problems of the magnitude facing the members of the Constituent Assembly after 1947. It can be argued with hindsight that it was unreasonable to put East and West Pakistan within the framework of a single nation. Reasonable or not, the politicians in the Assembly were presented with the task of bringing together two very different societies, separated by hundreds of miles of hostile territory, and amalgamating them by a constitutional formula which would apportion legislative representation and also incorporate Islamic values in a constitution based on a Western model. The magnitude of the task made success questionable. Yet the politicians in fact succeeded, and in 1954 produced a democratic constitution to which the religious factions were willing to accommodate themselves. The agreement hammered out in the Assembly dealing with legislative apportionment was the main achievement in the new constitution. Its Mohammad Ali Formula was a peer of the formula agreed on by Americans in Philadelphia in 1789, eleven years after their independence, and which they call their 'Great Compromise'.

The image which exists of Pakistan's politicians was created in large part, at least in the West, by their victorious enemies who succeeded in telling the story of democracy's downfall to the world. The wide circulation of Ghulam Mohammad's dissolution declaration and Mirza's press statements stand in contrast to the silence of the politicians of the Assembly. Munir expended considerable effort in his voluminous court decisions, not only to convince the public of the constitutional correctness of the dissolution, but also to make the point that democracy had failed because of the irresponsibility of the politicians in the Assembly. Fortunately, according to Munir, the constitution had been saved through his efforts.

Munir's opinions had profound effects on Pakistan. Beginning with *Umar,* he expanded the scope of military rule permissible in peacetime, and his Munir Report criticized the religious leaders and blunted their support for the new constitution. By employing a narrow and technical reading of the dominion constitution, he defeated the Constituent Assembly's move against dissolution and granted to the Governor-General new power over legislative functions. Making no mention of the negotiations between Jinnah and the British at the time of the transfer of power, he saw Pakistan as being less than independent. He contradicted what Mountbatten had told the people of Pakistan in his speech at the time of the transfer of power, that their new nation was a 'fully independent state'. Now they were told by Munir that because it was a dominion, Pakistan came into existence not as an independent nation but had been created only with the power to obtain independence by changing its dominion status. This conclusion was in direct opposition to Atlee's response when Churchill made the same assertion in 1947. Munir's distortion of the past created an oddity in the history of decolonization. Eight years after the transfer of power, a nation of ex-colonial subjects was claiming less independence than the departed colonial masters said they had been granted.

The people of Pakistan were told by Munir that they remained subject to the prerogative rights of the English Queen exercised through her representative, the Governor-General. Munir justified the use of the Queen's prerogative rights to uphold the dissolution of the Assembly on the ground that the Assembly had failed to produce a new constitution, a constitution which he in fact knew existed.

Munir hoped to leave Pakistan with his own unique brand of authoritian law which he presented as not inconsistent with the principles of democracy. His Law of Civil Necessity was a theory strongly influenced by the precepts of military rule. The effect of Munir's theory was that those in command of the coercive powers of the state had the right to suspend constitutional government when and for however long they thought necessary. His later Law of Revolution gave constitutional legitimacy to Ayub's military rule by creating an unprecedented and radical theory which guaranteed legitimacy to a rebel, be he brigand or liberator, so long as his seizure of power was successful. When Munir retired to private life, he had every reason to be satisfied that he had set in place the foundations of the autocratic government which he and Ghulam Mohammad believed in.

The second draft of the history of parliamentary democracy's destruction was written by the foreign Press. After censorship was eased, some newspapers in Pakistan began raising doubts about the legality of the Assembly dissolution and considering its constitutional implications. In contrast, the foreign Press, which formed much of the public opinion in the West, followed a different path. They accepted Munir's versions of events and saw Ghulam Mohammad's hand as having been forced by irresponsible politicians. The *Calcutta Statesman,* then British-owned, seemed to consider the existence of political differences sufficient justification for terminating democracy when it editorialized: 'In the particularly disturbing circumstances it appears that the Governor-General did well to be resolute. Provincialism and factionalism presented a grave threat to the country...It is difficult to think of Pakistan without the Muslim League, but its quarrels have brought it very low and threatened the foundation of the State.'[3]

Immediately after the dissolution, *The Times* of London seemed somewhat at a loss to grasp what had happened.[4] It concluded that the dissolution was 'less extreme' than the dismissal of Nazimuddin nineteen months earlier, but added that the events showed 'grave internal difficulties'. The *Economist* approved of the dissolution.[5] The *New York Times,* which the preceding year had heralded the Assembly's work on the new constitution as a 'key to the way the changing Muslim world may go politically in the next few years,' reported that it had attempted to discover the significance of the dissolution by interviewing unidentified constitutional lawyers.[6] The lawyers, however, could only give the opinion that the Governor-General had the power to dissolve the Assembly, his proclamation being 'complete in itself'. Nevertheless, they could cite no authority to support their opinion except to say that the Governor-General's action fitted into 'the highly involved and complicated structure of British law'. The paper also reported that Ghulam Mohammad had the backing of the Army and Civil Service, and his regime was friendly to the United States. A few days later, the paper noted that it was the Muslim League which had held East and West Pakistan together, and that now that bond was broken.[7] In official Washington the Assembly's dissolution attracted little attention.[8]

By 1 November, *The Times* of London was now able to form an opinion. It found that the legacy of the Raj, 'the trained administrators of the old Civil and Provincial Services with the Army behind them', had served as the 'remedy' for the plight facing Pakistan before that plight had become 'catastrophic'. It reported that the new regime was composed of 'ministers of all talents'. While some might regret the dissolution, 'anything, it is thought, must be better than a system which allowed the Civil Service and the Army to be exposed to the risk of manipulation by self-seeking and largely self-appointed political party causes…' In the United States, meanwhile, the idea took hold that Pakistan's underlying problem was the lack of a workable constitution. There was an absence of awareness that Pakistan had, since independence, had a constitution similar to those which had worked successfully in the senior dominions. It was sometimes asserted that what existed in Pakistan instead of a constitution were the 'patched-up remnants of the Government of India Act'.[9]

In its December edition, the *Round Table* pronounced its verdict. This British journal specializing in Commonwealth affairs reported that Pakistan had survived the greatest challenge in her history. It saw constitution-drafting as having reached a point where a show-down looked imminent. The Muslim League Parliamentary Party was 'a house divided against itself'. The political clash between the majority and a minority over the apportioning of power within the state was characterized as one where 'leadership had dismally failed to rise above narrow provincial and personal feuds.' The 'hydra-headed monster' of provincialism had been the cause of the Assembly's ruin. No mention was made of the various compromises and formulae which had been worked out over time addressing the problem of east-west representation, or how the Mohammad Ali Formula at one point had gained majority support from both wings. The *Round Table* warned that '...more than a fifth of [East Bengal] is Hindu and this is a fact which should constantly be borne in mind. If East Bengal's claims were met in full it would mean that the Hindu minority would dominate the whole of Pakistan.'

The *Round Table* lamented the fate of the common man who, along with Pakistan itself, had 'suffered long', and for that reason, '...if we now have people at the helm of affairs who we know are clear in their visions and have honesty of purpose we are inclined to wish them god-speed and *forget everything else*.' (Emphasis added.) That person of clear vision and honesty of purpose, in the opinion of the *Round Table*, was Ghulam Mohammad. '...[O]nce again the Governor-General stepped in and stopped the rot. Once again he proved from the hilt that he would never hesitate to take drastic steps to meet a situation rapidly getting out of control.' The Constituent Assembly had been 'wiped off the country's political map as one wipes spilled milk from a table.' Now '...a national government, as opposed to a one-party government, came into being. Talent and not party affiliation was now the principle.'

The *Round Table* had little patience with the idea that the Constituent Assembly was a sovereign body and could only be dissolved by its own action. '...[W]hen a people are confronted with a choice between anarchy and misery on one hand and authority and well-being on the other, it is unpardonable to take shelter behind constitutional maxims and create confusion by legislative interpretation.' It had to be admitted that the constitutional situation was unusual, but the *Round Table* reported that the Governor-General was supported by the majority. 'History provides many instances in which recourse had been had to extra-legal methods to serve democratic ends.' No example of the 'many instances' the editors had in mind were given. The *Round Table* was of the opinion that the end to be served by the dissolution was saving the country from 'irresponsible Muslim League politicians' who had made the Constituent Assembly their 'plaything'.[10] Keith Callard, who was at the scene in Karachi at the time, agreed. 'Perhaps the Prime Minister may have been right when he said Constitution-making is important. But most important by far is the security and stability of the country.'[11]

In its March 1955 issue the *Round Table* returned to what it saw as the plight of the common man in Pakistan. 'For years the petty politicians betrayed him...by years of maladministration, widespread corruption and never-ending petty jealousies and squabbles among politicians...' The common man had become 'a helpless spectator of the depressing political spectacle in the country.'[12] The report did not identify by name any of the petty politicians who had betrayed the common man, nor did this London journal reveal the source it used in ascertaining how the common man in Pakistan had reacted to the alleged squabbling and maladministration. Reports such as those in the *Round Table* passed into the analyses of Western scholars, who for the next twenty years placed heavy emphasis on the squabbling and banality of Pakistan's politicians as one of the main reasons for what they saw as democracy's failure.

In contrast, Ghulam Mohammad was headlined in the American news magazine *Time* as the 'Reluctant Dictator'. The magazine claimed that he had 'put his civil servants to work on what Pakistan's Constituent Assembly had for seven years failed to achieve—a constitution...A man disabled by a stroke, half paralyzed, and trained by crack British civil servants to rule by law, Ghulam Mohammad does not really like being a dictator.' *Time* intimated that Ghulam Mohammad wanted to reconvene the Assembly and hold elections but was dissuaded by his advisers, who had reportedly argued that 'restoring democracy would mean restoring chaos'.[13]

Ironically, Munir has emerged as somewhat of a hero. For some in the West he is the 'liberal' judge who in the Munir

Report rebutted the religious factions. Those who praise him are often unaware that in his report Munir was discrediting the religious activists who were at the time supporting a constitution which Ghulam Mohammad would not tolerate. Munir has been called 'a lion under the throne'.[14] He himself set the theme by which he wished to be remembered, claiming that he had built a 'bridge' to save the constitution.[15] Scholars in the West have echoed Munir. 'The Federal Court proved to be the guardian of the Constitution and indirectly also the saviour of the State and the democratic form of government. Thus, by its wise and learned decision it built a "legal bridge" which brought the nation back to constitutional government'.[16] It has been claimed that 'much of the credit for re-establishing Pakistan on the road to democracy is rightly given to the Federal Court, which showed no hesitation in questioning the validity of arbitrary actions on the part of the government.'[17] Pakistan has been described as 'plunged into a maze of legal problems from which it was eventually extricated by the Court.'[18] Some in their enthusiasm completely abandoned reality. 'Thus the Federal Court of Pakistan courageously raised its voice in defence of constitutional government while all others stood by as helpless spectators to the Governor-General's arbitrary use of power.'[19] 'The Court's judicial decisions had undoubtedly robbed the Governor-General of the fruits of his initial victories...The legal battle for supremacy between the Governor-General and the [Assembly] had ended in victory of the latter.'[20]

This almost unanimous praise arises from the fact that there are few who have read Munir's decisions.[21] Instead, they have relied on the analysis of Sir Ivor Jennings, whose *Constitutional Problems of Pakistan* was written shortly after *Reference No. 1* was decided, and contains the most comprehensive analysis of the dissolution cases in the English language. It had significant effect because of Jennings' reputation as an authority on British and Commonwealth constitutional affairs. Jennings' analysis reflects the position taken by the government in the case, a position based on the advice Jennings himself had furnished. Although he leaves the impression that his book is another in his long line of objective scholarly works, it actually reflects the memoranda he wrote on behalf of his client, Ghulam Mohammad. As with the efforts of any lawyer serving the interest of his client in an adversarial situation, Jennings avoided facts and theories unfavourable to the client's case and stressed those which were favourable.[22] Because of his unrivalled reputation as a constitutional scholar, the length and complexity of the courts' opinions, and the technical nature of the issues involved, Jennings' interpretation of *Tamizuddin* has been left unchallenged. Assured by Jennings of the constitutional soundness of Munir's decisions, historians and political scientists have been able to cross the constitutional 'bridge' Munir claimed he had constructed untroubled by doubts, and unaware that the constitutional wreckage spanned by that bridge was created by Ghulam Mohammad and by Munir himself.[23]

The religious leaders of Pakistan, while they have been less of a target, have not escaped the finger pointing from those in the West seeking the 'causes' for the failure of democracy. According to some critics, religion was partly at fault. The Muslims of Pakistan, it has been charged, were '...incapable of working the election process. The primary dilemma may be an obscure characteristic in their political culture. Islam may well be an impediment.' Such speculation ignores the role which the religious factions actually played in supporting the new constitution during its drafting.

While it is true that they were not from the beginning enthusiastic for democracy, they nevertheless supported the new constitution and feared its destruction at the hands of Ghulam Mohammad. Their conduct during the constitutional controversy rebuts those in the West who maintain that Pakistan is undemocratic because its core is Islam and Islam is undemocratic. Such an assertion is not only based on a misconception of the nature of Islam, but is inconsistent with how many Westerners see themselves and their own political world. For example, those in the West who do not consider that Roman Catholicism is a democratic religion would not conclude that democracy is not possible in Ireland, Italy, or Poland. Nor would they make the claim that parliamentary democracy cannot exist in Great Britain because the Church of England enjoys exclusive privileges in the nation's constitution. Yet such thinking does exist in the West about Islam and Pakistan. A not uncommon view is represented by one writer. '...[A] secular constitutional order and an Islamic system are scarcely compatible...The *Qur'an* is the only constitution a Muslim can genuinely subscribe to...It is pointless to speak of constitutional intentions.'[24]

Fortunately, there have been voices in the West able to reach conclusions more in line with what actually occurred in Pakistan during the years under review here. As Keith Callard characterized the role of the religions leaders, '...the *ulema* were willing to compromise with the mysterious machinery of parliamentary government.'[25] His position has found support from others who were able to see the *ulema* not as religious fanatics, but as persons capable of being gradualists who were often willing to compromise in applying the concepts of 'the sovereignty of God' and an 'Islamic State'. Since it was the construction of a twentieth century government which was at issue, it was understandable that it would be the *ulema,* rather than the secularists, who would have to make the greater moves away from their starting position. The secularists on their part found it necessary to compromise so as not to appear non-Islamic. There was, therefore, a basis for negotiating on constitutional issues. The *ulema* were flexible. 'It is probably that, like their medieval predecessors, they were more interested in establishing the supremacy of the Shari'a than they were in the specifics of the government's organization structure. They could live with a liberal or controlled democracy, a presidential or parliamentary government, as they had lived earlier, and even prospered, under pious and impious sultans. A commitment by the ruling elites to honor the Shari'a, even if hedged with qualifications, was therefore a welcome beginning. Later, at a more propitious time, pressure might be brought to bear on them to enlarge the commitment.'[26]

How adequate and appropriate was the dominion constitution for a nation emerging from colonial rule? The experience of the senior dominions argues that the constitution Pakistan inherited at independence provided a vehicle sufficient for the operation of a democratic government. The fact that the structure of the dominion constitution was imitated in succeeding constitutions of Pakistan after the Assembly's dissolution, attests to its attractiveness on the operational level. But there existed an important difference at the core between the constitution of Pakistan and those of the senior dominions, which had developed as British settlers in those dominions were granted self government. In contrast, the constitution of Pakistan was based on the Government of India Act, created in 1935 in response to nationalist pressures by a conquered people demanding freedom. The 1935 Act was an expediency intended to meet the security needs of the British first and to placate the aspirations of their Indian subjects second.

To fulfil the primary objective of security, the Government of India Act contained repressive measures. After independence, the Pakistan government did not have to continue the autocratic features of the Act. Nevertheless, because of the insecurity felt in the early years, party from real or imaginary threats presented by India, also because of the difficult task of amalgamating the east and west wings into a single government, as well as the inexperience of the nation's leaders in the affairs of government, Liaquat's ministry chose to follow the only example of government known to them, the British Raj. It re-established some of the repressive measures of that regime, to the extent of replacing sections of the Act which the British had removed at independence and adding new ones. Preventive detention, restrictions on the Press, and the restored powers of the central government under Section 92A, were accompanied by the passage of PRODA, and became part of the potential *modus operandi* by which Pakistan's constitution was implemented.

A second feature of the Government of India Act of 1935 was the grant of responsible government in the provinces while at the same time denying it to the government at the centre. In this way the British intended to defuse nationalist unity by diverting political activity to the provinces. This defusion of power became a major concern to Jinnah and Liaquat after independence. The actions taken by both these leaders against the provincial ministries was part of their efforts to change the power balance in the constitution by transferring powers from the provinces to the centre. In doing so they damaged the political vitality of the provincial governments and contributed to limiting the development of the Muslim League, which had its power base in the provincial legislatures. As a consequence, the federal structure and the Muslim League, potential barriers to the growth of autocratic government, were in weakened condition when Ghulam Mohammad moved to capture the power of the state.

At the time of independence, the central government lacked experience. Until independence India was ruled by a truncated central government which had remained essentially unchanged since it was constituted by the Government of India Act of 1919. The functioning of that government afforded limited opportunities for the development of the conventions necessary for the operation of a dominion constitution.

Without constitutional conventions, Pakistan lacked at birth what has been called 'the motor part of the constitution'. Conventions of a constitution are often more important than are its written parts. This is particularly true of constitutions which have their roots in the 'unwritten' constitution of England. So important are conventions that Jennings had described them in one of his scholarly works as being a part of every constitution and had to be obeyed.

Conventions had, however, been so disregarded by Jinnah and Liaquat, particularly in their dealings with the provinces, that it is not surprising that no serious opposition was voiced later when Ghulam Mohammad dismissed Nazimuddin. What happened to Nazimuddin was a repeat at the national level of what Liaquat had done to the provincial ministry of Mamdot, and Bogra was later to do to the United Front ministry after the elections in East Bengal. Munir was able to disregard two of the very few major conventions which had come into existence in Pakistan. By declaring Section 223A invalid because it lacked the assent of the Governor-General, he disregarded the convention that required a court to refrain from exercising jurisdiction over constitutional legislation enacted by the Constituent Assembly. He also disregarded the convention that the assent of the Governor-General was not necessary for legislation amending the constitution. The observance of either of those conventions would have prevented Munir from reaching his conclusions in Tamizuddin. Munir justified his disregard of convention by utilizing the Crown prerogative, which itself was an English constitutional convention.

On the positive side, there was considerable interest among the elite and the educated public in constitutional issues. This was shown in letters to the editors and editorial discussions, the debates of the Constituent Assembly, as well as the pro-constitution demonstrations conducted by Maududi and other religious leaders and by speeches in the mosques. There was also some showing of awareness of the importance of constitutional continuity. The legal right of the British to rule India was based on conquest and treaty, both internationally recognized as creating valid rights to rule at the time British rule was established. Although the people of the subcontinent desired to free themselves from that rule, the negotiations for independence conducted by their leaders were not based on a challenge to the legitimacy of British rule. Acceptance of dominion status was, at least by implication, a further recognition of that legitimacy. After independence, there was no denial by the new government that Parliament had had the right to legislate a constitution for Pakistan. Nor was it denied that the secular sovereignty of the state was in the Constituent Assembly because Parliament had exercised its legitimate right to vest that power there.

The fact that the right to draft a new constitution resided with the Constituent Assembly, a creation of Parliament, was also not a matter of serious contention. When Suhrawardy challenged the Assembly, he did not question this right but would replace it with 'morality', a concept vague enough to afford him better political opportunities. Even Ghulam Mohammad recognized the importance of constitutional legitimacy, which he sought by manipulating Munir's court rather than resorting to naked force. When the issues between the politicians and Ghulam Mohammad were fought out in the Sindh and Federal courts, legitimacy of the dominion constitution was an assumption accepted by the courts and by both sides to the dispute. This continued acceptance of the legitimacy of the constitution is a tribute to the British, who despite their mixed motives and their faltering, had imparted their lessons of constitutional government. It was also a tribute to those Pakistanis who had learned those lessons well.

A challenge to this legitimacy was voiced by the politicians who had prevailed in the East Bengal elections but who remained excluded from the Constituent Assembly. Under Suhrawardy's leadership they based their claim to seats in the Assembly on the ground that they were more representative than were the sitting members from East Bengal. Their claim had merit as to the fact of representation. The sitting members had been elected by the provincial legislatures which themselves had been elected before independence by a restricted electorate. But, as Pritt pointed out at one point in his oral argument to the court, the Constituent Assembly of Pakistan was no worse in that respect than was the English Parliament of 1830, which is often cited as a milestone in constitutional development.

The measure of a valid constitution is not whether its drafters represented the entire range of a society's population. While universal representation might be a positive attribute, it is not the essential attribute that legitimacy is. Certainly, the constitutions of England and the United States were not created by persons collectively representing directly all of the members of their society. The English avoid the undemocratic aspects of their constitution's creation by asserting that in the Parliaments which had created the constitution there had been 'virtual' representation of those parts of society which did not have the right to elect members. Among the delegates to the American constitutional convention in Philadelphia, the question of representation was not a serious issue. The delegates indulged in little pretence that their representation extended beyond the commercial, land-owning, and slave-owning elements of society.

The fact that the challenge to the Assembly's legitimacy was raised by Bengalis against Bengalis had the effect of weakening the one group which might have been able to offer effective resistance to Ghulam Mohammad. In part, their potential strength was due to the experience many Bengali leaders had gained in British India. In the decades leading up to independence, the Calcutta Municipal Corporation and the Bengal Assembly developed into the most advanced legislative bodies on the subcontinent. They served as incubators for Hindu and Muslim legislators, many of the latter afterwards playing important political roles in Pakistan. Nazimuddin, Huq, Suhrawardy, and Bogra were among those leaders who had gained this legislative experience not available elsewhere in British India. Nazimuddin and Suhrawardy had both headed ministries made up of Muslims, Hindus, and Europeans.

It was Ghulam Mohammad who was the beneficiary of the split among the Bengali leaders. Bengalis who hailed his dissolution of the Constituent Assembly had their opposition to constitutional legitimacy rewarded not with representative elections but with the imposition of autocratic rule.

When those who destroyed Pakistan's democracy wrote their histories, they placed a large part of the blame for the destruction on the victims. Supposedly it was the people, because they were not 'ready' for democracy, who were charged with being the underlying cause of the failure. Mirza, who became the spokesman for the regime which came to power after the dissolution, disdained the

Pakistani citizen as a political incompetent who needed a controlled government until he could be given proper training in the affairs of government.[27] This opinion has been reflected in the West. 'Public opinion was largely ill-educated, and was totally unused to the careful weighing of small issues that is required if the power of government is to be kept within bounds.' The same political scientist expressed his concern that the people's lack of education would lead them 'to an unreal estimate of the consequence of political action'.[28] Another influential Western commentator declared that Pakistanis were 'unsophisticated, essentially uneducated, tradition-bound,' and 'not capable of changing systems of social control that have endured for centuries.'[29] Professor Karl Newman, a German, lived among the Pakistanis before and after the Assembly's dissolution and later wrote and taught their history at Western universities. He too believed that poverty and lack of education had made them unready for democracy. He was also troubled by a contradiction: in the 1930s his own countrymen enjoyed almost one hundred per cent literacy and were far better off economically than were the Pakistanis in 1954, yet they had elected Adolf Hitler as their head of state.[30]

The people of Pakistan who witnessed the destruction of democracy in 1954 were not political fools, as Mirza would have them remembered. Newspaper editorials, letters to the editors, and debates in the Assembly amply demonstrated the understanding of the issues involved in drafting a new constitution. It was not the people who put Ghulam Mohammad in power. He seized power after having been appointed Governor-General by Nazimuddin, who had occupied the office as a ceremonial figure. Nor was it the people who wrote the court decisions which legitimized democracy's destruction. The Pakistanis of the mid-century who were demeaned by Mirza and patronized by Western experts were the same people who demonstrated their interest in and knowledge of democracy in the East Bengal election of 1954. Over sixteen million voters went to the polls then, and by a majority expressed their dissatisfaction with the existing political system by endorsing a second party, the United Front, as an alternative to the Muslim League. Their interest and participation in democracy was stamped out by the decision of the leaders in Karachi who refused to comply with the democratic requirement that they share power with those with whom they disagreed.

APPENDIX

INDIAN INDEPENDENCE ACT, SECTIONS 6 AND 8

6(1) The Legislature of each of the new Dominions shall have full power to make laws for that Dominion, including laws having extra-territorial operation.

(2) No law and no provision of any law made by the Legislature of either of the new Dominions shall be void or inoperative on the ground that it is repugnant to the law of England, or to the provisions of this or any existing or future Act of Parliament of the United Kingdom or to any order, rule of regulation made under any such Act, and the powers of the Legislature of each Dominion include the power to repeal or amend any such Act, order, rule or regulation in so far as it is part of the law of the Dominion.

(3) The Governor-General of each of the new Dominions shall have full power to assent to any law of the Legislature of the Dominion...

(6) The power referred to in sub-section (1) of this section extends to the making of laws limiting for the future the powers of the Legislature of the Dominion.

8(1)...[T]he powers of the Legislature of the Dominion shall, for the purpose of making provision as to the constitution of the Dominion, be exercisable in the first instance by the Constituent Assembly of the Dominion, and references in this Act to the Legislature of the Dominion shall be construed accordingly.

(2) Except in so far as other provision is made by or in accordance with a law made by the Constituent Assembly of the Dominion under sub-section (1) of this section, each of the new Dominions and all Provinces and other parts thereof shall be governed as nearly as may be in accordance with Government of India Act, 1935;...

Provided that:

(e) the powers of the Federal Legislature...under that Act, as in force in relation to each Dominion, shall, in the first instance, be exercisable by the Constituent Assembly of the Dominion, in addition to the powers exercisable by that Assembly under sub-section (1) of this Section.

ABBREVIATIONS

AC	Appellate Court (England)
AIR	All India Reports
FC	Federal Court
BPC	Basic Principles Committee
CAD (Con.)	Constituent Assembly Debates (Constitutional)
CAD (Leg.)	Constituent Assembly Debates (Legislative)
GGO 22/47	Governor-General's Order, No. 22 of 1947
GIA	Government of India Act
IIA	Indian Independence Act
IOL	India Office Library
PLD	Pakistan Legal Decisions
TP	*Transfer of Power,* N. Mansergh (ed.)
US	United States Reports

NOTES

Introduction

1. Lawrence Ziring, Pakistan: *The Enigma of Political Development* (Boulder: Westview Press, 1980) p. 220.

Chapter 1. Pakistan 1947

1. I CAD (Con.), p. 235.
2. Based on his personal conversations with Jinnah as recounted by Amjad Ali, a long-time associate of Jinnah, who after independence served as Ambassador to the United States during the Bogra administration and Finance Minister (1955-8). Amjad Ali interview (1992).
3. Memorandum of Mountbatten-Jinnah Meeting, 23 June 1947, F2/94, and letter, Mountbatten to Jinnah, 25 June 1947, F2/99, *Quaid-i-Azam Papers*, Department of National Archives, Islamabad.
4. Amjad Ali interview (1992).
5. Leonard Binder, *Religion and Politics in Pakistan* (Berkeley: University of California Press, 1963), p. 382.
6. *Civil and Military Gazette*, 30 April 1948. Three decades later, Ziring wrote of Pakistan as 'one of the few nation-states deprived of a fictitious air of inevitability: it does not have the appearance of a country that was meant to be.' Lawrence Ziring, op. cit., p. 59.
7. Charles Burton Marshall, Reflection on a Revolution in Pakistan, *Foreign Affairs,* January 1959, pp. 247, 251.
8. Ralph Braibanti, 'Public Bureaucracy and Judiciary in Pakistan' in Joseph La Palombra (ed.) *Bureaucracy and Political Development* (Princeton: Princeton University Press, 1962) p. 47.
9. *See,* Binder, op. cit., *passim.*
10. Quoted in Saeed Shafquat, *Political System of Pakistan and Public Policy* (Lahore: Progressive Publishers, 1989) p. 90.
11. Kalim Bahadur, *The Jamaat-e-Islami of Pakistan* (New Delhi: Chetana Publications, 1977) pp. 54-9. *See also,* Khalid B. Sayeed, 'The Jamaat-e-Islami Movement in Pakistan,' 30 *Pacific Affairs*, 59, 61 (1957).
12. I CAD (Con.) pp. 49-50.
13. For the uses made in Pakistan of the history of constitutional development of British India, *see,* Chs. 7 and 8, *infra.*

14. Macaulay quotes are from Reginald Coupland's *The Indian Problem 1833-1935* (Oxford, The Clarendon Press, 1942), pp. 19-20.
15. For discussion of these changes *see,* Lucy Sutherland, *The East India Company in Eighteenth-Century Politics* (Oxford: The Clarendon Press, 1952); Syed Razi Wasti, *Muslim Struggle for Freedom in British India* (Lahore: Book Traders, 1993), Ch. 3.
16. Parliament's Charter Act of 1833 had extended the legislative power of the East India Company to all the Company's holdings in India. The Act enlarged the Governor-General's Council by the addition of a fourth member and vested limited legislative functions in the Council. The Indian Councils' Act of 1861 (24 & 25 Vict. c. 67) further expanded the membership of the Council but its membership contained a large number of government officials. All members were appointed by the Governor-General until an indirect form of election of non-official members was introduced in the Indian Councils' Act of 1892 (55 & 56 Vict. c. 14). But the Council was strictly consultative in nature. Direct election of some non-official members was provided for in the Indian Councils' Act of 1909 (9 Edw. VII, c. 4). The Legislative Council remained small, continued to contain a large number of official members, was unrepresentative of the general public, was limited in its legislative functions, and remained under the control of the Governor-General.
17. Former Secretary of State for India Lord Kimberly. 342 H*ansard* (1890), p. 93.
18. Coupland, *op. cit.*, p. 51. Some Indians were not pleased with the prospect of democratic institutions. One to be noted, because he was to play an important political role during the early years of Pakistan, was A. K. Fazlul Huq. He complained that: 'Representative institutions have been thrust upon India, although there can be no doubt that [they] are utterly unsuited to Indian conditions.' Huq concluded that one could no more expect these institutions to flourish 'than you can expect a hot-house flower to blossom in the icy cold of the North.' Quoted, p. 75.
19. 9 & 10 Geo. V, c. 101.
20. An Indian historian, using Bengal as an example, has given an idea of the realities of the limitations of the new constitutional reform in operation. 'The subjects "transferred" to Indian ministers were not the most important. The changes inherent in this limited transfer of power were to be counterated by three factors: the predominantly White composition of the upper echelon of the bureaucracy, the weighted representation of the European community in the legislature and the fragmentation of the Indian electorate into communal categories.' Rajat Ray, *Social Conflict in Bengal* (New Delhi: Vikas Publishing House, 1987) p. 241.
21. Quoted, Coupland, op. cit., p. 81.
22. Ibid., p. 100.
23. Ibid., p. 106.
24. Stanley Wolpert, *A New History of India* (New York: Oxford University Press, 1977), p. 322.
25. 25 & 26 Geo. 5, C.2. The historical background of the 1935 Act and a detailed discussion of its provisions are found in Arthur B. Keith, *A Constitutional History of India 1600-1935* (London: Methuen & Co., 1936) p.323, *et seq.*

See also, H. Clokie, 'The New Constitution of India,' 30 *American Political Review*, 1152 (1935); K. Karve, 'The New Constitution Principles and Prospects,' 3 *University of Toronto Law Review*, 281 (1940); B. N. Rau, 'The Parliamentary System of Government in India,' 24 *University of Washington Law Review*, 91, 95 (1949). Rau was instrumental in developing the dominion concept for India and Pakistan at independence.

26. It has been said of the 1935 Act that, 'In the history of Indo-British relations it is an edifice deserving admiration.' H. V. Hodson, *The Great Divide* (Karachi, Oxford University Press, 1985), p.48. But the Act has not received universal praise. As Hodson himself points out, Winston Churchill called it 'a gigantic quilt of jumbled crochet work, a monstrous monument of shame built by pygmies.' (To Hodson, Churchill's colourful phrasing might be just another example of what Hodson called 'the puerility of his view of India.' Ibid., p. 200). Judith Brown's evaluation is, 'For all its limitations the 1935 Act was a major experiment in the devolution of power in a non-White part of Britain's empire. Its imperial framers hoped it would channel the interests and forces in Indian public life through institutions which protect Britain's diminishing interests on the subcontinent and require from Britain much lighter exercise of imperial control and decreased expenditure of resources; though by the time of its enactment it seemed a battered and much cobbled measure, disliked by most Indian politicians and a significant group of British MPs.' Judith Brown, *Modern India* (Delhi: Oxford University Press, 1985), p. 284.

Chapter 2. Jinnah and the Making of a Dominion

1. Michael Edwardes, *The Last Years of British India*, (London: Cassell, 1963), p. 175.
2. Quoted in Stanley Wolpert, *Jinnah of Pakistan* (New York: Oxford University Press, 1984), p. 52.
3. 22 Geo. V, c. 4.
4. *See*, Ivor Jennings, *Constitutional Problems of Pakistan* (London: Cambridge University Press, 1955) p. 20, and his 'The Making of a Dominion Constitution,' 65 *Law Quarterly Review*, 456, 478 (1949); D. R. Das, (ed.), *Transitional Constitutions of India and Pakistan* (Calcutta: The Indian Law Review Office, 1947) p. i.
5. *Quaid-e-Azam Papers*, National Archives, Islamabad, F2/72-4. Memorandum of Dominion Office, 'The Structure of the British Commonwealth'.
6. For the treaty and the constitutional aftermath, *see*, Lord Longford, *Peace By Ordeal, An Account...of the Anglo-Irish Treaty of 1921* (London: Sedgwick and Jackson, 1972) parts III-VI; *also*, George Dangerfield, *The Damnable Question* (Boston: Little, Brown and Co., 1976) part V; Nicholas Mansergh, *Prelude to Partition: Concepts and Aims in Ireland and India* (Cambridge; Cambridge University Press, 1978).
7. *Moore v. Attorney General for the Irish Free State*, (1935) A.C. 494.
8. Charles Loch Mowat, *Britain Between the Wars*, (Chicago: University of Chicago Press, 1955), p. 429.

9. Ibid., p. 601.
10. Ibid., p. 430.
11. 'Note of Zafrulla', I.O.L., MSS Eur. F/125/9, reprinted in S. S. Pirzada's *Quaid-e-Azam, Mohammad Ali Jinnah and Pakistan*, (Islamabad: Hurmat Publications, 1989), pp. 130-59.
12. Coupland, op cit., p. 43.
13. X, *TP*, No. 367, letter, Attorney-General Shawcross to Cripps, 9 May 1947.
14. XII, *TP*, No. 595, letter, Wavell to Pethick Lawrence, 2 February 1947.
15. Edward McWhinney, 'Sovereignty in the United Kingdom and the Commonwealth Countries at the Present Day,' 68 *Political Science Quarterly*, 511 (1953). See attempts to describe the Commonwealth in 'The Structure of the British Commonwealth, Note by the Dominion Officer', letter, Macke to Monteath, XI, *TP*, No. 131, 10 June 1947.
16. Quoted in E. W. R. Lumby, *The Transfer of Power in India* (London: George Allen and Unwin, 1954) p. 166.
17. X, *TP*, No. 33, minutes, Viceroy's Fifth Staff Meeting, 29 March 1947.
18. Ibid., No. 34, minutes, Viceroy's Sixth Staff Meeting, 31 March 1947.
19. Ibid., No. 87, minutes, Viceroy's Tenth Staff Meeting, 7 April 1947.
20. Ibid., No. 170, record of Mountbatten's discussion with officials, n.d.
21. *See*, F. J. Moore, *Retreat From Empire* (Oxford, Clarendon Press, 1966) pp. 229-31 for discussion of this opposition. *Also*, X, *TP*, No. 391, letter, Monteath to Brooke, 10 May 1947.

21A. Letter, Ismay to Jinnah, 4 July 1947, 'I have had very good reports of Mr Ivor Jennings,' *Quaid-e-Azam Papers*, op. cit., 12/175.

22. X, *TP*, No. 192, minutes, Viceroy's Twentieth Staff Meeting, 22 April 1947.
23. Ibid., No. 165, Viceroy's Personal Report No. 3, n.d.
24. Ibid., No. 220, record of interview, Mountbatten and V. K. Krishna Menon, 22 April 1947.
25. Ibid., No. 520, record of interview, Henderson and V. K. Krishna Menon, 22 May 1947.
26. Ibid., No. 372, record of discussion, Mountbatten and Nehru, 10 May 1947. Ibid., No. 381, minutes, Viceroy's Thirteenth Staff Meeting, 10 May 1947. As late as 14 April 1947, Nehru wrote: 'Under no conceivable circumstance is India going to remain in the British Commonwealth whatever the consequences...Any attempt to remain in the Commonwealth will sweep away those who propose it and might bring about major trouble in India.' Letter, Nehru to Singh, 14 April 1947, quoted in Moore, op. cit., p. 250.
27. XI, *TP*, No. 121, minutes, India and Burma Committee of the Cabinet, 9 June 1947.
28. X, *TP*, No. 437, minutes, Cabinet meeting, 14 May 1947. Moore, op. cit., pp. 251-5.
29. Ibid., No. 527, telegram, Attlee to Commonwealth Ministers, 23 May 1947.
30. Ibid., No. 442, record of interview, Mountbatten and Liaquat Ali Khan, 15 May 1947.
31. Ibid., No. 360, telegram, Mountbatten to Ismay, 8 May 1947.
32. Ibid., No. 282, minutes, Viceroy's Eleventh Miscellaneous Meeting, 10 May 1947.
33. Ibid., No. 392, telegram, Ismay to Mountbatten, 10 May 1947.

34. Ibid., No. 436, personal minutes, Prime Minister Attlee, 14 May 1947.
35. XI, *TP,* No. 118, minutes, Cabinet Commonwealth Relations Committee, 9 June 1947.
36. X, *TP,* No. 485, minutes, India and Burma Committee of the Cabinet, 19 May 1947.
37. Ibid., No. 367, letter, Shawcross to Cripps, 9 May 1947.
38. XII, *TP,* No. 122, letter, Mountbatten to Listowel, 25 July 1947.
39. Ibid., No. 314, letter, Abel to Harris (w/enc.) 2 August 1947. The advisers' opinions were in the enclosed memorandum by Rau who cited Arthur B. Keith and K. C. Wheare as the basis of his discussion and conclusions.
40. XI, *TP,* No. 445, letter, Churchill to Attlee, 1 July 1947.
41. Ibid., No. 504, letter, Attlee to Churchill, 4 July 1947.
42. X, *TP,* No. 513, record of interview, Mountbatten and Churchill, 22 May 1947.
43. Ibid., No. 494, minutes, India and Burma Committee of the Cabinet, 20 May 1947. Ibid., No. 513, record of interview, Mountbatten and Churchill, 22 May 1947.
44. *XI, TP,* No. 117, telegram, Ismay to Monteath 9 June, 1947.
45. *Quaid-e-Azam Papers,* op cit., F2/67. Under the GIA of 1935, 'The status of the Governor-General of India is higher than that of the Governor of a Colony. His appointment is a matter for the Cabinet and is made by the Crown on the Prime Minister's advice, not that of the Secretary of State alone. Similarly, the members of the Governor-General's Executive Council...are more like Cabinet Ministers, and share with the Governor-General in a collective responsibility to Parliament...' Coupland, op. cit., p. 8, n.1.
46. *XI, TP,* No. 204, letter, Listowel to Mountbatten, 22 July 1947; GIA §13; IIA §§5 and 6(3).
47. *Quaid-e-Azam Papers,* op cit., F2/85, 'Press Notice of Prime Minister Clement Attlee,' 10 July 1947.
48. *XII, TP,* No. 26, telegram, Ismay to Mountbatten, 7 July 1947.
49. *XII, TP,* No. 86, telegram, Mountbatten to Listowel, 12 July 1947. Ibid., No. 122, telegram, Listowel to Mountbatten, 15 July, 1947. At the time of the IIA's passage, some experienced India Office officials expressed uncertainty whether the Act created control of the executive by the legislature or simply carried on the *GIA. XI, TP,* No. 550, letter, Croft to Twinbull, 7 July 1947.
50. 10 & 11 Geo. 6, c. 30.
51. *Quaid-e-Azam Papers,* op cit., F1/149, F2/111-12, 149-70, letter, Mountbatten to Jinnah, 4 July 1947, and draft memoranda of meetings prior to the IIA being submitted to Parliament.
52. The participants made minor suggestions regarding the language of GIA Sections 6(2), 8(1), and 7(1), the latter with reference to the Indian princes. *XI, TP,* No. 428, Viceroy's Conference Paper, 30 June 1947. Ibid., No. 425, letter, Mountbatten to Listowel, 1 July 1947.
53. During the negotiations leading to the transfer of power, Mountbatten feared that Jinnah might refuse to convene the Constituent Assembly and thereby leave no constitutional body to which Parliament could transfer sovereignty

under the Independence Act. *XI, TP,* No. 437, telegram, Mountbatten to Listowel, 30 June 1947.

54. When he makes the point that 'The Constituent Assembly of Pakistan was born without the formal blessing of law,' Keith Callard in his *Pakistan: A Political Study* (London: George Allen & Unwin, 1957), p. 77, probably refered to the fact that the Assembly dates back to the Constituent Assembly for undivided India which first sat on 16 May 1946. That body was created in the Cabinet Mission plan, not by a statute of Parliament, and to that extent it might be said that it was without the 'formal blessing of law'. Although Muslim League members were elected to that Assembly, they did not take their seats until after independence, when the Constituent Assembly divided in two and separate assemblies began functioning, one for India and the other for Pakistan. This was the birth of Pakistan's Constituent Assembly and did have the authorization of the Indian Independence Act.
55. The federal legislature never came into existence although statutorily created by the GIA 1935. The legislature was to contain members from the States, and since no agreement was reached with the princes, the legislature at the centre remained as it had been constituted in the GIA of 1919.
56. Khalid B. Sayeed terms Jinnah 'an expert on constitutional law'. *Pakistan: The Formative Phase,* (Karachi: Civil and Military Gazette Press, 1967) p. 275. 'A man of unquestionable constitutional acumen', Ayesha Jalal, *The State of Martial Rule,* (Cambridge, Cambridge University Press, 1989) p. 28. As Callard described him, 'He had a mind for constitutional niceties and a thorough understanding of the government that prevailed in India.' Callard, *Pacific Affairs,* 5, 23 (1956). Early in his career Jinnah called attention to his constitutional expertise. In a speech as a member of the Governor-General's Council, newly formed at the centre under the GIA of 1919, he proclaimed, 'I have drunk deep at the fountain of constitutional law.' M. Rafique Afzal, *Quaid-e-Azam Mohammad Ali Jinnah: Speeches in the Legislative Assembly of India, 1924-30.* (Lahore: Research Society of Pakistan, 1976), p. xxi.
57. Quoted by M. A. H. Ispahani in his *Quaid-e-Azam Jinnah, as I Knew Him* (Karachi: Royal Book Company, 1970), p. 227. Ispahani was a close and long-time associate of Jinnah's.
58. Moore, op. cit., p. 162.
59. A copy of the note is in the possession of S. S. Pirzada who identifies himself as honorary secretary to Jinnah in the 1940s. Pirzada interview, 1992.
60. Sayeed, op. cit.
61. Pirzada interview, 1992. If Jinnah was referring to a dominion Governor-General whose constitutional position is likened to that of the monarch, then it is instructive to compare Geoffrey Marshall's explanation of executive power under the Westminster model. 'So, when Bagehot [in his *The English Constitution*] goes on to tell us that the Queen can do more things without consulting Parliament—that she can sell off the Navy, declare war, dismiss civil servants, create peers and pardon offenders—we are to understand that it is the Ministers who authorize and carry out those actions.' Geoffrey Marshall, *Constitutional Conventions* (Oxford: Clarendon Press, 1984) p. 19.

62. *Quaid-e-Azam Papers,* op. cit., F2/84, letter N. A. Faruqi to Jinnah, 23 June 1947.
63. *X, TP,* No. 119, minutes, Viceroy's Thirteenth Staff Meeting, 11 April 1947.
64. Sharif-al Mujahid, *Quaid-e-Azam Jinnah: Studies in Interpretation* (Karachi: Quaid-e-Azam Academy, 1978), pp. 128-32. Also, Pirzada interview (1991).
65. Aziz Beg, (ed.) *Quaid-e-Azam Centenary Bouquet* (Islamabad: Babur and Amer Publications, 1977) p. 728.
66. Ispahani, op. cit., p. 265. For the depth and longevity of the feeling against Mountbatten in Pakistan, *see also,* S. Hashim Raza, *Mountbatten and Pakistan* (Karachi, Quaid-e-Azam Academy, 1982).
67. Beg, op. cit., p. 724.
68. *XII, TP,* No. 26, telegram, Ismay to Mountbatten, 8 July 1947.
69. *XII, TP,* No. 14, letter, Lord Ismay to Mountbatten, 8 July 1947, mentioning Jinnah's 'overwhelming egotism'. *See also,* Raza, op. cit., p. 120.
70. Mountbatten quoted from personal interview reported in Larry Collins, *Freedom at Midnight* (New York: Simon and Schuster, 1975) p. 221. Similar but more contemporaneous statements were recorded by Mountbatten himself in his *Viceroy's Personal Report,* No. 11, 4 July 1947. When Mountbatten reminded Jinnah that as a constitutional Governor-General he would be limited to acting only on the advice of his Prime Minister, Jinnah replied, 'In my position it is I who will give the advice and others who will act on it.' *XI, TP,* No. 506. It was such remarks attributed to Jinnah which led some Britons and Indians at the time to charge that he planned to rule Pakistan as a dictator.
71. Chaudhri Mohammad Ali, *The Emergence of Pakistan* (New York: Columbia University Press, 1967) p. 30.
72. Golam Wahed Choudhury, *Democracy in Pakistan* (Decca: Green Book House, 1963) p. 37.
73. *Dawn,* 15 July 1947.
74. Consistent with this practice GIA §6(3), which originally read: 'The Governor-General of each of the new Dominions shall have full power to assent in His Majesty's name to any law of the Legislature of that Dominion...', was after Jinnah's death amended by the Constituent Assembly by deleting the words 'in His Majesty's name'. The effective date of the deletion was made retroactive to 15 August 1947. Constitution (Amendment) Act, 1950, Sect. 2.
75. Cabinet listings, September 1948 to September 1956, are given in Callard, *Political Study,* Appendix II.
76. *Quaid-e-Azam Papers,* op. cit., F1026/15.
77. M. A. Jinnah, *Speeches as Governor-General of Pakistan 1947-48* (Karachi: Government of Pakistan, n.d.) pp. 3 and 37.
78. Quoted in Mujahid, op. cit., p. 143.
79. *Dawn,* 26 January 1948.
80. Quoted in Mujahid, op. cit., p. 235.
81. Quoted in Matlubul H. Saiyed, *Mohammad Ali Jinnah: A Political Study* (Karachi: Elite Publishers, 1970) p. 462. According to Anwar Hussain Syed, when Jinnah referred to a Muslim government it is not correct to conclude that he equated this to an Islamic state. 'The Indian Muslim personality has

Islamic elements, but it also has many other elements that are non-Islamic and some that are, strictly speaking, un-Islamic.' Anwar Hussain Syed. *Islam, Politics and National Solidarity* (New York: Praeger, 1980) p. 58.

82. I CAD (Con.), p. 239.
83. Muhammad Munir, *Islam in History* (Lahore: Law Publishing Co., 1973), p. 290.
84. Wolpert, *Jinnah of Pakistan*, p. 340.
85. Hector Bolitho, *Jinnah: Creator of Pakistan* (London: John Murray, 1954) p. 197.
86. Mountbatten had wanted the Union Jack to be part of the flag of Pakistan. He acknowledged, however, that the Union Jack should be smaller than it was on the flags of the senior dominions because Pakistan would 'not want to emphasize the British connection quite as strongly as the other Dominions.' *Quaid-e-Azam Papers*, op. cit., F 1/3, letter, Mountbatten to Jinnah, 24 June 1947.
87. Quoted in Bolitho, op. cit., p. 198.
88. Ispahani, op. cit., p. 277.
89. Quoted in Jalal, *The State of Martial Rule* p. 279.
90. During the 1946 elections in which the Muslim League made its best showing and established the only Muslim provincial ministry, Jinnah was not invited to come to Bengal because the provincial League leaders were concerned least 'he upset the local Parliamentary Board'. H. S. Suhrawardy, *Memoirs* (Dhaka: University Press, 1987), p. 20.
91. *X, TP,* No. 291, telegram, Mountbatten to Listowel, 13 May 1947.
92. Sayeed, *Formative Phase*, p. 266.
93. *Cunningham Papers*, India Office Library, London, MSS Eur. D670/23. Cunningham to Jinna 8 September and 15 October 1947 for assessment of situation. *Also, Dawn*, 23 July and 27 August 1947.
94. Binder, op. cit., p. 131.
95. Section 51(5) provided: 'With respect to the choosing and summoning and dismissal of ministers, the Governor shall be under the general control, and comply with such particular directions, if any, as may from time to time, be given to him by the Governor-General.' GIA 51(5). For a description of the functioning of a provincial governor, *see,* Frederick Bourne, 'Constitutional Government Before and After the Transfer of Power,' 46 *Asiatic Review* No. 168 (1950), p. 1117. Bourne was the Governor of East Bengal. The Governor-General also had, under GIA §126(5), the right to 'at any time issue orders to the Governor of a Province as to the manner in which the executive authority thereof is to be exercised for the purpose of preventing any grave menace to the peace or tranquillity of India or to any part thereof.' These powers, were not intended as a means to solve political problems arising from the disapproval of the executive for a particular ministry.
96. GGO 20/47.
97. The limitations of a Governor-General under the GIA to have a provincial ministry removed when the ministry had lost the confidence of the provincial legislature was discussed between Secretary of State Amery and the incumbent Viceroy at the time of the 1946 Bengal Famine. *IV, TP,* Nos., 97, 104, 109, 131, 157, 277, 283, 301, 308, 311, and 315. *Also,* Sayeed, *Formative Phase*,

p. 282, and Ayesha Jalal, 'The Raj Survives' 19 *Modern Asian Studies*, 29 (1985), pp. 52-3.

98. Quoted in Sayeed, *Formative Phase*, p. 266.
99. Sir (Robert) Francis Mudie, member of the ICS (1914 to 1947), served mostly in UP until 1943. He was Governor of Bihar (1943-4), Home Member of the Viceroy's Executive Council (1944-5), Governor of Sindh (1946-7) and Governor of West Punjab (1947-9). Prior to independence, he was supportive of Jinnah and the Pakistan movement.
100. *Mudie-Jinnah Letters*, India Office Library, London, MSS Eur. F164/14-15.
101. Ibid., Mudie to Jinnah, 28 March 1948.
102. Ibid.
103. Ibid.
104. *Civil and Military Gazette*, 6 May 1948. For an account of Jinnah's attempt to settle the Mamdot-Daultana dispute and its results, *see*, *Mudie-Jinnah Letters*, op. cit., Mudie to Jinnah, 28 April, 6, 14, 17, 19, 25, 29 May, 1, 2 June 1948; Daultana to Mudie, 18 May 1948; Jinnah to Mudie, 18 May 1948; *Civil and Military Gazette*, 30 April, 16, 27 May and 2 June 1948; *Pakistan Times*, 18, 28 May and 2 June 1948.
105. Firoz Khan Noon took the same position in 1953 when he was requested by Nazimuddin to replace Daultana as chief minister of West Punjab. 'I could not say "no" on an occasion like this but I said I would only accept this position if the Punjab Muslim League Party would first elect me as their leader. I did not believe in accepting office at the order of the high command in Karachi and then command people through my influence and prestige to support me.' Firoz Khan Noon, *From Memory* (Lahore: Feroz Sons, 1966) p. 234.
106. Daultana interview (1992).
107. *Quaid-e-Azam Papers*, op. cit., F499/17, letter, Daultana to Mudie, 17 May 1948.
108. Undated translations of newspaper clipping are included in the Mudie IOL file. *Nawa-i-Waqt*, with a circulation of 18,000, was much smaller in that regard than were the Urdu *Jang* and *Aman*, with circulations of 70,000 and 32,000 respectively. Mudie often sent clippings along with his correspondence to Jinnah and Liaquat. He probably used *Nawa-i-Waqt* because it was published in Lahore, Multan, and Rawalpindi, while *Jang* and *Aman* were Karachi and Rawalpindi newspapers. The *Civil and Military Gazette* had a circulation of 18,000, compared with *Dawn*, 32,000, *Pakistan Times*, 33,000 and the *Pakistan Observer*, 12,000. The *Gazette* was founded in 1870 and had a high reputation for the quality of its political reporting and analysis. Rudyard Kipling had worked for the paper as a reporter.
109. *Civil and Military Gazette*, 6 May 1948.
110. *Mudie-Jinnah Letters*, op. cit., 18 May 1948. Beg, op. cit., p. 841, claims that 'Governor's rule was suggested to the Quaid, but he rejected this suggestion on the grounds that such action could be taken only when the security of the state was threatened. In this case it was an internal Party matter.'
111. *Quaid-e-Azam Papers*, op. cit., F499/11, letter, Mudie to Jinnah, 14 May 1948.

112. *Pakistan Times*, 22 May 1948. Beg, op. cit., p. 842, cites a *Pakistan Times* article reporting that 'Public opinion has more or less crystallized against the "unwarranted Central interference" in provincial ministerial politics. Although there is unquestioned loyalty and devotion for the Quaid-e-Azam, there is perceptible resentment against the wire-pulling from the Centre in favour of individuals in the provincial arena.'
113. *Civil and Military Gazette*, 2 June 1948.

Chapter 3. Pakistan Under Liaquat

1. Liaquat's main source of strength was the trust Jinnah placed in him. 'Had it not been for this fact the clever Khaliquzzaman or the dynamic Suhrawardy would have replaced him.' Sayeed, *Formative Phase*, p. 277.
2. To at least one later commentator, the prospects for the success of permanently shifting power away from the office of Governor-General was questionable. 'Liaquat believed there was still time to make the post of Governor-General a ceremonial non-political one. Unfortunately for him, and for Pakistan it, was already too late. Jinnah had proved that the parliamentary system was not sacrosanct and that the colonial tradition of the Viceroy, now in the office of the Governor-General, had not been discarded.' Lawrence Ziring, *Pakistan: Enigma of Political Development* (Boulder: Westview Press, 1980) p. 73.
3. Sayeed, *Pakistan: Formative Phase*, p. 411. *See also,* K. K. Aziz, *Party Politics in Pakistan 1947-1958,* (Islamabad: National Commission of Historical and Cultural Research, 1976) p. 14; Mushtaq Ahmed, *Government and Politics,* (Karachi: Pakistan Publishing House, 1959) p. 32; Lawrence Ziring, *The Failure of Democracy in Pakistan*, (Ph.D. Dissertation, Columbia University, 1962) p. 80.
4. For discussion of Muslim League weaknesses and the growth of opposition, *see,* M. Rafique Afzal, *Political Parties in Pakistan* op. cit., p. 89; Ahmad, *Government and Politics,* p. 145; Keith Callard, *Political Study*, ch. II.
5. The only organized non-Muslim League representation in the Constituent Assembly whose members were Muslim was the Azad Pakistan Party, founded and led by Mian Iftikharuddin. It began in November 1950 in West Pakistan as a leftist breakaway from the Muslim League, and maintained its existence until suppressed by the action of the central government in 1954. The party's objectives included the repeal of the Pakistan Safety Acts because they allowed imprisonment without trial, dissolution of the Constituent Assembly and the election of a new one on the basis of adult franchise, complete provincial autonomy, the abolition of the landholding *zamindari* system, changing Pakistan to a republic with no connection with the Commonwealth, compulsory military training, an independent foreign policy, and the sponsoring of an uprising against India in Kashmir. The party never gained significant popular support or organized itself effectively for political action. It won only one seat in the Punjab Assembly in the election of 1951, and failed to gain any seats in the North-West Frontier election in the next

year. It held its first and last annual conference in September 1952. The party's principal activity was within the Constituent Assembly where it had only three seats, and its opposition to the government's policies was nullified by the Muslim League's successful effort to equate the party's opposition with Hindu opposition.

6. I. Hussain, *The Failure of Parliamentary Politics in Pakistan* (Ph.D. Dissertation, Oxford University, 1967) pp. 46-8. Hussain reported on the many interviews he had with some of the leading figures of Pakistan's early political history.
7. The *Civil and Military Gazette*, 23 May 1948, said of the Muslim League ministry in Punjab, 'There could be no difference on policy, simply because there is no policy. It is a Ministry of landlords preaching the gospel of Communism.' Mudie also takes notice of the lack of policy in a letter to Liaquat of 26 May 1948. *Mudie-Liaquat Letters*, op. cit.
8. *Mudie-Nazimuddin Letters*, India Office Library, London, MSS Eur. F 164/51.
9. For the advice tendered to Liaquat by Mudie, *see, Mudie-Liaquat Ali Khan Letters,* India Office Library, London, MSS Eur. F 164/49, Mudie to Liaquat 13 February, 26 March, 20 August 1948. For letter by Mudie expressing (or feigning) reservations about the use of Section 92A, *see,* his 9 September letter to Liaquat, written when Jinnah was still alive and Mudie was theorizing to Nazimuddin about the difference between Sections 93 and 92A in his letter to Nazimuddin of 30 January 1949. *Mudie-Nazimuddin Letters*, ibid.
10. For the events of January 1949 leading to, and the execution of, the suppression of Mamdot's Administration, *see, Mudie-Liaquat Letters*, 10 January 1949; *Pakistan Times*, 25 January 1949; *Dawn*, 27 January 1949; *Civil and Military Gazette*, 25 and 26 January 1949.
11. Daultana claims that he was unaware at the time that he had lost favour with Mudie. Daultana interview (1992).
12. *Dawn*, 25 January 1949; Munir, *Highways and Bye-Ways of Life,* p. 75. Sayeed projected the importance of Mamdot's dismissal into the future. 'Ghulam Mohammad has often been accused of having committed the original sin when he dismissed Nazimuddin's Ministry in 1953 and later dissolved the Constituent Assembly in 1954. But is must be remembered that the spade-work for all this had been done in the provinces. If Liaquat could dismiss a provincial ministry in West Punjab and dissolve the House in 1949 on the plea that both the ministers and the Legislators were a pack of selfish and irresponsible men, Ghulam Mohammad could advance the same arguments for his action.' Sayeed, *Formative Phase*, pp. 449-50.
13. 2 February 1949.
14. For Mudie's theories on the interim government and the adviser's plan, *see, Mudie-Liaquat Letters*, op. cit., Mudie to Liaquat 28 February, 1 and 22 June 1949.
15. 31 January 1949.
16. *The Civil and Military Gazette* of 6 March 1949 criticized the appointment as rewarding the person who caused section 92A to be imposed.
17. Examples of the campaign: *Civil and Military Gazette*, 24 and 26 April 1949; *Dawn*, 25 April and 25 May 1949; *Pakistan Times*, 24 May 1949.

18. *Mudie-Liaquat Letters,* op. cit., Mudie to Liaquat, 26 May 1949.
19. Ibid., 26 May and 1 June 1949.
20. 14 June 1949.
21. *Mudie-Liaquat Letters,* op. cit., Mudie to Liaquat, 16 June 1949.
22. Ibid., Liaquat to Mudie.
23. Ibid., Mudie to Liaquat, 1 June 1949.
24. 9 July 1949.
25. For fuller discussion, *see,* Binder, op. cit., *passim*; Callard, *Political Study,* ch. VI.
26. For party structure in East Bengal, *see,* Rounaq Jahan, *Pakistan: Failure in National Integration* (New York: Columbia University Press, 1972) Ch. II; Ziring, *Failure of Democracy in Pakistan*, p. 85, *et seq.* For the background of Bengal politics prior to independence, *see,* Shila Sen, *Muslim Politics in Bengal 1937–1974* (New Delhi, Impex India, 1974); Kenneth McPherson, *The Muslim Microcosm, Calcutta 1918 to 1935* (Wiesbaden: Franz Steiner Verlag, 1974).
27. Noon, op. cit., p. 296. Viceroy Lord Wavell said about Suhrawardy, 'I have always regarded him as one of the most inefficient, conceited and crooked politicians in India, which is saying a good deal...I dislike him and distrust him intensely. I have always thought him a dishonest and self-seeking careerist with no principles.' Wavell, *A Viceroy's Journal*, (Lindom: Oxford University Press, 1973), pp. 239, 348. In July of 1946, Suhrawardy was elected to the Muslim League's Central Parliamentary Board. His importance in pre-partition Muslim politics is indicated by the make-up of the board. Suhrawardy's fellow members were Jinnah, Liaquat, Nishtar, Noon, Begum Shah Nawaz, Nazimuddin, and Sir Azizul Haq.
28. *See, Mahatma Gandhi, Collected Works* (New Delhi Ministry of Information and Broadcasting, 1983) Vol. 89, pp. 17–67, *passim; also see,* correspondence, Gandhi to Suhrawardy, *Gandhi Papers* (New Delhi: National Archives) No. 8965, 21 March and 18 April 1947. Robert Trumbull of the *New York Times* commented, 'Hussain Shaheed Suhrawardy...is about as Gandhian a personality as the Aga Khan.' Trumbull, *As I See India*, (New York: William Sloane Associates, 1956), p. 49.
29. '[Suhrawardy's] loss to the Muslim League is considered enormous. There is some justification for the view that the history of Pakistan would have been far different had he not been forced from the Muslim League.' Ziring, *Enigma of Political Development,* p. 10.
30. Ziring, *Failure of Democracy,* p. 98.
31. Ibid., pp. 92, 102, and 104.
32. Quoted ibid., p. 96. Suhrawardy makes no mention of this incident in his *Memoirs,* although he does claim that Abdul Qayyum threatened to arrest him if he campaigned at in the NWFP during the 1951 election. p. 84.
33. Karl J. Newman believes, based on his personal contacts with Liaquat, that Liaquat had little interest in constitutional matters. Newman interview (1991).
34. *Dawn*, 9 October 1950.
35. For Liaquat's public statements on the subject of opposition to Muslim League, *see,* Ziring, *Failure of Democracy in Pakistan*, pp. 96-105.

36. Geoffrey Marshall described some difficulties of incorporating existing constitutional principles into a written constitution by enumerating how the British constitution could be reduced to a written document. Marshall wrote: 'Perhaps we could start with enacting an improved version of the 1688 Bill of Rights and then set about codifying the Act of Settlement, the Scottish and Irish Acts of Union, the Parliament Acts and the Representation of the People Acts. Possibly some bits of Magna Carta and the Statute of Westminster should go in. But what about, say, the Crown Proceedings Act, the Judicature Acts, the House of Commons (Disqualification) Act, the Royal Titles legislation and the European Communities Act? What should we do about all the vital parts of our Constitution that derive from convention, such as ministerial responsibility and the rules that govern the exercise of the Queen's prerogative powers? What, again, about some central common law principles such as, it might be, the sovereignty of Parliament?' *Times Literary Supplement*, 7 March 1986.
37. Quoted in Bahadur, op. cit., p. 52.
38. Ibid., p. 60.
39. V CAD (Con.), p. 4.
40. Ibid., pp. 100-1.
41. 2 March 1949.
42. V CAD (Con.), p. 51.
43. The importance of the role played by the concept of sovereignty in a new nation has been pointed out by Professor Marshall. Geoffrey Marshall, *Parliamentary Sovereignty and the Commonwealth* (New York: Oxford University Press, 1957), p. 31. *See also,* H. W. R. Wade, 'The Basis of Legal Sovereignty', *1955 Cambridge Law Journal*, pp. 172, 189.
44. *Report of the Court of Inquiry Constituted Under Punjab Act II of 1954* (hereinafter *Munir Report*) (Lahore: Government of the Punjab Press, 1954) p. 203 *et seq.*
45. V CAD (Con.), p. 3.
46. Ibid., p. 42.
47. Ibid., p. 86.
48. Ibid., p. 46.
49. 'The real issue of the nature of an Islamic state was not yet joined, nor was it even clearly defined.' The Objectives Resolution '...was in fact only an agreed formulation which both sides interpreted in their own way.' What was intended by its drafters and the Assembly was only 'a deposit' on the constitution. Binder, op. cit., pp. 150-4. *See also,* Callard, *Political Study*, Ch. VI.
50. The Objectives Resolution was in subsequent years made the preamble of the Interim Report, the BPC Report, the 1954 draft of the constitution, and the 1956 and 1962 constitutions. *See,* discussion of the Objectives Resolution in *Zeaur Rehman v. State*, dec'd 1972, reported PLD 1986 Lahore 428, 514 (opinion by Justice Zafarullah). *See also, Ahmad Tariq Rahim v. Federation of Pakistan,* 44 A.P.L.D. 646 (S.C. 1991); *Hakim Khan v. Government of Pakistan,* 44 A.P.L.D., 595 (S.C. 1992).
51. Binder, op. cit., p. 159. But *see,* Sayeed, *Formative Phase*, p. 418: 'Parliamentary government had not taken deep roots in the soil of Pakistan.

It had been adopted as a legacy from the British and also because it was fashionable to do so in the modern world.'

52. *Dawn*, 18 December 1949.
53. *Dawn*, 18 December 1949 (editorial).
54. *Basic Principles Committee Interim Report* (Karachi: Constituent Assembly, 1950); VII CAD (Con.), pp. 13-50.
55. VIII CAD (Con.), p. 181.
56. VII CAD, (Con.), pp. 182 *et seq.*
57. VII CAD (Con.), p. 183.
58. Afzal, op. cit., p. 145.
59. According to Rehman, op. cit., p. 42, his review of the press coverage of the Interim Report showed that in one newspaper alone, the *Pakistan Observer,* there was detailed public reaction in the form of letters to the editor on at least six days and that four articles appeared in the newspaper on a single day, 13 October 1950.
60. 5 October 1950.
61. Hussain, op. cit., p. 54; *Dawn*, 22 January 1951.
62. 30 September 1950.
63. VIII CAD (Con.), pp. 181-5. To some, like Karl Newman, the withdrawal was a crucial event in Pakistan's constitutional history. 'Above all, he [Liaquat] was too slow in constitution making for the new state. Instead of applying Franklin D. Roosevelt's maxim that a statesman should suggest to the electorate what the electorate is to suggest to him, he threw his constitutional proposals wide open to public discussion. If he had chosen to submit a finished draft constitution to the Constituent Assembly not later than 1950, it would have been passed easily by the large Muslim League majority. Pakistan would have had a fundamental law and its subsequent development might have been different and happier.' Newman, 'Pakistan's Preventive Autocracy and Its Causes', 32 *Pacific Affairs*, p. 21 (1959). Newman's observation assumes that Liaquat had answers to the questions of east-west representation and the Islamic nature of the state which the Constituent Assembly would have been able to accept. His comment also overlooks the fact that Pakistan under Liaquat was not lacking fundamental law. Such law had existed since independence, embodied in the constitution made up of the amended Government of India Act of 1935. Pakistanis, like the people of any new nation, might wish to draft their own constitution if for no other reason but that the attempt itself would force the diverse groups making up the nation to consider important issues and reach agreements which would become contractual political terms of the new constitution. But regardless of the benefits of drafting their own constitution, that there was no immediate *need* to do so is attested to by the fact that when new constitutions were completed in 1954 and 1956, they contained such a high degree of the form and substance of the Government of India Act of 1935 as amended in 1947.
64. VIII CAD (Con.), p. 181. In response to Liaquat's assertion that further clarification of religious ideas of the constitution was needed, the *ulema* called a conference in January 1951. Despite their often sharp disagreement with him, the *ulema* invited Maududi to attend. The purpose of the meeting

seems to have been to prove to the Liaquat administration that they were able to agree on constitutional ideas. They succeeded only because Maududi dominated the conference. The *ulema* themselves appeared as disunited as ever, but this had little effect on the course of events because the suggestions of the conference were by and large ignored by the administration. Bahadur, op. cit., p. 61.

65. G. W. Choudhury, *Constitutional Development in Pakistan* (London: Longman, 1969) p. 72.
66. Binder's conclusion that 'Liaquat was well on his way to producing a constitution for Pakistan' seems to have little to support it. Op. cit., p. 244.
67. Suhrawardy, whose Awami League won 32 of out of 175 seats in the West Punjab election, gave his version of the provincial elections: 'These elections were rigged with a vengeance in the interest of the Muslim League.' He characterized the results of the election and those in the NWFP and Sindh as resulting in 'no difference in the complexion of the legislatures. The same League governments and party were in power and the same kind of people had been returned. Namely, those belonging to the feudal aristocracy, except in the NWFP where Khan Abdul Qayyum Khan had taken care to see that a large number of illiterates were elected so that no one in the legislature would ever be able to challenge his supremacy.' Suhrawardy, *Memoirs*, p. 83.

Chapter 4. Ghulam Mohammad Ends Cabinet Government

1. Amjad Ali interview (1992).
2. Newman interview (1991).
3. Hussain, op. cit., p. 57.
4. Amjad Ali interview (1992).
5. Sir Frederick Bourne, 'Constitutional Government Before and After the Transfer of Power,' 46 *Asiatic Review*, No. 168 (1950) p. 1111.
6. Chaudri Mohammad Ali, op. cit., p. 284.
7. Munir, *Highways and Bye-Ways*, p. 74, and in his *Chief Justice Muhammad Munir, His Life, Writings and Judgments* (Lahore: Research Society of Pakistan, Nazir A. Choudhury [ed.], 1973) p. 19. Some historians and political scientists have not viewed Nazimuddin as kindly as did his contemporaries. While G. W. Choudhry credits Nazimuddin with being a respected leader and one of the few Pakistani politicians who appear to have had a genuine regard for parliamentary government, Sayeed describes him as being 'extremely affable' but 'weak, indecisive and depending entirely on the counsel of his shrewd brother, Khwaja Shahabuddin.' Jalal assesses him as 'a man whose reputation for weakness was tempered only by that of religious piety' and charges him with a 'talent for making wrong decisions at critical moments.' Choudhury, *Democracy in Pakistan*, p. 10; Sayeed, *Formative Phase*, p. 231; Jalal, *State of Martial Law*, p. 137.
8. Newman, *Preventive Autocracy*, op. cit., p. 24, and interview (1991).
9. Jalal, *State of Martial Law*, p. 108.

10. Chaudhri Muhammad Ali, op. cit., p. 375.
11. Qudratullah Shahab, *Shahab Nama* (Lahore: Sang-e-meel Publications, 1987) p. 656.
12. Newman interview (1991).
13. Amjad Ali interview (1992).
14. Mohammad Ayub Khan, *Friends Not Masters, a Political Autobiography* (New York: Oxford University Press, 1967) p. 51.
15. Munir, *Life, Writings and Judgments*, p. 19. Ghulam Mohammad was later described as 'a man of immense willpower...unwilling to interpret his own role as merely ornamental.' Callard, *Political Study*, p. 23. He was also referred to as 'perhaps the most controversial figure of Pakistan's political history...Ghulam Mohammad knew only one method of dealing with opponents: their ruthless elimination.' Khalid B. Sayeed, 'The Political Role of the Pakistan Civil Service,' 31 *Pacific Affairs* 131, 134 (1958).
16. *Quaid-i-Azam Papers*, op. cit., F.264/3, 4, 6, and 7.
17. Muhammad Munir, *Constitution of the Islamic Republic of Pakistan* (Lahore: All Pakistan Legal Decisions, 1975) p. 30. Further on Ghulam Muhammad's background, that of Iskander Mirza, and on the make-up of the Punjab group, *see*, Ziring, *Failure of Democracy in Pakistan*, p. 116; Goodnow, op. cit., pp. 72-3.
18. D. G. Karve, 'The New Constitution—Principles and Prospects,' 3 *University of Toronto Law Journal* 281, 296 (1940).
19. Amjad Ali interview (1992).
20. But *see*, Jalal, *The State of Martial Rule*, *passim*.
21. *See*, his *Friends Not Masters*, *passim*, and Callard, *Political Forces*, p. 20.
22. Shafqat, op. cit., pp. 143-5. Jalal asserts that: 'It was the skillful manipulation of international connections that eventually cleared the ground for the development of the institutional imbalances that have plagued Pakistan's history.' *The State of Martial Rule*, p. 124.
23. For an account of the language incident, *see*, Ziring, *Failure of Democracy in Pakistan*, pp. 118-39. For economic problems, *see*, Ahmad, *Government and Politics*, p. 37. A summary of an investigation of the violence arising from the language controversy, conducted by Mr Justice Ellis of the High Court of Judicature at Dhaka, was published as *Report of the Enquiry into the Firing by the Police at Dhaka on 21 February 1952* (Dhaka: Government of East Bengal Press, 1952) and appeared also in the *Pakistan Times*, 1 June 1952.
24. Jamiluddin Ahmad (ed.), *Speeches and Writings of Mr Jinnah*. (Lahore: 1964) Vol. III, pp. 496-7. A Bangladesh journalist, the chief of the news bureau of the *Daily Hindustan*, later charged, 'A man of impeccable tastes, Jinnah was also a first class hypocrite. He knew full well that Urdu could not become the lingua franca of Pakistan. Not only was it not the language of Bengalis but it was also not the language of Sindh, Balochistan, and NWFP...He was not echoing the sentiments of the vast majority of the Pakistanis but a handful of people of the Punjab whose real mother-tongue was something other than Urdu.' Yatindra Bhatnagar, *Mujeb* (Delhi: ISSD, 1971), p. 57.
25. Aziz, op. cit., p. 7, n. 3, states that there were reports that Jinnah was heckled. Bhatnagar's account, written in 1971, placed long-term significance in Jinnah's speech. After Jinnah concluded his speech, 'There was a hush but

only for a fraction of a second. It was broken by a daring student and his bold band of fire-eating friends.' They declared they wanted Bengali as the national language. 'It was the beginning of the revolt (for Bangladesh).' Bhatnagar, op. cit., p. 57.

26. Sayeed, *The Political System of Pakistan,* (Karachi: Civil and Military Gazette Press, 1967), p. 189.
27. The Muslim League was Urdu-oriented from its founding. Kenneth McPherson, *The Muslim Microcosm,* p. 27. Also ibid., Ch. I, Rafat Roy, *Urban Riots of Indian Nationalism* (New Delhi: Vikas, 1979) p. 165.
28. Ziring, *Failure of Democracy,* p. 121. Chaudhri Muhammad Ali blamed the disturbances on 'a small group of politicians in East Pakistan, mainly to embarrass the Nazimuddin ministry...' He also saw the hand of the Calcutta Hindu Press playing a part. Chaudhri Mohammad Ali, op. cit., p. 365.
29. *Nawa-i-Waqt,* 5 December 1951.
30. Binder, op. cit., p. 246.
31. *Dawn,* 7 December 1951.
32. Inamur Rehman, *Public Opinion and Political Development in Pakistan* (Karachi: Oxford University Press, 1982) p. 19.
33. Bahadur, op. cit., p. 62.
34. Rehman, op. cit., pp. 19-20.
35. Binder, op. cit., p. 254.
36. XII CAD (Con.) pp. 80-160.
37. *Dawn,* 22 November 1952; *Pakistan Times,* 26 November 1952.
38. Punjab, Sindh, NWFP, Tribal Areas, Bahawalpur, Balochistan, Balochistan State, Khairpur State, and Karachi.
39. *Dawn,* 24 and 25 December 1952; Afzal, op. cit., p. 148.
40. For a review of press coverage, *see,* Riaz Ahmed, *Constitutional and Political Development in Pakistan October 1951-October 1954,* (M. Phil. Dissertation, Quaid-i-Azam University, Islamabad, 1954).
41. 26 December 1952.
42. Excerpts from letters to the editor columns quoted in Rehman, op. cit., pp. 32-3.
43. 31 December 1952.
44. 11 January 1953.
45. Binder, op. cit., p. 258.
46. Tamizuddin Khan, *Test of Time* (Dhaka: University Press, 1960), p. 150.
47. Afzal, op. cit., p. 148; Riaz Ahmed, op cit., p. 39.
48. Firoz Khan Noon, *From Memory* (Lahore: Ferozsons, 1966) p. 234. 'This situation was brought about by people who wanted to get into power in the Centre. They thought that by creating unrest, the men at the helm of affairs in the centre would have to go. The old tried method of attacking a religious minority sect called Ahmadis was used to inflame the minds of otherwise peaceful people.' Noon identified those 'at the helm of affairs in the centre,' after the murder of Liaquat, as being Ghulam Mohammad, Chaudhuri Mohammad Ali, and Iskander Mirza, who Noon pointed out were all unelected officials. Ibid., p. 246. Noon was appointed to replace Daultana, who was removed by the central government's Section 92A action during the Ahmadi riots.

49. According to information based on personal interviews he conducted in Pakistan, K. B. Sayeed has informed the author that it was Mirza who ordered the army to take action in the Punjab when he believed Nazimuddin was vacillating. Sayeed was unable to get affirmation or denial when he interviewed Nazimuddin, who was so sensitive on this point that he terminated the interview when Sayeed broached the subject.
50. Bahadur, op. cit., p. 67-75.
51. Daultana believed that it was his opposition to Nazimuddin's constitutional plan, not the Ahmadi controversy, which was the cause of his dismissal. Daultana interview (1992).
52. *Dawn*, 9 April 1953.
53. 11 April 1953.
54. Hussain, op. cit., p. 75; Amjad Ali interview (1992).
55. *Dawn*, 19 April 1953.
56. *Pakistan Times*, 19 April 1953.
57. Hussain, op. cit., p. 79. Jalal, *The State of Martial Rule*, p. 179, also states that Nazimuddin's house was placed under guard and his telephone line disconnected. She claims that Nazimuddin contacted the British High Commission who, however, (in Jalal's words) 'thought it politic not to transmit the Prime Minister's telegram to the Queen'. Jalal also reports that Mirza and Ayub were active participants in the removal of Nazimuddin and had the army in readiness in case there was opposition. *See also,* Nur Ahmed Syed, *From Military Law to Martial Law* (Boulder: Westview, 1985) p. 321.
58. Quoted in Hussain, op. cit., p. 79.
59. *Pakistan Times*, 19 April 1953. Binder claims that: 'In a matter of days Nazimuddin accepted his dismissal, and a life pension of 2,000 rupees per month, provided he would stay out of public life' op. cit., p. 297. Unfortunately Binder gives no further information. Nazimuddin did not stay out of public life. He remained in the Constituent Assembly and was active and effective in the attempt to complete the new constitution. Afzal accepts Nazimuddin's claim that he did not challenge his dismissal because he did not wish to harm Pakistan's image abroad. *Political Parties*, p. 52.
60. *Pakistan Times*, 21, 23 April and 27 May 1953. For editorial protests as well as protests by the Azad Pakistan Party, *see, ibid.*, 27 July 1953.
61. 20 April 1955.
62. Quoted in Callard, *Political Study*, p. 135.
63. Binder, op. cit., p. 299.
64. Jalal, *State of Martial Rule*, p. 178.
65. Munir, *Life, Writings and Judgments*, p. 19.
66. K. B. Sayeed, 'The Political Role of the Pakistan Civil Service,' 31 *Pacific Affairs*, (1958), p. 331, maintains that because of the breakdown of political government in the provinces, the civil service effectively controlled the entire administration of the provinces, and the politicians were kept in office subject to their willingness to obey central government directives. Altaf Gauhar, who served as a magistrate in East Bengal during this period, supports Sayeed's conclusion as to East Bengal. He states that the Muslim League depended on the civil service to manage a hoped-for victory for the League in the March 1954 election. Gauhar interview (1992). But *see*, Henry F. Goodnow,

The Civil Service of Pakistan (New Haven: Yale University Press, 1964) Ch. 4.

67. Binder, op. cit., p. 239.
68. Ambassador Emerson, quoted in Jalal, *State of Martial Rule*, p. 179. *See also,* Wayne A. Wilcox, *Pakistan: The Consolidation of a Nation* (New York: Columbia University Press, 1963) p. 171.
69. Ayub, op. cit., p. 50.
70. *New York Times*, 21 June 1953. Noon of West Punjab and Nur Amin of East Bengal, chief ministers of their respective provinces, were among the seven who refused to serve.
71. While Callard was willing to admit that certain principles of parliamentary government were breached when Nazimuddin was dismissed, he did not place much emphasis on that fact but instead stressed the allegation that Nazimuddin was not an efficient administrator. Callard adopted the view that no one in the Cabinet or the Assembly really cared, the Assembly did not even consider Nazimuddin's dismissal as 'worthy of debate.' The matter seemed to Callard little more than an inconvenient interruption in government affairs. 'Ghulam Mohammad was left with an awkward political situation on his hands.' Callard ignored the possibility that the dismissal was carried out accompanied by the use of police. He seemed to completely misread what happened when he concluded that, 'The Governor-General's action was not a personal seizure of power.' *Political Study*, pp. 135-7.
72. *Dawn*, 19 April 1953. But after leaving office Brohi later wrote, 'Over and above the law of the Constitution, is invariably to be found a set of rules, rules which are habitually obeyed by those who are concerned in the administration of public affairs, and these are called conventions of the Constitution or, what comes to the some thing, the political understandings—and they form the hard core of the ethics of constitutional behaviour or constitutional morality.' Brohi, *Fundamental Laws of Pakistan*, p. 3.
73. Under GIA of 1935 the Governor-General in British India chose ministries to assist him to conduct the affairs of government. The ministers were to serve 'during his pleasure' (§10). He was however 'enjoined' to chose his ministers by consulting 'the person who in his judgment is likely to command the largest following in the legislature'. *Joint Committee on Constitutional Reforms (1933-34 Session)* (London: HM Stationery Office, 1934) Vol. I, Part 1. *See,* Geoffrey Marshall, *Constitutional Conventions* (Oxford: Oxford University Press, 1984) pp. 25-34; Jennings, *Cabinet Government* (Cambridge: Cambridge University Press, 1955) pp. 368, 530-8. At independence the British believed that the Prime Minister would be a person possessing the confidence of the Assembly. *See, supra*, Ch.2.
74. GIA §10. 'A proposition more destructive of the parliamentary system could not be advanced as it meant that no administration could survive the displeasure of the Governor-General however much it might enjoy the confidence of the Parliament or the people. It made the Governor-General an arbiter of the fate of governments, which he could dismiss or appoint at his will or whim.' Mushtaq Ahmad, *Government and Politics,* p. 13.
75. *Dawn*, 19 April 1953.
76. Ibid., 21 April 1953.

77. Ibid., 29 April 1953.
78. *Morning News*, 26 April 1953.
79. 20 April 1953.
80. 21 April 1953.
81. 22 April 1953.
82. 21 April 1953.
83. 23 April 1953.
84. Interview with Amjad Ali (1992), who in 1953 was Pakistan's Ambassador in Washington.

Chapter 5. The 1954 Constitution and the Dissolution of the Assembly

1. *See, Munir Report*, op. cit., Part III.
2. 24 August, 1952.
3. *Dawn*, 7 September 1952.
4. Hussein S. Suhrawardy, *Memoirs* (Dhaka: University Press, 1987), p. 79. There were originally sixty-nine members of the Assembly. Five members were added after independence.
5. Of the original sixty-nine members of the Constituent Assembly, forty-nine belonged to the Muslim League Parliamentary Party, with twenty-four from East Bengal and fourteen from West Punjab. Both the Bengali and the West Pakistani membership were internally disunited, the latter because West Pakistan consisted of several provinces and the Punjabis were badly split within their own delegates; the Bengalis were not united because twenty-five per cent of its Assembly delegation was Hindu.
6. Nur Ahmad, op. cit., p. 345.
7. 7 October 1953.
8. 26 August 1953. Suhrawardy was at first reluctant to endorse One Unit even as he moved into alliance with Ghulam Mohammad. While he termed the concept as being fostered as 'a solid front against East Pakistan,' he appreciated that it could afford administrative efficiency. Perhaps to avoid conflict with Ghulam Mohammad, Suhrawardy gave as his reason for opposition the unreadiness of West Pakistan for unity because the people needed more information to convince them of the advantages of the One Unit Plan else there was danger of failure, which Suhrawardy maintained would be of greater harm than if the idea was never tried. Suhrawardy, *Memoirs*, p. 92. When he took office after the Assembly's dissolution he supported One Unit, much to the displeasure of many of his Bengali allies. His support of West Pakistani unity continued when he became Prime Minister, at which time he may have won over some of the Bengali politicians. Unfortunately for Suhrawardy, by that time One Unit was becoming unpopular in West Pakistan. *Economist*, 19 October 1957.
9. Ayub, op. cit., pp. 186-92.
10. Munir, *Highways and Bye-Ways*, p. 77.
11. Ayub, op. cit., p. 50; Amjad Ali interview (1992).

12. Jalal, *State of Martial Rule*, p. 180. Callard, *Political Study*, p. 138.
13. *See,* example in Ziring, *Failure of Democracy in Pakistan*, p. 115.
14. Munir, *Life, Writings and Judgments*, p. 20.
15. One party, the Peasant-Workers Party (Krishak Sramik Party) was a resurrection of Fazlul Huq's pre-independence party which had been disbanded when he joined the Muslim League. Huq again led the party, which was re-established in May 1953. It was intended that this party, which enjoyed the backing of the religious factions in East Bengal, would represent the interests of a growing working class, as well as representing the interests of the peasants. Other parties formed were the Democratic Party (Ganatantri Dal), Islamic Order Party (Nazam-i-Islam Party), and Divine Sovereignty Party (Khilâfat-i-Rabbani Party).
16. Bahadur, op. cit., p. 62. The Jamaat-e-Islami Party also entered the provincial elections in West Punjab and the NWFP. It did not field its own slate of candidates, hoping only to instruct public opinion. If provincial leadership could be changed, the Jamaat believed, the work of building an Islamic state could perhaps begin. While the Jamaat made little impact on the outcome of the elections, the fact that the party participated was itself a significant departure from its previous policy that elections were un-Islamic. After the Objectives Resolution was adopted that changed, and the Jamaat declared that Pakistan was now an Islamic state, at least in principle.
17. Altaf Gauhar interview (1992).
18. Goodnow, op. cit., p. 58, claims that the Assembly's reaction was to 'gloss over' the situation presented by the dismissal of Nazimuddin. Goodnow does not deal with the fact that Ghulam Mohammad was backing his claimed right to dismiss the Cabinet with police power, which he had demonstrated he was willing to use. Ziring, *Enigma of Political Development*, p. 77, is not correct when he indicates that Nazimuddin could have challenged his dismissal in court. Nazimuddin was dismissed in April of 1953. Section 223A, authorizing the writ action upon which the Assembly later challenged its dissolution, was not made law until July of 1954. Government of India (Amendment) Act, 1954; 26 Geo. V, c. 2.
19. F. Innes, 'The Political Outlook in Pakistan,' 26 *Pacific Affairs*, 303, 306 (1953). After leaving the ICS, Innes was adviser to the Pakistan Central Commercial Committee and was correspondent for the *Economist, Round Table,* and *Manchester Guardian.*
20. *New York Times,* 8 October 1953
21. 6 October 1953. *See also,* 'New Brooms in Pakistan,' *New Statesman*, 6 November 1953.
22. Ayub, op. cit., p. 50.
23. Binder, op. cit., p. 309. Ardath W. Burks, 'Constitution Making in Pakistan,' 69 *Political Science Quarterly*, 550 (1954). Burks visited Pakistan and wrote at the time of the events related here. He saw Bogra as representing 'the younger, more progressive elements in the Muslim League,' and saw his 'decisive views' as a powerful behind-the-scenes influence.

24. XV CAD (Con.), pp. 13-14. The Mohammad Ali Formula was as follows:

	Upper House	Lower House	Total
East Bengal	10	165	175
Punjab	10	75	85
NWFP, Frontier States, Tribal Areas	10	24	34
Sindh and Karachi	10	19	29
Balochistan, BSU, Bahawalpur	10	17	27
Total	50	300	350

25. Sayeed, *Political System*, p. 72. For a detailed account of the debates on the formula, *see*, Binder, op. cit., pp. 315-44. Karl Newman claims that he, at the request of Bogra, devised the formula. Newman interview (1991).
26. According to Newman, Bogra presented 'a constitutional draft which was acceptable both to East and West Pakistan.' 'Pakistan's Preventative Autocracy' op. cit., p. 25. Burks, op. cit., p. 562, reported that '...the federal formula was unanimously accepted by the government, by the Chief Ministers of East Bengal, the Punjab, Sindh, the North-West Frontier Province, and Bahawalpur, all members of the Muslim League Parliamentary Party, as well as by the Constituent Assembly.' Sayeed asks, 'Did this mean that the entire Punjabi group accepted this formula?' Sayeed, who had interviewed many of the contemporary figures involved, answered his question by stating that he had found no evidence to the contrary. He also points out that Punjabi leaders like Noon and Daultana, as well as newspapers as diverse as *The Civil and Military Gazette* and *Nawa-e-Waqt*, welcomed the compromise formula. Sayeed, *Formative Phase*, p. 419. *See also*, Binder, op. cit., p. 312; G. W. Choudhury, *Constitutional Development in Pakistan* (London: Longmans, 1964), p. 79; Afzal, op. cit., p. 155.
27. *New York Times*, 8 October 1953.
28. XV CAD (Con.), p. 11 *et seq*. A blank copy of a workbook used is in *Jennings Papers*, op cit., B/XV/1-2.
29. 8 October 1953.
30. Several years later, Callard, based on his experience in Pakistan at the time of constitution-making, recounted his impression of the Assembly in action. 'Constitutional issues were intricately involved in the manoeuvring of control of a province or of influence within the federal cabinet. Each decision was one of a series of hard-fought compromises. Each new issue and each fluctuation of real political power, altered the balance of the whole and opened the way for fresh manoeuvres. At no stage did the leaders of the League make up their minds to endorse an entire scheme of government, and to demand its acceptance or rejection as a whole. Each issue was resolved after hard bargaining, accepted "unanimously" by the Muslim League Parliamentary Party, and presented as a *fait accompli* to the Assembly.' Callard, *Political Study*, p. 99.
31. Unfavourable: *Pakistan Times*, 7 October 1953; *Pakistan Observer*, 15 October 1953. Favourable: *Dawn*, 6, 8, 9, and 20 October 1953.
32. 15 October 1953.
33. 9 October 1953.
34. *New York Times*, 22 October 1953.

35. 6 October 1953.
36. XV CAD (Con.), pp. 480-748.
37. *New York Times*, 1 November 1953. Cf. 'It can be argued that Pakistan's leaders never intended to rest the national foundation on a constitutional rock. It was fashionable and perhaps even necessary to pay lip-service to constitutional enactments, but it is doubtful that many were serious about their commitment to such abstract, legal contrivances.' Ziring, *Enigma of Political Development*, p. 168.
38. XV CAD (Con.), p. 748. Burks, op. cit., p. 559, reported: 'Beginning 22 September 1953 Federal Cabinet members and Chief Ministers of provinces met daily to try to resolve the problem of representation in the House of the People, reflected specifically in the dispute between the Punjab and East Bengal.'
39. Ibid., p. 748.
40. Ibid., p. 749.
41. Ibid., p. 753.
42. Ibid., p. 750. The Islamic nature of the constitution caused concern to be expressed by the Indian government because of the large Hindu population in East Bengal. Addressing these concerns, Minister of Justice Brohi announced that Pakistan government would submit legislation protecting minority rights. *New York Times*, 8 November 1953. Nehru publicly announced that Pakistan's constitution, because it was Islamic, was 'a rather medieval conception' and one totally opposed to democratic ideals. Burks, op. cit., p. 563.
43. IIA §8(1).
44. For coverage of the elections, *see,* Goodnow, op. cit., p. 61; Callard, *Political Study*, pp. 110, 140; Afzal, *Political Parties*, p. 85.
45. Newman, 'Pakistan's Preventative Autocracy,' 32 *Pacific Affairs*, 18, 22 (1959). According to Altaf Gauhar, who acted as one of the officials in charge of the East Bengal election, there was abundant public indication well in advance of the election of how the Bengalis intended to vote but the leaders of the Muslim League and the officials of the central government seemed not interested in listening. Gauhar interview (1992).
46. Suhrawardy, *Memoirs*, p. 85.
47. *Dawn*, 17 June 1953. A, op. cit., p. 23, reports that after the 1951 election in West Punjab the newly-elected legislature of that province made a demand that the Punjab members of the Constituent Assembly resign because the provincial election had shown them to be no longer representative.
48. Ibid., 28 March 1954.
49. IIA§ 8(1).
50. 18 March 1954.
51. *Dawn,* 9 April 1954.
52. Ibid., 21 March 1954.
53. XVI CAD (Con.), p. 93.
54. Ibid., pp. 217-495.
55. *Pakistan Times*, 20, 21, 23, 24, and 29 April, 8 May, 1, 2, and 6 June 1954.
56. *New York Times*, 23 May 1954; *Pakistan Times*, 26 May 1954. *The Statesman* (Calcutta) of 4 May 1954, reported Huq as having said, 'I do not believe in

the political division of a country. I am, in fact, not familiar with the words—Pakistan and Hindustan—when I speak of India I mean both the countries.' Huq's sometime ally Suhrawardy described Huq's statement: 'With his usual emotionalism and want of balance when in the presence of an audience, [Huq] made a speech at a meeting in Calcutta which was calculated to draw the acclaim and plaudits of his Hindi-Indian audience. The newspapers reported him stating that he could not understand the *raison d'etre* of Pakistan and would bend his energies to bring the two parts of Bengal together.' Suhrawardy, *Memoirs*, p. 86. At the time of independence, Huq and Suhrawardy had advocated an independent undivided Bengal and Huq had at times been a political ally of Hindu politicians during his long career in Bengal under British rule.

57. *Dawn*, 25 and 31 May 1954.
58. *New York Times*, 31 May 1954. Binder states: 'Some additional troops were also dispatched, but their numbers are not known. In any case, no important disorders occurred. Bengalis themselves are swift to admit that the central government was seriously provoked.' Op. cit., p. 351, n. 12. Jalal claims that there was a serious 'law and order problem' in the province. *State of Martial Rule*, p. 190. On 5 June 1954 *Dawn* reported that 400 people had died in a riot at the Adamjee Mills but that the authorities appeared to be doing nothing. Newman, however, who lived in East Bengal at the time, agrees that the situation was violent, but no more so than usual in what he considers a turbulent society. Newman interview (1991).
59. *Pakistan Times*, 7 June 1954; *Dawn*, 30 June 1954.
60. *Pakistan Times*, 1 June1954.
61. Ibid., 2 June 1954.
62. *Pakistan Times*, 1 June 1954.
63. *Dawn*, 2, 19, and 21 June 1954; *Pakistan Times*, 27 May, 1, 2, and 6 June 1954. Raids were made on the headquarters of the Communist Party in East Bengal, and the party was put out of operation. *Dawn*, 26 July 1954.
64. Ziring, *Failure of Democracy*, p. 191.
65. Suhrawardy, *Memoirs*, p. 86.
66. Binder, op. cit., p. 353.
67. XVI CAD (Con.), p. 353-65.
68. Suhrawardy, *Memoirs*, pp. 88-91.
69. *Pakistan Times*, 3 and 14 September 1954.
70. XVI CAD (Con.), p. 353.
71. XVI CAD (Con.), pp. 356-9. After seizing power Ghulam Mohammad dismissed Noon's Punjab Ministry because, according to Noon, he, Noon, was thought to be not a strong enough supporter of One Unit. Noon, op. cit., p. 245. One Unit also later brought Suhrawardy to grief when in 1962 it became an issue between him and then President Mirza and led to his dismissal as Prime Minister.
72. XVI CAD (Con.), pp. 359-63; *Dawn* and *Pakistan Times*, 16 September 1954.
73. XVI CAD (Con.), p. 361.
74. Binder, op. cit., p. 357. '[T]he climax was reached when the Governor-General hinted to the Prime Minister himself that he also could be a victim

of PRODA.' Sayeed, *Formative Phase*, p. 420. Sayeed asserts that it was a combination of the Bengali-Sindh-Frontier groups which enabled the Assembly to move against Ghulam Mohammad by repealing PRODA and amending the constitution. Ibid., p. 421. For a discussion of PRODA, *see*, Ch. VI *infra*.

75. XVI CAD (Con.), p. 419.
76. XVI CAD (Con.), p. 451; Government of India (5th Amendment) Act, 1954, amending Sections 9, 10, 10A, 10B, and 17. *Pakistan Times*, 22 September 1954; *Dawn*, 21 September 1954. *For*, Munir's comments on the clash between the Assembly and the Governor-General, *see*, Munir, *Life, Writings and Judgments*, p. 119.
77. Statement accompanying the bill, quoted in Callard, *Political Study*, p. 107. Although he did not discuss this point in any of the litigation following the dissolution of the Constituent Assembly, Chief Justice Munir was aware of the political significance of these legal moves by the Assembly. Munir, *Life, Writings and Judgments*, p. 20.
78. *See*, Marshall, *Constitutional Conventions*, p. 19.
79. Cf. Callard, *Political Study*, pp. 102-13. Callard held to the theory that the Assembly's actions were a 'conspiracy' by 'rebels' against the Governor-General. The term 'conspiracy' was also used by Suhrawardy in his *Memoirs*, p. 85. Binder terms the Assembly's actions part of a 'vendetta against the constitutional counterpart of the Governor-General.' Op cit., p. 352. Stephens, who served as editor of the *Calcutta Stateman* from 1942 to 1951 and was historian to the Pakistan Army from 1957 to 1967, adopted Callard's conspiracy approach, and blamed what he termed a 'seizure of power' by Fazlur Rahman. Ian Stephens, *Pakistan* (London: Ernest Benn, 1963) p. 241.
80. *Dawn*, 22 September 1954.
81. 23 September and 9 October 1954.
82. 7 and 9 October 1954.
83. XVI CAD (Con.), pp. 499-510, 570-2.
84. Under the rules of the Assembly, legislation, including constitutional legislation, was enacted if it received the votes of the majority present.
85. The date was subsequently changed to 28 October.
86. Karachi: Manager Government Press, 1954. Burks, op. cit., p. 544, n. 5a.
87. Jennings' corrections on the final draft of the constitution are shown in his handwriting in the *Jennings Papers*, Institute of Commonwealth Research, London, B/XV/4-5.
88. *Dawn*, 2 October 1954. Rehman, op. cit., p. 76.
89. *Pakistan Times*, 5 October 1954.
90. Part III, based on the *Report of the Committee on Fundamental Rights of Citizens of Pakistan and the Matters Relating to Minorities*, adopted by the Assembly on 7 September 1954. An earlier report on the same subjects had been passed on 6 October 1950, as an interim report.
91. *Draft Constitution of Pakistan, Confidential*, Preamble.
92. Ibid.
93. Ibid., Part V, ch. III.
94. Ibid., §1.
95. Ibid., §3(1).

96. Ibid., §§1 and 2.
97. Ibid., Pt. III
98. Ibid., §75.
99. Ibid., Second Schedule, Part III.
100. Ibid., Part XII.
101. Ibid., §§45 and 85.
102. Ibid., Part V, ch. II.
103. Ibid., Part V and Fifth Schedule.
104. Newman, 'Pakistan's Preventative Autocracy,' op. cit., p. 25.
105. *Draft Constitution of Pakistan, Confidential,* Section 63.
106. Burks, 'Constitution-Making in Pakistan,' op. cit., p. 360.
107. Binder op. cit., p. 268. *See also,* Callard, *Political Study,* pp. 93-7. Syed, *Islam, Politics and National Solidarity,* pp. 80-1. Cf. Ziring, *Enigma of Political Development,* pp. 137, 168, 174.
108. *Dawn,* 23 October 1954; Binder, op. cit., p. 361.
109. *Dawn,* 15 October 1954; Bahadur, op. cit., p. 75.
110. Rehman, op. cit., p. 149.
111. 10 October 1954.
112. *Dawn,* 7 October 1954; *Pakistan Observer,* 10 October 1954.
113. Binder, op. cit., p. 358.
114. (Karachi, Manager Government Press, 1954.) It contained the printed notation preceding the text of the constitution: 'TO BE INTRODUCED IN THE CONSTITUENT ASSEMBLY OF PAKISTAN'.
115. *Dawn,* 14 October 1954. Noon was known not to favour the dissolution of the Assembly.
116. G. W. Choudhury, *The First Constitution of Pakistan,* Ph.D. Dissertation, Columbia University, 1956, p. 209.
117. *Dawn,* 2 and 10 October 1954.
118. Tamizuddin Khan, *The Test of Time,* p. 151. Ziring, *Failure of Democracy,* p. 198, claims that Ghulam Mohammad encouraged Bogra to leave the country to place his children in school in England. Sayeed claims that Bogra thought because Ghulam Mohammad was a sick man, he would not contest the Assembly's actions against him, and that Bogra also believed that Ghulam Mohammad would do nothing which would embarrass Pakistan while the Prime Minister was negotiating in Washington. Sayeed, *Formative Phase,* p. 421.
119. *Pakistan Times,* 10 August 1954; Ziring, *Failure of Democracy,* p. 196, recounts the verbal lashing Ghulam Mohammad gave Bogra when the latter reported the action of the Assembly over the telephone.
120. *Pakistan Times,* 21 October, and editorial comment 22 October 1954.
121. *New York Times,* 21 October 1954.
122. *Pakistan Times,* 10 and 16 October 1954; *Dawn,* 16 and 27 October 1954; Afzal, op. cit., p. 162.
123. *New York Times,* 24 October 1954.
124. *Dawn,* 24 October 1954.
125. *Dawn,* 19 October 1954. For some of the pro-constitution activities of the religious groups and the statements of their leaders *see,* ibid., 15, 16, 19, and 20 October 1954.

126. Ibid., 24 October 1954.
127. *New York Times*, 21 October 1954.
128. Ibid., 23 October 1954.
129. Ayub, op. cit., p. 51.
130. Ziring, *Failure of Democracy*, p. 200. It is Binder's opinion that the Assembly would have had to actually have removed the Governor-General before the Queen would have acted, op. cit., p. 306.
131. *Dawn*, 24 October 1954.
132. *Dawn* and *Pakistan Times*, 24 October 1954.
132A 8 November 1954. According to this account, Bogra's wife was 'elbowed' out of the car and two Generals escorted him to the Governor-General's residence.
133. Ayub, op. cit., p. 52.
134. Mohammad Musa, *My Chief* (Lahore: Longmans, Green & Co., 1960) p. 1.
135. Ibid., p. 4
136. According to Wheeler, *The Times* of London reported that Bogra protested against the takeover for two hours, then went home to sleep on the question. Wheeler, *Governor-General's Rule*, p. 4. Ziring, presumably based on personal interviews, claims that after leaving his meeting with the Governor-General, Bogra met with his Muslim League associates who were waiting for him and claimed that it was he who had saved the country from Army rule. Ziring terms Bogra's claim 'an empty, false and pompous statement.' *Failure of Democracy*, p. 135.
137. *Dawn*, 25 October 1954.
138. Ibid., 23 October 1954.
139. Reprinted in Ziring, *Failure of Democracy*, p. 203. Even if it could be said that Ghulam was acting with the advice of his Prime Minister his act would still have to be authorized by the GIA or the IIA. *See,* Ch. 8, n. 70, *infra*.
140. *Pakistan Times*, 31 October 1954.
141. *New York Times*, 28 October 1954.
142. *Dawn*, 31 October 1954.
143. *Calcutta Statesman*, 29 October 1954.
144. *New York Times*, 29 October 1954.
145. June 1955, p. 28.

Chapter 6. Ghulam Mohammad's Pakistan 1954

1. *Calcutta Statesman*, 26 October 1954.
2. Mirza was described at the time by an American adviser to the Pakistan government as a man who lacked imagination. 'Mirza understands the routines of administration, the negative business of maintaining order and the techniques of divide and rule. Politics as a business of producing consensus was beyond him—something fearful and strange.' Charles B. Marshall, 'Reflections on a Revolution in Pakistan', *Foreign Affairs* (January 1959) 247, 251.
3. *Dawn*, 31 October 1954.
4. Ibid., 30 and 31 October 1954.

5. *Dawn*, 15 November 1954. *See,* Philip Deane, 'The Men Who Really Run Pakistan', 12 *The Reporter* 33 (1955).
6. 30 October 1954.
7. Ibid.
8. *New York Times*, 30 October 1954.
9. Ibid.
10. 27 October 1954.
11. 3 November 1954.
12. 3 November, 7 and 8 December 1954.
13. 26 October 1954.
14. 3 November 1954.
15. 26 and 27 October 1954.
16. Rehman, op. cit., p. 153.
17. Shafqat, op. cit., Ch. 4.
18. Jalal, *State of Martial Rule,* p. 187.
19. Keith Callard, 'The Political Stability of Pakistan,' 29 *Pacific Affairs,* 5, 18 (1957); Ayub, op. cit., p. 50; Amjad Ali interview (1992). Jalal, *State of Martial Law*, Ch. 4, attributes a very important role to the military in manipulating political events from behind the scene during this period.
20. *See,* his plan set out in Ayub, op. cit., pp. 186-92.
21. Ziring, *Failure of Democracy*, p. 199.
22. *Calcutta Statesman*, 21 October 1954.
23. Suhrawardy, *Memoirs*, p. 86. Although rivals, Suhrawardy at first was able to work closely with Mirza. Stephens observed them as a strange but effective team. 'Temperamentally indeed, they had resemblances. Clever, and aware of it; bold; personally ambitious, and rejoicers in power for its own sake; thoroughly westernized and secular; and not noticeably shackled by ethical scruples, they were well-qualified, in partnership, to give the country resolute leadership.' Stephens, op. cit., p. 244.
24. Binder, op. cit., p. 361.
25. *Pakistan Observer*, 10 November 1954.
26. Aziz, op. cit., p. 263.
27. Stephens, op. cit., p. 243.
28. Aziz, op. cit., p. 245.
29. Quoted in Charles Haines, *The American Doctrine of Judicial Supremacy* (New York: Russell & Russell, 1959) p. 25.
30. F. A. Mann, 'Britain's Bill of Rights,' 94 *Law Quarterly Review* 512, 514 (1977). Mann characterized the opposition of Britain's intellectual community as being 'hostile' to fundamental rights and cited Harold Lasky as an example. Ibid., p. 516.
31. Francis Wormuth, *The Origins of Modern Constitutionalism* (New York: Harper & Brothers, 1949) p. 210. Dicey observed that 'a modern judge would not listen to a barrister who argued that an Act of Parliament was invalid because it was immoral or went beyond the limits of Parliamentary authority.' Quoted in Mann, op. cit., p. 515. For more recent effects of the absence of guaranteed rights with reference to the Thatcher government's policy in Northern Ireland, *see,* 'The Appeal for a British Bill of Rights', *New York Times*, 11 December 1988.

32. Ivor Jennings, *The Approach To Self Government* (London: Cambridge University Press, 1956) p. 20.
33. *All Parties Conference Report of a Committee to Determine Principles of the Constitution of India* (Nehru Report), pp. 89-90.
34. *Report of the Joint Parliamentary Committee, 1934*, H.C. Pt. I, pp. 215-16.
35. GIA §12, pp. 297-300.
36. For general discussion of preventive detention, *see,* Mohammed Iqbal, *Law of Preventive Detention in England, India and Pakistan* (Lahore: The Punjab Religious Book Society, 1955); S. S. Pirzada, *Fundamental Rights and Constitutional Remedies in Pakistan* (Lahore: All Pakistan Legal Decisions, 1960), p. 191-207.
37. Preventive detention represented a substantial departure from the practices of criminal justice found in Great Britain, the Commonwealth, and the United States. In the western democracies, such extraordinary power is resorted to only as a temporary measure in a period of grave emergency. During the two World Wars, for example, powers of preventive detention were exercised in Great Britain in the interests of security of the realm. *Liversidge v. Anderson*, 1942 A.C. 206. *See,* Clinton Rossiter, *Constitutional Dictatorship* (New York: Harcourt, Brace and World, 1945), Ch. V. Sections 57 and 58 of the Government of India Act of 1935 vested broad police powers in the Governors of each province. This power was to be exercised completely at the discretion of the Governor, and was put into the Act by Parliament because of the anxiety at the time over 'terrorist' activities in Bengal. Keith, *Constitutional History of India*, p. 538. They were amended by Mountbatten's Transition Schedule, GGO 22 of 1947.
38. The Code of Criminal Procedure covered persons suspected of being likely to cause a breach of peace or to disturb the public tranquillity, and persons suspected of disseminating, orally or in writing, seditious matter calculated to cause communal tension. It was similar in many respects to Regulation III. The basic concept of the Code allowed a person to be imprisoned if the detaining authority was satisfied the detainee was likely to act to the prejudice or the safety of the state, the public tranquillity or what has been characterized as 'some similar very wide conglomeration of notions'. Iqbal, op. cit., p. 202-8. For example, a person who 'brings or attempts to bring into hatred or contempt or excites or attempts to excite disaffection toward the government established by law in the provinces' could be sentenced to a maximum sentence of banishment for life. GIA §124A. This was the provision utilized to imprison Abdul Ghaffar Khan on two sentences totaling six years. The Liaquat administration was thereby able to suppress the separatist movement in the NWFP.
39. The extraordinary police powers were unpopular. Such leaders as Suhrawardy, Firoz Khan Noon, Nawab of Mamdot, Mumtaz Daultana, Shaukat Hayat, and R. O. H. Malik were among those who made public statements condemning the Public Safety Ordinances. Afzal, *Political Parties*, p. 92. *See also*, Willard Berry, *Aspects of the Frontier Crimes Regulation in Pakistan* (Durham, N. C., Duke University Press, 1966) p. 97. The Jamaat-e-Islami also criticized the Safety Act, claiming that it '...miserably fails to fulfil even the minimum demands of justice'. Khurshid Ahmad (trans. & ed.)

An Analysis of the Munir Report (Karachi: Jamaat-e-Islami Publications, 1956). The Azad Party and the Awami League also made abolition of the Safety Acts a part of their programmes.

40. Security of Pakistan Act XXXV (1952). This latter legislation made the general use of preventive detention a concurrent power exercisable by the central government, which previously had been restricted to matters concerning defence and external affairs, while matters of public order were within the powers of the provinces.
41. Government of India (Second Amendment) Act of 1952.
42. The Frontier Safety Act created by the British in 1873 was also continued. North-West Frontier Province Public Safety Acts II and XXI of 1948 and the Frontier Province Ordinance III of 1949. I CAD (Leg.), p. 400. This Act was originally intended to meet what the British considered to be the special problems of administering law and order among the Pukhtoons in the North-West Frontier. As with Regulation III of 1818, it was used where a person was suspected of an offence but available evidence was not sufficient for conviction under the Penal Code, or where the government believed the suspect might commit an offence in the future. It contained the interesting provision allowing the detention of persons and the reference of cases to tribal elders. Administration of criminal law in the border areas as designated in the regulation was treated more as an administrative matter than a judicial one, and contained neither the safeguards of customary law nor the Western constitutional concept of due process. A hearing before a government official was usually held, but the hearing could be held in secret, no pleaders were allowed to appear on behalf of the detainee, and with few exceptions no appeal to a court was allowed. *See,* Berry, op. cit., R. N. Iyer and A. R. Khosl (eds.) *The Punjab and North-West Province Acts Annotated* (Madras: Government Printing Office, 1934).
43. Callard, *Political Study*, p. 285. Henry F. Goodnow, *The Civil Service of Pakistan* (New Haven: Yale University Press, 1964) p. 61.
44. It was with the arrival of the Second World War that preventive detention was extensively used by the British. A. Glendhill, *Pakistan: Development of its Law and Constitution* (London: Stevens & Sons, Ltd., 1957) pp. 130 and 234. Regulation III was, however, used in 1932 to detain Subhas Bose. *See,* Leonard A. Gordon, *Brothers Against the Raj* (New York: Columbia University Press, 1995) p. 254. Paul Scott in his novel *The Day of the Scorpion* (London: William Morrow & Co., 1974) p. 301 *et. seq.*, gives an informed fictionalized account of a detainee's arrest and imprisonment.
45. PLD 1953 Lahore 331.
46. *See,* David Bayler, 'The Indian Experience With Preventative Detention,' 35 *Pacific Affairs* 99 (1960). Granville Austin was of the opinion that as of 1966, India's use of preventive detention had been restrained and was not employed for partisan purposes. Granville Austin, *The Indian Constitution* (Oxford: Clarendon Press, 1966), p. 113.
47. Public Safety Ordinance XIV (1949) §6; Security of Pakistan Act XXXV (1952) §7.
48. I CAD (Leg.), p. 671. A, op. cit., p. 219, claims that during the period 1952-3, fifty newspapers received warnings from the government of Press

Law violations, that in February 1957 the government disclosed that it had required thirty-nine newspaper to post security, and that anti-government newspapers were frequently harassed by government agents.

49. Judith Brown, *Modern India (*Delhi: Oxford University Press, 1985), p. 288. The reluctance of the home government to sanction the use of Section 93 in India even in the face of the Bengal Famine of 1943 serves as perhaps an extreme example of the application of non-interference in provincial affairs. *See,* IV *TP* Nos. 100, 283, *et passim.*
50. After Liaquat employed Section 92A against the Mamdot ministry, federal government rule continued in the Punjab from January 1949 to April 1951, a period of twenty-seven months. Federal government control was imposed in Sindh in 1951 under Section 92A and was not withdrawn until 1953. In the same manner, the Daultana ministry was removed in the Punjab in 1953. Section 92A was employed again the next year, when the Muslim League-controlled central government, faced with the loss by the Muslim League to the United Front in the East Bengal provincial elections, dissolved that provincial ministry and replaced it with a government appointed by the centre. Between 1947 and 1955, the central government removed a total of ten provincial ministries, four in Sindh, three in Punjab, two in NWFP, and the Huq ministry in East Bengal. The potential of the provinces to act as a buffer within the federal framework to check the growth of central power was eliminated.
51. The emergency powers vested in the central government of Pakistan were not necessarily on the face of it more repressive than powers which were exercised by the other parliamentary democracies in times of emergency such as the two World Wars. *See,* Rossiter, op. cit., *passim.* What was different in Pakistan was that these emergency powers were not legislated to meet emergencies as they arose, as was the constitutional practice in England and the senior dominions, but were a part of the Pakistan constitution itself and contained no adequate safeguards or specifications for when and how these extraordinary powers were to be employed.
52. Keith Callard, *Political Forces in Pakistan 1947-1959* (New York: Institute of Pacific Relations), p. 20.
53. Ahmad, *Government and Politics,* p. 92-102.
54. Callard, *Political Forces,* p. 22.
55. For example, on 16 December 1948, D. N. Dutta of the Pakistan Congress Party made an adjournment motion to consider the arrest and incarceration of Khan Abdul Ghaffar Khan. The Speaker of the Assembly, Tamizuddin Khan, with the support of Liaquat, responded by ruling that the federal government was not concerned with the matter because the Frontier Crimes Act, under which the prisoner was detained, was a provincial administrative matter. In May 1954, the question of the arrests, under Section 144 of the Code of Criminal Procedure, of political workers and journalists in Karachi, and the police search of the Azad Pakistan Party's offices, was raised. This motion was ruled out of order, again by the Speaker, Tamizuddin Khan, on the ground that these actions had been taken by legally-constituted authorities against which legal remedies were available. Thus, the matter of government

abuse of police power did not receive discussion. II CAD (Leg.) pp. 65-9, 1576-83; VIII CAD (Con.) p. 56.

56. 26 Geo. V, c. 2.
57. For discussion of PRODA, *see*, Callard, *Political Study*, p. 102; Goodnow, op. cit., p. 65.
58. Jalal, *State of Martial Rule*, p. 109 n. 159.
59. VII CAD, (Con.) pp. 74-118 and XII, pp. 1-35. D.N. Pritt gives a description of the Act in operation, pp. 1338-9 of his *Autobiography*, Manuscript Room, British Library, London. *See*, Jalal, *State of Martial Rule*, p. 119, *et seq.*, for details of the Rawalpindi Conspiracy, which she characterizes as 'a tragic watershed in Pakistan's history. Tragic because it provided the ostensible justification for insulating the army from the nascent nationalism combining some parts of the land and because it marked a break in critical thinking from which the people of Pakistan one generation later have still not recovered.' Ibid., p. 121.
60. VII CAD, (Con.), p. 94.
61. According to Jalal, during the Liaquat administration there was a strengthening of the central police power. An example was the granting to the Army of overriding powers of arrest and search in West Punjab, powers previously vested exclusively in the provincial police. This power was granted to the army not by Constituent Assembly legislation but by a Governor-General's ordinance. *State of Martial Rule*, p. 68.
62. Callard, *Political Forces*, p. 18.
63. Binder, op. cit., p. 239.
64. Goodnow, op. cit., p. 71, but *see,* Sayeed's assessment in his *Formative Years,* Ch. XII.
65. *See,* Shafqat, op. cit., pp. 127-59.
66. *See,* Geoffrey Marshall, *Parliamentary Sovereignty and the Commonwealth* (New York: Oxford University Press 1957) p. 31.

Chapter 7. A Clash of Ideas

1. Amjad Ali, who served as Finance Minister in the Cabinet appointed by Ghulam Mohammad after the dissolution of the Constituent Assembly, is of the opinion that Ghulam Mohammad would have backed down had the litigation gone against him. Amjad Ali interview (1992). But *see infra* the preparations made by the government for a take-over if the decision of the Federal Court went against the government.
2. Braibanti, op. cit., p. 412.
3. Ibid., p. 411.

3A. Callard reported from Karachi immediately after the Assembly's dissolution, 'The proclamation does not explicitly dissolve the existing Constituent Assembly. Indeed, it is a matter of argument whether the Governor-General, even with the support of the Cabinet, has the power of dissolution.' Callard pointed to the fact that the Governor-General's power to dissolve had been deleted from the GIA. 'Pakistan Puzzle', *Nation*, 13 November 1954.

4. *New York Times*, 28 October 1954.

5. Section 223A of the Government of India Act. *Moulvi Tamizuddin Khan v. Federation of Pakistan*, PLD 1954, Sindh, 96. Section 223A of the Government of India Act had not been available to Nazimuddin at the time of his dismissal. It became law on 6 July 1954. It is interesting to note that it was A. K. Brohi, Law Minister in the Cabinet appointed by Ghulam Mohammad after he dismissed Nazimuddin, who introduced the constitutional change for Assembly action. XVI CAD (Con.) p. 188. Such writs as provided for in Section 223A are regularly found in England and in Commonwealth jurisdictions. *See*, Pritt's discussion of the procedural role of Section 223A in the context of English law, in his *Autobiography*, p. 1384.
6. The following account of the court filing and the subsequent attempt to settle the controversy is based on interviews with S. S. Pirzada in 1991 and 1992 and is consistent with the facts related in Tamizuddin Khan, *The Test of Time* (Dhaka: University Press, 1960) p. 151, by the editor of that work, Mirza Nurul Huda.
7. Pirzada was at the time a comparatively junior member of the bar but he was experienced in constitutional matters. He had previously represented Chief Minister Khuhro of Sindh in his dispute with the central government.
8. Pirzada interview (1992). Also, Tamizuddin Khan, *Test of Time*, p. 151.
9. Pritt's account is given in his *Autobiography*, pp. 1384 *et seq.*
10. *Jennings Papers*, London, Institute of Commonwealth Studies, B/XV/4-5, Letters: Snelson to Jennings, 3 and 6 November 1954.
11. Ibid., B/XV/4-5, Letter: Jennings to Snelson, 1 December 1954.
12. 28 October 1954.
13. Quoted in Karl J. Newman, 'Pakistan's Preventative Autocracy and its Causes,' 32 *Pacific Affairs*, (1959), pp. 18, 23.
14. Where the GIA gave the Governor-General the right to act 'at his discretion', he need not consult with his ministers. Where he was empowered to act 'on his individual judgment', he was first to consult with his ministers but was then free to disregard their advice and act on his own. In all other situations convention required that he act on the advice of his ministers. These were 'terms of art—familiar to lawyers and administrators who had to interpret and work the Act but esoteric to everyone else...' Hudson, op. cit., p. 49.
15. *See*, C. L. Amand, *The Government of India Act 1935* (Lahore: The University Book Agency, 1944) p. 220. The tenure of the ministers was set by the Legislature. Keith, *Constitutional History of India*, p. 334.
16. §6(3) IIA.
17. *Jennings Papers*, op. cit., B/XV/4-5, Memorandum.
18. 3 State Trials, 826 (1640).
19. *Jennings Papers*, op. cit., B/IV/4-5, 'The Status of the Constituent Assembly', p. 11.
20. 13 Geo. III c. 16 & 63.
21. 3 & 4 Will. IV, c. 85.
22. 21 & 22 Vict. c. 106.
23. 26 Geo. V, c. 2, §2(1).
24. Jennings avoided the fact that the Crown prerogative was executive power and that the Queen was not the repository of executive power in Pakistan as she was in the senior dominions. *See*, for example, Australian Constitution

§61. In contrast, Section 2 of the GIA provided that all rights previously exercised by the East India Company (which had never possessed or exercised the Crown's prerogative powers) were to be exercised by the Crown except as otherwise provided in the Act. At the same time, the entirety of that power was transferred by Parliament to the Governor-General leaving no power personally in the Crown, including executive power. Sections 7 and 8 of GIA. *See,* Arthur Keith, *The Constitutional History of England from Queen Victoria to George VI* (London: Macmillan, 1940) Vol. II, pp. 6, 314; *also,* Keith, *Constitutional History of India*, p. 331; Clokie 'The New Constitution of India,' 30 *American Political Science Review* (1935) p. 1152. It was therefore meaningless to place significance, as did Jennings, in the fact that the Governor-General was the representative of the Queen. While the Governor-General of Pakistan was the representative of the Queen, under the constitution of Pakistan he was the representative of a Queen who did not herself possess executive power in Pakistan, including the executive power of the Crown prerogative. It follows that the Governor-General could not exercise, as representative of the Queen, prerogative powers which she herself did not possess. If he were to exercise prerogative powers in Pakistan he would do so only if he possessed those powers independently of his position as representative of the Queen. But such powers, other than symbolic executive powers, were not given to him by Crown Instructions, the dominion constitution, or any statute. In contrast, the new dominion of Ceylon was an example of one of the dominions where the Queen's prerogative rights were exercised by the Governor-General as her agent. For a fuller discussion, *see,* Ivor Jennings *The Constitution of Ceylon* (London: Oxford University Press, 3rd ed., 1953) Ch. 5.

25. *Jennings Papers*, op cit., B/XV/4-5, 'The Prerogative in Pakistan.'
26. Ibid., p. 8. IIA§6(3).
27. Jennings held the opinion that the former territories of British India remained what he termed 'technically' dominions of the Crown after independence. Ivor Jennings, *Constitutional Law of the Commonwealth*, (Cambridge, Cambridge University Press, 1955) p. 148. Cf. K. C. Wheare, 'The Nature and Structure of the Commonwealth,' 47 *American Political Science Review* (1953) p. 1017.
28. *Jennings Papers,* B/XV/4-5, 'The Status of the Constituent Assembly,' p. 11, citing *Attorney General vs. De Kayser's Royal Hotel*, 1920 A.C. 508. In that case, Lord Atkins, while disliking the suggestion that the prerogative is 'merged' in the statute, held that if the King in Parliament gave authority to do a thing in a specific manner, it must be held that the statute 'abridges the royal prerogative while it is in force to this extent: that the Crown can only do the particular thing under and in accordance with the statutory provisions, and that its prerogative power to do that thing is in abeyance.'
29. Ibid., p. 9.
30. Ibid., p. 20.
31. Ibid., p. 20.
32. Ivor Jennings, *Constitutional Problems of Pakistan,* (London: Cambridge University Press, 1955) p. 50.
33. An act which Karl Newman labelled as 'clearly unconstitutional since the

Governor-General's powers had been specifically amended so as to exclude the power to dissolve the Constituent Assembly.' Newman, 'Preventive Autocracy,' op. cit., p. 25; GGO 22/47; §19 IIA, para. 526.

34. *See,* text of §6(3) in Appendix, *infra.*
35. Indian Independence (Amendment) Act, 1949, §2, amended. IIA. §19(3),
36. *Jennings Papers,* B/XV/4-5, 'The Status of the Constituent Assembly,' p. 5.
37. W. S. Holdsworth, 'The Conventions of the Eighteen Century Constitution,' 17 *Iowa Law Review,* (1966) pp. 101, 162.
38. Arthur Keith, *Sovereignty in the British Commonwealth,* (Cambridge. Cambridge University Press, 1933), p. 161.
39. Jennings, *Cabinet Government,* p. 2. *Also,* Ivor Jennings, *Law and the Constitution* (London, University of London Press, 1959), p. 74. Jennings believed there was 'no distinction of substance or nature' between law and convention. He pointed out that statutes often recognized conventions. As an example, the Prime Minister, the Cabinet, and the Leader of the Opposition, all offices created by convention, are named in the Ministerial and Other Salaries Act of 1974. Jennings, ibid., p. 223.
40. Pirzada later held the offices of Attorney-General, Foreign Minister, and Ambassador. Chundrigar, a noted lawyer originally from Delhi, had been a member of the pre-independence interim government Cabinet and the Muslim League Working Committee. Wavell, observing his work in the interim Cabinet, pronounced Chundrigar 'slow and dull'. Wavell, op. cit. p. 413. He was a close friend of Mirza, introduced the 1956 Constitution in the Second Constituent Assembly, and was appointed by Mirza to be Attorney-General and later Prime Minister.
41. *New York Times,* 7 December 1955. *See,* Jennings' discussion in his *Cabinet Government* at p. 368 *et seq.,* and statement of the government, *Pakistan Times,* 14 December 1954. There is only one example of a forced dissolution in the British Empire. That took place in Nova Scotia in 1873. It has been viewed as an exception in constitutional history and has not been considered precedent. Eugene A. Fossey, *The Royal Power of Dissolution of Parliament in the British Commonwealth* (Toronto: University of Toronto Press, 1943) p. 71. The politics involved in that dissolution made it distinguishable from the facts of *Tamizuddin.* For further discussion of parliamentary dissolution, *see,* Arthur Keith, *Sovereignty in the British Commonwealth* (London: Macmillan, 1938) p. 162; B. J. Markesinis, *The Theory and Practice of the Dissolution of Parliament* (Cambridge: Cambridge University Press, 1972) p. 56; Robert Campbell, 'The Prerogative Power of Dissolution,' 1961 *Public Law,* p. 165.
42. 26 Geo. V, C.2, passed on 16 July 1954, by amendment to the GIA. XVI CAD (Con.) No. 17, p. 181. This provision is known as §223A of the Government of India Act (amended), 1954.
43. Pirzada interview (1992).
44. GIA, §32. The extent to which the requirement for assent was only a formality was discussed by members of the Pakistan public. For example, a contributor to the *Pakistan Observer,* 23 April 1955, called attention to the proposition that by the precedents of constitutional history there was serious doubt concerning a Governor-General's right to withhold his assent to any

legislation which had been sponsored by a ministry and passed by the Assembly.

45. III CAD (Con.), p. 45.
46. Rule 48.
47. GIA §32.
48. The issue first arose in the Punjab High Court in 1949 when Mohammad Munir was Chief Justice of that court. In *Khan Iftikhar Hussain Khan v. Province of Punjab* it was held that the Constituent Assembly was a sovereign body and that no assent of the Governor-General was required for constitution-making legislation. PLD 1950 Lahore 384. The next year, the case of *M. A. Khuhro v. Federation of Pakistan* was decided by the Chief Court of Sindh. PLD 1950 Sindh 59. In that case the plaintiff claimed that the legislation under which proceedings had been brought against him was invalid because it did not receive the assent of the Governor-General. It was the government which took the position in that case that assent was not necessary because the legislation in issue was passed by the Constituent Assembly when acting in its capacity as a constitution-making body and not as the ordinary legislature. The government prevailed. Two months later, in May 1950, the same question came before Pakistan's highest court. On appeal from the Punjab High Court in *Mamdot v. Federation of Pakistan*, the appellant argued to the Federal Court that the same legislation considered in *Khuhro* was improperly passed by the Constituent Assembly acting as a constitution-making body rather than as the ordinary legislature, and, therefore, the Act was void because it did not have the assent of the Governor-General. PLD 1950 FC 15. To this the government again responded that the legislation was properly enacted by the Constituent Assembly functioning as a constitution-making body and the Federal Court agreed with the government that the Governor-General's assent was not required. A fourth case, *Ex-Major General Akbar Khan and Faiz Ahmad Faiz v. The Crown*, involved convictions under the Rawalpindi Conspiracy (Special Tribunal) Act of 1953. PLD 1954 FC 87. The issue was the same as the preceding two cases, and on the same rationale the appeals were dismissed. In India, the Supreme Court rejected the necessity of Governor-General's assent, Justice Das writing, 'This Court has no jurisdiction to examine the legislation passed by a sovereign body.' *State of Seraikella v. Union of India*, AIR (38) 1951 S.C. pp. 253, 254.
49. Pritt, op. cit., p. 1386. S. S. Pirzada claims that when he served as Law Minister in the 1960s he conducted a search of his department's files but found no memorandum in which the advice was given that the Governor-General's assent was necessary for constitutional legislation. He did, however, find a memorandum from Zafrulla Khan, written when he was Law Minister, to Liaquat, in which the opinion was given that no such assent was required. Pirzada interview (1992). Cf. Jennings, *Constitutional Problems of Pakistan*, p. 24.
50. *See*, text of IIA §6(3) in Appendix, *infra*.
51. The question of the Assembly's sovereignty when passing ordinary (non-constitutional) legislation was not an issue. When so functioning the Assembly was acting under the IIA as the Federal Legislature of British India was to

have functioned under the GIA of 1935. The Federal Legislature of British India was subordinate to Parliament and therefore not sovereign. Because of this relationship, the assent of the Governor was required in Pakistan after independence for ordinary legislation. GIA §32. *See*, N. 64 *infra*.

52. *Jennings Papers*, op. cit., B/XV/4-5, undated Memorandum: 'Note for H. M. Law on the Validation Bill.'
53. *Jennings Papers*, op. cit., B/XV/4-5. Memorandum: 'Tamizuddin Khan vs. Federation of Pakistan.'
54. Ibid.
55. Ibid.
56. Pirzada is of the opinion that had Bogra contacted the Queen, Ghulam Mohammad would have retaliated and Bogra would have had reason to fear for his safety. Pirzada interview (1992).
57. *Tamizuddin Khan v. Federation of Pakistan*, PLD 1955 Sindh, p. 157.
58. Ibid., p. 138.
59. Ibid., p. 106.
60. Ibid., p. 104. The Federal Legislature was designated in the GIA of 1935 as the legislature for British India. It was not a sovereign body, possessing no constituent (constitution-making) powers, but was limited to the enactment of ordinary legislation. After independence, its functions were to be performed by the Constituent Assembly which both enacted ordinary legislation and performed the constituent function of drafting a new constitution. In exercising this dual function, the Assembly operated much like the British Parliament which also exercises ordinary and constituent legislative powers. Prior to the enactment of a completed new constitution, the constituent functions of the Assembly included the power to amend the GIA and the IIA. The Federal Legislature never came into existence because of the failure of the Princely States to join. The provision for its existence remained in the GIA (1947). After independence the Assembly exercised its constituent function by enacting forty-three statutory changes in the GIA. The Legislature of the Dominion, referred to in the IIA, was to come into existence as the permanent legislature of Pakistan after the Constituent Assembly had defined that body either by a constitutional statute or in a new constitution.
61. Vellani cited a leading English case which had enunciated the principle that after Parliament had passed a statute and while that statute remained in force 'the thing it empowers the Crown to do can thenceforth only be done by and under the statute and subject to all the limitations, restriction, and condition by it imposed, however unrestrained the Royal Prerogative may theretofore have been'. *Attorney General v. DeKeyser's Hotel*, (1920) AC, 509, 540.
62. Ibid., p. 118. The Federal Court itself had become the court of highest appellate jurisdiction by constitutional legislation which had amended the Government of India Act of 1935, but which did not receive the assent of the Governor-General. Privy Council (The Abolition of Jurisdiction) Act of 1950; VII CAD (Con.) pp. 43-51. There was further irony in that the Crown's prerogative, upon which so much of Jennings' and Munir's conclusions were based, existed because of constitutional convention.
63. IIA §9(1)(c).

64. *Moulvi Tamizuddin Khan v. Federation of Pakistan*, PLD 1955 Sindh 115. In effect, the British Parliament, by including 6(3) in the Independence Act, was affording the Dominion of Pakistan the opportunity to utilize the royal assent as part of its legislative process. Pakistan never chose to employ this option.
65. *Pakistan Times*, 10 February 1955; *Pakistan Observer*, 11 February 1955. Gauhar interview (1992); Syed Sami Ahmad, *Tamizuddin Khan's Case*, (Karachi: Justice Kayani Memorial Law Society, 1991), Ch. 3.
66. Pirzada interview (1992).
67. *Jennings Papers*, op. cit., B/XV/4-5, undated memorandum: 'Tamizuddin Khan vs. Federation of Pakistan.' Who the author of this memorandum was is not indicated. It was probably the work of Jennings himself. The internals of the document indicate that, if not authored by Jennings, it was written by someone involved in the litigation on the government side and high enough in standing to be addressing the Governor-General, and that what was said was considered significant enough by Jennings to be included in his papers.
68. Ibid.
69. Ibid. Chief Justice Shah recalls that the government did have contingency plans of an 'emergency nature' to be put into effect if the decision of the court finally went against the government. As a junior member of the government's litigation team he was not privy to the details of those plans. Shah interview (1992).
70. *Pakistan Observer*, 4 March 1955.
71. *Pakistan Times*, 4 and 8 March 1955.
72. Rehman, op. cit., p. 160.
73. *Pakistan Observer*, 10 March 1955; *Pakistan Times*, 11 March 1955. For the negotiations and failure of the attempts to settle the case, *see*, *The Times* of London, 4, 8, 10, 11 March 1955.
74. Interview of Nizami (1990) who was Deputy Clerk of Court and was in the courtroom at the time of Munir's statement. For reports of hearings, *see*, *The Times* of London, 17, 26, 28 April and 9 May 1955.
75. Pirzada interview (1992).
76. Pirzada interview (1992).
77. Shah interview (1992).
78. Munir, *Introduction to the Islamic Constitution*, p. 31; Jennings, *Constitutional Problems*, p. vii.
79. Munir, *Highways and Bye-Ways*, p. 270. The law reporter citation for the case before the Federal Court is *Federation of Pakistan v. Moulvi Tamizuddin Khan*, PLD, 1955 FC 240. The case is reproduced in full in Jennings' *Constitutional Problems.* Because of the wide availability of that work citation to that work instead of the law reporter will be made in this footnote as *Tamizuddin* (Jen.), pp. 169-72, for Diplock's Argument and that form of citation will be followed hereafter.
80. Interview of former Chief Justice Cornelius (1990).
81. Interview of former Chief Clerk Nizami (1990), who was present, having been invited to attend the judges' conference for the purpose of preparing the press release.
82. Munir's court opinion is at *Tamizuddin* (Jen.), pp. 79-160. Cornelius' dissenting opinion is ibid., pp. 165-231.

83. No transcript exists of what Diplock and Chundrigar argued to the court. The summaries of their arguments given here are from the comments made by the Justices in their written opinions and from interviews of Cornelius, Shah, and Pirzada. Discussions of some of the arguments as they were made in court can also be found in Jennings' introduction to his *Constitutional Problems.*
84. Munir's understanding of the nature of the agreement differs from Mountbatten's at the time he proposed dominion status, according to Mountbatten's press aide, Campbell-Johnson. Mountbatten was reported as saying, 'Some people seem to have some doubts about the word "Dominion Status". It is absolute independence in every possible way, with the sole exception that the Member States of the Commonwealth are linked together voluntarily'. Campbell-Johnson, op. cit., p. 109.
85. *Tamizuddin* (Jen), p. 156. Jennings reported that during oral argument, 'The Chief Justice made some caustic comments upon the attitude of the Constituent Assembly which acted as the Constituent Assembly for a Dominion but did not accept the implications of Dominion status, and at the same time neglected to frame a Constitution by which Pakistan could cease to be a Dominion.' Jennings, *Constitutional Problems,* p. 20. Munir did not mention that the constitution adopted by the Assembly, and aborted by Ghulam Mohammad's dissolution of that body, created a republic.
86. Also known as *Calvin's Case* (1606). This case dealt with the effects on the status of a subject arising from the union of Scotland and England. Unlike most of the other ideas in Munir's opinion this one is not discussed in Jennings' notes.
87. Jennings, *Constitutional Problems,* p. 20.
88. *Tamizuddin* (Jen.), p. 154.
89. IIA §8.
90. Due to the fact that from Jinnah to the time of *Tamizuddin,* the almost universal understanding of the meaning of §6(3) was otherwise, it is difficult to accept Munir's assertion that a reasonable reading of §6(3) could only lead to the conclusion he arrived at. His stand on ambiguity was important to his case because if §6(3) was unambiguous, no evidence was allowable to show what Parliament intended by the section when they passed the Independence Act. Where a statute is ambiguous the intent of the legislative body which enacted the legislation is usually determinative. Counsel for Tamizuddin Khan offered records of the debates of Parliament to establish what Parliament meant, but Munir refused to hear the evidence, on the ground that the section was unambiguous. However, in his written court opinion he cited 440 H. C. Debates, 5th Series (1946-7) to support his own position on the assent issue. Jennings, *Constitutional Problems,* p. 7.
91. *See,* A. K. Brohi, *Fundamental Law of Pakistan* (Karachi: Din Muhammadi Press, 1958) p. 601.
92. IIA §7(1).
93. *Tamizuddin* (Jen.), p. 188. In its original form, GIA §18 provided that the King was to be a part of the then Federal Legislature. When amended in 1947 the section omitted the King. Section 6(3) of the IIA, which originally provided that assent by the Governor-General was to be given 'in His

Magesty's name' was amended by the Constituent Assembly in 1950 to omit that phrase retroactively to 15 August 1947. Constitution (Amendment) Act 1950, §2. No reference was made to this amendment in the arguments to the Sindh and Federal courts nor in the written opinions of these courts. This change in the IIA would have been irrelevant to Munir because the Constitutional (Amendment) Act of 1950 lacked the Governor-General's assent.

94. *Tamizuddin* (Jen.), pp. 184 and 188. 'For India's benefit there was conceived a remarkable piece of pragmatic nonsence, the Headship of the Commonwealth. Perhaps "nonsense" puts the position too strongly, but the sense and meaning of the term is certainly obscure and uncertain. It is a position of no power, prerogative, or characterization except that of being acknowledged by those who acknowledge it...Perhaps the most striking change in the Commonwealth relationship is the virtual disappearance of the United Kingdom Crown and Parliament's former centrality of status.' Marshall, *Constitutional Conventions,* pp. 170-1.

95. The history of the Irish Free State, relied on by Cornelius, was, like the evolution of the Statute of Westminster, an example of the constantly-changing composition of the Commonwealth and the dominions themselves. What De Valera had brought about in Ireland by his gradual moves away from dominion status as it existed at the time of the First World War was reflected in the Indian Independence Act. There was no need for Pakistan to go through the process of statutory devolution with regard to Crown allegiance as had the Irish Free State. The Indian Independence Act had accomplished the same goal by creating Pakistan and India as fully independent states.

96. *Sarfaraz Khan v. The Crown,* PLD 1950 Lahore 658. The assent referred to in this case was the assent required under GIA §32 for ordinary legislation.

97. *Tamizuddin* (Jen.), p. 222. William Cooley, *the General Principles of Constitutional Law in the United States of America* (New York: Brown, Little, Brown & Co.) p. 144. *See also,* Brohi, op. cit., p. 601. Courts exercising judicial review often find that strong evidence of intent of a legislature, such as Parliament in passing §6(3), can be deduced from the actions of persons who were in a position to know the intent of the creators of a constitution and who had the responsibility of carrying out the provisions of that constitution at a time prior to pending litigation in which the meaning of the constitution is in issue. *Pocket Veto Case,* 279 US 655; *Field v. Clark,* 143 US 655; *O'Gorman & Young, Inc. v. Hartford Fire Insurance Co.,* 282 US 251. For further on judicial review and the relevancy of American cases in the judicial process of Pakistan, *see,* Ch. 8, *infra.*

98. *Tamizuddin* (Jen.), p. 222. Where established practice has allowed significant rights to vest over time, only for the most compelling reasons and where a statute is clear in its meaning will that practice be overturned by a court. *United States v. Curtis-Wright Export Corp.,* 299 US 304. Pursuant to the power vested in him by IIA §9, Viceroy Mountbatten on 3 June 1947 granted to the Constituent Assembly the right to frame its own rules. The Assembly, under the presidency of Jinnah, approved Rule 48 on 25 May 1948 which provided that constitutional legislation enacted by the Assembly

would become law upon being authenticated by the Assembly's President without the assent of the Governor-General. American courts have given great weight to the interpretation to the constitution arrived at by the first Congress convened after independence, because the Congress contained a substantial number of members who had participated in the making of the constitution. *Missouri Ry. Co. v. Kansas,* 248 US 276. The general rule is that the interpretation of a constitutional exercise of powers followed by general acquiescence therein for a substantial period of time, especially if commencing with the organization of the government, may be treated as fixing the construction of the constitution. *United States v. Curtis-Wright, supra.*

99. *Tamizuddin* (Jen.), p. 229.
100. Ibid., p. 160, *also,* the official report at PLD 1955 FC 240. *See also,* the report of the case in *The Times* of London, pp. 11, 17, and 23 May 1955.
101. *Tamizuddin* (Jen.), p. 149. The Governor-General's assent was considered a formality because by convention his assent was given to legislation as a matter of routine and without any reference to his opinion on the legislation. If he were to withhold his assent he could be removed from office by the Queen acting on the advice of the dominion's Prime Minister. Later, at p. 9 of his *Islamic Constitution,* Munir wrote the principle of statutory construction which was applicable in a situation such as the one presented by *Tamizuddin,* '...[A] constitutional enactment should be interpreted liberally and not in a narrow and pedantic sense...'

Chapter 8. Munir and Judicial Politics

1. For an account of Munir's life, *see,* Munir, *Life, Writings and Judgments, passim.*
2. Quoted in Chaudhri Muhammad Ali, op. cit., p. 361, who gives his version of the incident.
3. The report is officially *The Report of the Court of Inquiry constituted and Punjab Act II of 1954 to Enquire into the Punjab Disturbances of 1953* (Lahore: Government of Punjab Press, 1950).
4. Richard S. Wheeler, 'East Bengal Under Governor-General's Rule,' *Far East Survey*, 8 (1970).
5. *Munir Report*, p. 387.
6. PLD 1953 Lahore 528.
7. 'The rules and conventions that govern the use of the armed forces for purposes internal to the government of a community are an important segment of its constitutional framework. As such their character and content need to be clearly established. In Britain there is little help to be had in the matter from the traditional sources of constitutional doctrine.' Marshall, *Constitutional Conventions*, p. 155.
8. *Munir Report*, p. 364.
9. *See,* Bahadur, op. cit., pp. 72-4 for an account of Maududi's arrest and imprisonment during the same period.

10. A. K. Brohi in his *The Fundamental Law of Pakistan* (Karachi: Din Mohammad Press, 1958), p. 645, cites with approval the summary of the nature of martial law given by Blackstone in his *Commentaries*, Vol. I, p. 413, 'For Martial Law, which is built on no settled principles, but is entirely arbitrary in its decisions, is...in truth and reality no law, but something indulged in rather than allowed as law...[I]t ought not to be permitted in time of peace, when the King's Courts are open for all persons to receive justice according to the laws of the land.'
11. *Umar v. The Crown*, PLD 1953 Lahore, pp. 528, 541-4. The exercise of martial law was judicially recognized in British India in peacetime, thus distinguishing India from the rule applicable in England itself where the Petition of Rights absolutely barred martial rule except in wartime. *Chanappa v. Emperor*, AIR 1931 Bombay, p. 57. For development of the martial law concept in England, *see generally*, Herbert Fairman, *The Law of Martial Rule* (Chicago: Collaghay & Co., 1943); *also* H. W. Ballantine, 'Unconstitutional Claims of Military Authority', 24 *Yale Law Journal* 198 (1924).
12. A. V. Dicey, *Law and the Constitution*, (9th ed.), p. 287, quoted in Khurshid Ahmad (ed.), *Analysis of the Munir Report* (Karachi: Jamaat-e-Islami Publications, 1956).
13. It is for the courts to decide if the necessity existed for military rule. Blackstone, op. cit., p. 413; Brohi, op. cit., p. 645-50. Keith, *Constitutional History of India*, pp. 389-92. *See also,* Carl Friedrich, *Constitutional Government and Democracy* (Waltam, Mass.: Blarsdell Publishing, 1968) p. 561.
14. Because Britain had been comparatively free of domestic disturbance in modern times, its judiciary has had little experience with questions arising from military rule. The United States Supreme Court stated the rule of necessity justifying martial rule as follows: 'Martial law cannot arise from a threatened invasion. The necessity must be actual and present, the invasion real, such as to effectually close the courts and depose the Civil Administration....Martial rule can never exist where the courts are open and in proper and unobstructed exercise of their jurisdiction.' *Ex parte Milligin*, 71 US 2 (1866). Cf. *Korematsu v. United States*, 323 US 214 (1944).
15. For a description of the use of military law in Ireland after the Revolt of 1798, *see*, R. B. McDowell, *Ireland in the Age of Imperialism and Revolution* (Oxford: Clarendon Press, 1979) pp. 659-68.
16. Marshall, *Constitutional Convention,* p. 154.
17. James G. Randall, *Constitutional Problems Under Lincoln* (Urbana: University of Illinois Press, 1964) p. 143.
18. The potential effect of a case such as *Umar* was commented on by Justice Jackson of the United States Supreme Court in *Korematsu v. US* 323 US pp. 214, 246 (1944). 'A military commander may overstep the bounds of constitutionality, and it is an incident. But if we review and approve, that passing incident becomes the doctrine of the Constitution. There it has a generative power of its own, and all that it creates will be in its own image.' Following *Umar* martial law administration was upheld in *Muhammad Ayub Khuhro v. Pakistan*, 1960 2 PSCR 29; *Gulab Din v. Major A. T. Shaukat*, PLD 1961 Lahore 952; *Mir Hassain v. State*, PLD 1969 Lahore 786. PLD

1972 S.C. 139. These cases do not support Wheeler's claim that after *Umar* the 'judicial interpretation defined and restricted the powers of martial-law tribunals.' He is correct, however, in concluding that the court decisions did help develop a 'martial law constitutionalism'. Richard S. Wheeler, *The Politics of Pakistan, A Constitutional Quest* (Ithaca: Cornell University Press, 1970) p. 137. Munir later denied that there was a relationship between martial law and his law of necessity.

19. *Pakistan Times*, 2 June 1954.
20. Interviews of Chief Clerk of Court Nizami (1990) and Chief Justice Huq (1990).
21. Interview of Chief Justice Cornelius (1990). Jalal, *The State of Martial Rule*, p. 103, n. 23.
22. Qudratullah Shahab, *Shahab Nama* (Lahore: Sang-e-meel Publications, 1987) pp. 652-4. Nizami questions whether such correspondence took place, asserting that his relationship, as Clerk of Court, with Munir was such that he knew of all of the Chief Justice's correspondence. Nizami interview (1990).
23. Nizami interview (1990).
24. Cornelius interview (1990).
25. Munir, *Islam in History* (Lahore: Law Publishing Co., 1973) p. 21.
26. Pirzada interview (1992).
27. Shah interview (1992).
28. Pirzada interview (1992).
29. Shah interview (1992).
30. Pirzada interview (1992).
31. Ayesha Jalal, in D. A. Low's *Constitutional Heads and Political Crisis* (London: Macmillan, 1988) p. 57.
32. *See,* Jennings, *Constitutional Problems*, pp. 38-40, for further details of the effect of *Tamizuddin* on existing laws and institutions.
33. *Tamizuddin* (Jen.), p. 140.
34. GIA§223A, was constitutional, as distinguished from ordinary legislation, because it amended the GIA.
35. To the point that in England a court will not pass on the validity of a parliamentary act for any reason, an often quoted 1871 court opinion of an English judge stated the rule in all its certainty. '[The Court does] not sit here as a court of appeal from Parliament. We sit here as servants of the Queen and the legislature. Are we to act as regents over what is done by Parliament with the consent of the Queen, Lords, and Commons? I deny that any such authority exists.' *Lee v. Bude and Torrington Junction Rly Co.* (1871) LR 6CP 576, 582. An English court would restrict itself to statutory interpretation, limited to the words of a statute, to determine what the intent of Parliament was in enacting the legislation in issue. The courts then see that the statute is construed and applied in conformity with the intent of Parliament as the court understands that intent to be. For the differing approaches to constitutional interpretation among the Commonwealth nations, *see,* Chester J. Antieu, *Constitutional Construction* (London: Oceana Publications, Inc., 1982), pp. 4-6.

36. The courts of British India were not subject to the extraordinary powers of the Governor-General as was the legislature. H. McD. Clokie, 'The New Constitution of India,' 30 *American Political Science Review*, 1152, 1162-4 (1935). The Federal Legislature was subordinate to Parliament and hence not a sovereign body. As such, its legislation was reviewable by the courts. Chakradhar Jha, *Judicial Review of Legislative Acts* (Bombay: M. M. Tripathi Private Ltd., 1974), pp. 54, 131. The legislation under review after the Ahmadi riots (*Umar*) was ordinary legislation passed by the Constituent Assembly as successor to the Federal Legislature of British India, and although the court did not invalidate the legislation in *Umar,* it had the power to do so.
37. *Tamizuddin* (Jen.), p. 139. The sovereignty recognized by the courts in England is legal, not political, sovereignty. According to A. V. Dicey: 'The electors can in the long run always enforce their will. But the courts will take no notice of the will of the electors. The judges know nothing about any will of the people except and so far as that will is expressed by an Act of Parliament and would never suffer the validity of a statute to be questioned on the ground of its having been passed or being kept alive in opposition to the wishes of the electors. The political sense of the word "sovereignty" is, it is true, fully as important as the legal sense or more so. But the two significations, though intimately connected together are essentially different...' Quoted in Ivor Jennings, *Law and the Constitution* (London: University of London Press, 1959), p. 31.
38. For a contemporaneous discussion of sovereignty, *see,* Edward McWhinney, 'Sovereignty in the United Kingdom and the Commonwealth at the Present Day,' 58 *American Political Science Quarterly*, p. 511 (1953).
39. The fact that Munir's decision in *Tamizuddin* was effecting a fundamental change in Pakistan's judicial system by assuming the powers of judicial review was not discussed at the time. The only commentator who expressed awareness of the creation of judicial review in Pakistan in *Tamizuddin* was Keith Callard in his *Political Study,* pp. 5 and 281. He, however, did not develop the significance of judicial review, nor did he analyse the *Tamizuddin* case itself. He indicated the need for further work by commenting, '...it is for the constitutional lawyers to decide upon the merits of the judgment.' Ibid., p. 147.
40. Judicial review originated in the United States. *See,* Charles G. Haines, *The American Doctrine of Judicial Supremacy* (New York: Russell & Russell, 1959). Pirzada, *Fundamental Rights,* p. 38, places the origin of judicial review in *Bonham's Case* of seventeenth century England. However, even if that case can be read to sanction the subjecting of Parliment to judicial review, any of the case's influence disappeared in later English legal history when judicial review found no adherents. Consequently, *Bonham's Case* exerted no influence when judicial review came into existence in the United States. The dilemma faced by a new nation when creating its judicial system was of concern to B. R. Ambedkar, one of the drafters of the Indian constitution after independence. 'I cannot altogether omit the possibility of a legislature packed with party-men making laws which may abrogate or violate what we regard as certain fundamental principles affecting the life and

liberty of an individual. At the same time, I do not see how five or six gentlemen sitting in the Federal or Supreme Court examining law made by the legislature and by dint of their own individual conscience or their bias or their prejudices [can] be trusted to determine which law is good or which is bad. It is rather a case where a man has to sail between Charybdis and Scilla.' Quoted by C. W. Alexandrowicz, *Constitutional Development in India,* (Bombay: Oxford University Press, 1967). Judicial review had found favour in some of the emerging nations. *See,* Mauro Cappellette, *Judicial Review in the Contemporary World* (Indianapolis: Bobb Merrill, 1970) Ch. VIII; Edward McWhinney, *Judicial Review in the English-speaking World* (Toronto: Toronto University Press, 1956) p. 75 *et seq.* The move made by some ex-colonial nations to the American constitutional model after they had begun on the Westminster constitution is noted in C. J. Antieu, *Constitutional Construction* (Oceana Publications 1982) p. 1. Nigeria and Ghana are two prominent African nations which abolished their Westminster constitutions. Pakistan's aborted 1954 constitutional draft provided for judicial review. The 1954 constitution, however, played no part in Munir's decision. He created judicial review on his own authority.

41. The paradox of the absence of judicial review in England is that the courts refrain from exercising such review because of the existence of Parliamentary sovereignty, yet the sovereignty of Parliament itself exists because the courts acknowledge that it exists. Professor Wade identifies the basis of parliamentary sovereignty as the relationship between the courts and Parliament and points out that the relationship is 'first and foremost a political one'. The sovereignty of Parliament rests on 'a political fact for which no purely legal explanation can be given'. H. W. R. Wade, 'The Basis of Legal Sovereignty', 1955 *Cambridge Law Journal*, pp. 172, 189. An argument can be made that parliamentary sovereignty is not a rule of any sort but only a statement or prediction about the behaviour of the courts in a particular system of government.

42. *Marbury v. Madison*, 1 Cranch 137, 2 L. Ed. 60 (1803). The Congressional law which Marshall struck down as unconstitutional in the first case of judicial review had been drafted by Marshall's predecessor, Chief Justice William Ellsworth, when Ellsworth was a member of the Constitutional Convention in Philadelphia. The law had been passed by a Congress containing many members who had been members of the Constitutional Convention, and it was signed by President George Washington, who had presided over that convention. Marshall, who played no part in the constitution-making process, used judicial review against James Madison, a litigant in *Marbury v. Madison*, the first case in which judicial review was used. Madison had been perhaps the most influential member of the Constitutional Convention in shaping the ideas of the constitution. Yet it was Marshall who decreed what the true meaning of the constitution was. Munir did the same in *Tamizuddin*, holding that it was his understanding of Pakistan's dominion constitution that made it necessary to strike down a law that had been passed by a procedure approved of by Jinnah but which Munir found to be in violation of the dominion constitution. Munir had played no part in negotiations which Jinnah had conducted for a constitution from the

British Parliament. In the case of both Munir and Marshall, it was a judge who established the intent of the constitution, not those like Madison and Jinnah who had participated in the making of the constitution.

43. Fred Rodell, *Nine Men, A Political History of the Supreme Court from 1790 to 1955* (New York: Random House, 1955), p. 90.
44. *See,* Felix Frankfuter, 'Marshall and the Judicial Foundation,' 69 *Harvard Law Review* 217 (1955); Wright, op. cit., p. 35. For Chief Justice Marshall's use of history, *see,* Maria C. Klenkhammer, 'John Marshall's Use of History,' *Catholic University Law Review*, 77, 87 (1957). Cf. William Foran, 'John Marshall As a Historian,' 43 *American Historical Review*, 51 (1937).
45. Rodell, op. cit., p. 74.
46. Munir, *Life, Writings and Judgments*, p. 91. There were, however, important differences. Marshall set an example which has served as a cornerstone of American political and constitutional life, while *Tamizuddin* signalled the end of parliamentary democracy in Pakistan. Marshall was also dealing with a much different constitution than was Munir. Munir had to discard parliamentary sovereignty, the centrepiece of Pakistan's dominion constitution, before he could exercise judicial review. Marshall did not face the same barrier because under the United States constitution sovereignty was vested in the people, not Congress. Further, while Marshall felt obliged to justify his exercise of judicial review by reasoning from the terms of the constitution, Munir did not acknowledge that he was departing from the constitution and cited no basis for his exercise of the power of judicial review. His will was the basis of judicial review in Pakistan. Marshall would not have agreed with Munir's assumption of judicial review on that basis, having set for himself the principle that: 'Judicial power, as counter-distinguished from the power of the laws, has no existence. Courts are the mere instruments of the law, and can will nothing.' Marshall in *Osborn vs. US Bank*, 9 Wheat. 738 (1824).
47. In addition to Munir and Cornelius, three other justices of the court filed written opinions. Their opinions were short and agreed with Munir.
48. *See,* Braibanti, op. cit., Ch. 5.
49. Interviews of Chief Justice Huq and S. M. Zafar (1990). The latter gave an interesting reason for the lack of legal literature or written comment in Pakistan. Zafar, a Muslim lawyer and former Cabinet minister, explained that prior to partition it was the Hindu members of the bar who did the writing and when they left West Pakistan the Muslims never filled their place. *See, also,* Braibanti, op. cit., Ch.5.
50. A leading case on contempt is *M. Inayat Khan v. M. Anwar*, 28, PLD 1976 S.C. 254, where a prominent attorney was held in contempt for criticizing Munir's 'poisonous mind' in *Tamizuddin*. 'Since that fateful day we have not been able to put our derailed train back on the rails.' He accused the Munir court of placing 'this great country at the very mercy of adventurers'.
51. Mir Chand Mahajan in his *Looking Back* (London: Asia Publishing House, 1963), pp. 88 and 108, gives an account of what he calls a 'reign of terror' by Sir Douglas Young, Chief Judge of the Punjab High Court prior to independence. This is a partisan account but it gives an idea of the scope of the courts' contempt power. *See,* Judge Young's opinion *In re K. L. Gauba,*

Barrister-at-Law, A. I. R. (29) 1942 Lahore 105. The incident with Young could have been in the minds of some when *Tamizuddin* was decided a dozen years later. Munir had been a member of Young's court. *See also,* Braibanti, op. cit., pp. 14-44, 246-61. In a 1990 interview, Ms Hina Jilani, Lahore attorney and political activist, recounted to the author that in the 1970s she refrained from joining any protests against decisions of the court on human rights and women's legal rights for fear that as a lawyer she might be subject to contempt action by the courts. Professor Aslam Sayeed, Quaid-i-Azam Professor at Columbia University, in 1988 told the author that when a graduate student, he was advised by the head of his department in Pakistan not to do his dissertation on the *Tamizuddin* case because of the danger of contempt of court. Sayeed had this advice confirmed by a member of the Pakistan Supreme Court with whom he was acquainted. Contempt powers had a long life in public matters. On the date of the author's interview of Altaf Gauhar in April 1992, his newspaper, *The Muslim*, was cited by the court in Islamabad to show cause why the paper should not be held in contempt for criticism it had printed concerning a new pension plan established for the judiciary.

52. Interview of Nizami (1991).
53. 11 February 1955. This conclusion ignored the fact that no consensus had been reached in Pakistan about the people's sovereignty and such a claim could not be supported by the terms of the Objectives Resolution.
54. 22 March 1955.
55. 22 March 1955.
56. *Pakistan Times*, 30 March 1955; *Pakistan Observer*, 30 March and 7 April 1955. A columnist in the *Pakistan Observer* of 16 March 1955 commented that, for the dissolution of the first Constituent Assembly to have been correctly carried out according to accepted parliamentary procedure, the dissolution should have been followed by elections within six weeks. The writer added, 'that was how the continuity of legislative bodies was maintained'.
57. *Pakistan Observer*, 2 February 1955.
58. Emergency Powers Ordinance IX, 1955; *The Gazette of Pakistan, Extraordinary*, Karachi, 27 March 1955, §§3, 4, 6, & 8. *Also,* Snelson's 23 & 24 March 1955, memoranda marked 'Secret' in *Jennings Papers*, op. cit., B/XV/2-3, for the listing of those GIA sections which were validated by the order. It was reported at the time that it was Sir Eric Snelson, Law Secretary, who advised Ghulam Mohammad that he possessed the constitutional right to retrocatively validate legislation, *Dawn,* 23 March 1955.
59. 28 March 1955.
60. 28 March 1955.
61. 30 March 1955.
62. 30 March 1955.
63. *Dawn*, 21 March 1955.
64. Ibid., 24 April 1955; *Pakistan Times*, 23 April 1955.
65. PLD 1955 FC 387.
66. *Jennings Papers*, op. cit., B/XV/4-5, Memoranda: 'Note for H. M. Law on the Validation Bill,' 'The New Constituent Assembly.' *Also,* Jennings, *Constitutional Problems*, p. 46.

67. The *Usif Patel* case has been interpreted not as the result of confusion, which it was, but as an example of Munir's court exerting its independence and courageously standing up to Ghulam Mohammad. Wilcox made the claim that *Usif Patel* 'brought Pakistan back to its democratic roots'. Op. cit., p. 189. A Lahore lawyer has made the claim that Ghulam Mohammad was 'thwarted' by the *Usif Patel* decision. Hamid Yusif, *Pakistan in Search of Democracy* (Lahore: Afrasia Publications, 1980), p. 49. The case is also the basis for Newman's 'preventive autocracy' theory, whereby Munir supposedly gave some and then took some from Ghulam Mohammad, thereby preventing complete autocracy. Newman interview (1991).
68. PLD 1955 FC 240, decided 10 May 1955. This case is also reprinted in full in Jennings, *Constitutional Problems,* and will be cited hereafter as *Special Reference* (Jen.).
69. Munir, *Highways and Bye-Ways*, p. 79.
70. §32, amended. Munir recognized that 'whether the Governor-General was acting with the advice of the Prime Minister or without his advice, some authority, express or implied, must be found in the Constitutional Acts to make the action of the Governor-General legal.' *Special Reference* (Jen.) p. 265.
71. The matter was submitted to the court under GIA §213, which restricted advisory opinions to questions of law. In an advisory opinion the legislature or executive branch seeks advice from the court. Such opinions properly are based on hypothetical facts which may occur in the future, such as when the legislature contemplates the passing of a statute and seeks advice before enacting the statute to ensure that it will be legal. Such advice would have been appropriate before the dissolution, when the Governor-General could have obtained advice from the court as to whether he possessed the authority to dissolve the Assembly under the constitution. GIA §213; Brohi, op. cit., p. 690-1; Keith, *Constitutional History of India*, pp. 521-3. Advisory opinions are not appropriate where, as here, facts concerning the dissolution of the Assembly and its ability to frame a constitution were being contested. The framers of the United States Constitution were wary of advisory opinions, which for that reason were not permitted in federal courts. For a criticism of advisory opinions, *see*, Felix Frankfurter, 'A Note on Advisory Opinions,' 37 *Harvard Law Review* 1002 (1924). Justice Frankfurter admonished: 'It must be remembered that advisory opinions are not merely advisory opinions. They are ghosts that slay.' Ibid., p. 1008. For use of advisory opinions in British India, *see, In Reference Under Section 213 Government of India Act,* A I R 1944 FC 73, 74.
72. Pirzada interview (1992).
73. Munir's opinion is found at *Special Reference* (Jen.), pp. 259-309.
74. Prerogative was understood to mean the residue of discretionary or arbitrary authority which at any time is left by Parliament in the hands of the Crown. *Attorney-General v. De Keyser's Royal Hotel* [1920] AC 508.
75. §8(1).
76. *Special Reference* (Jen.), p. 284. In reaching this conclusion Munir listed twenty nations and the time each took to draft its constitution. He gave one

year and nine months as the time taken by the United States when it ratified its constitution in 1789. He made no note of the fact that 1789 was eleven years after the United States gained its independence. Before being able to arrive at a federal constitutional formula it had experimented with the Articles of Confederation, which had proven unsatisfactory in the opinion of the ruling elite.

77. Ibid., p. 291.
78. Ibid., p. 292.
79. Ibid., p. 293. On this point, Munir made no mention of the statute in issue, the Indian Independence Act, which was a statute of Parliament.
80. Ibid.
81. For Munir's citations to and decision of these authorities *see*, *Special Reference* (Jen.), pp. 291-306.
82. He cited Joseph Chitty, A. V. Discy, and Thomas Waitland as authorities for this proposition. While the proposition is true, the examples cited dealt with emergencies arising from war or civil disturbance and none was an emergency created in peacetime by a person such as Ghulam Mohammad, who was justifying the exercising of power based on an emergency he himself had created by dissolving the Constitutent Assembly.
83. The doctrine of necessity was later discussed in *Jalani v. Federation of Pakistan*, op. cit., where it was observed that the doctrine could be applied 'where the ignoring of it would result in disastrous consequences to the body politic and upset the social order...' In the celebrated case of Zulfikar Ali Bhutto, Chief Justice Anwarul Huq utilized the doctrine of necessity with disastrous results, leading to his resignation and the resignations of two Associate Justices. *Begum Nusrat Bhutto v. The Chief of the Army Staff and the Federation of Pakistan*, 29 PLD 1977, 657, 702, 715, and 722. *See*, Syed, op. cit., p. 138. For its use on a less auspicious occasion, *see*, the account of journalist Emma Duncan of her interview, thirty years after Munir's decision, when the doctrine of necessity was used to support a position in an interview with the Chief Judge of the Punjab High Court, a jurist who had read for the bar at Lincoln's Inn. Duncan, *Breaking The Curfew. A Political Journey Through Pakistan* (London: Arrow Books, 1988), p. 263. Generally, *see*, Leslie Wolf-Phillips, *Constitutional Legitimacy: A Study of the Doctrine of Necessity* (London: Third World Foundation, 1980). Cf. Justice Jackson's opinion in *Korumatsu*, *M. 18, supra.*, Munir's *Umar* decision's Law of Necessity, to use Jackson's term, had 'generative power of its own, and all that it [created was] in its own image'.
84. 'Necessity may be an occasion for the proclamation of Martial Law,' Munir wrote, 'but Martial Law is a law *sui generis* and has its own corpus comprising rules of international law, Common Law and the statute law of certain countries such as the state of siege in France, and is entirely different from the law of civil necessity.' Munir, *Highways and Bye-Ways*, p. 272. No previous mention of the Law of Civil Necessity had been made by the courts in Pakistan. It could reasonably be expected that Munir would supported his position by giving specific citations to court decisions in other jurisdictions, which he did not do. His only authority seems to have been himself.
85. Pritt, op. cit., p. 1386.

86. In *Usif Patel* Munir had ordered the Governor-General to change the name of the Murree meeting from Constitutional Convention to Constituent Assembly.
87. 16 April 1955.
88. 17 April 1955.
89. This was sound advice not only because the new Assembly may have lacked legitimacy under the Independence Act. Assuming legitimacy, and granting that the Assembly had erred in the procedure by which it had enacted legislation, '...Parliament is not controlled in its discretion and when it errs, its errors can only be corrected by itself.' Erskin May, *Parliamentary Practice*, 16th ed., p. 28. Jennings, in his *Constitutional Problems*, p. 40, recognized that sending the challenged legislation back to the Assembly was a possible remedy but rejected it because of the political implications it would have. According to Chief Justice Shah, who served the government as an associate counsel in *Tamizuddin*, this solution was not argued to the court. Shah interview (1992). G. W. Choudhury, who remains of the position that the decision reached by Munir was necessary to get the country 'back on the track', and basing his conclusion on the Law of Necessity, acknowledged to the author (1991) the existence of this alternative but, like Jennings, rejects it on political grounds.
90. *Pakistan Times*, 18 April 1955.
91. Suhrawardy, *Memoirs*, p. 87.
92. 18 April 1955. One Unit had been put into operation by Ghulam Mohammad on 4 April 1955, GGO No. 6 of 1955.
93. *Pakistan Observer*, editorial, 7 April, and articles 20, 22, 23 April 1955. The opinions of the *Observer* and *Times* can be compared with the conclusion of Callard that with the 1956 Constitution, '... the transition from Government of India Act to the provisions of the constitution took place smoothly and without any disruption of the normal process of government.' *Political Study*, p. 123. The process went so smoothly because it was merely a facade once the Governor-General's usurpation of power had not been set aside by the court in *Tamizuddin*.
94. Suhrawardy, *Memoirs*, pp. 88-9.
95. *Jennings Papers*, op. cit., B/XV/2-3, *passim*.
96. *Pakistan Times*, 16 April 1955.
97. Chief Justice Hamoodur Rehman, in *Asma Jilani v. Government of Pakistan*, PLD 1972 SC 139, 161, discussed the allegations that the constitution of 1956 was framed by an illegally-constituted body which conducted its business under the threat of the Governor-General to refuse his assent to any measure which displeased him, and which was also coerced into electing Iskander Mirza as the nation's first President. Cf. *Constitutional Development* p. 95, where he calls the constitution of the Second Constituent Assembly 'the miracle of '56'.
98. For several years, Ghulam Mohammad had suffered physical impairment from illness, but he hung on to power. Charles Burton Marshall, serving as an adviser at the time to the Pakistan government, wrote of Ghulam Mohammad: 'I had often read of Ghulam Mohammad being another Ataturk before going to Pakistan in 1955. I found instead a sickened man, vague and

fitful of will, pitifully possessive of power vastly beyond his capabilities. With his articulation impaired by paralysis of the palate and with too much pride to admit his weakness, he spent his official hours trying to whisper incomprehensible orders.' Marshall, op. cit., p. 250.

99. Munir's Speech to the Bar Association, reprinted in Munir, *Life, Writings and Judgments*, p. 22, *et seq.*
100. Ibid.
101. Ibid., p. 523.
102. Ayub, op. cit., p. 74.
103. *Dosso v. Federation of Pakistan*, PLD 1958 SC. 533.
104. Munir, *Life, Writings and Judgments*, op. cit., p. 523.
105. Ibid.
106. Munir's claim that his theory of revolution in *Dosso* found support in Kelsen was denied by Kelsen in 17 *Stanford Law Review*, 1128, 1135 (1964). Unlike *Tamizuddin*, the *Dosso* case did attract some international attention. It was cited favourably in the South Rhodesian case of *Lardner Burke*, 1960 RLD 756 (Gen. Div.), the Uganda case of *Ex parte Michael Mortovu*, 1964 CLR 1958, and on appeal to the Privy Council, *Madjimabamute*, All England Law Reports 561. It was also discussed in 83 *Law Quarterly Review*, 67 (1967) and received favourable comment by I. M. Eiklaar, 'Principles of Revolutionary Legitimacy' in *Oxford Essays on Jurisprudence*, (1972). *Dosso* was overruled by *Jilani v. Federation of Pakistan*, PLD 1958 SC 533, and Kelsen's theory was repudiated. As Munir himself said of *Dosso*, 'the name of the case began to be shunned like the devil,' and he came under heavy attack in comments made in Pakistan. Munir, *Highways and Bye-Ways*, p. 253. In the *Ziaur Rehman* case, op. cit., *Dosso* was compared with the American case *Dred Scott* as being a 'self-inflicted wound' and a 'public calamity'. Munir took comfort in the fact that, 'however hated in Pakistan it (*Dosso*) may be, it has acquired an international fame'. Ibid., p. 254.
107. Munir, *Life, Writings and Judgments*, p. 257.
108. Ibid., p. 270.
109. *Pakistan Times*, 23 April 1960. Munir's speech to the Lahore High Court Bar Association, 1960 is reprinted in his *Life, Writings and Judgments*, p. 21. Munir claimed that in such situations, 'I not only look into the papers and books but also around myself.' Law must change with society, stated Munir. He called this 'pragmatic interpretation'. Ibid., p. 33.
110. Munir, *Highways and Bye-ways*, p. 257, and *Islamic Constitution*, p. 31.

Chapter 9. Pakistan the 'Undoubted Failure'

1. Callard referred to the Assembly's 'undoubted failure'. *Political Study*, p. 118.
2. During this period Walter Lippman argued the cause of liberal democracy but described most democratic legislatures in the West as 'boss-ridden oligarchies'. Lippman, *The Public Philosophy*, (New York: The American Library, 1956), p. 488.
3. 29 October 1954.

4. 30 October 1954.
5. 30 October 1954.
6. 25 and 28 October 1954.
7. 31 October 1954.
8. Amjad Ali interview (1992).
9. Callard was among those who so characterized the constitution. *Political Study,* p. 25. *See also, Time,* 8 November 1954.
10. 9 December 1954.
11. Callard, *Pakistan Puzzle,* op. cit., p. 424.
12. March 1955, p. 28.
13. 11 April 1955
14. Callard, *Political Forces,* p. 26.
15. Munir, *Life, Writings and Judgments,* p. 22.
16. Karl J. Newman, *Essays on the Constitution of Pakistan* (Dhaka: Pakistan Co-operative Book Society Ltd., 1956), p. 207.
17. Callard, *Political Study,* p. 300.
18. Goodnow, *Civil Service,* pp. 30, 58.
19. Sayeed, *Political System,* p. 80.
20. Ahmad, *Government and Politics,* pp. 18, 44. Cf. Jalal, 'Constitutional Heads,' p. 57. Jalal seems to be a writer on the period who has understood the significance of *Tamizuddin.*
21. Munir himself lodged this complaint after his retirement from the Bench, advocating that his decisions dealing with the Assembly should be evaluated on their legal merits independent of political considerations. Munir, *Highways and Bye-Ways,* p. 206; *also,* interview of Chief Justice Shah (1992).
22. Jennings described the efforts to draft a constitution: '...the process of constitution-making proceeded in a desultory fashion for seven long years and had not been completed when the Assembly was "dissolved" on 24 October 1954.' *Constitutional Problems,* p. 22. Jennings' statement is unusual even for a lawyer arguing the cause of his client. He had reviewed and approved the final draft of the constitution which the Assembly adopted. *Jennings Papers,* op. cit., BX/V 4-5. Munir later described the Assembly's efforts as follows: 'As a constitution-making body it had held 115 settings without doing anything material in that direction.' Munir, *Highways and Bye-Ways,* p. 67. Yet, prior to the Assembly's dissolution, Munir had given a public address on the subject of the completed constitution. *See,* Ch. 5. *supra,* M. 89. According to Pirzada's notes, taken at the time of the court hearing, Munir stated his awareness of the drafted constitutions existence and inquired of the Advocate-General whether the government was willing to assent to the new constitution; and if not why not. S.S. Pirzada *Dissolution of Constituent Assembly of Pakistan* (Karachi: Asia Law House, 1995) p. 196
23. Despite his wide-ranging discussion of the dissolution cases, Jennings specifically avoids the one issue upon which *Tamizuddin* was decided. In discussing the relevant selections of the Indian Independence Act, when he arrived at Section 6(3) he stated: 'Since the meaning of this sub-section was the main question in controversy in the *Mouvli Tamizuddin Khan's* case, it would be inappropriate to analyze it at this point.' *Constitutional Problems,* p. 17.

24. Ziring, *Engima of Political Development,* pp. 93-97.
25. Callard, *Political Forces,* pp. 93-97.
26. Sayed, *Islam, Politics and National Solidarity,* pp. 80-81.
27. *Dawn,* 18 November 1954.
28. Callard, *Political Study,* pp. 9 and 125.
28. Ziring, *Engima of Political Development,* p. 58.
30. Interview (1991).

SELECT LIST OF PERSONS INTERVIEWED

(Date of interview 1990 unless otherwise indicated)

Anwar-ul-Huq, Lahore, retired Chief Justice, Pakistan Supreme Court.

Ijaz Hussain Batalvi, Lahore, Senior Advocate, Pakistan Supreme Court.

Nasim Hassan Shah, Lahore (1990 and 1992), attorney in *Tamizuddin* and later Chief Justice, Pakistan Supreme Court.

S. M. Zafar, Lahore, Senior Advocate and former Cabinet Minister.

Hina Jilani, Lahore, Advocate and political activist.

A. R. Cornelius, Lahore, retired Chief Justice, Pakistan Supreme Court, dissenting Justice in *Tamizuddin*.

Sajjad Sipra, Lahore, Associate Justice, High Court of West Punjab.

L. A. Nizami, Islamabad, retired Chief Clerk, Pakistan Supreme Court, Clerk of the Federal Court during *Tamizuddin*.

Karl J. Newman, Bonn (1991). Retired Professor of Political Economy, Cologne University; former Chairman of the Department of Political Science, Dhaka University; constitutional adviser to Prime Minister Mohammad Ali Bogra.

S. S. Pirzada, Karachi (1991 and 1992), Senior Advocate, diplomat and historian, former Attorney-General and Foreign Minister, represented Tamizuddin Khan in the Assembly dissolution cases.

Syed Amjad Ali (1992), former Ambassador to the United States and Finance Minister.

Mian Mumtaz Daultana, Lahore (1992), former Chief Minister of West Punjab.

Altaf Gauhar, Islamabad (1992), Editor of *The Muslim*; former Editor, *Dawn*; served as election official in East Bengal during the election of March 1954

BIBLIOGRAPHY

Books Journals and Dissertations

Afzal, M. Rafique. *Political Parties in Pakistan 1947-1958.* Islamabad: National Commission on Historical and Cultural Research, 1976.

Ahmad, Khurshid (ed.). *An Analysis of the Munir Report.* Karachi: Jamaat-e-Islami Publications, 1956.

Ahmad, Mushtaq. *Government and Politics in Pakistan.* Karachi: Pakistan Publication House, 1959.

Ahmad, Riaz. *Constitutional and Political Development in Pakistan October 1951-October 1954.* M Phil. Dissertation. Islamabad: Quaid-i-Azam University, 1975.

Alexandrowicz, Charles H. *Constitutional Developments in India.* Bombay: Oxford University Press, 1957.

Ali, Chaudhri Muhammad. *The Emergence of Pakistan.* New York: Columbia University Press, 1967.

Amad, Mohammed. *My Chief.* Lahore: Longmans, Green & Co., 1960.

Amand, C L. *The Government of India Act 1935.* Lahore: The University Book Agency, 1944.

Antieau, Chester J. *Constitutional Construction.* London: Oceana Publications, Inc., 1982.

Austin, Granville. *The Indian Constitution: Cornerstone of a Nation.* Oxford: Clarendon Prcss, 1966.

Ayub Khan, Mohammad. *Friends Not Masters, A Political Autobiography.* New York: Oxford University Press, 1967.

Azfar, Kamal. *Pakistan Political and Constitutional Dilemmas.* Karachi: Pakistan Law House, 1987.

Aziz, Khursheed K. *Party Politics in Pakistan 1947-1958.* Islamabad: National Commission of Historical and Cultural Research, 1976.

Bahadur, Kalim. *The Jamaat-e-Islami of Pakistan.* New Delhi: Chetana Publications, 1977.

Bakhsh, Ilahi. *With the Quaid-i-Azam During His Last Days.* Karachi: Quaid-i-Azam Academy. 1978.

Banerjee, A C. *The Constituent Assembly of India.* Calcutta: A. Mukherjee & Co. 1947.

Bayler, Daniel H. 'The Indian Experience With Preventive Detention,' 35 *Pacific Affairs,* 99 (1960).

_______, *Preventive Detention in India.* Calcutta: Firma K. L. Mukhopadhyay, 1962.

Beg, Aziz (ed.) *Quaid-i-Azam Centenary Bouquet.* Islamabad: Babur and Amer Publications, 1977.

Berry, Willard. *Aspects of the Frontier Crimes Regulation in Pakistan.* Durham, N. C.: Duke University Press, 1966.

Bhatnagar, Yatindra. *Mujib.* Delhi: ISSD, 1971.

Binder, Leonard. *Religion and Politics in Pakistan.* Berkeley: University of California Press, 1963.

Bolitho, Hector. *Jinnah: Creator of Pakistan.* London: John Murray, 1954.

Bourne, Sir Fredrick. 'Constitutional Government Before and After the Transfer of Power,' 46 *Asiatic Review,* No. 168. (1950).

Braibanti, Ralph. 'Public Bureaucracy and Judiciary in Pakistan,' in Joseph La Polombara (ed.). *Bureaucracy and Political Development.* Princeton: Princeton University Press, 1962.

Brohi, A K. *Fundamental Law of Pakistan.* Karachi: Din Mahammadi Press, 1958.

Brown, Judith. *Modern India.* Delhi: Oxford University Press, 1985.

Burks, Ardath W. 'Constitution-Making in Pakistan,' 69 *Political Science Quarterly,* (1954).

Calder, G J. 'Constitutional Debates in Pakistan,' 45 *Muslim World,* 40, 144, 253 (1956).

Callard, Keith. *Pakistan, A Political Study.* New York: The Macmillan Company, 1957.

_______, *Political Forces in Pakistan 1947-1959.* New York: Institute of Pacific Relations, 1959.

_______, 'The Pakistan Puzzle.' 179 *Nation,* 422 (1954).

_______, 'The Political Stability of Pakistan,' 29 *Pacific Affairs,* 5 (1956).

Campbell, Robert. 'The Prerogative Power of Dissolution,' 1961 *Public Law*, 165.

Campbell-Johnson, Alan. *Mission with Mountbatten*, New York: Dutton, 1953.

Cappellette, Mauro. *Judicial Review in the Contemporary World.* Indianapolis: The Bobb-Merrill Co., 1971.

Chand, Dewan Khan. *The Constituent Assembly.* Lahore: Lion Press, 1946.

Choudhury, Golam Wahed. 'Constitution-Making in Pakistan,' *Western Political Quarterly*, (December 1955).

_______, 'Failure of Parliamentary Democracy in Pakistan,' 12 *Parliamentary Affairs*, 60(1959).

_______, *The First Constituent Assembly of Pakistan.* Ph.D. Dissertation, Columbia University, 1956.

_______, *Constitutional Development in Pakistan.* London: Longman, 1969.

_______, *Democracy in Pakistan.* Dacca: Green Book House, 1963.

_______, *Documents and Speeches on the Constitution of Pakistan.* Vancouver: University of British Columbia Press, 1967.

Clokie, H McD. 'The New Constitution of India,' 30 *American Political Science Review*, 1152 (1935).

Collins, Larry. *Freedom at Midnight.* New York: Simon and Schuster, 1975.

Cornelius, A. R. *Law and Judiciary in Pakistan.* Lahore: Lahore Law Times Publications, 1981.

Coupland, Reginald. *The Indian Problem, 1833-1935.* Oxford: The Clarendon Press, 1942.

Das, D R (ed.). *Transitional Constitutions of India and Pakistan.* Calcutta: The Indian Law Review Office, 1947.

Deane, Philip. 'The Men Who Really Run Pakistan,' *The Reporter.* (7 January 1955).

Dhar, Pannalal, *Preventive Detention Under Indian Constitution.* New Delhi: Deep and Deep Publications, 1986.

Duncan, Emma. *Breaking the Curfew. A Political Journey Through Pakistan.* London: Arrow Books, 1988.

Edwardes, Michael. *The Last Years of British India.* London: Cassell, 1963.

Fairman, Charles. *The Law of Martial Rule.* Chicago: Callaghan and Company, 1943.

Feldman, Herbert. *A Constitution for Pakistan.* Karachi: Oxford University Press, 1955.

Foran, William. 'John Marshall as a Historian,' 43 *American Historical Review*, 51 (1937).

Fossey, Eugene A. *The Royal Power of Dissolution of Parliament in the British Commonwealth.* Toronto: University of Toronto Press, 1943.

Gilmartin, David. 'Religious Leadership and the Pakistan Movement in the Punjab,' 13 *Modern Asian Studies*, 485 (1979)

Glendhill, A. *Pakistan; The Development of its Law and Constitution.* London: Stevens & Sons, 1957.

Goodnow, Henry F. *The Civil Service of Pakistan.* New Haven: Yale University Press, 1964.

Gordon, Leonard. *Brothers Against the Raj.* New York: Columbia University Press, 1990.

Greer Steven C. 'Military Intervention in Civil Disturbances: the Legal Bases Reconsidered,' 1983 *Public Law,* 573.

Haines, Charles G. *The American Doctrine of Judicial Supremacy.* New York: Russell & Russell, 1959.

Hardy, Peter. *The Muslims of British India.* Cambridge: Cambridge University Press, 1972.

Hayes, Louis D. *The Struggle for Legitimacy in Pakistan.* Lahore: Vanguard Books, 1986.

Hodson, H. V. *The Great Divide.* Karachi: Oxford University Press, 1985.

Holdsworth, W S. 'The Conventions of the Eighteenth Century Constitution,' 17 *Iowa Law Review,* 101 (1966).

Hussain I. *The Failure of Parliamentary Politics in Pakistan.* Ph.D. Dissertation, Oxford University, 1967.

Huq, Mahfuzul. *The Electorate System in Pakistan: an Analysis of the Problem of Minority Representation.* Ph.D. Dissertation, Columbia University, 1964.

The India and Pakistan Yearbook and Who's Who. Bombay: The Times of India, 1945-53.

Innes, F. M. 'The Political Outlook in Pakistan,' 26 *Pacific Affairs,* 303 (1953).

Iqbal, Mohammed. *Law of Preventive Detention in England, India and Pakistan.* Lahore: The Punjab Religious Book Society, 1955.

Ispahani, A. H. *Quaid-i-Azam Jinnah, as I Knew Him.* Karachi: Forward Publications Trust, 1967.

Iyer, R. N. and Khosla, A. R. (eds.). *The Punjab and North West Province Acts Annotated.* Madras, Government Printing Office, 1934.

Jahan, Rounaq. *Pakistan: Failure in National Integration.* New York: Columbia University Press, 1972.

Jalal, Ayesha and Seal, Anil. 'Muslim Politics Between the Wars,' 15 *Modern Asian Studies,* 416 (1981).

Jalal, Ayesha. *The State of Martial Rule.* Cambridge: Cambridge University Press, 1989.

———, 'The Raj Survives,' 19 *Modern Asian Studies,* 29 (1985).

_______, In D. A. Low (ed.). *Constitutional Heads and Political Crisis.* London: MacMillan, 1988.

James, Frederick. 'The Indian Legislature in War-time,' 1945 *Asiatic Review,* 225.

Jennings, Ivor. *The Law and the Constitution.* London: University of London Press, 1959.

_______, *The Constitutional Law of the Commonwealth.* Cambridge: Cambridge. University Press, 1952.

_______, *Cabinet Government.* Cambridge: Cambridge. University Press, 1936.

_______, *Constitutional Problems of Pakistan.* London: Cambridge University Press, 1955.

_______, *The Approach to Self-Government.* London: Cambridge University Press, 1956.

_______, 'The Making of a Dominion Constitution,' 65 *Law Quarterly Review*, 456 (1949).

_______, 'Crown and Commonwealth in Asia,' 32 *International Affairs*, 137. (1956).

_______, *The Constitution of Ceylon.* London: Oxford University Press 3rd ed., 1953.

Jha, Chakradhar. *Judicial Review of Legislative Acts.* Bombay: N M Tripathi Private Ltd, 1974.

Jinnah, Mohammad Ali. *Speeches as Governor-General of Pakistan 1947-1948.* Karachi: Government of Pakistan, n.d.

_______, *Speeches, Statements, Writings, Letters, etc.* Lahore: Sang-e-Meel Publications, 1976.

Karve, D. G. 'The New Constitution Principles and Prospects,' 3 *University of Toronto Law Journal*, 281 (1940).

Keith, Arthur B. *A Constitutional History of India. 1600-1935.* London: Methuen, 1936.

_______, *The Constitutional History of England from Queen Victoria to George VI.* London: Macmillan, 1940.

_______, *Sovereignty in the British Commonwealth.* London: Macmillan, 1938.

Kelly, Alfred H. 'Clio and the Court: An Illicit Love Affair,' *Supreme Court Reporter,* 119 (1965).

Khaliquzzaman, Chaudhry. *Pathway to Pakistan.* Lahore: Pakistan Longman, 1961.

Lester, Anthony. 'Fundamental Rights in the United Kingdom: The Law and the British Constitution,' 125 *University of Pennsylvania Law Review*, 337 (1976).

Liaquat Ali Khan. *Pakistan, The Heart of Asia.* Cambridge: Harvard University Press, 1950.

Low, D. A. *Constitutional Heads and Political Crises.* London: Macmillan, 1988.

Lumby, E. W. R. *The Transfer of Power in India.* London: George Allen and Unwen, 1954.

La Porte, Robert, Jr. *Power and Privilege, Influence and Decision-Making in Pakistan.* Berkeley: University of California Press, 1975.

McWhinney, Edward. 'Sovereignty in the United Kingdom and the Commonwealth Countries at the Present Day,' 58 *Political Science Quarterly*, 511. (1953).

———, 'Constitutional Conventions,' 35 *Canadian Bar Review*, 92 (1957).

———, *Judicial Review in the English-Speaking World.* Toronto: Toronto University Press, 1956

Mahajan, Mir Chand. *Looking Back.* Lahore: Asia Publishing House, 1963.

Majahid, Sharif-al. *Quaid-i-Azam Jinnah.* Karachi: Quaid-i-Azam Academy, 1978.

Mann, F A. 'Britain's Bill of Rights,' 94 *Law Quarterly Review*, 512 (1977).

Mansergh, Nicholas. *Prelude to Partition: Concepts and Aims in Ireland and India,* Cambridge: Cambridge University Press, 1978.

Markesinis, B. S. *The Theory and Practice of Dissolution of Parliament.* Cambridge: Cambridge University Press, 1972.

Marshall, Charles B., 'Reflection on a Revolution in Pakistan.' *Foreign Affairs,* January 1959, 247.

Marshall, Geoffrey. *Parliamentary Sovereignty and the Commonwealth.* New York: Oxford University Press, 1957.

———, *Constitutional Conventions.* Oxford: Clarendon Press, 1984.

Menon, V. P. *The Transfer of Power in India.* London: Longmans Green, 1957.

Miller, Charles A. *The Supreme Court and the Uses of History.* Cambridge, Mass.: Harvard University Press, 1969.

Misra, K. P. *Pakistan's Search for Constitutional Consensus.* New Delhi: Impex India, 1967.

Moore, F. J. 'Jinnah and the Pakistan Demand,' 17 *Modern Asian Studies*, 529 (1983).

———, *Retreat From Empire.* Oxford: Clarendon Press, 1966.

Mujahid, Sharif-al, *Quaid-i-Azam Jinnah: Studies in Interpretation.* Karachi: Quaid-i-Azam Academy, 1978.

Muneruzzaman, Talukdar. 'Group Interests in Pakistan Politics, 1947-1958,' 39 *Pacific Affairs*, p. 85 (1966).

Mowat, Charles L. *Britain Between the Wars*, Chicago: University of Chicago Press, 1955.

Munir, Muhammad *From Jinnah to Zia*. Lahore: Vanguard Books, 1980.

______, *Highways and Bye-Ways of Life*. Lahore: Law Publishing Co., 1978.

______, *Constitution of the Islamic Republic of Pakistan*. Lahore: Law Publishing Co. Legal Decisions, 1975.

______, *Principles of the Law of Evidence*. Lahore: Law Publishing Co., 1974.

______, *Islam in History*. Lahore: Law Publishing Co., 1973.

______, *Chief Justice Muhammad Munir, His Life, Writings and Judgments*. Lahore: Research Society of Pakistan, 1973. Chaudhri, Nazir H (ed.).

Munro, C. R. 'Laws and Convention Distinguished,' 1975 *Law Quarterly Review*, 218.

Newman, Karl J. *Essays on the Constitution of Pakistan*. Dhaka: Pakistan Co-operative Book Society Ltd., 1956.

______, 'Pakistan Preventative Autocracy and its Causes,' 32 *Pacific Affairs*, 18 (1959).

Nizami, Majid. *The Press in Pakistan*. Lahore: University of Punjab Press, 1958.

Noon, Firoz Khan. *From Memory*. Lahore: Ferozsons, 1966.

Oldenburg, Philip. 'A Place Insufficiently Imagined'; Language, Belief, and the Pakistan Crisis of 1971,' 44 *Journal of Asian Studies*, 741 (1985).

Oracion, Lossier. *Constitution Making in Pakistan 1947-1956*. Ph.D. Dissertation, Karachi University, 1968.

Park, Richard L. 'East Bengal: Pakistan's Troubled Province,' 23 *Far Eastern Survey*, 70 (1954).

Phillips, O Hood. 'Constitutional Conventions, Dicey's Predecessors,' 29 *Modern Law Review*, 137 (1966).

Pirzada, Syed Sharifuddin. *Fundamental Rights and Constitutioanl Remedies in Pakistan*. Lahore: All Pakistan Legal Decision, 1966.

______, *Quaid-i-Azam Mohammad Ali Jinnah and Pakistan*, Islamabad: Hurmat Publications, 1989.

Rashiduzzaman, M. *Pakistan: A Study of Government and Politics*. Dhaka: Ideal Library, 1967.

Rau, B. N., 'The Parliamentary System of Government in India,' 24 *University of Washington Law Review*, 91 (1949). R.

Raja, S. Hashim, *Mountbatten and Pakistan*. Karachi: Quaid-i-Azam Academy, 1982.

Rehman, Inamur. *Public Opinion and Political Development in Pakistan, 1947-1958*. Karachi: Oxford University Press, 1982.

Rittenberg, Stephen. *Ethnicity, Nationalism and the Pathans.* Durham, N.C., Carolina Academic Press, 1988.

Rodell, Fred. *Nine Men, A Political History of the Supreme Court from 1790 to 1955.* New York: Random House, 1955.

Rosenthal, Erwin I. J. *Islam in the Modern National State.* Cambridge: Harvard University Press, 1965.

Rossiter, Clinton. *Constitutional Dictatorship.* New York. Harcourt Brace and World, 1945.

Saharay, H. K. A. *A Legal Study of Constitutional Development in India.* Calcutta: Nababharat Publishers, 1970.

Saiyed, M. H. *Mohammad Ali Jinnah: A Political Study.* Karachi: Elite Publishers, 1970.

Sayed, Anwar Hussain. *Pakistan: Islam, Politics and National Solidarity.* New York: Praeger, 1982.

Sayeed, Khalid B. *Politics in Pakistan.* New York: Praeger. 1980.

———, 'Federalism and Pakistan,' 23 *Far Eastern Survey*, 139 (1954).

———, 'Collapse of Parliamentary Democracy In Pakistan,' 13 *Middle East Journal*, 389 (1959).

———, 'The Governor-General of Pakistan,' *8 Pakistan Horizon*, 1 (1955).

———, 'Jamaat-e-Islami Movement in Pakistan,' 30 *Pacific Affairs*, 59 (1957).

———, *Pakistan: the Formative Phase.* Karachi: Civil and Military Gazette Press, 1967.

———, *The Political System of Pakistan.* Karachi: Civil and Military Gazette Press, 1967.

———, 'The Political Role of the Pakistan Civil Service,' 31 *Pacific Affairs*, 131 (1958).

Schuler, Edgar A. *Public Opinion and Constitutional Development in Pakistan 1958-62.* East Lansing: Michigan State University Press, 1967.

Shafqat, Saeed. *Political System of Pakistan and Public Policy.* Lahore: Progressive Publishers, 1989.

Shahab, Qudratullah. *Shahab Nama.* Lahore: Sang-e-meel Publications, 1987.

Stephens, Ian. *Pakistan.* London: Earnest Benn, 1963.

Suhrawardy, Husain S. 'Political Stability and Democracy in Pakistan,' 35 *Foreign Affairs*, 422 (1956-57). *Memoirs.* Dhaka: University Press, 1987.

Suleri, Z. A. *Pakistan's Lost Years; Being a Survey of a Decade of Politics*, 1948-58, Lahore: Progressive Papers, 1962.

Syed, Nur Ahmed, *From Military Law to Martial Law.* Boulder: Westview Press, 1985.

Talbot, I. A. 'The 1946 Punjab Elections,' 14 *Modern Asian Studies*,'65 (1980).

Tamizuddin Khan. *The Test of Time*. Dhaka; University Press, 1960. (ed. Mirza Nurul Huda).

Tinker, Hugh. *India and Pakistan: A Political Analysis*. London: Pall Mall, 1962.

Von Vorys, Karl. *Political Developments in Pakistan*. Princeton: Princeton University Press, 1965.

Wade, H. W. R. 'The Basis of Legal Sovereignty,' 1955 *Cambridge Law Journal*, 172.

Wasti, Syed Razi. *Lord Minto and the Indian Nationalist Movement, 1905-1910*. London: Oxford Unversity Press, 1965.

_______, *Muslim Struggle for Freedom in British India*. Lahore: Book Traders, 1993.

Wavell, Archibald. *A Viceroy's Journal*. London: Oxford University Press, 1973.

Wheare, K. C. 'The Nature and Structure of the Commonwealth,' 47 *American Political Science Review*, 1016 (1953).

_______, *The Statute of Westminister and Dominion Status*. Oxford: Oxford University Press, 1947.

Wheeler, Richard S. *The Politics of Pakistan, A Constitutional Quest*. Ithaca: Cornell University Press, 1970.

_______, and Park, Richard. 'East Bengal Under Governor's Rule,' 23 *Far Eastern Survey*, 129 (1954).

_______, *Government and Constitution-Making in Pakistan*. Ph.D. Dissertation, University of California, Berkeley, 1957.

Wilcox, Wayne A. *Pakistan: The Consolidation of a Nation*. New York: Columbia University Press, 1963.

Wolf-Phillips, Leslie. *Constitutional Legitimacy: A Study of the Doctrine of Necessity*. London: Third World Foundation, 1980.

Wolpert, Stanley. *Jinnah of Pakistan*. New York: Oxford University Press, 1984.

Wright, Benjamin F. *The Growth of American Constitutional Law*. Chicago: University of Chicago Press.

Yusuf, Hamid. *Pakistan in Search of Democracy*. Lahore: Afrasia Publications, 1980.

Ziring, Lawrence. *The Failure of Democracy in Pakistan*. Ph.D. Dissertation, Columbia University, 1962.

_______, *Pakistan: The Enigma of Political Development*. Boulder: Westview Press, 1980.

Public Documents

Basic Constitutional Documents. Vol. 1. Islamabad: National Assembly Secretariat, n.d.

Basic Principles Committee Interim Report. Karachi: Constituent Assembly. 1950.

Basic Principles Committee Report (as passed on 21 September 1954). Islamabad: Printing Corporation of Pakistan Press, 1971. (Reprint).

Constituent Assembly Debates. Official Reports. (*Constitutional*). Karachi: Government of Pakistan Press, 1947-54.

Constitutent Assembly Debates. Official Reports. (Legislative). Karachi: Government of Pakistan Press, 1947-54.

Constitution of the Islamic Republic of Pakistan, Karachi: Manager of the Government Press, 1954.

Draft Constitution of Pakistan, Confidential. Karachi: Manager of the Government Press, 1954.

Government of India Act, 1935. *Constitutional Documents (Pakistan)* Vol. II. Karachi: Manager of the Government Press, 1964.

Joint Committee on Indian Constitutional Reform. Session 1933-4. 2 Vols. London: His Majesty's Stationary Office 1934.

Report of the Court of Inquiry Constituted under Punjab Act II of 1954 to Enquire into the Punjab Disturbances of 1953. Lahore: Government of the Punjab Press, 1954.

Report of the Enquiry into the Firing by the Police at Dhaka on the 21 February, 1952. Dhaka: Government of East Bengal Press, 1952.

Transfer of Power, Nicholas Mansergh (ed.) London: H.M. Stationary Office, 1970-2.

Private Documents

Cunningham Papers. India Office Library, London

Gandhi Papers. National Archives, New Delhi.

Jennings Papers. Institute of Commonwealth Research, London.

Jinnah Papers. National Archives, Islamabad.

Mudie Papers. India Office Library, London.

Nehru Papers. Nehru Memorial Library, New Delhi.

Pritt Autobiography. Manuscript Room. British Library, London.

Newspapers and Periodicals

Civil and Military Gazette (Lahore)

Dawn (Karachi)

Times (London)

Pakistan Times (Lahore)

New York Times (New York)

Pakistan Observer (Dhaka)

Economist (London)

Round Table (London)

Statesman (Calcutta)

Time (New York)

INDEX